DATE DUE

DEMCO 38-296

CONTEMPORARY MUSICIANS

ISSN 1044-2197

CONTEMPORARY MUSICIANS

PROFILES OF THE PEOPLE IN MUSIC

MICHAEL L. LaBLANC,
Editor

VOLUME 5

Includes Cumulated Indexes

 *Gale Research Inc.* · DETROIT · LONDON

STAFF

Michael L. LaBlanc, *Editor*

Julia M. Rubiner, *Associate Editor*

Christine Ferran, *Assistant Editor*

David Bianco, Marjorie Burgess, John Cohassey, David Collins, Margaret Escobar, Peter W. Ferran,
Joan Goldsworthy, Anne Janette Johnson, Kyle Kevorkian, Jeanne M. Lesinski, Meg Mac Donald, Greg
Mazurkiewicz, Louise Mooney, Nancy Pear, Nancy Rampson, Calen D. Stone, Elizabeth Wenning,
Contributing Editors

Peter M. Gareffa, *Senior Editor*

Jeanne Gough, *Permissions Manager*
Patricia A. Seefelt, *Permissions Supervisor (Pictures)*
Margaret A. Chamberlain, *Permissions Associate*
Pamela A. Hayes and Keith Reed, *Permissions Assistants*

Mary Beth Trimper, *Production Manager*
Shanna Philpott Heilveil, *External Production Assistant*
Arthur Chartow, *Art Director*
Cynthia Baldwin, *Graphic Designer*
C.J. Jonik, *Keyliner*

Special thanks to the Biography Division Research staff

Cover Illustration by John Kleber

The paper used in this publication meets the minimum requirements
of American National Standard for Information Sciences—Permanence
Paper for Printed Library Materials, ANSI Z39.48-1984. ∞™

ISBN 0-8103-2215-3
ISSN 1044-2197

Computerized photocomposition by
Roberts/Churcher
Derby Line, Vermont

Contents

Introduction

Fills the Information Gap on Today's Musicians

Contemporary Musicians profiles the colorful personalities in the music industry who create or influence the music we hear today. Prior to *Contemporary Musicians,* no quality reference series provided comprehensive information on such a wide range of artists despite keen and ongoing public interest. To find biographical and critical coverage, an information seeker had little choice but to wade through the offerings of the popular press, scan television "infotainment" programs, and search for the occasional published biography or expose. *Contemporary Musicians* is designed to serve that information seeker, providing in one ongoing source in-depth coverage of the important figures on the modern music scene in a format that is both informative and entertaining. Students, researchers, and casual browsers alike can use *Contemporary Musicians* to fill their needs for personal information about the artists, find a selected discography of the musician's recordings, and read an insightful essay offering biographical and critical information.

Provides Broad Coverage

Single-volume biographical sources on musicians are limited in scope, focusing on a handful of performers from a specific musical genre or era. In contrast, *Contemporary Musicians* offers researchers and music devotees a comprehensive, informative, and entertaining alternative. *Contemporary Musicians* is published twice yearly, with each volume providing information on 80 to 100 musical artists from all the genres that form the broad spectrum of contemporary music—pop, rock, jazz, blues, country, new wave, New Age, folk, rhythm and blues, gospel, bluegrass, rap, and reggae, to name a few, as well as selected classical artists who have achieved "crossover" success with the general public. *Contemporary Musicians* will occasionally include profiles of influential nonperforming members of the music industry, including producers, promoters, and record company executives.

Includes Popular Features

In *Contemporary Musicians* you'll find popular features that users value:

- **Easy-to-locate data sections**—Vital personal statistics, chronological career summaries, listings of major awards, and mailing addresses, when available, are prominently displayed in a clearly marked box on the second page of each entry.

- **Biographical/critical essays**—Colorful and informative essays trace each personality's personal and professional life, offer representative examples of critical response to each artist's work, and provide entertaining personal sidelights.

- **Selected discographies**—Each entry provides a comprehensive listing of the artist's major recorded works.

- **Photographs**—Most entries include portraits of the artists.

- **Sources for additional information**—This invaluable feature directs the user to selected books, magazines, and newspapers where more information on listees can be obtained.

Helpful Indexes Make It Easy to Find the Information You Need

Contemporary Musicians features a Musicians Index, listing names of individual performers and musical groups, and a Subject Index that provides the user with a breakdown by primary musical instruments played and by musical genre.

We Welcome Your Suggestions

The editors welcome your comments and suggestions for enhancing and improving *Contemporary Musicians*. If you would like to suggest musicians or composers to be covered in the future, please submit these names to the editors. Mail comments or suggestions to:

The Editor
Contemporary Musicians
Gale Research Inc.
835 Penobscot Bldg.
Detroit MI 48226-4094
Phone : (800) 347-4253
Fax: (313) 961-6241

Photo Credits

PHOTOGRAPHS APPEARING IN *CONTEMPORARY MUSICIANS*, VOLUME 5, WERE RECEIVED FROM THE FOLLOWING SOURCES:

AP/Wide World Photos: pp. 1, 3, 6, 8, 11, 13, 19, 21, 23, 25, 28, 32, 36, 39, 48, 50, 53, 55, 58, 62, 66, 71, 74, 76, 78, 82, 88, 93, 97, 102, 105, 112, 119, 122, 124, 131, 133, 139, 142, 144, 147, 150, 153, 157, 160, 163, 166, 172, 175, 184, 187, 190, 200, 204, 206, 214, 218; **Photograph by Paul Cox,** © **1990 CBS Records:** p. 16; **Courtesy of Rounder Records:** p. 34; **Courtesy of Jive Records:** p. 42; **Courtesy of Black Top Records:** p. 45; **Photograph by Blake Little, courtesy of Kronos Quartet:** p. 99; **Photograph by Jeff Katz, courtesy of MCA Records:** p. 110; **UPI/Bettmann;** p. 127; **Photograph by Mike Rutherford, courtesy of MCA Records;** p. 178; **Photograph by Robert John, courtesy of Warner Bros. Records:** p. 194; **The Bettman Archive:** p. 197; **Photograph by Christian Steiner, courtesy of ICM Artists Ltd.:** p. 209. As this book was going to press, the photograph on p. 107 supplied by **AP/Wide World Photos.**

John Anderson

Singer, songwriter

Singer-songwriter John Anderson is "one of country music's most distinctive talents," according to critic Alanna Nash of *Stereo Review*. Ralph Novak of *People* has lauded his "throaty, bluesy voice," and Nash noted further that Anderson "was among the forefront of the return to a hard country style." With hits like "Wild and Blue," "Would You Catch a Falling Star," and his biggest smash, "Swingin'," he became one of the most popular country artists of the early 1980s. Though his hit production has slacked off somewhat since, his albums continue to fare well both with what *Country Music* reporter Patrick Carr labeled "backward hard-core" country fans and "too-sophisticated college graduates who don't listen to the right kind of radio station."

Anderson was born in Florida during the mid-1950s. As Carr put it, "he had . . . served his time in the honky tonks and songwriting rooms [and] honed his road show and writing craft" before signing with Warner Bros. Records. His first three albums for that company were fairly successful, and the songs "Wild and Blue," "I'm Just an Old Chunk of Coal," and "Would You Catch a Falling Star" traveled a good way up the country charts and gained him a good reputation with many fans. But Anderson's fourth album included "Swingin'," a song he wrote himself about sitting on a porch swing with a girl. That single shot to number one on the country charts, and made Anderson a major country star.

Unfortunately, Anderson did not realize the extent of his own success; he told Carr, speaking for himself and his accompanying band: "Frankly, we just didn't realize what a big record 'Swingin'' was. It didn't dawn on us that we should quit what we were doing and change the way we did things; go for bigger [concert] dates, pay attention to what was going on with the record company, all that stuff." Thus, while he was the proud owner of the United States' top country hit, he was still performing in small clubs. Anderson partially attributes his later difficulty repeating the success of "Swingin'" to the fact that neither he nor his record company promoted his music well enough at that time.

Carr, however, also offered a different explanation for Anderson's decline on the charts, having to do with the way country music's audience has become more suburban and mainstream. "The result is that there are no more sharp edges in mainstream Nashville music," he protested. "Virtually all the new artists contracted and promoted with any real effort by Nashville record companies in the past decade have been . . . unlikely to offend the consumers in a 'soft' marketplace with music that is too hard in any way." Carr therefore theorized that Anderson, with his hard, rough-edged style of

For the Record. . .

Born c. 1956. in Florida; married; wife's name, Janie. Singer, songwriter. Recording artist and concert performer since the early 1980s.

Awards: Won two awards from the Country Music Association, both in 1983.

Addresses: *Record company*—Capitol Records, 1750 N. Vine St., Hollywood, CA 90028.

singing, along with his long-haired, faded-jeans appearance, does not fit the image that country music promoters are looking for. Anderson conceded to Carr that this might be a factor: "They found guys that *would* cut their hair, and wear rhinestones, and change their names, and they figured that was just fine because sure enough, those guys were 'easier to work with.' And those were the guys they spent their money on. Right now they're at the top of the charts, and I'm working 300-seaters."

Other critics, however, have other theories. Reviewing Anderson's 1988 album, *Blue Skies Again,* Rich Kienzle of *Country Music* blamed co-producer Jimmy Bowen for "[trying] to put Anderson into styles that simply don't fit." Nash, reviewing Anderson's 1987 effort, *Countrified,* in *Stereo Review,* claimed that Anderson "has slacked off on the honky-tonk, barroom weepers that he does best and chosen some particularly airless songs that do nothing to boost his career."

But while it is true that Anderson has yet to equal the success he has had with "Swingin'," he did score moderate hits with "Black Sheep," from 1983's *All the People Are Talkin',* and with "Countrified," from the album of the same name. At any rate, Anderson's album sales are large enough to merit continuing releases by major record companies, including late 1988's *John Anderson 10,* which Novak praised as displaying his "uncommon musical common sense," and 1989's *Too Tough to Tame.*

Selected discography

Singles; released by Warner Bros.

"Swingin'," 1983.
"Black Sheep," 1983.
"Countrified," 1987.

Also released "Wild and Blue," "I'm Just an Old Chunk of Coal," and "Would You Catch a Falling Star" during the early 1980s.

LPs

All the People Are Talkin', Warner Bros., 1983.
Countrified, Warner Bros., 1987.
Blue Skies Again, MCA, 1988.
John Anderson 10, MCA, 1988.
Too Tough to Tame, Capitol, 1989.

Sources

Country Music, January-February 1987; May-June 1988; May-June 1989.
People, December 19, 1988.
Stereo Review, March 1987; March 1988.

—*Elizabeth Wenning*

Asleep at the Wheel

Country band

The sounds of old-time Texas swing bands live on today in the work of Asleep at the Wheel, a group that marked its twentieth anniversary in 1990. Asleep at the Wheel has earned considerable critical reputation—and a devoted following—by wandering over a wide spectrum of America's musical roots. The group plays traditional Texas swing jazzed up with big band overtones, standard country fare, zydeco-Cajun, blues, rock, and boogie, all in a high-spirited style that one critic described as "sweatily entertaining."

Akron Beacon Journal correspondent Jack Hurst wrote: "There arguably is no more musically wide-ranging band in the whole country field than Asleep at the Wheel, yet its maintenance of country identity—albeit non-mainstream—tends to be pretty unswerving." For many years an ever-changing group of musicians made a modest living working with Asleep at the Wheel, mostly in live appearances across the United States and Canada. Today the band has become the latest rage on radio; its 1990 album, *Keepin' Me Up Nights*, has sold better than any of its previous work.

For the Record. . .

Band formed in 1970 in Philadelphia, PA; original members included **Ray Benson** (vocals, horn, guitar), **Chris O'Connell** (vocals, guitar), and **Lucky Oceans**. More than seventy-five musicians have played with Asleep at the Wheel on instruments ranging from fiddle and steel guitar to saxophone and accordion. Current membership includes Benson, **John Ely, Mike Francis, David Sanger, Tim Alexander, John Mitchell,** and **Larry Franklin.**

Group signed with United Artists, 1971, and produced first album, *Comin' Right at Ya,* 1971. Currently recording with Arista Records.

Awards: Grammy awards, 1978, for "One O'Clock Jump," and 1988, for "String of Pars"; named best touring band by the Academy of Country Music, 1977; nine nominations for outstanding work from the Country Music Association, 1973-89.

Addresses: *Record company*—Arista Records, 6 West 57th Street, New York, NY 10019.

Odd as it may sound, Asleep at the Wheel had its origins in Philadelphia, Pennsylvania, where founding member Ray Benson grew up. Benson left Philadelphia in 1970, at the age of seventeen, with two pals, Chris O'Connell and Lucky Oceans. While performing in West Virginia, Oceans coined the name Asleep at the Wheel—a brainstorm he received in an outhouse near Paw Paw. After playing several months in West Virginia, the group moved to Marin County, California, where they signed with United Artists. Their first album, *Comin' Right at Ya,* was released in 1973.

Benson told the *Lexington Herald-Leader* that he had strong convictions about the kind of music he wanted to make professionally. "I wanted to return to the roots of American country music," he said. "I wanted to reinterpret country music. In 1969, country music entertainers and musicians were ashamed of their hillbilly and bluesy roots. They were watering down country music and making it like pop and middle-of-the-road music. This disturbed me. They called it 'countrypolitan,' and I didn't like it."

Benson and his associates began to re-create the style and sound of traditional western swing at a time when it seemed distinctly out of vogue. In *down beat* magazine Dave Helland wrote: "AATW has been the prime, if not sole, musical example of the juncture of hillbilly and dixieland music; a juncture which took place just about

50 miles east of the 'x' in Texas, and came to be known as western or Texas swing, with Bob Wills as its band-leader exemplar. . . . What the audience gets is a brew of country-swing instrumentation (fiddle, steel guitar, as well as saxophone); big band jazz standards, and cowboy songs. The albums as well as the gigs mix hoedowns and big band swing, reels, fox trots, and blues."

To quote Hurst, Asleep at the Wheel gradually evolved into a "seven-piece aggregation of hot-time crowd-pleasers." The group performed an average of 250 live concerts per year for more than a decade, traveling literally millions of miles on a series of custom-made buses. Mainstream success may have eluded them, but the musicians found enthusiastic crowds wherever they played, especially in their home base of Austin, Texas. Benson—who is the only original member still associated with the group—surrounded himself with a cadre of talented sidemen (and women), who played everything from steel guitar and fiddle to saxophone, trumpet, and accordion. All told, more than seventy-five people have played with Asleep at the Wheel over its twenty-year run.

The band has always been a favorite with music critics. Two singles, "One O'Clock Jump" and "String of Pars" have won Grammy Awards, and the Academy of Country Music named the group best touring band of 1977. Still, before 1990 Asleep at the Wheel had never earned a gold album. Benson told *down beat* that his act works best in live appearances with a crowd that wants to dance. "Country-western, big band jazz: both those titles will fit us," he said, "but we're definitely a dance band. We're happiest in a dance setting. And in a dance setting it makes a lot more sense musically. We bebop around so many different styles that are really not very consistent musically except that they are connected by the fact that people dance to them. . . . We don't make set lists or nothing. We do an opening four numbers, assess situations, and then do whatever is called for. . . . If we're not an opening act, we regularly play as long as two or three hours straight."

Although a 1988 album, *Western Standard Time,* sold some 100,000 copies and earned the group its second Grammy, CBS Records released the band in 1989. Undaunted, Benson took his act to the Arista label, a newcomer to Nashville circles. There he worked out a deal for an album that would be classic Asleep at the Wheel, but more "radio-friendly" than previous works. The result was *Keepin' Me Up Nights,* a release Hurst called "a highly entertaining collection that, in contrast with so many other Nashville albums, is strongly uptempo and unabashedly joyous."

Keepin' Me Up Nights proved not only radio-friendly,

but video-friendly as well; videos have gained Asleep at the Wheel a number of new fans. The band has been able to confirm its message on a bumper sticker handed out at concerts—"Western Swing Ain't Dead, It's Asleep at the Wheel."

The hectic touring schedule continues, though Asleep at the Wheel now has the extra media coverage that keeps bands in business. Benson credits his group's success to the new interest in traditional American music. "Who knows what country music is supposed to sound like anymore," he told the *Lexington Herald-Leader*. "I describe what we do as roots music. That's what I always wanted to play to begin with. I experiment with things all the time, but after a few years you start to realize what you do best, and you just say, 'Golly, this fits me.'"

Selected discography

Comin' Right at Ya, United Artists, 1971.
Asleep at the Wheel, Epic, 1974.
Wheelin' and Dealin', Capitol, 1976.
Texas Country, United Artists, 1976.
The Wheel, Capitol, 1977.
Collision Course, Capitol, 1978.
Served Live, Capitol, 1979.
Fathers and Sons, Epic.
Framed, MCA, 1980.
Pasture Prime, MCA, 1985.
Asleep at the Wheel, MCA, 1985.
Asleep at the Wheel Ten, Epic, 1987.
Western Standard Time, Epic, 1988.
Keepin' Me Up Nights, Arista, 1990.

Sources

Books

Vaughan, Andrew, *Who's Who in New Country Music,* St. Martin's, 1989.

Periodicals

Akron Beacon Journal, July 8, 1990.
down beat, May 1988.
Lexington Herald-Leader, October 13, 1985; January 15, 1988.

—*Anne Janette Johnson*

Rick Astley

Pop singer

When pop singer Rick Astley burst upon the music scene in 1987, his album, *Whenever You Need Somebody,* debuted in the number one spot on the British charts. He quickly conquered more of the world, his first single—"Never Gonna Give You Up"—rising to the tops of charts in Belgium, Germany, Finland, Denmark, Australia, and the United States. Critics attribute Astley's success to what Edwin Miller in *Seventeen* labeled his "confident romantic baritone"; David DeNicolo in *Glamour* called Astley "the little white kid with the big black voice," and concluded that "Never Gonna Give You Up" is "the ultimate in happy pop."

Astley was born in or near 1966, in the small town of Newton-le-Willows, Lancashire, England. He suffered briefly through piano lessons, but was not particularly entranced by the instrument and soon quit. As he told Miller, he "was dragged into the choir, like anybody else who could half sing, and into school plays." But as an adolescent Astley reserved his true musical enthusiasm for the drums, and he formed a band called Give Way with friends when he was about fifteen years old. "We never did play many gigs," he confessed to Miller. "We were too young, and none of us could drive."

After Astley *had* learned to drive, he played drums for a group named FBI. When FBI found itself playing in small local clubs, Astley found himself writing songs. His fellow band members urged him to fight his shyness and sing them; they liked the results so much that they hired another drummer so Astley could devote himself to vocals. Late in 1985 the production team of Mike Stock, Matt Aitken, and Pete Waterman—who also handle artists such as Bananarama and Samantha Fox—were part of one of Astley's audiences. Waterman recounted his reaction in *People* magazine: "He had a phenomenal voice. It was like hearing a 40-year-old black man while seeing this 19-year-old white pimply kid." Waterman and his partners signed Astley to a contract almost immediately, but they put him through an intensive grooming process before they began working on an album. Astley recalled for Miller: "I'd play one of my songs to them, and they'd say, 'That's good, but don't you think. . . .'"

At last he was ready, and *Whenever You Need Somebody* was recorded and released. In addition to the aforementioned smash "Never Gonna Give You Up," Astley scored hits with "Together Forever," "It Would Take a Strong, Strong Man," and the title track. Critics had praise for his striking voice, but many complained that the songs lacked substance. Astley, however, is untroubled by their opinion; he explained his own philosophy about his work to Miller: "Popular music should be popular music—lighthearted. Something that you look back on in your thirties and say, 'That was fun.' I

For the Record. . .

Full name, Richard Paul Astley; born c. 1966, in Newton-le-Willows, Lancashire, England; father sold plants.

While a teenager played drums in groups, including Give Way and FBI; drove a plant truck; recording artist and concert performer, 1987—.

Awards: Received Grammy nomination for best new artist.

Addresses: *Record company*—RCA, c/o 1133 Ave. of the Americas, New York, NY 10036.

don't think politics and pop music mix. I don't think it's right to make people aware of your own views." Similarly, he told *People:* "I'm not particularly trying to put any messages across. I'm not Peter Gabriel. We can't all be."

Astley released his second album, *Hold Me in Your Arms,* in 1989; it received a similar critical response. David Hiltbrand of *People* carped at Stock, Aitken, and Waterman's method of employing "a beat so solid you could balance a herd of elephants on it," but conceded that "Astley's voice is still an intriguing instrument." Nevertheless, the young singer's danceable tunes continue to make him popular with Top Forty music fans.

Hits from *Hold Me in Your Arms* include "She Wants to Dance With Me," and a remake of the Temptations' smash, "Ain't Too Proud to Beg."

Selected discography

Albums

Whenever You Need Somebody (includes "Whenever You Need Somebody," "Never Gonna Give You Up," "Together Forever," "It Would Take a Strong, Strong Man," and "When I Fall in Love"), RCA, 1987.
Hold Me in Your Arms (includes "Hold Me in Your Arms," "She Wants to Dance With Me," "Ain't Too Proud to Beg," "Till Then," "I Don't Want to Be Your Lover," "Dial My Number," "I Don't Wanna Lose Her," "Take Me to Your Heart," and "Giving Up on Love"), RCA, 1989.
Free, RCA, 1991.

Sources

Glamour, August 1988.
People, February 8, 1988; June 27, 1988; February 20, 1989.
Rolling Stone, March 23, 1989.
Seventeen, July 1988.
Stereo Review, July 1988; May 1989.

—Elizabeth Wenning

Chet Atkins

Guitarist, songwriter

A more important contributor to the genre of country music than famed guitarist and composer Chet Atkins is difficult to imagine. Not only has the man labeled "Mr. Guitar" by fans and critics alike gifted music audiences with his own recordings of classics such as "Gallopin' Guitar," "Country Gentlemen," and "Snowbird," but for many years he helped RCA Records recruit other talented country artists, including Waylon Jennings and Charley Pride.

And while Atkins is credited by some with helping country music retain its popularity throughout the boom of rock and roll, he has not limited himself to performing in the country genre—he seems equally adept at picking out the strains of jazz, classical, and pop music on his guitar, and during the 1980s has released records that find airplay on New Age music stations. Atkins has also received numerous awards for his talent, including several Grammy awards and nominations, and was for many consecutive years named top guitarist by *Cash Box* magazine.

Chester Burton Atkins was born June 20, 1924, in a secluded, rural area near Luttrell, Tennessee. His family was poor, and large—both his mother and father had children from previous marriages. But Atkins was surrounded by music from the beginning, and in addition to listening to his older family members sing and play, he also listened to the records of country pioneer Jimmie Rodgers. When he was very small, his older brothers did not want him playing their guitars, so he first learned the violin, or fiddle. Then, when he was nine, he traded a gun for an old, beat-up guitar, but he continued with the fiddle, and also the ukulele. Atkins and his brother would play at various gathering places, putting a hat before them on the ground for people to throw change in, and, for the Depression years, were fairly successful.

Atkins liked the guitar best, however, and more or less taught himself to play. As a boy he would listen to guitarists on a radio crystal set he had assembled himself, and try to imitate their styles. One of his favorites was Merle Travis, but, as he told Bill Milkowski in *down beat,* "I didn't see his fingers so I didn't know he was playing with just one finger and a thumb. I started fooling around with three fingers and a thumb, which turned out to be this pseudoclassical style that I stuck with. So I guess I was lucky that I didn't see him and copy him any more than I did." Thus Atkins developed his distinctive finger style guitar, which, in turn, has been imitated by many other aspiring artists.

While Atkins was still in high school, he landed his first job with a radio station, playing both country and jazz for WRBL in Columbus, Georgia, where he had gone with some of his family to live in order to improve the

Full name, Chester Burton Atkins; born June 20, 1924, near Luttrell, Tenn.; son of James Arley (a music teacher, piano tuner, and evangelical singer), and Ida (maiden name, Sharp) Atkins; married Leona Pearl Johnson (a singer), July 3, 1946; children: Merle (daughter).

Played fiddle in the street for small change as a child; during the 1940s played fiddle and/or guitar for various radio stations and radio shows, including "The Parson Jack Show," WRBL, Columbus, Ga., "The Jumpin' Bill Carlisle and Archie Campbell Show" and "Midday Merry-Go-Round," also member of staff band, WNOX, Knoxville, Tenn.; member of staff band, WLW, Cincinatti, Ohio; worked at WPTF, Raleigh, N.C.; performed on Grand Ole Opry, c. 1946; performed on "Sunshine Sue Show" and "Old Dominion Barn Dance," WRVA, Richmond, Va.; member of Slim Wilson and the Tall Timber Trio, KWTO, Springfield, Mo.; featured on the Mutual radio network show "Corn's a' Crackin'"; member of cowboy band in Denver, Colo.; recording artist, 1947—. Also performed again on the Grand Ole Opry during the late 1940s and 1950s, forming acts with Homer and Jethro and the Carter Family. Served as session musician for RCA Victor Records, 1949-53, consultant, 1953-57, part-time producer, 1957, manager, 1957-68, Division Vice President, 1968-c. 1982.

Awards: Elected to the Country Music Hall of Fame, 1973; several Grammy Awards, including Best Contemporary Instrumental Performance of 1967 for *Chet Atkins Picks the Best*, Best Country Instrumental Performance of 1970 for *Me and Jerry*, Best Country Instrumental Performance of 1971 for "Snowbird," and another Grammy in 1976 for *Chester and Lester*. Has been named top guitarist for many years during the 1960s and 1970s by *Cash Box* magazine. Humanitarian Award, 1972, from the National Council of Christians and Jews.

Addresses: *Record company*—Columbia Records, 51 West 52nd Street, New York, NY 10019.

country picking, or for missing performances due to asthma flare-ups. He even had a brief stint with the "Grand Ole Opry."

Atkins was playing with a cowboy band in Denver, Colorado, when Steve Sholes of RCA caught up to him. Sholes had seen a transcription—despite the fact that Atkins never learned to read or write music, and memorizes all of his pieces—of the young guitarist's "Canned Heat" and was favorably impressed, but Atkins moved from job to job so much that he proved somewhat difficult to locate. Sholes offered Atkins a recording contract with RCA, and Atkins traveled to the company's Chicago studios. Some of the numbers from this session included Atkins's own vocals; he has since tried to destroy many of the master tapes that include his singing. Though his first instrumental cuts—"Canned Heat," "Bug Dance," and "Nashville Jump" (released in 1947)—did not garner much public attention, disc jockeys liked them and gave them a lot of airplay.

But Atkins was not convinced that his recording career would take off, and he continued to play on radio

A more important contributor to the genre of country music than famed guitarist and composer Chet Atkins is difficult to imagine.

shows. During the late 1940s he was invited to play with the Carter Family, and with them performed again on the "Grand Ole Opry" in 1950. In 1949, however, he had recorded more tracks for RCA, including the hits "Gallopin' Guitar" and "Main Street Breakdown." At last, he was brought to the attention of a widespread audience, and his fame continued to grow with album releases like *Chet Atkins In Three Dimensions* and *Stringin' Along*. Eventually, of course, Atkins became popular worldwide, making successful tours of Europe and Africa in addition to the United States.

Meanwhile, RCA decided to make Atkins a session musician as well as a featured attraction. Recording executives quickly noticed that his suggestions on other artist's work made for more successful products, and they increasingly involved him in management decisions. He became an artist and repertory man for them, in charge of finding and recruiting new talent, and his discoveries include Don Gibson, Waylon Jennings, Dottie West, Bobby Bare, and pianist Floyd Cramer. Atkins was also instrumental in signing the first

severe asthma he had suffered since childhood. He dropped out of high school, however, and returned to Tennessee, winning a job playing fiddle at Knoxville's WNOX. He served there on programs such as "The Jumpin' Bill Carlisle and Archie Campbell Show" and "Midday Merry-Go-Round." From then on, Atkins spent most of the 1940s playing for various radio stations throughout the United States, often impressing management and other artists with his virtuosity, but often getting fired, either for mixing a little jazz into his successful black country singer, Charley Pride. By 1968, after he had managed their Nashville operations for over ten years, RCA had named Atkins its division vice president in charge of country music.

In his management work for RCA, Atkins helped country music adapt itself for consumption by increasingly modern audiences. He was able to do this because, in addition to having a certain knack for predicting what performances would make for hit records, he continually experimented with his own music. Atkins has played jazz for festival audiences at Newport, strummed the classical notes of Bach with symphonies, and recorded with Arthur Fiedler and the Boston Pops, as well as many country artists. One of the first country musicians to recognize the talent of the Beatles, Atkins's *Chet Atkins Picks on the Beatles* proved to be one of his best selling albums.

Though Atkins left RCA in 1982, he continues to be active as a recording artist for Columbia. In addition, compact disc releases of some of his older albums are still producing raves from the critics. One such compilation, including the albums *Pickin' My Way, In Hollywood,* and *Alone,* prompted reviewer Jon Sievert in *Guitar Player* to declare that "Chet's masterful tempo shifts, subtle vibrato technique, intimate feel, and uncommon taste make him required listening for all pretenders to the throne." Atkins's Columbia recordings, however, increasingly stray from the country genre, including *Chet Atkins, C.G.P.* (initials stand for Certified Guitar Player), which Alanna Nash of Stereo Review lauded for its "complex musical images in startlingly vivid colors." Cuts from *C.G.P.* and a few albums previous to it are often heard on progressive and new age music radio stations, and Milkowski in *down beat* concluded that Atkins's 1980s efforts "are really a natural progression for the man who has always been stretching, probing other idioms, and interpreting these modes through his own signature approach."

Selected discography

LPs; released by RCA, except as noted

Chet Atkins Plays Guitar, 1951.
Chet Atkins in Three Dimensions, 1951.
Hi-Fi in Focus, 1957.
At Home, 1958.
In Hollywood, 1959.
Mister Guitar, 1960.
Teensville, 1960.
Other Chet Atkins, 1960.
Workshop, 1961.
Most Popular, 1961.
Down Home, 1962.

Caribbean Guitar, 1962.
Back Home Hymns, 1962.
Our Man in Nashville, 1963.
Travelin', 1963.
Guitar Country, 1964.
Best, 1964.
Progressive Pickin', 1964.
Reminiscing, 1964.
My Favorite Guitars, 1965.
Chet Atkins Picks on the Beatles, 1966.
From Nashville, 1966.
Guitar World, 1967.
Chet Atkins Picks the Best, 1967.
Class Guitar, 1967.
Solid Gold '69, 1969.
Warmth, 1969.
Best, Volume 2, 1970.
Love and Guitars, 1970.
Standing Alone, 1970.
(With Jerry Reed) *Me and Jerry,* 1970.
This Is Chet Atkins, 1970.
Portrait of My Woman, 1971.
For the Good Times, 1971.
Welcome to My World, 1971.
Then You Can Tell Me Goodbye, 1971.
Pickin' My Way, 1971.
Lovin' Her Was Easier, 1971.
Now & Then, 1972.
Chet Atkins Picks on the Hits, 1972.
(With Merle Travis) *The Atkins-Travis Travelin' Show,* 1974.
Atkins String Band, 1975.
(With Les Paul) *Chester and Lester,* 1976.
Stay Tuned, Columbia, 1985.
Chet Atkins, C.G.P., Columbia, 1989.

Other

(Compact disc compilation) *Pickin' My Way/In Hollywood/Alone,* Mobile Fidelity Sound Lab, 1989.

Also recorded *Stringin' Along* and *Finger Style Guitar* on RCA during the 1950s.

Sources

Books

Atkins, Chet, *Country Gentleman,* Regnery, 1974.

Periodicals

Country Music, May-June 1989.
down beat, May 1989.
Guitar Player, November 1989; December 1989.
Stereo Review, May 1989.

—Elizabeth Wenning

Frankie Avalon

Singer, actor

Perhaps best known for his roles in a series of 1960s musical films about young people on the beach, pop singer Frankie Avalon was also an important part of the Philadelphia sound of the late 1950s and early 1960s. He had hits like "Dede Dinah" and his smash "Venus" during this period; later Avalon concentrated more on film and television, appearing in the 1978 film musical *Grease,* and guesting on shows like *Fantasy Island.* In 1987, he reunited with his beach movie partner Annette Funicello to make the comedy musical *Back to the Beach.*

Avalon was born Frank Avallone on September 18, 1940, in Philadelphia, Pennsylvania. He became interested in music during his childhood, and was taking lessons on the trumpet while still in grade school. The boy began playing professionally when he was almost thirteen years old, playing with a teenage group in Atlantic City, New Jersey. In this way, Avalon became something of a local celebrity, and he was soon playing on Paul Whiteman's television show in Philadelphia. Within a few years, he had gone on to nationally-broadcast programs, including Jackie Gleason's.

Meanwhile, Avalon had also developed a good singing voice. He was discovered by songwriters Bob Marcucci and Peter de Angelis, who, in addition to their creative activities, also owned Chancellor Records. They signed Avalon to a contract; his first recordings were released in 1957. These singles enjoyed a small measure of success, but Avalon's 1958 release, "Dede Dinah," became a nationwide hit. The young singer had his best year as a recording artist, however, in 1959. Avalon scored with "Just Ask Your Heart," which was quite popular, and then followed it up with the musical plea to the Roman goddess of love, "Venus." The latter tune climbed to the Number 1 spot on the charts. In 1960, Avalon had another hit, "Why."

But Avalon had been exploring a career as an actor concurrent with his one as a vocalist. Even before "Dede Dinah" made him a celebrity throughout the United States, he had won his first screen role, making his debut in the motion picture *Disc Jockey Jamboree.* Avalon also made films such as *Guns of the Timberland* and *The Carpetbaggers* during the early 1960s before settling into the series of beach movies he starred in with Funicello. The first of these low-budget fun-fests, which always featured Avalon's vocal talents as well, was simply titled *Beach Party,* and it was released in 1963. In the next two years he starred in four more such motion pictures—*Muscle Beach Party, Bikini Beach, Beach Blanket Bingo,* and *How to Stuff a Wild Bikini.*

Though Avalon continued to be interested in his singing career—like many other popular artists of the late 1950s and early 1960s—the demand for his talents was drastically reduced with the advent of the British Invasion. He still performed in small clubs, though he admitted to Eric Sherman in the *Ladies' Home Journal* that "sometimes there wouldn't be more than forty people in the audience." Avalon supplemented his income with guest appearances on television shows, including *Love, American Style* and *Fantasy Island.* For almost a decade he did not record, but in 1975 he cut a disco version of his old hit "Venus" that made it into the Top 40. In 1978, Avalon made a winning cameo appearance in the musical film *Grease,* performing the song "Beauty School Drop Out."

But the 1980s nostalgia for the music of the 1950s and 1960s brought an upswing in Avalon's fortune. The audiences for his concerts grew way beyond forty people; in fact, according to Sherman, the performances were often sellouts. From this, Avalon got the idea to make another beach movie. At first, screen producers were skeptical about the film's appeal, but television people were interested. But Avalon told Jeff Yarbrough in *People:* "I didn't want to do a movie of the week that would be on one night and be over." Eventually, however, he got the backing of film producer Frank Mancuso Jr., famed for the *Friday the Thirteenth* series of horror films, and *Back to the Beach* was made in 1987. The musical motion picture took a look at the Avalon and Funicello characters of the old beach movies as middle-aged adults with children of their own. According to Yarbrough, Avalon and Funicello have considered doing a sequel to *Back to the Beach.*

Selected discography

Single releases

"Dede Dinah," Chancellor, 1958.
"Just Ask Your Heart," Chancellor, 1959.
"Venus," Chancellor, 1959.
"Why," Chancellor, 1960.
"Venus," (disco version), De-Lite Records, 1975.

LPs

Hits of Frankie Avalon, United Artists, 1964.

Sources

Ladies' Home Journal, July 1987.
Maclean's, August 17, 1987.
People, August 10, 1987.

—Elizabeth Wenning

Pearl Bailey

Singer, actress

Pearl Bailey's sudden death at the age of 72 deprived America of one of its best-known goodwill ambassadors. The energetic and personable Bailey was beloved by three generations of theater and movie fans, and was the favorite of presidents Dwight D. Eisenhower, Lyndon Johnson, and Gerald Ford. In the *Washington Post,* Joseph McLellan called Bailey "America's ambassador of love," adding: "She used her voice—and her heart—to become an eloquent advocate for the poor, oppressed and suffering, working to promote interracial harmony and more recently to help those worldwide suffering from AIDS."

Bailey began singing on the lightly comic vaudeville theater circuit in the early 1930s, eventually carrying her special talents into the largest nightclubs and onto the Broadway stage. "Here was no skinny starlet of small renown," wrote Karl Stark in the *Philadelphia Inquirer.* "Bailey . . . was a star of the old school, a performer who could wow you with the expressive power of her art or bowl you over with the acuity of her intellect. She was, first and foremost, a vaudevillian who relished the intimacy of live performances."

Pearl Mae Bailey was born in the small town of Newport News, Virginia, in 1918. Her father was an evangelical minister, and from her earliest years she sang and danced during his church services. When she was only four her parents divorced, and she moved with her two sisters and brother, first to Washington, D.C. and then to Philadelphia, Pennsylvania.

It was in Philadelphia, during her teens, that Bailey was introduced to show business. Her brother was a professional tap dancer who often worked at the city's Pearl Theatre. One night when he was late returning home for dinner, she went down to get him and wound up entered in an amateur-night contest. She sang "Poor Butterfly" and won first prize—five dollars and a two-week engagement at the theater. Unfortunately, the theater had hit hard times, and it closed before Bailey could be paid for her services. She was undaunted, however; the brief experience on stage convinced her that it was the only career for her.

Bailey entered and won another amateur contest, this time at the renowned Apollo Theatre in New York City. Soon thereafter she set out on a club circuit that took her through the rough-and-tumble coal mining towns of central Pennsylvania. For 15 dollars a week she sang in Scranton, Wilkes-Barre, and Pottsville before graduating to larger venues in Washington, D.C. and Baltimore. The onset of World War II found her touring the country with a U.S.O. (United Service Organizations) troupe, entertaining stateside U.S. servicemen.

For the Record. . .

Full name Pearl Mae Bailey; born March 29, 1918, in Newport News, VA; died of heart failure, August 17, 1990, in Philadelphia, PA; daughter of Joseph James (a minister) and Ella Mae Bailey; married fourth husband, Louis Bellson, Jr. (a jazz drummer), November 19, 1952; children: Tony, DeeDee. *Education:* Georgetown University, B.A., 1985.

Singer and actress, 1933-90. Had debut in an amateur-night contest at Pearl Theatre in Philadelphia, 1933; became professional singer, 1933. Became soloist at major New York City nightclubs, 1944; worked as stand-in with Cab Calloway's band, 1945. Had Broadway debut on March 30, 1946, in *St. Louis Woman.* Also appeared on Broadway in *House of Flowers,* 1954, and *Hello, Dolly!,* 1967.

Film appearances include *Isn't It Romantic,* 1948; *Carmen Jones,* 1954; *Saint Louis Blues,* 1957; *Porgy and Bess,* 1959; *All the Fine Young Cannibals,* 1960; *The Landlord,* 1970; and *Norman, Is That You?,* 1976.

Star of television series *The Pearl Bailey Show,* 1971, and *Silver Spoons,* 1982-85; made numerous guest appearances on variety and holiday television shows, including *Night of 100 Stars,* 1982.

Awards: Donaldson Award, 1946, for *St. Louis Woman;* Entertainer of the Year citation from *Cue* magazine, 1967; Antoinette Perry Award (Tony), 1968, for *Hello, Dolly!;* March of Dimes Award, 1968; Woman of the Year citation from the U.S.A., 1969; named special advisor to the U.S. Mission of the United Nations General Assembly, 30th session, 1975.

After the war Bailey became a headliner in her own right. She was working at the Village Vanguard in New York City in 1944, when the owner suggested she loosen up and be herself onstage. That advice helped her to create a signature style—easy and personal, with throwaway lines and jokes added between and during songs. McLellan wrote: "The public image projected through Bailey's songs was less earth mother than earthy. Her voice had a pleasant tone, an impressive clarity and a way of projecting words with exquisite care. She had a special way of styling a song, with a flavor of jazz and often some worldly wise aside on the music's sentiment." The critic added: "Bailey inherited a special tradition of earthy, sexually aware singing from such pioneers as [American blues singers] Ma Rainey and Billie Holiday, tidied it up a bit for general

consumption and won an enthusiastic following in nightclubs."

The entertainer's fame was assured in 1945, when she signed on as a stand-in with Cab Calloway and his orchestra. Bailey worked 20 weeks with Calloway at the Zanzibar nightclub on Broadway and forged a friendship with him that would last for decades. In 1946 she made her Broadway debut with a major role in *St. Louis Woman,* an all-black musical. Her two numbers, "A Woman's Prerogative" and "Legalize My Name," were considered the highlights of an otherwise average show, and Bailey received the 1946 Donaldson Award as best newcomer on Broadway.

Thereafter Bailey kept busy with a steady round of nightclub appearances, stage plays, and movies. She appeared in both major all-black musical films of the 1950s, *Carmen Jones* and *Porgy and Bess,* and won a wide following with her live performances of the songs "Birth of the Blues," "Bill Bailey, Won't You Please Come Home," "Let's Do It," "Come Rain or Come Shine," and "St. Louis Blues." In 1957 she was a featured entertainer at the second inauguration of President Eisenhower.

The high point of Bailey's career came in 1967, when she headed the cast of a new Broadway staging of *Hello, Dolly!* The all-black show featured Bailey as the husband-hunting Dolly Gallagher Levi, and her friend Cab Calloway as the reluctant suitor Horace Vandergelder. The show opened in November of 1967 to rave reviews. *New York Times* theatre critic Clive Barnes, for one, wrote that Bailey "took the whole musical in her hands and swung it around her neck as easily as if it were a feather boa. Her timing was exquisite, with asides tossed away as languidly as one might tap ash from a cigarette, and her singing had that deep throaty rumble that . . . is always so oddly stirring." Barnes concluded: "The audience would have elected her governor if she'd only name the state." Bailey was awarded a Tony for her work in *Hello, Dolly!*

After touring extensively with *Hello, Dolly!,* Bailey was offered her own television show. *The Pearl Bailey Show* lasted only one season, but the performer made numerous guest appearances on other variety and dramatic shows. For several years in the 1980s she portrayed Lulu Baker in the situation comedy *Silver Spoons,* but Bailey always preferred working before live audiences—her greatest joy, she said, was singing to a crowd.

Bailey numbered several United States presidents among her fans, and she was named a public goodwill ambassador to the United Nations four times. By the mid-1980s she had written five books and had earned, at age 67, her bachelor's degree in theology from

Georgetown University. After receiving her degree, Bailey told the *Philadelphia Inquirer:* "I have a go-for-it attitude about education, about life, about everything. . . . My religion is action. You can't spend your life waiting around. You go for it."

Bailey had suffered from heart trouble as early as the 1960s, but she seemed in good health in the summer of 1990 when she traveled to Philadelphia for knee surgery. She was recuperating from the operation when she died unexpectedly on August 17th in her Philadelphia hotel room. She was survived by her devoted husband of 38 years, jazz drummer Louis Bellson, Jr., and two adopted children.

Karl Stark remembered Bailey as a "wise, witty, and exuberant woman" whose accomplishments in many fields were staggering. The entertainer undoubtedly made her finest mark as a singer—perhaps the most famous black woman singer of her generation. Stark concluded of Bailey: "She was sultry and statuesque, a muse in high heels. When she sang a song, she squeezed it with an earthy embrace that could warm a listener from the back of the neck to the soles of his feet."

Writings

Raw Pearl, Harcourt, 1969.
Talking to Myself, Harcourt, 1971.
Pearl's Kitchen: An Extraordinary Cookbook, Harcourt, 1973.
Duey's Tale (juvenile), Harcourt, 1975.
Hurry Up, America, and Spit, Harcourt, 1976.

Selected discography

Hello, Dolly!, RCA, 1968.

Sources

Books

Contemporary Theatre, Film, and Television, Volume 4, Gale, 1985.
Current Biography Yearbook 1969, H.W. Wilson, 1970.
Bailey, Pearl, *Raw Pearl,* Harcourt, 1969.
Bailey, Pearl, *Talking to Myself,* Harcourt, 1971.

Periodicals

Cue, January 6, 1968.
Life, December 8, 1967.
Newsweek, December 4, 1967.
New York Post, January 16, 1955; April 27, 1965; November 18, 1967.
New York Times, November 13, 1967; November 20, 1967; November 26, 1967.

Obituaries

Philadelphia Inquirer, August 18, 1990; August 20, 1990.
Washington Post, August 19, 1990.

—*Anne Janette Johnson*

Basia

Singer, songwriter

"**A** potent cosmopolitan cocktail," wrote Cathleen McGuigan in *Newsweek,* Basia "sings a brand of jazzy Brazilian-flavored blend that could melt ice." Born and raised in Poland, Basia—who lives in London, and writes and records in English—shows influences of samba, Brazilian bossa nova, and American soul in her music. "Such creative poaching," though, commented Andrew Abrahams in *People,* "has left her with her own unmistakable style." Basia flaunts a "rich, freewheeling voice" and "stylish urbanity," according to McGuigan; hers "is music for grown-ups, but it's not too smooth—no one could sit still through its irresistible bossa nova beat." Basia's solo albums, *Time and Tide* and *London Warsaw New York,* have been hits on both contemporary jazz and pop listings in the United States and Europe, and the singer holds the distinction of being the first Pole to appear on U.S. top-forty charts.

Basia grew up in the southern Polish industrial city of Jaworzno, where her parents ran an ice cream enterprise. She was influenced early by recordings of various American artists. "I was hungry for everything," she told Abrahams. Among her favorites was Aretha Franklin's *Greatest Hits.* She also listened to Stevie Wonder, Carole King, James Taylor, Pink Floyd, and King Crimson. At 15 Basia won a national talent contest and joined an all-girl group named Alibabki, which toured Eastern Europe and the Soviet Union for two years. At the age of 18 she made her way to Warsaw, where she joined a group that came to the attention of an agent, who signed them to perform at Polish-American centers in the United States. In 1980 Basia sang pop music—in both Polish and English—at the Polonia club in Chicago, and frequented the city's blues and jazz establishments. The singer was homesick for Poland, however, and in 1981 moved to London to be nearer her family.

In England Basia met keyboardist Danny White and worked briefly with a jazz-funk group, Bronze, before joining Matt Bianco, a pop trio that sported a smooth jazz style, classy designer suits, and a name contrived to give the group an Italian feel. Matt Bianco was very popular throughout Europe and Basia was able to further develop her samba style while with the group. Her love affair with the bossa nova and samba came from her admiration for Brazilian singer Astrud Gilberto, who provided vocals on the original recording of "The Girl from Ipanema." Basia told Abrahams that she particularly liked Gilberto's "very light feel." In fact, Basia's "Astrud" pays tribute to the singer's influence: "One-note samba will never be the same," the song goes.

Basia longed for more autonomy, however, than she found with Matt Bianco and in 1985 she and White broke away to do their own music. "All I had to do was record my parts in the studio and look pretty onstage," she told Abrahams about her role with the band. "I even had to get permission to wear a certain kind of shirt or dress." Basia and White began to collaborate on songs that would eventually comprise her 1986 debut solo album *Time and Tide.*

A contributor to *Melody Maker* called the release a "cool, classy concoction of Latin, funk and jazz rhythms," while other reviewers similarly praised it as one of the year's most stylish releases. Two songs, "Promises" and "New Day for You," were number-one hits on the adult contemporary charts, while the title track was a top pop single. On the strength of the album—which turned platinum in 1989—Basia and her band, led by White, embarked on a successful 22-city tour of the United States.

In 1989 Basia released a second album, *London Warsaw New York,* which contained a collection of jazz-influenced pop songs. That effort turned gold and generated two new hits, "Cruising for Bruising" and "Until You Come Back to Me," a remake of Aretha Franklin's 1973 hit. "Overall, popular music doesn't get much better than this," wrote a contributor to *Stereo Review.* He added: "As before, Basia and White have collaborated as writers and arrangers, coming up with a delightful group of original compositions. Basia performs the vocals in styles ranging from the pensive to the teasing, but she is always irresistible. . . . The melodies flow naturally yet evolve into all sorts of unexpect-

ed shapes." Basia explained the message behind the songs on *London Warsaw New York:* "All the songs on this album share a common theme. People have the same hearts, the same needs and desires. They all want to love and be loved, wherever they live, be it Europe, America, or Asia."

While some critics have dubbed Basia a jazz artist, she disagrees: "I'm a pop singer, not a jazz singer," she told Angie Daniell in *Melody Maker.* "I like elements of Fifties jazz which I put into my music because I feel comfortable with them, but it's a million miles away from [legendary jazz singers] Sarah Vaughan or Ella Fitzgerald. I could never be in the same league as them." Some have compared Basia to the singer Sade, but, as talent agent Muff Winwood commented to Janice C. Simpson in *Time,* "Sade has a more soulful, laid-back style. . . . Basia is much more vibrant and up front."

In interviews Basia has been quick to comment about being close to her Polish heritage. "Did you ever meet a Polish person who wasn't emotional?" she was quoted by Abrahams. "Chopin? The Pope? We start talking about our country or our mothers, and all of a sudden everyone's crying!" She enjoys her success outside of her native country, yet one day hopes to return to Poland—where she also enjoys a large popular following. "I miss the passion of Poland," she told Abrahams. "If something is wrong, the British won't tell you what it is. . . . I know I'm doing well now, but when I stop someday and I'm old, I will go back to Poland. There's no superficial politeness there. They tell you exactly what they feel."

Selected discography

Time and Tide (includes "Promises," "Run for Cover," "Time and Tide," "New Day for You," "Astrud," and "Miles Away"), Epic/Columbia, 1986.
London Warsaw New York (includes "Cruising for Bruising," "Best Friends," and "Until You Come Back to Me"), Epic/Columbia, 1989.

Also appeared on several recordings with group Matt Bianco under WEA label, including the album *Whose Side Are You On,* and sang lead on the hit single "Half a Minute." Released video collection *A New Day,* CBS, 1990.

Sources

BMI: Music World, winter 1989.
Glamour, June 1990.
Jazziz, April/May 1990.
Los Angeles Times, February 11, 1990.

Melody Maker, December 13, 1986; July 4, 1987; July 18, 1987;
   February 6, 1988.
Newsweek, August 22, 1988.
People, January 30, 1989.
St. Petersburg Times (Florida), March 9, 1990.
Stereo Review, June 1990.
Time, April 23, 1990.

—Michael E. Mueller

Adrian Belew

Guitarist

Rock guitarist Adrian Belew has had a long and distinguished career recording with other rock artists, including Frank Zappa and David Bowie, as well as holding memberships in bands and putting out solo recordings. Noted for his unusual experimentation with the guitar, Belew finally achieved widespread popularity with the release of his 1989 album, *Mr. Music Head,* which featured the hit single, "Oh, Daddy." As reviewer Andrew Nash noted in *High Fidelity,* Belew's "guitar work has always been distinctive."

Belew was heading his own band, Sweetheart, and playing small clubs in the southern United States during the late 1970s. At one such engagement he was performing at Fanny's in Nashville, Tennessee; Frank Zappa was in the audience, and, impressed with what he heard, asked Belew to audition for his band. He did so, and successfully recorded with Zappa for a while. Belew's reputation for fine and unusual guitar playing grew, and over the years he has played not only for Zappa and Bowie, but for Talking Heads, Laurie Anderson, Jean-Michel Jarre, and Paul Simon.

In the early 1980s, Belew was part of the rock group King Crimson, winning critical acclaim for his contribution to their recordings. But, as he explained to *Rolling Stone*'s Moira McCormick, he was not happy. "A great band, but not an entirely pleasant experience. It isn't publicly known, but I had a very hard time in King Crimson." Belew did derive some pleasure, however, from his solo career during the same period. While he was not widely known to fans, critics noticed the three albums he cut on the Island label, including 1982's *Lone Rhino,* which Nash pronounced a "masterpiece."

When King Crimson broke up in 1984, Belew was looking forward to devoting more time to his solo work, in addition to playing on the albums of others. According to McCormick, "he vowed he'd never be in a band again." But in 1985 he was scheduled to produce an album for a local Cincinnati, Ohio, band called the Raisins, whose members he had met while he was still performing with Sweetheart. When Belew arrived on the scene, however, he found the Raisins at the point of breaking up. He told McCormick that he spent the night "trying to figure out what I thought about the whole thing. At three o'clock in the morning, it just hit me that I wanted to be in a band with these guys. That I in fact had always wanted to be in a band with these guys, and why didn't we just start one?"

Thus, with former Raisins members Rob Fetters, Bob Nyswonger, and Chris Arduser, Belew formed the Bears. "We wanted a generic name, one that sounded like a Little League team," Belew quipped to McCormick. By 1987, they had released their self-titled debut album on IRS's sister label, Primitive Man. Featuring a blend of

For the Record. . .

Born c. 1950; children: Audie, Ernie, Iris. Guitarist, songwriter, vocalist, pianist. Has been a professional guitarist since the 1970s; played with group, Sweetheart, in 1976; served as guitarist for various artists, including Frank Zappa, David Bowie, Talking Heads, Laurie Anderson, Jean-Michel Jarre, and Paul Simon; member of King Crimson, c. 1981-84; member of the Bears, beginning c. 1987; solo recording artist.

Addresses: *Home*—Lake Geneva, Wisconsin. *Record company*—Atlantic Records, 75 Rockefeller Plaza, New York, NY 10019.

Eastern and Western style music, *The Bears* was called "a collection of fresh, artful pop songs set provocatively askew by the alluring modalities of the Orient" by McCormick. Nash proclaimed that "the Bears sound like a charged-up, adventurous improvement on Huey Lewis and the News."

In 1989 Belew released the album *Mr. Music Head* on Atlantic Records, which spawned his first solo hit, "Oh, Daddy." Accompanying him on this track—and in the song's video, which received much airplay on cable music video stations, is his eldest daughter, Audie. Critic David Hiltbrand of *People* described "Oh, Daddy" as "a bopping little pop song in which a young girl, her head full of lurid MTV images, asks her rock musician father such logical questions as 'Daddy, when you gonna put on some stretch pants?'" Reviewer Wif Stenger in *Rolling Stone* also noted the question: "'When you gonna be a big star,'—to which Belew responds, 'Well, don't hold your breath/'Cause it'll make you blue!'"

Other tracks, including "Hot Zoo," "One of Those Days," and "1967," have also been singled out for acclaim; Hiltbrand called "1967" the album's "most sustained achievement." Similarly, Stenger called the cut "a whimsical, Beatlesque ramble into the attic of a restless musical mind," and declared that *Mr. Music Head* contained "some of [Belew's] most imaginative guitar exploration ever." In 1990, Belew released another album on the Atlantic label, *Young Lions*.

Selected discography

Lone Rhino, Island, 1982.
Desire Caught By the Tale, Island, 1987.
(With the Bears) *The Bears* (includes "Man Behind the Curtain," "Raining," "None of the Above," and "Figure It Out"), Primitive Man, 1987.
Mr. Music Head (includes "Oh, Daddy," "Coconuts," "Hot Zoo," "One of Those Days," "Bad Days," "1967," and "Motor Bungalow"), Atlantic, 1989.
Young Lions, Atlantic, 1990.

Also recorded with other groups and artists, including King Crimson, Frank Zappa, David Bowie, Talking Heads, Laurie Anderson, Jean-Michel Jarre, and Paul Simon; also recorded another solo album on Island Records.

Sources

High Fidelity, August 1987.
People, August 14, 1989.
Rolling Stone, June 4, 1987; August 10, 1989.

—Elizabeth Wenning

Clint Black

Singer, songwriter, guitarist

Throughout 1990 the country charts were dominated by a new young star—Clint Black, a Houston-based honky tonker with an expressive voice and movie star good looks. Black's debut album, *Killin' Time,* went platinum and spent a phenomenal eight months at number one on the *Billboard* lists, and he placed no less than five singles in the country top ten as well. Few stars have climbed to fame so quickly on the strength of just one album.

"Boy, it's like jumpin' into a car doing eighty," Black told *Rolling Stone* of his sudden success. Once the front singer in an anonymous bar band, Black is now hounded by the press and is a headlining entertainer who can draw crowds of 85,000. Women beg him for locks of his hair and even his fingernail clippings, and in the summer of 1990 fans stood in line all day to get his autograph at a fair in Nashville. "I'd pretty much been living off nightclub gigs for the past eight or nine years," Black told *Country America* magazine. "I made ends meet, but I never could keep up with the bills. Now I find I can keep up with the bills and have a little extra too."

Such modest expectations are typical of Clint Black, a singer who has sought success because he dearly loves to perform. Black was born in New Jersey in 1962 but was raised in Texas, where his father worked as a crane operator. The youngest of four boys, he barely missed being called Cole by a father who loved Cole Porter. His father backed off the name Cole Black, he told *Country America,* only "because we thought he'd take a ribbing for it." Black was "painfully short" and described himself in *People* magazine as "a loner" who "wasn't popular with girls." In high school Black began to pick guitar and sing. He entered a school talent show as a junior and won second place. From then on, he told *People,* "I took my guitar everywhere I went. I was obsessed."

Soon after he graduated from high school in 1980, Black hit the nightclub circuit in Houston, playing and singing covers of Merle Haggard, Loggins and Messina, Charlie Daniels, Willie Nelson, and even Dire Straits. The living was meager, to say the least, and to help make ends meet he also worked in construction. "I hated that kind of work," he admitted in *People.* Slowly Black began to incorporate his own material into his act, mainly Haggard-esque honky tonk ballads and tales of lost love. In order to publicize his appearances, he used his own pocket money to print fliers which were distributed in the Houston area.

In 1987 Black met guitarist Hayden Nicholas at a gig. Nicholas joined Black's band and began providing tunes for Black's lyrics. The following year, producer Bill Ham (ZZ Top and others) caught Black's perform-

Born February 4, 1962, in Long Branch, N.J.; son of G. A. (a crane operator) and Ann Black. *Education:* High school graduate.

Country singer, guitarist, and songwriter, 1980—. Has also worked in construction in Houston, Tex. and as a bait cutter in Galveston, Tex. Signed with RCA Records c. 1988; released first album, *Killin' Time,* 1989. Had first number one country single, 1989, with "A Better Man."

Band includes Hayden Nicholas (guitar, vocals), Jeff Peterson (steel guitar, dobro), John Permenter (fiddle), Jake Willemain (bass guitar), and Dick Gay (drums).

Awards: Horizon Award for career development from the Country Music Association, 1989; named male vocalist of the year by the Country Music Associaton, 1990.

Addresses: *Record company*—1133 Avenue of the Americas, New York, NY 10036.

ance at a Houston club. Ham was impressed and offered his considerable services to the band. Black recalled in *People:* "[Ham] said, 'Clint, do you want to be a star?' And I said, 'Yup.'" Within five months Black had a recording contract with RCA Records. When he arrived in Nashville to cut his album, he had never been inside a recording studio before.

Most country musicians—especially newcomers—record with seasoned studio veterans as backup. Black insisted on recording with his road band, thus preserving the intimate quality of his live work. On *Killin' Time,* Black sings lead and plays guitar; the album is entirely composed of songs he wrote alone or with Nicholas. *Killin' Time* was released in 1989, and the debut was auspicious from the start. Black's first single release, "A Better Man," climbed to number one on the country charts—the first debut single to do so in fourteen years. Subsequent number-one hits from *Killin' Time* include the title cut as well as "Walkin' Away" and "Nothing's News."

Many of Black's lyrics deal with the consequences of a broken heart. A bachelor, Black has mined his relationships—especially the breakups—for song material. Some of the tunes are traditional heartbreak fare, but others reflect the lessons to be learned from any life experience. In "A Better Man," for instance, Black thanks a departed sweetheart for giving him confidence to pursue his goals. "Walkin' Away," also a hit, suggests that it's best to end a bad relationship and search for "the right one" instead. Black's superhit "Killin' Time" takes the message a step further in a frank disavowal of "drinking to forget." All of Black's music is Texan in flavor, with a honky tonk beat and plenty of steel guitar accompaniment. Black's voice has a remarkable range and is strong, full-bodied, and distinctive.

When fame found Clint Black so did women. Fellow honky tonker Buck Owens described Black as "the kind of guy you'd want to take home to meet your father, if you could trust your mother." His talents as a songwriter and singer notwithstanding, it is probably Black's looks and stage presence that helped propel his album to platinum sales. Whatever the source of his success, Black is more than satisfied that he finally has huge audiences for his work wherever he goes. "I have to make sure that I stop and tell myself, 'Wait a minute—this is a moment I've been dreaming about and living for,'" he told *Country America.* "I used to say, with a sigh, 'I wonder if this could ever happen to me?' Well, this is it!"

Selected discography

Killin' Time (includes "Straight from the Factory," "A Better Man," "Nobody's Home," "Walkin' Away," "You're Gonna Leave Me Again," "I'll Be Gone," "Nothing's News," "Winding Down," "Killin' Time," and "Live and Learn"), RCA, 1989.
Put Yourself in My Shoes (includes "Put Yourself in My Shoes," "The Gulf of Mexico," "One More Payment," "Where Are You Now," "The Old Man," "This Nightlife," "Loving Blind," "Muddy Water," "A Heart Like Mine," and "The Goodnight-Loving"), RCA, 1990.

Sources

Country America, September 1990.
New York, October 2, 1989.
People, September 11, 1989.
Rolling Stone, September 21, 1990.

—Anne Janette Johnson

Patsy Cline

Vocalist

Up until Patsy Cline's recordings in the late 1950s and early 1960s there were only a handful of country and western female singers; and the title of queen belonged solely to Kitty Wells. It was Cline who dethroned Wells with classic performances on cuts like "Walkin' After Midnight" and the Willie Nelson composition "Crazy," which combined the pop characteristics of Patti Page and Kay Starr with the hillbilly traits of Hank Williams. All three singers were major influences on Cline's style.

Cline's entertainment career began at the tender age of four, when she won a local amateur contest for tap dancing in her hometown of Winchester, Virginia. By age eight she was playing the piano and singing in her church's choir. In 1948 the drugstore counter girl began singing in nightclubs with Bill Peer and his Melody Boys. Wally Fowler of the Grand Ole Opry convinced the 16-year-old to go to Nashville for an appearance on Roy Acuff's "WSM Dinner Bell" radio program. Cline hung around Nashville trying to break into the industry but ended up working as a club dancer.

Cline headed back home shortly thereafter and continued singing with Peer's band until 1954, when she returned to Nashville and signed a contract with William McCall's 4 Star Sales Co. out of Pasadena, California. Cline's first recording session was on June 1, 1955, and her first three songs were leased to Coral Records, a subsidiary of Decca. Part of her deal with 4 Star, which included one-time session fees with no royalties, stipulated that she could only record material that belonged to McCall's company. This may have been part of the reason that the majority of her early work did not sell very well. She was also tackling a wide variety of styles that made it hard to categorize her.

Producer Owen Bradley was trying to create a new genre with Cline by bathing her voice in full, jazzy orchestrations at his Quonset Studios in an effort to counter the rising popularity of rock and roll. According to *The Listener's Guide to Country Music,* "Patsy Cline was his ultimate country success. For him, she played down her country characteristics. For her, he played down his popular music background. The results were records full of tension and dynamics."

It would, however, take some time before the formula caught on, as the country scene was changing from hillbilly to country and western and was still mainly dominated by male artists. Cline's radical image as a two-fisted, hard-drinking woman definitely made her stand out from the rest of the Nashville crowd, but any chance of success would rely on her voice and songs. Her talents shined on both slow torchers and up-tempo cuts but her 4 Star sessions never did fully realize her potential, with the exception of "Walkin' After Midnight."

Cline recorded the tune on November 8, 1956, but it was the rendition of the song she performed on *Arthur Godfrey's Talent Scouts* television program on January 28, 1957, that got the industry's attention. She had debated performing the song but was finally convinced by one of the regulars on Godfrey's show, Janette Davis. The television audience went wild and gave Cline a standing ovation.

4 Star rushed to release the single on February 11 and it shot all the way to number three on *Billboard*'s country chart. More importantly, however, "Walkin'" also rose to number 17 on the pop charts. Donn Hecht had originally written the tune for Kay Starr, who turned it down, but Cline and Bradley managed to use it as a vehicle to bridge the gap between hillbilly and pop. McCall, whose company was eventually shut down as a result of questionable business dealings, was unfortunately too slow in following up on the hit. He did convince Cline to renew her contract, but it took another six months before she recorded another session, "Fingerprints"/"A Stranger in My Arms." Her remaining work with 4 Star was unspectacular and in 1959 she jumped to Decca Records, insisting upon a $1,000 advance.

It wasn't until 1961, one year after she became a regular cast member of the Grand Ole Opry, that Cline had her second hit, "I Fall to Pieces." The song went to number one on the country charts and was joined by "Crazy," another Top 10 hit of 1961. Cline's vocals began to soar to new heights on material that was less restrictive than 4 Star's catalog. For the next two years she recorded major hits with "She's Got You" (a number-one hit), "When I Get Through With You, You'll Love Me," "Faded Love," and "Leavin' On Your Mind" (all Top 10's).

Cline was just coming into her own when tragedy struck on March 5, 1963. On the way home from a Kansas City benefit for disc jockey Cactus Jack Callat, Cline, Randy Hughes, Cowboy Copas, and Hawkshaw Hawkins were killed when the airplane they were flying in crashed near Camden, Tennessee. At the age of 31 she had been performing for over twenty years, yet recording for less than eight.

Ironically, perhaps her most identifiable tune, "Sweet Dreams," was released posthumously and also broke the Top 10. Even with her relatively small collection of songs, Cline managed to break new ground and influence hundreds of female, and some male, country singers since. Loretta Lynn, undoubtedly Cline's most successful pupil, recorded a tribute LP, *I Remember Patsy*, featuring nine of Cline's songs.

"Patsy Cline knew how to cry on both sides of the microphone," wrote Donn Hecht in *The Country Music Encyclopedia*. "And the why of it all, explained by many, understood by few, is slowly becoming a legend unparalleled by any other country entertainer since Hank Williams."

Selected discography

Patsy Cline Portrait, Decca, 1965.
How a Heartache Begins, Decca, 1965.
Greatest Hits, Decca, 1967.
Golden Hits, Evergreen, 1963.
In Memoriam, Evergreen, 1963.
Patsy Cline Legend, Evergreen, 1964.
Reflections, Evergreen, 1965.
Here's Patsy Cline, Vocalion, 1965.
Great Patsy Cline, Vocalion, 1969.
Gotta Lot of Rhythm, Metronome, 1965.
The Patsy Cline Story, MCA, 1988.
12 Greatest Hits, MCA, 1988.
Walkin' Dreams—Her First Recordings, Vol. 1, Rhino, 1989.
Hungry For Love—Her First Recordings, Vol. 2, Rhino, 1989.
Rockin' Side—Her First Recordings, Vol. 3, Rhino, 1989.
Here's Patsy Cline, MCA.

Sources

Lazarus, Lois, *Country Is My Music!*, Messner, 1980.
Malone, Bill C., *Country Music U.S.A.—A Fifty-Year History*, American Folklore Society, 1968.
Oermann, Robert K., with Douglas B. Green, *The Listener's Guide to Country Music*, Facts on File, 1983.
Stambler, Irwin, and Grellun Landon, *The Encyclopedia of Folk, Country & Western Music*, St. Martin's Press, 1983.
Stars of Country Music—Uncle Dave Macon to Johnny Rodriguez, edited by Bill C. Malone and Judith McCulloh, University of Illinois Press, 1975.
Shestack, Melvin, *The Country Music Encyclopedia*, KBO, 1974.

—Calen D. Stone

The Coasters

Vocal group

The Coasters "walked the line between novelty record[s] and vocal-group record[s]," according to Ed Ward in his book, *Rock of Ages: The Rolling Stone History of Rock and Roll.* Growing out of the rhythm and blues tradition of the early 1950s, the Coasters had their first successful release in 1956 with "Down in Mexico," but bigger smashes, such as "Young Blood," "Yakety Yak," and "Charlie Brown," quickly followed. Typically, the group's songs combined humorous lyrics with skilled vocal arrangements that were pleasing to the ear. Like many artists of the 1950s, the Coaster's popularity waned with the coming of the 1960s and the advent of the British rock invasion, but—throughout various personnel changes—they continued to record and perform, benefitted by the nostalgic resurgence of 1950s music during the 1970s and 1980s.

Two of the Coasters' original members, lead singer Carl Gardner and bass vocalist Bobby Nunn, first experienced musical success as part of the Robins, a rhythm and blues group based in Los Angeles, California. Founded in 1950, the Robins scored hits on the rhythm

For the Record...

Group formed by songwriting-producing team of Jerry Leiber and Mike Stoller in Los Angeles, Calif., in February 1956; original members included **Carl Gardner** (lead and backup vocals), **Bobby Nunn** (bass vocals); **Billy Guy** (lead and backup vocals); and **Leon Hughes** (second tenor). Nunn was replaced by **Will "Dub" Jones,** c. 1958; Jones was replaced by **Ronnie Bright** in the 1960s; Hughes was replaced by **Young Jessie,** who was replaced by **Cornell Gunther,** who was in turn replaced by **Earl "Speedo" Carroll.** Current lineup includes Gardner, Carroll, Bright, and **Jimmy Norman.**

Addresses: *Record company—c/o* Atlantic Records, 75 Rockefeller Plaza, New York, NY 10019.

and blues charts with songs that told stories, including "Riot in Cell Block No. 9," and "Smokey Joe's Cafe." This latter song, especially, attracted executives from Atlantic Records who wished to sign the Robins to their subsidiary label, Atco. Management for the group did not think it a good idea, however, and while they stalled negotiations, Atlantic lured Gardner and Nunn away from the group on their own. To this duo, Atlantic added tenors Billy Guy and Leon Hughes, and christened the new ensemble the Coasters.

The Coasters were assigned to the songwriting and production team of Jerry Leiber and Mike Stoller, and together they set about to make hit records. "Down in Mexico," the Coaster's first single, was a solid success, selling a million copies, but it was far more prominent on the rhythm and blues charts than on the pop ones. Their next release, however, 1957's double-sided hit of "Searchin'" and "Young Blood," struck a major chord with the young, burgeoning rock and roll audiences. As Ward described it, in "Searchin'" the narrator "is searching for his runaway girlfriend, vowing to track her down with the tenacity of a Northwest Mountie or a Bulldog Drummond, as the group executes a fiendishly tricky vocal arrangement built around the chant of 'Gonna find her.'" The other side, "Young Blood," tells of seeing a beautiful girl on the street, following her home, and being banished by her father. Interjected into the singing are comic comments on the situation by each member of the Coasters. Ward summed: "Funny, true, sexy, and innocent, it captured the entire teenage experience in just over two minutes . . . reminded America that teenagers could be black, and that adolescence forged a bond of desires and concerns that even transcended race."

Two other Coasters hits, "Yakety Yak," and "Charlie Brown," were somewhat controversial because they fueled the late 1950s debate over whether rock and roll music was a serious form of rebellion on the part of young people. "Yakety Yak" is the humorous lament of a teenager "bedeviled by his parents," in Ward's words, a young man who has no time to hang out with his friends because his mother and father burden him with a seemingly endless list of chores. Ward called it "yet another teenage classic of social commentary, yet another record that would set parents and school authorities against rock and roll." Similarly, "Charlie Brown"—completely unrelated to Charles Schultz's "Peanuts" character—proved "just as incendiary as 'Yakety Yak' had been," according to Ward. Its hero smoked in the auditorium and mocked his teachers.

The Coasters underwent some major personnel changes in 1958; Nunn retired to be replaced by Will "Dub" Jones, and Young Jessie was substituted for Hughes. Other men who became Coasters over the years included Cornell Gunter and Earl Carroll. But the composition of the group did not seem to affect their ability to release hit songs. Some of their smashes during the late 1950s were "Along Came Jones" and "Poison Ivy." Their last major hit, however, came in 1961 with "Little Egypt," a song about falling in love with an exotic dancer. Though the Coasters continued to record through the early 1970s, and though some critics have offered the opinion that the later songs were as good as their early hits, changes in musical tastes and stylings caused them to be largely ignored by the predominantly young record-buying audience.

Selected discography

Single releases; on Atco

"Down in Mexico," 1956.
"Searchin'"/"Young Blood," 1957.
"My Baby Comes to Me," 1957.
"Yakety Yak," 1958.
"The Shadow Knows," 1958.
"Charlie Brown," 1959.
"Along Came Jones," 1959.
"Poison Ivy," 1959.
"I'm a Hog for You," 1959.
"Shopping for Clothes," 1960.
"Little Egypt," 1961.
"T'ain't Nothin' to Me," 1963.
"Let's Go Get Stoned," 1965.

LPs

The Coasters, Atco, 1958.
The Coasters' Greatest Hits, Atco, 1959.
One by One, Atco, 1960.
Coast Along With the Coasters, Atco, 1962.
The Coasters: Their Greatest Recordings/The Early Years, Atco,
    1971.
It Ain't Sanitary, Trip, 1972.
On Broadway, King, 1973.

Sources

Books

Helander, Brock, *The Rock Who's Who,* Schirmer Books, 1982.
Ward, Ed, Geoffrey Stokes, and Ken Tucker, *Rock of Ages: The
    Rolling Stone History of Rock and Roll,* Summit Books, 1986.

Periodicals

Jet, December 1, 1986.

—Elizabeth Wenning

Ornette Coleman

Jazz saxophonist, composer, trumpeter, violinist

Ornette Coleman enjoys the paradoxical reputation of being a genuine revolutionary in modern jazz, but one who is still less than fully embraced by the listening and critical establishment. From the start, his singular playing style (rooted in his idea of free jazz—"everybody is soloing, harmolodically") outraged some critics and fellow musicians and bewildered many jazz lovers; but it also inspired rhapsodic praise from players and writers alike.

In 1990, at age 60, he has composed over a hundred songs, a symphony, a string quartet, and a woodwind quintet, and he has released more than thirty long-playing records. But in this same life's span he has suffered material deprivation, commercial exploitation, racial brutality, and professional humiliation, all on a scale which rather befits a false prophet than an acknowledged musical genius. *New Yorker* jazz writer Whitney Balliett referred to this uneven motion of life and career when he said: "Few twentieth-century innovators have got in their own way as often as Ornette Coleman. . . . He is a stubborn and brilliant visionary and a man of great integrity, and these attributes have hobbled him."

Born in 1930 of a poor black family in Fort Worth, Texas, Ornette taught himself alto saxophone by age 14, and before graduating from high school he was supporting his widowed mother and a sister by playing tenor saxophone in local rhythm and blues bands. He learned to play marches and hymns in school and church bands, but at the same time he was listening to honky-tonk, blues, and funk. After he heard Lester Young in a Fort Worth jam session playing show tunes "with bridges," he set about memorizing popular songs off the radio, buying sheet music, and teaching new songs to his own band. He quickly figured out commercial tricks like distinguishing among white, black, country, and Mexican repertoires, and liked mimicking the rhythm and blues tenor men's leaping, bending, and honking moves. This aptitude enabled the young Coleman in the year 1947 to earn a hefty hundred dollars a week as a gigging musician.

His jazz styling was already being influenced by a combination of Charlie Parker, Jimmy Dorsey, and Pete Johnson. At 18, instead of accepting any of the music scholarships offered by several black colleges, he joined a touring minstrel show, which soon left him stranded in Natchez, Mississippi. He found his way to New Orleans and then Baton Rouge, where he was beaten up one night after a dance gig by "guys who didn't like my clothes or my hair." Taking a look at his locks, beard, and eloquently careless garb, the police warned him to get out of town before they finished him off themselves. Returning home, he started playing alto again, using a horn borrowed from a New Orleans friend. By late 1949, at age 19, these experiences had solidified both his character and his playing style. Both would bring him distinction and trouble.

He spent most of the 1950s in Los Angeles, initially with the rhythm and blues band of Pee Wee Crayton. "His style, already formed," Balliett explained, "alienated club owners and other musicians, and he found little work." Indeed, he was ignored, scorned, and even shunned at jam sessions by the likes of Dexter Gordon, Clifford Brown, Sonny Rollins, and Max Roach. However, he found compatible spirits in trumpeter Don Cherry, bassist Charlie Haden, and drummer Billy Higgins, with whom he formed an early quartet for gigs around Los Angeles and, eventually, Chicago and New York. Contemporary Records produced his first two LPs in 1958 (*Something Else* and *Tomorrow is the Question*), and a year later Atlantic jumped on the fashionable "free jazz" wave, issuing seven disks of Coleman's groups between 1959 and 1962. This rush followed the celebrated debut of the original quartet at New York's Five Spot in 1959, with Haden and Higgins making innovative harmony and rhythm, Cherry blowing a provocative "pocket trumpet," and Ornette sailing over everyone on his soon-to-be-notorious white plastic alto saxophone.

His flash flood of post-be-bop popularity carried an unhealthy amount of controversy. There were sometimes fights in the Five Spot during the quartet's five-month appearance there. The New York music avant-garde quickly lined up pro and con Ornette Coleman, with Leonard Bernstein, Gunther Schuller, and the Modern Jazz quartet's pianist John Lewis asserting Coleman's brilliance against dismissals by prominent performers like bassist Charlie Mingus and trumpeters Kenny Dorham and Miles Davis. (In a 1986 *People* article, David Grogan reports that it was Davis who pronounced the adventuresome altoist "all screwed up inside.") Coleman soon developed an antagonism towards the recording companies, who he knew were exploiting him.

Coleman began demanding extraordinary fees for recording and live appearances, justifying it by pointing to the discrepancy between the sums of money he attracted and the amount he took home. His free-style playing and conception, along with his theoretical comments about "harmolodics," only amplified the argument about his talent and genuineness. (The titles no less than the substance of the early Atlantic albums—*The Shape of Jazz to Come, Change of the Century, Free Jazz*—set the tone and drew the boundaries for this dispute.) He grew an initial reputation for deliberate obscurity, fakery, and self-indulgence. All this was happening in the heated-up climate of mid-1960s America, with the explosions of pop-rock, pop-psychology, the sexual revolution, and Vietnam protests just around the corner.

Like many of his black jazz compatriots of an earlier generation, Ornette Coleman withdrew from this emotionally taxing scene and did not re-emerge often until the early 1980s. In the meantime he learned to play trumpet and violin, toured Europe and North Africa with several groups, and began composing in different idioms and for alternative instrumental combos. His 1972 symphony, *Skies of America,* is written for jazz quartet and full orchestra. The 1977 *Dancing in Your Head* contains a live "jam" between Ornette and Moroccan tribal musicians, along with compositions of his own that were inspired by this mid-1970s visit; it is performed by a new electronic rock-funk-blues band, Prime Time, which features two electric guitars, one or two bassists, and two drummers. This fusion group has been his combo of choice for most of the 1980s, featuring himself on alto, soaring freely above the high-energy polytonality and polyrhythmics of drummers Ronald Shannon Jackson and Denardo Coleman (Ornette's son), bassist Jamaladeen Tacuma, and guitarists James Blood Ulmer, Bern Nix, or Charles Ellerbee.

Veteran Coleman fans and musicians whom he has influenced agree that the combination of his theoretical pronouncements and his steadfast commitment to his own vision has complicated the public's appreciation of his music. Among the younger musicians who owe a large debt to Coleman's ground-breaking artistry, saxophonists Branford Marsalis and Dewey Redman, popular jazz guitarist Pat Metheny, and Grateful Dead guitarist Jerry Garcia tell the same story: Ornette begins sessions by explaining his musical conception in very dense, puzzling terms, but when it comes time to perform he says "Just go ahead and play, man." His oldest sideman, Charlie Haden, had already been similarly drawn to this free-jazz experience in the late 1950s, when, as he relates in the *People*, Ornette told him: "Here are some chord changes, but you don't have to play them. Just play what you hear." Haden's response was like that of many a modern jazz player since: "Man, I had so much fun I couldn't believe it. It was spontaneity like I had never experienced before. Each note was a universe. Each note was your life."

This is a good characterization of free jazz. Coleman himself described it this way to Balliett: "'Improvising' is an outdated word. I try and play a musical idea that is not being influenced by any previous thing I have played before. You don't have to learn to spell to talk. The theme you play at the start of a number is the territory, and what comes after, which may have very little to do with it, is the adventure." Most fans agree that Charlie Parker is his biggest alto influence—the similarly voice-like tone, the bursts of lyrical runs, the rhythmic irregularity—but Coleman's melodic conceptions are much freer than Parker's. Detroit-area bassist Ted Harley, who has been an Ornette devotee since first hearing the quartet in 1958 at Chicago's southside Sutherland Hotel, declared: "His playing is almost purely melodic, but the key to his group sound is the bass player: his melodic invention varies according to who's on bass. Listen to him with Charlie Haden, then with Jimmy Garrison, then Scott La Faro. Ornette and the bass, that's it."

"Harmolodics" is the name Coleman concocted (from "harmony," "movement," and "melodic") in an early attempt to explain what he was doing, possibly in answer to the furiously negative responses his playing received. This is Branford Marsalis's opinion (as quoted by David Fricke in his 1989 *Rolling Stone* article): "Coleman was dismissed as a heretic simply because he couldn't explain what he was doing." For all the bewilderment, however, Coleman's theorizing makes perfect post-modern sense. "In America you can know

exactly who you would like to pattern yourself after and what you'd like to do," Balliet quoted him as telling Leonard Feather, "but the moment you find something you can do that outdates that . . . it's no longer the same idea anymore, it's a different thing . . . [this] problem . . . could be even more healthy if a solution could be made where every person could express his consciousness to its fullest without outdating the particular information he's gotten to do that or to enhance it. The world would be ten times more productive."

"What I'm saying," he continued in *Rolling Stone*, "if you take an instrument right at this very moment and play it, it's not impossible that you will play something that no one has ever heard before. . . . The melody can be a rhythm note. It can be a key note. The time can be the melody. It's like the difference between spelling cat with a k or a c. It still sounds the same. To me, that is the tool in harmolodics, how to convert sound into your own language." His longtime friend John Snyder told Balliett: "It's his theory of music, and it has nothing to do with what they teach you in music school. It's the sound in the instrument. It's the structure he's built around his feelings."

Ornette Coleman's musical life has received a rejuvenating jolt from the surge of youthful interest in jazz after be-bop, the birth of rock-jazz fusion, and the spreading movie and news treatment of American jazz careers. Add to this his new business relationship with the Fort Worth recording company, Caravan of Dreams, the recent albums with Prime Time and Pat Metheny, all reinforced by his son Denardo's job as personal business agent, and the artistic future for Ornette Coleman promises to be much healthier than his past. For listeners to the post-modern jazz of this embattled innovator, these words to *down beat* interviewer Howard Mandel should be instructive: "Here I am with a band based upon everyone creating an instant melody, composition, from what people used to call improvising, and no one has been able to figure out that that's what's going on. All my disappointment about it just makes me realize how advanced the music really is."

Selected discography

Something Else!, Contemporary, 1958.
Tomorrow is the Question!, Contemporary, 1958.
The Shape of Jazz to Come, Atlantic, 1959.
Change of the Century, Atlantic, 1959.
This is Our Music, Atlantic, 1960.
The Art of the Improvisers, Atlantic, 1961.
Free Jazz, Atlantic, 1961.
Broken Shadows, Columbia.
Science Fiction, Columbia.

Crisis, Impulse.
Friends and Neighbors, Flying Dutchman.
Ornette at 12, Impulse.
Who's Crazy, Affinity.
Love Call, Blue Note.
New York is Now, Blue Note.
Chappaqua Suite, Columbia (Japan).
The Great London Concert, Artista/Freedom.
At the Golden Circle, Vol. 1, Blue Note.
At the Golden Circle, Vol. 2, Blue Note.
Ornette, Atlantic Jazzlore, c. 1962.
Ornette on Tenor, Atlantic, 1962.
Town Hall 1962, ESP, 1962.
The Empty Foxhole, Blue Note, 1966.
Dancing in Your Head, A&M Horizon, 1977.
Body Meta, Artist House, c. 1980.
Soapsuds, Soapsuds, Artist House, c. 1983.
Skies of America, Columbia, 1972, rev. c. 1986.
(With Pat Metheny) *Song X*, Geffen, 1986.
Of Human Feelings, Antilles, 1986.
Opening the Caravan of Dreams, Caravan of Dreams, 1986.

In All Languages, Caravan of Dreams, 1987.
Prime Design/Time Design, Caravan of Dreams, c. 1987.
Virgin Beauty, CBS Portrait, 1988.

Sources

Books

Balliett, Whitney, *American Musicians: Fifty-six Portraits in Jazz*, Oxford University Press, 1986.

Periodicals

down beat, August 1987.
Horizon, November 1986.
People, October 13, 1986.
Rolling Stone, March 9, 1989.

—*Peter W. Ferran*

Marshall Crenshaw

Singer, guitarist, songwriter

For a rock and roll artist who set out to write and perform *hits,* guitarist Marshall Crenshaw has achieved an unexpected bounty of recognition. Regarded by some music critics as one of the best songwriters and performers of the 1980s, Crenshaw creates and records songs that have been acclaimed as highly crafted, with infectious melodies and heartfelt lyrics. However, while critical recognition has not abated since the debut of his much-praised 1982 album *Marshall Crenshaw,* Crenshaw and his self-proclaimed "singles band" have had only one Top 40 hit among four albums: 1982's "Someday, Somewhere." "Can you beat it?" asked Craig Zeller in *Creem.* "Marshall Crenshaw makes impassioned rock'n'roll, is a wizard with pop dynamics, and remains well aware of the fact that the magic's in the music. Yet he's a virtual stranger to the airwaves." Crenshaw commented to Bill Beuttler in *down beat* on his so-called success: "We were well-received right from day one; we've never had a record come out that's been totally ignored. I was surprised and sort of confused by it because . . . just about every track on the record was conceived as a single. . . . I thought we would be—a singles band. We're not; we're a cult band."

Crenshaw's career started with the influence of his musical family, which included his guitar-playing father, in addition to a cousin who was a back-up singer for country artist Ronnie Milsap, and his brother Robert, who is the drummer in Marshall's band. He grew up in a suburb of Detroit, and as a teenager he enjoyed listening to music—an activity he still enjoys as much as playing music. He was particularly interested in rockabilly: the early recordings of rock and roll which combine elements of blues, bluegrass, and country music—typified by such artists as Elvis Presley, Roy Orbison, and Jerry Lee Lewis. After graduating from high school, Crenshaw played in a variety of bands, including a country band, a Hawaiian band, an oldies band, and even accompanied the rockabilly artist Jack Earls. After a move to Los Angeles in the mid-1970s did not work out, Crenshaw auditioned for—and won—the role of John Lennon in the traveling stage show, *Beatlemania.* He continued to aspire to write and perform his own music, however, and after tiring of *Beatlemania* in 1980, set out for New York City. There, with his brother Robert and bassist Chris Donato, Crenshaw played gigs in clubs around Manhattan, while making demo tapes and sending them to record producers and performers. He eventually caught the attention of Warner Bros., who in 1981 signed him to a recording contract. The next year, *Marshall Crenshaw* debuted to overwhelming critical praise. The album was listed among many critics' Top Ten lists, while Crenshaw received numerous Best New Artist accolades.

For the Record. . .

Born c. 1954; grew up in a suburb of Detroit, Mich. Toured with the stage show, *Beatlemania*, 1978-80; solo artist, singing and touring, 1980—. Appeared in the films *La Bamba* (as Buddy Holly), and *Peggy Sue Got Married*.

Addresses: *Record company*—Warner Bros. Records, 3300 Warner Blvd., Burbank, CA 91510.

Crenshaw's music has been described as "authentic" rock and roll, and his songs show influences of such artists as Presley, Conrad Birdie, and the Beatles—the latter to whom he is frequently compared. Among Crenshaw's favorite guitarists are Bo Diddley and Duane Eddy, and he has recorded songs by Gene Vincent, the Jive Five, and Buddy Holly. However, despite carrying echoes of earlier artists, "Crenshaw is no copycat revivalist," Scott Isler remarked in *Musician*. "He accomplishes the much harder task of writing contemporary music rooted in the values of past craftsmanship." Crenshaw commented to Isler on his ideal method of composing: "I find a really good technique is just to pick up a guitar and start beating on it and give it absolutely no thought beforehand. You start with the germ of an idea and just sorta build it up from there. The best ideas are the ones that materialize out of nowhere. Those are the ones I try to capture and develop." Although he is also praised for his personalized, often wrenching lyrics, Crenshaw states that the *music* is most important to him. "As far as words go, I feel I'm just groping along, trying to finish the songs," he told Isler. "Music is a much more powerful form of communication than language. There are hundreds of songs I love, and I don't know what the lyrics are." A self-described "sound fanatic," Crenshaw agrees with Iggy Pop that "good music should be like an hallucination," he told Karen Schlosberg in *Creem*. "What's important is just the *impression* of it, rather than the specific little notes and stuff like that. I think that's really a great, simple explanation for a feeling that I share, too."

Although all of Crenshaw's albums receive high marks from critics, his debut album remains one of his best. Schlosberg wrote that Crenshaw "found a direct line between heart and music resulting in an album that was a joyful celebration of pop music at its purest. Not happy, but joyful—happy doesn't give you goosebumps, but joy does." Isler called it "a stunning debut, full of memorable phrases (verbal and musical) and rhythmic byplay." The cut "Someday, Somewhere," which sold over 200,000 copies, stands as Crenshaw's biggest single to date. Although he has not had major hits, he finds satisfaction in recording, as he related to Isler: "I still think of us as a singles band, even though we've only had one single that got in the top forty. My impression was that we would be like Abba or Creedence Clearwater. It just hasn't fallen that way, and I'm at a loss to understand why. But life goes on, and I'm still more than happy to be doing things the way I'm doing them. . . . I wanted to make records all my life, so I'm not complaining."

In addition to his own recordings, Crenshaw has had his songs recorded by other artists and groups, including Bette Midler, the Nitty Gritty Dirt Band, and Robert Gordon. While the music industry continues to appreciate Crenshaw's talents, commercial success remains a question mark. In a review of 1987's *Mary Jean and 9 Others*, Zeller wrote: "I don't know if the release of his fourth album will inspire mass cries of 'Giddyup'; I do know that Crenshaw is one of the best we have, and it's a real shame that more people haven't had a chance to realize that. . . . Crenshaw strikes me as a never-say-die kind of person and on *Mary Jean and 9 Others* he sounds better than ever, as glad to be alive as he was on his debut five years ago."

Selected discography

Marshall Crenshaw (includes "Someday, Somewhere" and "There She Goes Again"), Warner Bros., 1982.
Field Day, Warner Bros., 1983.
Downtown, Warner Bros., 1985.
(Contributor) *La Bamba: Original Motion Picture Soundtrack*, Slash, 1987.
Mary Jean and 9 Others, Warner Bros., 1987.

Sources

Creem, August 1983; September 1987; October 1987.
down beat, March 1986.
Musician, January 1986.

—*Michael E. Mueller*

J. D. Crowe

Banjo player, singer, songwriter

For more than 20 years the name J. D. Crowe has been synonymous with experimental bluegrass music. A first-rate banjo player in his own right, Crowe has been the leader of two progressive bands—the Kentucky Mountain Boys and the New South—both of which have made stylistic forays into rock, jazz, and country. In *The Big Book of Bluegrass,* Herschel Freeman called Crowe "the quintessential [Earl] Scruggs-style picker, a consummate craftsman with flawless timing and classic tone." Freeman added that Crowe's solid playing and willingness to let fellow band members create their own styles "produced a stunningly contemporary sound within a traditional context, . . . catapulted bluegrass into the forefront of progressive American music and drew a whole new generation of young musicians into the acoustic fold."

J. D. Crowe was born and raised in Lexington, Kentucky, the heart of bluegrass country. He told Freeman that he literally learned to pick the banjo at the knee of its greatest pioneer, Earl Scruggs. When Crowe was a boy, his parents would take him to the studio where Scruggs and his partner Lester Flatt rehearsed in preparation for their radio show. Crowe sat by the hour drinking in Scruggs's every move; then the youngster would go home and try to imitate the sound. "Back then there weren't many instruction books," Crowe said. "You learned the hard way, by watching and memorizing it. There weren't all that many pickers to learn from—maybe two or three, and you took your choice. For me, it was mainly Scruggs. I loved the way his right hand worked."

By the time he was a teenager, Crowe could pick well enough to find professional work, and by eighteen he had landed a spot in a major bluegrass band. His first big job was with Mac Wiseman in 1955. Touring the country with Wiseman's group and the companion band of Don Reno and Red Smiley, Crowe was able to spend hours jamming with some of the creators of the bluegrass sound. In 1956 Crowe joined the Sunny Mountain Boys, a band headed by Jimmy Martin. With this group Crowe was not only expected to pick but also to sing, in a style somewhat different from the one he'd developed. "Jimmy's timing was more outgoing," he said. "He wanted all the backup instruments going real hard all the time to match his singing, so I had to simplify my style. . . . It was straighter playing and hard driving. Jimmy always stressed rhythm and timing, and playing what fit the song."

Martin's was a traditional bluegrass band in many respects, and it served as an excellent apprenticeship for the more progressive Crowe. The 1960s found Crowe listening to rock 'n' roll, folk, and jazz, and although he adhered to the bluegrass tradition onstage,

For the Record. . .

Born in August, 1937, in Lexington, Ky. Banjo player, singer, songwriter, 1955—; leader of The Kentucky Mountain Boys (with **Doyle Lawson** and **Red Allen**), c. 1965-74; leader of J. D. Crowe and the New South, 1974—; New South members have included Tony Rice, Ricky Skaggs, Jerry Douglas, Bobby Slone, Wendy Miller, Steve Bryant, Keith Whitley, Paul Atkins, and Randy Hayes. Has recorded albums with Rebel Records, Starday Records, and Rounder Records.

Addresses: *Record company*—Rounder Records, 1 Camp St., Cambridge, MA 02140.

he was beginning to experiment on his own. Finally he formed his own group, the Kentucky Mountain Boys, a trio completed by the talented pair Doyle Lawson and Red Allen. Powerhouse instrumentals and fine vocal harmonies quickly made the Kentucky Mountain Boys a favorite on the bluegrass scene.

The group disbanded in the early 1970s and Crowe formed a new band, J. D. Crowe and the New South. The original New South included Tony Rice, Ricky Skaggs, and Jerry Douglas—all young, wide-ranging musicians like Crowe; the band's debut album caused a sensation. *The New South,* released in 1975, offered a revolutionary blend of the contemporary and the traditional, with electrifying instrumental riffs in a series of up-tempo songs. In *Country Music U.S.A.,* Bill C. Malone wrote: "J. D. Crowe's New South never lost their identity as bluegrass musicians, nor their rapport with older fans, even though they roamed far and wide for material and pushed their instruments to limits generally not sought by other performers. Superb musicians, such as Larry Rice, Tony Rice, Doyle Lawson, and Ricky Skaggs, moved in and out of the New South, but all of them learned something from the timing, precision, and clarity exhibited by Crowe himself."

The popular New South served as a training ground for a number of superstars in country and bluegrass, especially Skaggs, Lawson, and Keith Whitley, who joined in the early 1980s. Each time the personnel changed, the band's sound changed too, much to the chagrin of bluegrass purists. Crowe's albums have become slightly more country-oriented over time, blending drums and electric instruments with the bluegrass strings. Freeman noted that for Crowe, "change is a matter of expanding rather than abandoning his bluegrass base. . . . It is a posture that is uniquely suited for a man with the myriad talents of J. D. Crowe."

Recent years have seen further changes in the New South lineup, and Crowe has begun to produce recordings in Nashville and been known to work solo as well. "I don't want to continue doing what I did in 1970," he said. "It's like riding a dead horse. . . . That's where progress comes from, how new groups evolve." Crowe was quick to add, however, that he has nothing but pleasant memories of his accomplishments with the New South, a band that many have considered the "outlaws" of bluegrass. "Anybody that's been a part of the New South, I don't feel they can say anything but that we enjoyed it, burnt hell out of a lot of songs, and put it down like it should have been done," he said. "Everybody had a good time." He added that at present, "we're looking forward to playing new places and for new audiences. Basically, it's a matter of playing what you like and what you feel, and hopefully, the people will like it too."

Selected discography

With Jimmy Martin and The Sunny Mountain Boys

Good 'n' Country, Decca.
Country Music Time, Decca.
Widow Maker, Decca.
Big 'n' Country Instrumentals, Decca.

With The Kentucky Mountain Boys

Bluegrass Holiday, Rebel.
Blackjack, Rebel.
Model Church, Rebel.

With The New South

J. D. Crowe and the New South, Starday.
The New South, Rounder.
You Can Share My Blanket, Rounder.
My Home Ain't in the Hall of Fame, Rounder.
Somewhere Between, Rounder.
Straight Ahead, Rounder.
J. D. Crowe Live in Japan, Rounder, 1987.

Sources

Kochman, Marilyn, editor, *The Big Book of Bluegrass,* Morrow, 1984.
Malone, Bill C., *Country Music U.S.A.,* 2nd edition, University of Texas Press, 1985.

—Anne Janette Johnson

Ray Davies

Singer, songwriter, guitarist

"**D**uring more than two decades," according to *People* critic Michael Small, British rock musician and composer Ray Davies has "written some of the most clever, sexy and thoughtful pop-rock songs ever," and helped make the Kinks "one of the coolest rock bands in history." As the driving force behind the Kinks—a group which has also included Ray's brother Dave Davies and artists Mick Avory, Peter Quaife, and John Gosling—Davies has brought rock fans hits like "You Really Got Me," "Lola," "Destroyer," and "Come Dancing." Though other members of the Kinks have come and gone, Davies has always served as the band's leader and as such, has released over 40 albums, including concept discs, rock operas, and outstanding live recordings. He has also earned the respect of his peers; in another *People* article Small quoted Davies's fellow rock star Pete Townshend of the Who as saying that when it came to lyrics, "in British rock Ray Davies is our only true and natural genius."

Davies was born June 21, 1944, in the Muswell Hill area of London. He was introverted as a child, but during his adolescence developed an affinity for soccer and considered becoming a professional player. He was also deeply interested in music, and learned to play the guitar and piano. Especially fond of the blues, he listened to recordings of the genre's greats, including Leadbelly and Bill Broonzy. When Davies was 16 he began playing rhythm and blues numbers in local bars with his younger brother Dave. He also performed in a local group called the Dave Hunt Band. Nevertheless, Davies did not look toward music as a career; after completing secondary schooling he enrolled in college to major in drama and fine arts.

Davies did not last long at college, however, and at the age of 19 dropped out to join the Ravens, a band in which his brother played. The Ravens played straightforward rock and roll in the style of American rock pioneer Chuck Berry. As Small put it, "with their wildly ragged sound and long hair, the Ravens became a hot act at society parties." Davies almost immediately assumed leadership of the band, which met with rapid success and was signed to a contract with Pye Records. In the early days Davies took to wearing mismatched outfits; someone took note of one clashing ensemble at a recording session and labeled him a "kink." Davies explained to Small: "He meant it as a put-down, but I thought, 'Why the hell not use the name?'" Thus the Ravens became the Kinks, just in time for the release of their first album, *You Really Got Me,* which in 1964 was issued in the United States on the Reprise label.

Although the first two singles from the album did nothing on the charts, Davies's confidence in his abilities

For the Record. . .

Full name, Raymond Douglas Davies; surname pronounced "Davis"; born June 21, 1944, in Muswell Hill, London, England; son of a gardener and a homemaker; married Rasa Dictpatris c. 1964 (divorced, 1973); married Yvonne Gunner (a teacher), 1976 (divorced c. 1980); married Pat Crosbie (a ballet dancer); children: (first marriage) two daughters, one named Louisa; (with singer Chrissie Hynde) Natalie. *Education:* Attended art school.

Singer, songwriter, guitarist. Played during the early 1960s with the Dave Hunt Band; joined the Ravens, c. 1963; member of the Kinks (previously the Ravens), 1964—. Has recorded most recently with MCA Records.

Addresses: *Record company*—MCA Records, Inc., 70 Universal City Plaza, Universal City, CA 91608.

was undiminished. One of the Kinks' producers had come up with what Small described as a "polished version" of the title track, "full of the overdubs and echoes that were popular in 1964," and wanted the band to release it. But Davies insisted on his rougher-sounding original, and, as he recounted for Small, told the producers, "If you release this, I'm never going to make another record." He got his way and "You Really Got Me" soared to Number One in England; it also fared well in the U.S. The song contained what Small deemed "an aggressive guitar sound that became a mainstay of heavy metal."

"You Really Got Me" was followed by the hits "All Day and All of the Night," "Who'll Be the Next in Line," and "Tired of Waiting for You." But Davies did not restrict himself to straight rock; he also composed satires on society and fashion, including "Well Respected Man" and "Dedicated Follower of Fashion." While the Kinks churned out hits, they also gained a reputation as rowdy and violent concert performers, often fighting amongst themselves on stage—conflicts between the Davies brothers the primary root of these battles. Though the circumstances are still cloudy, Davies believes it was this behavior that caused the American Federation of Musicians to bar the Kinks from playing in the United States from 1966 to 1968.

Perhaps because they were not allowed to promote their releases in the U.S., Davies and the Kinks fell into something of a popular slump during the late 1960s. Despite rave reviews from critics for their 1969 rock concept album *Arthur*, which was compared favorably with the Who's rock opera *Tommy*, the work yielded only the moderate hit single "Victoria." The band came back in a big way, however, with their 1970 album *Lola versus Powerman and the Moneygoround*. The smash hit single "Lola" was controversial as the first pop hit to deal blatantly with transvestitism and homosexuality. Although Small claimed that the infamous lyric "I know what I am and I'm glad I'm a man and so is Lola" is "ambiguous—was Lola glad the narrator was a man, or was Lola also a man?"—Davies confided that the song was inspired by an incident from his own life that took place in a French nightclub. "One night I was dancing with this really attractive woman till dawn," he explained to Small. "Then she said, 'Come on back to my place,' and I said, 'Okay.' It wasn't until we got in the daylight that I saw the stubble on her chin. So I blew that one off."

During the early 1970s the Kinks returned to concept albums. Davies revived the character Mr. Flash from the band's 1969 effort, *The Kinks Are the Village Green Preservation Society,* for the albums *Preservation, Act I* and *Preservation, Act II;* like *Arthur* these were more warmly received by critics than fans. *Soap Opera,* the Kinks' early 1975 concept release fared slightly better, but *Schoolboys in Disgrace*—a set of unrelated songs that came out later that year—was even more popular. *Schoolboys* marked the return of Dave Davies to the Kinks; he had left the band in 1973 over disagreements with his brother.

Despite other personnel changes, including the loss of longtime drummer Mick Avory—again due to personality conflicts—Davies and the Kinks continued to produce hits throughout the 1980s, among them "Destroyer" and "Come Dancing." They led off the 1990s with the album *UK Jive,* which prompted Small in a third *People* review to assert that Davies's music "still comes straight from the heart, the gut, and the soul." His impressive musical achievements notwithstanding, Davies modestly told Small: "I don't feel I've done enough with my life. I don't want to be known only as a guy who made hit records."

Selected discography

You Really Got Me, Reprise, 1964.
Kinks-Size, Reprise, 1965.
Kinda Kinks, Reprise, 1965.
Kinks Kinkdom, Reprise, 1965.
Kink Kontroversy, Reprise, 1966.
Greatest Hits! Reprise, 1966.
Face to Face, Reprise, 1967.
"Live" Kinks, Reprise, 1967.
Something Else, Reprise, 1968.
Four More Respected Gentlemen, Reprise, 1968.

The Kinks Are the Village Green Preservation Society, Reprise, 1969.

Arthur, Reprise, 1969.

Lola versus Powerman and the Moneygoround, Reprise, 1970.

Muswell Hillbillies, RCA, 1971.

Kink Kronicles, Reprise, 1972.

Everybody's in Showbiz, RCA, 1972.

The Great Lost Kinks Album, Reprise, 1973.

Preservation, Act I, RCA, 1973.

Preservation, Act II, RCA, 1974.

Soap Opera, RCA, 1975.

Schoolboys in Disgrace, RCA, 1975.

Celluloid Heroes—The Kinks' Greatest, RCA, 1976.

Sleepwalker, Arista, 1977.

Misfits, Arista, 1978.

Low Budget, Arista, 1979.

One for the Road, Arista, 1980.

Second Time Around, RCA, 1980.

Give the People What They Want, Arista, 1981.

Word of Mouth, Arista, 1984.

Think Visual, MCA, 1986.

UK Jive, MCA, 1990.

Sources

People, May 11, 1987; July 6, 1987; February 19, 1990.

Rolling Stone, January 15, 1987.

—Elizabeth Wenning

Depeche Mode

Avant garde techno-pop group

The latest British band to take America by storm is Depeche Mode, a group of post-punk pop performers who have broken new ground in the field of computer-assisted music. Depeche Mode has enjoyed great success in England almost since its debut in 1981. In the United States its following was limited to a sizeable cult until 1990, when the album *Violator* brought the group into the mainstream. Since then Depeche Mode has had little trouble placing singles on the top forty charts and selling albums by the millions.

The group's success has come without compromise or pretense—Depeche Mode's members call themselves pop musicians and seem quite comfortable in that format. In fact, Depeche Mode has been one of the few recent bands to infuse pop with some sense of credibility. "Most pop songs just don't reflect life the way it really is," songwriter Martin Gore told *Spin* magazine. "You can't be happy all the time. Throughout our career, I've tried to write good serious songs as well as escapist songs. I know we get accused a lot of being depressive, but our songs also have a certain get-on-

with-it attitude. If life is bad, there's always something to give you solace."

Most pop bands tend to bask in the limelight and court the press. The members of Depeche Mode do almost the opposite—they save their performances for the arena and do little to court favor among the media. Depeche Mode interviews and features are so uncommon that many new fans still do not recognize the individual band members—a state of affairs the musicians do nothing to correct. This reluctance to speak in print stems from the band's earliest days in England.

Depeche Mode formed outside London in 1980, fronted by songwriter Vince Clarke. Other founding members include Martin Gore, Andy Fletcher, and Dave Gahan, all of whom grew up in the suburbs of London. Rock music had spawned a whole new generation of machines for making music—synthesizers and drum simulators, to name two—and Depeche Mode's members gravitated to these machines. "We started doing something completely different," Gahan told *Rolling Stone.* "We had taken these instruments because they were convenient. You could pick up a synthesizer, put it under your arm and go to a gig. You plugged directly into the PA. You didn't need to go through an amp, so you didn't need to have a van. We used to go to gigs on *trains.*"

The group also did not need a grange hall in which to practice. In fact, they didn't even need to be together—any individual's bedroom could become a studio. Within a year of founding Depeche Mode, Clarke had put together a demo tape and was making the rounds trying to find a record label. Finally the band signed with an independent British company, Mute Records, and released a debut album, *Speak and Spell,* in 1981. The music was entirely synthetic, but it was original nonetheless. At a time when most techno work revolved around gloomy themes, Depeche Mode offered a dance beat, provocative lyrics, and that "get-on-with-it" attitude. *Speak and Spell* became one of the ten best-selling albums in Great Britain in 1981, and Depeche Mode was launched.

Not surprisingly, fans and press hounded the young performers mercilessly, and soon Vince Clarke had had enough. After Clarke quit, Gore became the principal songwriter, and Alan Wilder was added to help with vocals. "Under Gore's direction," wrote Jeff Giles in *Rolling Stone,* "Depeche Mode's music became—to quote the title of an album that many of the group's fans hold dearest—a 'black celebration.' His songs, a few of which have made American radio programmers blush, have been both profane . . . and kinky." Almost virtually without radio station support, Depeche Mode began to attract an audience in America. They had one Top 10 hit in 1985, with "People Are People," but they became immensely popular as live performers. For a time the group was even compared to the heavy metal bands of the 1970s who regularly sold out in concert without ever earning a gold record.

Gradually, however, Depeche Mode began to make inroads in the all-important radio market. This was not an easy task for a group one critic called "synth wimps"—the standard rock format radio stations simply would not play Depeche Mode. The group was saved by dance hall crowds and New Wave fans who could groove to the band's techno-pop beat and provocative lyrics. Gore told *Rolling Stone:* "A lot of people get swayed by the 'real' music thing. They think you can't make soul music by using computers and synthesizers and samplers, which we think is totally wrong. We think the soul in the music comes from the song. The instrumentation doesn't matter at all."

Early on the members of Depeche Mode realized that their brand of music would not translate well in live performance. They have therefore become one of the few major pop groups be open about enhancing their concerts with pre-recorded material. This has allowed the group to be as outrageous as any of its contemporaries and has contributed in no small part to its fantastic success. "Using . . . tapes to enhance a band's performance is less a case of deliberate misrepresentation than of keeping up with the times technologically and giving the audience what it wants," Peter Watrous wrote in the *New York Times.* "People weaned on music from the 1960's may go to an Eric Clapton concert to hear how well he plays his guitar, but an audience for

Depeche Mode, whose concerts seem almost completely prerecorded, attend for different reasons. The combination of post-punk performance ideas, in which improvisation is beside the point, and consumer-driven images, in which people come to share space with a performer, has produced an audience that goes out for more than the pleasure of music."

If the sold-out 1990 World Violation Tour is any indication, Depeche Mode is reaching its fans even with prerecorded concerts. Fletcher told *Spin* that Depeche Mode's whole aim is to avoid the ego-trip legacy of the big rock bands. "We don't think you have to be a great musician to be allowed to play and get a message out," he said. "I guess that's what punk was all about, getting rid of the ego and getting right down to it without having to be a session guitarist." Wilder put it more bluntly in *Time* magazine. While working with Depeche Mode, Wilder said, "nobody is allowed to be pretentious." The music speaks for itself—and it speaks volumes.

Selected discography

Speak and Spell, Sire, 1981.
People Are People, Sire, 1985.
Catching Up with Depeche Mode, Sire, 1986.
Black Celebration, Sire, 1986.
Music for the Masses, Sire, 1988.
101, Sire, 1989.
Violator, Sire, 1990.
A Broken Frame, Sire.
Construction Time Again, Sire.
Some Great Reward, Sire.

Sources

New York Times, July 22, 1990.
Rolling Stone, May 3, 1990; July 12-26, 1990.
Spin, July 1990.
Time, July 16, 1990.

—*Anne Janette Johnson*

DJ Jazzy Jeff and the Fresh Prince

Rap duo

DJ Jazzy Jeff and the Fresh Prince have done more to bring rap music into the mainstream than any other hip-hop group. The Philadelphia-based duo, who infuse their work with satire and playfulness—a departure from the hostile tone of some rap acts—in 1988 produced one of the best-selling rap albums of all time, *He's the DJ, I'm the Rapper*. The group also proved outstanding by receiving the first ever Grammy in the rap music category for their quintessential teenage lament, "Parents Just Don't Understand." Because their work is funny and accessible to teens of all races, DJ Jazzy Jeff and the Fresh Prince are welcome where other rap groups are rarely invited—to live concerts, teen magazines, and even network television.

Rolling Stone contributor Jeffrey Ressner noted that DJ Jazzy Jeff and the Fresh Prince "have distinguished themselves by avoiding rap's traditionally angry tone. . . . Rather than tackling themes like urban violence and drug abuse, Jazzy Jeff and the Fresh Prince prefer to satirize frothier middle-class subjects like video games, monster movies and going shopping with parents." The

music is not entirely sanitized, however—it may be self-mocking one moment and bitterly sarcastic the next, the mood more exasperated than militant. "The music comes from us and it reflects who we are," Jazzy Jeff told the *Philadelphia Inquirer.* "We don't approach the music with the idea of getting a message across. We just sing about our experiences, and the audience finds it funny or can relate to it."

Although they have been heralded as the first middle-class rappers, Jazzy Jeff and the Fresh Prince did not exactly grow up in the suburbs. Jeffrey Townes, or Jazzy Jeff, grew up in a working-class neighborhood of South Philadelphia and the Fresh Prince, born Willard Smith, was raised in nearby Wynnefield, Pennsylvania. Both began perfecting their musical craft at an early age. Jazzy Jeff started spinning records at parties when he was only ten, using his family's basement as a training ground for his expert mixing and double scratching. The Fresh Prince, a rapper from age 13, attended Philadelphia's Overbrook High School, where he earned sufficient grades to qualify for a full scholarship to the academically rigorous Massachusetts Institute of Technology (M.I.T.).

The two musicians knew of one another while they were still young teens. Their paths crossed from time to time because they each performed in different rap groups. Early in 1986 they got together at a party; the rapport was instantaneous. "I worked with 2,000 crews before I found this maniac," Jazzy Jeff told *People.* "There was a click when I worked with him that was missing before." Jazzy Jeff, who had released an album in 1985, was already a local celebrity when he took on the Fresh Prince. As a result the duo had little trouble finding a

record label. Their first single, "Girls Ain't Nothing but Trouble," hit the charts in 1986.

DJ Jazzy Jeff and the Fresh Prince's first album, *Rock the House,* made a strong showing in 1987, selling some 600,000 copies. Stardom came the following year with the double LP *He's the DJ, I'm the Rapper,* one of the first rap albums to go double platinum. Both albums, but especially the second, offer raps about what the musicians understand best—the day-to-day troubles of modern teens. "Parents Just Don't Understand," for instance, details the nightmares of shopping for school clothes with a mother who is hopelessly out of touch with current styles; the Prince pleads with his mom to "put back the bell-bottom Brady Bunch trousers."

Not surprisingly, the "clean rap" image proved a mixed blessing for DJ Jazzy Jeff and the Fresh Prince. Some other rap artists scorned them for selling out to the white audience and for ignoring legitimate problems of black youths. On the other hand, the musicians found themselves invited to perform live concerts far more often than many of their cohorts because promoters saw less chance for violence at their shows. As a consequence DJ Jazzy Jeff and the Fresh Prince toured extensively, performing throughout the Midwest and in Canada. Jazzy Jeff told the *Philadelphia Inquirer:* "We like to give the audience a lesson in rap. It's not hard, anyone can do it. It's not about black or white, it's just about having fun."

By 1989 the duo had far more competition in the mainstream market; their release *And in This Corner* sold just under a million copies. That album contained the hit "I Think I Could Beat Mike Tyson," a piece that pokes fun at an over-active ego. Music videos accompanying "I Think I Could Beat Mike Tyson" and "Parents Just Don't Understand" brought the Fresh Prince to the attention of a new audience—television producers. On the basis of his work in videos, he was invited to take a leading role in a network situation comedy, *The Fresh Prince of Bel Air.*

The demands on the Fresh Prince of filming a television show have greatly curtailed the rap duo's musical work. The two still perform and record together, however, and Jazzy Jeff makes frequent guest appearances on the show. The Fresh Prince told the *Lexington Herald-Leader* that he took the television work in order to continue his quest to educate people about rap. "Rap music—which a lot of white America doesn't understand—rap music is not just a music," he said. "Rap music is a subculture: hip-hop. It's a style of dress, an attitude, a look, a language. It's more than just music."

Though perhaps not as visible as the Fresh Prince, there is little chance that Jazzy Jeff will return to obscurity. With his wide-ranging knowledge of modern jazz, eerie mixes of fine music and trashy television theme songs, and masterful record scratching, he will remain in demand on the rap circuit. Jazzy Jeff explained his performance philosophy in the *Philadelphia Inquirer*. "We're not from the suburbs, so we don't pretend to know what growing up there is like," he said. "But there are certain experiences or feelings that everyone has in common." He added: "We don't care if the audience is black or white, inner city or suburban, as long as they show up and are having a good time."

Selected discography

Rock the House, Jive, 1987, reissued, 1989.

He's the DJ, I'm the Rapper, Jive, 1988.
And in This Corner, Jive, 1989.

DJ Jazzy Jeff also recorded the solo album *On Fire*, Jive, 1985.

Sources

Lexington Herald-Leader, July 8, 1990.
People, October 3, 1988.
Philadelphia Daily News, June 7, 1989; May 4, 1989.
Philadelphia Inquirer, March 18, 1990; March 26, 1990.
Rolling Stone, December 1, 1988.

—Anne Janette Johnson

Ronnie Earl

Guitarist

Blues guitarist Ronnie Earl once told Guitar Player: "My whole approach is based around playing with feeling. I just let it tip out." Listening to Earl play guitar, one would assume that he had virtually grown up with the instrument in his hands. His sound displays a taste and authority that usually takes years and years to develop. But, amazingly enough, Earl did not start his musical career until he was twenty-three, just after witnessing a Muddy Waters concert in 1975. "I decided that this was it," he told Dan Forte in *Guitar Player,* "he changed my life."

Earl had already been teaching retarded children for four years after graduation from Boston University with a degree in special education. He immediately purchased a $35 Harmony guitar and began to absorb the "feel" of the instrument, rather than copying the licks of the master bluesmen like Magic Sam and Guitar Slim. Unlike many of his contemporaries, Earl avoided the rock and roll phase and went straight to the source.

He began sitting in at Boston jam sessions and soon landed a gig at the Speakeasy club backing up artists like Big Mama Thornton, Otis Rush and Albert Collins. He hooked up with an east coast unit, Johnny Nicholas and the Rhythm Rockers, before moving to Texas where he lived with Fabulous Thunderbirds Jimmie Vaughan and Kim Wilson. Vaughan's impact on Earl is evident in his choice of guitars (Fender Stratocaster) and amps (a Fender Super Reverb) and the ability to play clean, economical leads. Earl also prides himself, like Vaughan, on his knowledge of chords and considers himself to be more of a sideman pumping the rhythm than a flashy lead guitarist. "That's what being a blues player is," he told *Guitar Player,* "to know it, but not necessarily show all your cards."

Earl went from Texas to Louisiana before heading back to Boston to join Sugar Ray and the Blue Tones. In 1979 he hooked up with the premiere east coast blues unit, Roomful of Blues, whose guitarist, Duke Robillard, had just quit. "I literally was having nightmares of crowds chanting in unison, 'Where's Duke?'," he confessed in *Guitar Player.* Three days after quitting Roomful and joining Robert Gordon, Robillard wanted back in Roomful, but they stuck with their decision to hire Earl. His stint with Roomful lasted eight years and produced six excellent albums, including two Grammy nominations with Eddie Cleanhead Vinson and Big Joe Turner.

Earl didn't just fill Robillard's shoes, he wore a whole new outfit: "Every single night I try to take people's heads off and try to get my soul into their soul," he stated in *Guitar Player.* The cut "Three Hours Past Midnight" from the *Live at Lupo's* LP is a prime example of just that. Earl controls the tempo and the crowd like a master; building up tension and then releasing it at just the right moment, a technique that can only come from within. "I lost a lot of my family in a concentration camp. So there's a feeling of oppression or whatever in my background," he told *Guitar World.* "Blues just hit me real hard."

Earl ventured outside Roomful's horn-based format ("I feel like I got all this other stuff stirring up in my soul, which is to play, like, real filthy blues," he told *Guitar Player*) in 1983 to release his first solo album on the Black Top label. *Smoking,* observed Dan Forte in *Guitar Player,* is "a bare-knuckled, sweat-drenched R & B blowout . . . that may amount to the best recorded example of the so-called 'blue wave' movement. . . . [Earl] takes charge with a vengeance." Taking a cue from the late Earl Hooker, Earl displayed some fine slide work (in regular tuning, no less) on "Baby Doll Blues" and literally tore up a version of Freddie King's "San-Ho-Zay." All in all, it was quite an impressive debut.

In 1986, while still working with Roomful, he recorded *I Like It When It Rains,* a basically acoustic outing with Earl plugging in his electric guitar for only a few cuts. The results were as authentic and pure as any contemporary blues LP in recent memory, with Earl proving that the genre knows no color boundaries. "I think that blues is American music, it's not white or black," he explained to *Guitar Player.* "I always try to have enough pride in myself to feel like I'm out there just like they're out there. They were my fathers, but I'm doing it now. And I think I'm doing it the right way." For those who were just looking for licks, Earl had plenty to spare also. In *Guitar Player,* Dan Forte called the LP "a guitar player's dream. . . . Throughout, he plays with the finesse of a Sugar Ray Leonard and the intensity of a Jake LaMotta." The album was dedicated to Earl Hooker,

Walter Horton and Clifford Antone (owner of the Austin, Texas, nightclub, Antone's, as well as the label that recorded the album).

For his second solo effort, Earl called on his old cronies, Sugar Ray and the Blue Tones, for 1985's *They Call Me Mr. Earl.* He ripped into six originals, a Buddy Guy classic ("Let Me Love You") and proved that he could whammy bar with the best of them on "Waitin' For My Chance." In 1987 Earl felt it was time to move ahead and left Roomful to form his own band, the Broadcasters. "It got a little more commercial and I wanted to stay in a more traditional blues bag," he told *Guitar World.* In 1988 *Soul Searching* was released and featured former Muddy Waters sideman Jerry Portnoy on harp. On "Backstroke" Earl swapped licks with Robillard and then played an impassioned dedication to the father of electric blues guitar, T-Bone Walker, on "Blues For Bone."

In the latter part of the 1980s Earl finally overcame a nagging drug and alcohol habit, got married, and lectured at Berklee College of Music in Boston with hopes of one day opening a school devoted to the blues. One can only imagine how far he will go now that he seems to be in total control of his life and even more dedicated to music.

"I do what I do with my band and hope that one day people will catch on to it," he told the *Detroit News.* "I am looking forward to making a good living with the people in my band and getting a wider audience. I'm trying to become a better musician and a better person."

Selected discography

Solo albums

Smoking, Blacktop, 1983.
They Call Me Mr. Earl, Black Top, 1985.
I Like It When It Rains, Antones, 1986.
Soul Searching, Black Top, 1988.

With Roomful of Blues

Hot Little Mama, Blue Flame, 1980.
Dressed Up To Get Messed Up, Varrick, 1984.
Live At Lupo's Heartbreak Hotel, Varrick, 1986.
Big Joe Turner With Roomful of Blues, Blues Train, MUSE, 1984.
Eddie Cleanhead Vinson And Roomful of Blues, MUSE, 1983.
Earl King And Roomful of Blues—Glazed, Black Top, 1986.

With others

(With Lou Rawls) *Shades of Blue,* Phil. International.
(With Walter Horton) *Little Boy Blue,* JST.
(With Ron Levy) *Wild Kingdom,* Black Top, 1986.
(With Levy) *Safari To New Orleans,* Black Top, 1988.
(With Hubert Sumlin) *Blues Party,* Black Top, 1987.
(With Snooks Eaglin) *Baby, You Can Get Your Gun!,* Black Top, 1987.
(With Eaglin) *Out of Nowhere,* Black Top, 1989.
(With William Clarke) *Tip Of The Top,* Satch, 1987.
(With Nappy Brown) *Something Gonna Jump Out The Bushes,* Black Top, 1987.
(With Various Black Top Artists) *Blues-A-Rama, Vols. I and II,* Black Top, 1988.

(With Bobby Radcliff) *Dresses Too Short,* Black Top, 1989.

Sources

Detroit News, February 2, 1990.
down beat, September 1986, May 1987.
Guitar Player, September 1984; April 1985; January 1986; February 1987; September 1988.
Guitar World, September 1988; September 1989.

—*Calen D. Stone*

Cass Elliot

Pop singer

"**M**ama" Cass Elliot's strong contralto voice attracted much of the attention focused on the popular late 1960s vocal group the Mamas and the Papas. She helped provide harmony on all the quartet's hits, including "California Dreaming," "Monday, Monday," and "Dedicated to the One I Love." Following The Mamas and the Papas' breakup in 1968, Elliot enjoyed a successful solo career until her death in 1974.

Born Ellen Naomi Cohen in Baltimore, Maryland, on September 19, 1940, Elliot demonstrated her musical interests early in life. During grade school she took piano lessons; later, she tried the guitar, feeling it was more useful for the folk genre. By the time she reached high school, she focused more on her vocal abilities, and often sang in school shows. After graduation, Elliot rebelled against her parents' wishes that she attend a prestigious women's college, and moved to New York City to become involved in the folk scene a few years later. She adopted the name Cassandra Elliot, thinking it would help her in show business.

In New York's Greenwich Village, Elliot joined a folk group called the Big Three. The Big Three also included James Hendricks, to whom she was married for a time. They were successful enough to record two albums, *The Big Three* and *Live at the Recording Studio* on the FM label. By 1964, Elliot and her husband were singing with the Mugwumps. This group, too, was able to make a self-titled album, but it was not put out by Warner Bros. until Elliot had gained fame with the Mamas and the Papas.

Meanwhile, Elliot's career was being admiringly followed by musician John Phillips, and when he decided to form a vocal group in 1965, he recruited her and fellow Mugwump Denny Doherty. Elliot, Phillips, Doherty, and Phillips's wife Michelle traveled to the Virgin Islands to practice their distinctive sound for five months before heading for Los Angeles, California, to look for a record deal. There, they were discovered by producer Lou Adler, who had just formed the Dunhill label and offered not only to record them but to be their manager.

The Mamas and the Papas' first album, *If You Can Believe Your Eyes and Ears,* was released in 1966. And the first single from it, "California Dreamin'," was an attention-gaining smash for them. Geoffrey Stokes explained in *Rock of Ages: The Rolling Stone History of Rock and Roll* that the tune "might have been a hit no matter what it was about, for the group's hallmark harmonies—controlled, elaborate, cool—were an extraordinarily beautiful pop sound. . . . It also offered a vision of California that was as romantic as the Beach Boys' 1965 "California Girls," without any of that song's holdover teenage ethos . . . tantaliz[ing] Easterners with a California that was enigmatically magical."

death as a heart attack. Elliot's "crystal voice" was recalled in her *Newsweek* obituary.

Selected discography

With the Big Three

The Big Three, FM, 1963.
Live at the Recording Studio, FM, 1964.

With the Mamas and the Papas

If You Can Believe Your Eyes and Ears (includes "California Dreamin'," "Monday, Monday," "Go Where You Wanna Go," and "I Call Your Name"), Dunhill, 1966.
The Mamas and the Papas (includes "I Saw Her Again," "Words of Love," "No Salt on Her Tail," "Dancing Bear," "Strange Young Girls," and "Trip, Stumble, and Fall"), Dunhill, 1966.
Deliver (includes "Dedicated to the One I Love" and "Creeque Alley"), Dunhill, 1967.
The Papas and the Mamas (includes "Twelve Thirty," "Safe in My Garden," "Dream a Little Dream of Me," and "Glad to Be Unhappy"), Dunhill, 1968.

With others

(With The Mugwumps) *The Mugwumps,* Warner Bros., 1967.
(With Dave Mason) *Dave Mason and Cass Elliot,* Blue Thumb, 1971.

Solo LPs

Dream a Little Dream (includes "Dream a Little Dream"), Dunhill, 1968.
Bubblegum, Lemonade, and Something for Mama, Dunhill, 1969.
Make Your Own Kind of Music (includes "Make Your Own Kind of Music"), Dunhill, 1969.
Cass Elliot, RCA, 1972.
The Road Is No Place for a Lady, RCA, 1972.
Don't Call Me Mama Anymore, RCA, 1973.

Sources

Books

Helander, Brock, *The Rock Who's Who,* Schirmer Books, 1982.
Ward, Ed, Geoffrey Stokes, and Ken Tucker, *Rock of Ages: The Rolling Stone History of Rock and Roll,* Summit Books, 1986.

Periodicals

Newsweek, August 12, 1974.
New York Times, July 30, 1974.
Time, August 12, 1974.

—*Elizabeth Wenning*

Full Name, Cassandra Elliot; name originally Ellen Naomi Cohen; born September 19, 1941, in Baltimore, Md.; died as a result of choking (one source says heart attack) July 29, 1974, in London, England; married James Hendricks (a musician; marriage ended) children: Owen (daughter).

Member of The Big Three, 1963-64; member of The Mugwumps, 1964-65; member of The Mamas and the Papas, 1965-68; solo recording artist and concert performer, 1968-74.

If You Can Believe Your Eyes and Ears also included the classic "Monday, Monday," a recording of the John Lennon and Paul McCartney tune "I Call Your Name," and the enthusiastically upbeat "Go Where You Wanna Go." Elliot and the Mamas and the Papas followed up their initial success with a late 1966 self-titled album that included two big hits, "I Saw Her Again" and "Words of Love." Their 1967 effort, *Deliver,* also produced two chart-climbers—a remake of the Shirelles' "Dedicated to the One I Love," which Stokes lauded as a "three-minute chorale," and "Creeque Alley," which more or less told the group's story. But 1968's *The Papas and the Mamas* produced only minor singles like "Twelve Thirty" and "Glad to Be Unhappy." In addition, the Phillips's souring marriage, along with musical differences among the members, was creating tension within the group, and the Mamas and the Papas broke up.

Elliot, still recording for Dunhill, wasted no time in launching her solo career. She took a song from the last Mamas and Papas album and turned it into the title track for her debut album, released late in 1968. Her solo rendition of "Dream a Little Dream" became a much bigger hit for her than it had for the group. Elliot made two albums the following year, *Bubblegum, Lemonade, and Something for Mama,* and *Make Your Own Kind of Music,* the title tune of the latter scoring another hit for her. In 1971, Elliot made an album with musician Dave Mason, which Brock Helander in his book *The Rock Who's Who* kindly remembered as "an ill-received but underrated album."

Though Elliot changed to the RCA label in 1972, she never had another hit. She did, however, continue to be a popular nightclub and concert performer. Elliot had just finished a 1974 stint at the Palladium Theater in London, England, when she was found dead in her hotel room. She reportedly had choked on a ham sandwich, but at least one source listed the cause of

Emerson, Lake & Palmer/Powell

Rock group

One of the most innovative rock groups in pop music history, ELP—initially Emerson, Lake and Palmer, later Emerson, Lake and Powell—was organized in the late 1960s and quickly rose to become the "leading force in classically oriented electronic rock," or what Keith Emerson preferred to call "progressive rock with a lot of regard for the past." Their rich, orchestral sound, popular remakes of age-old classics, and romping stage act made them one of the most notable contemporary musical acts of their generation.

Keith Emerson is perhaps the best-known member of ELP, a brilliant composer and show stealer. Even before the days of ELP, the flamboyant keyboardist was known, as a member of the English band the Nice, to have wild stage behavior, including "stabbing and assaulting his electric organ." While ELP was on its debut tour of the United States, *Billboard*'s Nancy Ehrlich commented on Emerson, "Here is a man who has to keep running constantly to work off too much energy for one person to handle." Emerson's early musical influences included classical pianists, an influ-

ence that would follow him into his own music and give ELP one of the most unusually sophisticated sounds in the rock-pop world. While still a member of the Nice, Emerson met bassist/vocalist Greg Lake, one of the founding members of King Crimson, at San Francisco's Filmore West in 1969. At home in England, the duo recruited drummer Carl Palmer, formerly of Atomic Rooster and The Crazy World of Arthur Brown. After several months of rehearsing, the group made a memorable debut concert at the Isle of Wight Festival in 1970, impressing the audience with their virtuosity, onstage antics, and the firing of two cannons at the start of the gig. Shortly after, the trio was signed by Island Records in England, producing their first, self-titled album in 1971. It was an immediate success not only in England, but also in the United States, where it was released a short time later. A minor hit single at the time, Greg Lake's haunting ballad "Lucky Man" continued as a radio standard for years to come. Their second album, *Tarkus* arrived the same year as their first. Both were certified gold before 1972.

The band's classical sound was explored deeply in ELP's live third album, featuring an impressive piece based on the classical composition *Pictures at an Exhibition* by Modest Mussorgsky. While critics were surprised the 45-minute set could hold the attention of the average rock fan, Palmer pointed out that the piece was greatly varied, covering styles from 12-bar blues to light singing. "Everything imaginable can be gotten from it," he said. "It's just a glorious work." *Trilogy,*

released later the same year, Included the moderate hit "In the Beginning," as well as rocked-up, romping variations of Maurice Ravel's "Bolero" and Aaron Copland's "Hoedown." Both proved to be crowd pleasers.

In 1973 the band formed their own label, Manticore, and after nearly a year and a half of vacation, they recorded the infamously-titled *Brain Salad Surgery.* Soon after, they headed out for a monster tour across America, dragging 36 tons of equipment with them. Not only did the tour boast the first true quadraphonic sound system, but it involved timpani, gongs, chimes, a church bell, six moog synthesizers, an electric piano, two organs, and a Steinway. It resulted in a live triple gold album, *Welcome Back My Friends.* After several years of pursuing solo projects, the group returned in 1977 with a double-record set and two unique concepts. First, the album dedicated a side each to individual efforts, with the fourth side featuring their combined talents. Again Greg Lake would produce a hit in the form of another eerie ballad, "C'est la Vie." Second, the band launched a major American tour, the likes of which had never been seen before. This time they brought along not only a large crew but a choir and a 50-piece-plus symphony orchestra (over one hundred people altogether), costing them an estimated $250,000 per week. After fifteen concerts, the orchestra was dismissed.

Somewhere along the line, attitudes shifted, and by the end of the decade ELP disbanded. Their last album, *Love Beach,* released in 1977, was "greeted by scathingly hostile reviews." Almost ten years later, when Emerson and Lake returned with drummer Cozy Powell, much of the hostility remained. Whether audiences had become more sophisticated and ELP failed to challenge them, or whether "classical and progressive" had simply come to mean "pomp" is difficult to judge. In either case, the self-titled 1986 album, *Emerson, Lake & Powell,* was met with disdain by some reviewers who complained about the songs being too lengthy, sappy, and pretentious. Said one reviewer for *Stereo Review,* "the term 'heavyhanded' was coined for their stuff. 'Overwrought,' 'bombastic,' and 'hopelessly silly,' might have been too." The same reviewer called Greg Lake's fantasy ballad "The Miracle" another "ersatz epic," claiming that the artist "blubbers on for seven eternal minutes and two merciful seconds about swords and dragons and jesters." With a crushing indirect compliment, *Rolling Stone's* Jim Farber wrote, "These guys are literally the only ones left in 1986 who still have the balls to serve up vintage crap like this . . . tracks . . . with titles and lyrics that would make the Moody Blues blush." On the brighter side, another critic applauded the group's effort and the creativity evident in such pieces as "The Score" and "The Miracle," saying, "Emerson's bravura keyboard playing is especially penetrating . . . he still produces that unique tone, a cross between an organ and a trumpet."

Mixed reviews did not keep the group from touring, though they found the audiences far different from those they played to in the seventies—more sophisticated, perhaps, and often much younger. Said Lake, "It is a strange feeling to see your old fans bringing their children . . . but it's not an unsavory one." Why should the newer generation be so fascinated with yesterday's supergroups? Lake commented again, offering a personal insight: "What you have now is rock & roll product. The music ceased to be a culturally meaningful art form. The groups of the late Sixties and Seventies had very individual identities . . . you'd know immediately who you were listening to, today it's hard to say who's who."

In 1988 the group reformed again. This time, Emerson joined forces with the first P of ELP, drummer Carl Palmer. The third spot was filled by American songwriter-guitarist Robert Berry, chosen because, according to the band's promotional materials, he had a "West coast sort of voice." Also, sources indicated Palmer appreciated Berry's ability to write shorter songs. Unfortunately, the resulting album, *To the Power of Three,* was received poorly. Berry was criticized for lack of vocal range; Emerson's keyboard playing and Palmer's drumming seemed restricted in the short pop songs featured. Even on their remake of the Byrds' "Eight Miles High" the band failed to produce anything more than another "pedestrian cover song." It makes critics and fans alike long for the days of grand ELP fare— when they were still on the forefront of a new sound, the classically-based rock music that charged a genera-tion. Progressive and innovative, they flourished in a time before synthesizers became commonplace and computers took over the basics.

Selected discography

Emerson, Lake and Palmer, Island Records, 1970.
Tarkus, Island Records, 1971.
Pictures at an Exhibition, Island Records, 1971.
Trilogy, Island Records, 1972.
Brain Salad Surgery, Island Records, 1973.
Welcome Back My Friends, Manticore, 1974.
Works, Manticore, 1977.
Works Vol. 2, Atlantic, 1977.
Love Beach, Atlantic, 1978.
In Concert, Atlantic, 1979.
Best Of Emerson, Lake and Palmer, Atlantic, 1980.
Emerson, Lake and Powell, Polydor, 1986.
To the Power of Three, Geffen, 1988.

Sources

Books

Anderson, Christopher P., *The Book of People,* Putnam, 1981.
Stambler, Irwin, *Encyclopedia of Pop, Rock and Soul,* St. Martin's Press, 1989.

Periodicals

People, June 23, 1986; May 2, 1988.
Rolling Stone, August 14, 1986; December 18, 1986.
Stereo Review, October 1986.

—*Meg Mac Donald*

Fabian

Pop singer

Though many critics complained of his lack of vocal talent, singer Fabian used his good looks and publicity to become an extremely popular teen idol during the late 1950s and early 1960s. Viewed at the time as being the leading pretender to the pop throne vacated by Elvis when the king was drafted into the Army in 1958, Fabian scored Top Forty hits with "Tiger" and "Turn Me Loose," and gained even more exposure when he began to appear in films, featured along with actors such as Bing Crosby and John Wayne. As Ed Ward summed up in his book *Rock of Ages: The Rolling Stone History of Rock and Roll,* Fabian "was a very clever, very calculated product," but also, for a time, a very successful one.

Fabian was born Fabian Forte on February 6, 1943, in Philadelphia, Pennsylvania. Not displaying any particular interest in music beyond that of a normal teenager, it was perhaps as much a surprise to him as to anyone else when he was discovered by the writing-producing-recording team of Bob Marcucci and Pete DeAngelis—the owners of the Chancellor record label who were also instrumental in the career of Frankie Avalon. There are varying accounts of how Forte was recruited; Fabian himself was quoted in the *Los Angeles Times* as saying that it happened while his father was being carried out to an ambulance after suffering a heart attack. "Marcucci was walking by and we were introduced. He was intrigued by my name and he wondered if I'd be interested in the recording business."

Marcucci, however, quoted by Ward, claimed that Avalon was responsible for the meeting, and recounted his reactions: "Somehow I sensed that here was a kid who could go. He looks a little bit like both [Elvis] Presley and Ricky Nelson. I figured he was a natural. It's true that he couldn't sing. . ." But it was a fairly common practice during the late 1950s for record producers to look for handsome young men that could induce joyful sighing and screaming in young female music fans, and thus, while still in his late teens, Fabian was signed to a contract with Chancellor Records. The young man took it in stride; he told Dennis Hunt in another *Los Angeles Times* article that "when I got the offer . . . I took it because I thought it might be exciting. Besides, my father was sick and the family needed money."

Despite the fact that DeAngelis and Marcucci provided Fabian with singing lessons, his career did not take off right away. His first single, "I'm in Love," met with little but critical derision when it was released. But the proprietors of Chancellor were unwilling to give up; they stirred up massive amounts of publicity about Fabian, and booked him for an East Coast tour of many theaters and auditoriums. Fabian began to build up a following among teenagers, and by 1959 he was having hit

Full name, Fabian Forte; born February 6, 1943, in Philadelphia, Pa.

Worked for a time in a drugstore and as a janitor's assistant; recording artist and concert performer, beginning in 1957 and temporarily ending during the early 1960s; performer in clubs and in nostalgia shows, beginning in the 1970s. Appeared in films and television shows, including *Hound Dog Man*, 1959, *High Time*, 1960, *North to Alaska*, 1960, *Love in a Goldfish Bowl*, 1961, and *Bus Stop*.

records—his first was "I'm a Man." "Tiger" and "Turn Me Loose" followed quickly.

But after his banner year of 1959, Fabian's ability to produce hits began to fail him. For a time this mattered little, because he was exploring a career as an actor. Because of his popularity, he was approached by Hollywood, and his first featured role was in 1959's *Hound Dog Man*. He began to rise above the teen music exploitation film genre the following year, when he appeared with Bing Crosby in *High Time* and John Wayne in *North to Alaska*. Unfortunately, though, as his musical fame faded, Fabian's film offers grew scarcer; one of his last memorable roles was the portrayal of a psychopath in *Bus Stop*.

Like many other performers of his period, however, Fabian experienced a resurgence in popularity when music fans in the late 1970s and 1980s began to feel nostalgic for the songs of the 1950s and 1960s. He still sings his hits in oldies' shows, though he has not recorded any new material.

Selected discography

Singles; on Chancellor Records

"I'm in Love"/"Shivers," c. 1957.
"I'm a Man," 1959.
"Tiger," 1959.
"Come on and Get Me," 1959.
"Got the Feeling," 1959.
"Hound Dog Man," 1959.
"This Friendly World," 1959.
"Turn Me Loose," 1959.
"String Along," 1960.
"About This Thing Called Love," 1960.
"Kissin' and Twistin'," 1960.

Sources

Books

Stambler, Irwin, *The Encyclopedia of Pop, Rock, and Soul,* St. Martin's, 1989.
Ward, Ed, Geoffrey Stokes, and Ken Tucker, *Rock of Ages: The Rolling Stone History of Rock and Roll,* Summit Books, 1986.

Periodicals

Los Angeles Times, January 3, 1973; July 5, 1974.

—Elizabeth Wenning

Roberta Flack

Singer, songwriter, pianist

When Roberta Flack's debut album, *First Take,* appeared in 1969, a war-weary public embraced the mellow sound: Flack's warm, velvety voice weaving intimate ballads, touched by the vitality of gospel and jazz. Also including rock, swing, and folk songs in her repertoire, the performer challenged the conventions of popular black music at the time, opening the door for the musical innovations of succeeding black artists like Stevie Wonder, Maurice White, and Marvin Gaye. A canny judge of musical material, Flack enjoyed a string of Number 1 hit singles during the early 1970s, and became known in the industry not only for her outstanding artistry but for her exacting professionalism and dedication.

No stranger to taking several months and studios to complete an album, Flack once insisted that her record company recall 500,000 singles of her "Killing Me Softly With His Song" so that she could provide a better ending. Becoming increasingly involved in all aspects of the music business, the singer has selected, arranged, conducted, and edited her own recording material since the mid-1970s, engaging in music publishing and producing as well. Always appreciative of talented new songwriters and singers, she has helped launch the careers of vocalists like Danny Hathaway and Peabo Bryson by performing and recording with them. Flack explained her artistic independence in *The Best of the Music Makers:* "I am going to be who and what I am, not what agents, promoters, record companies, producers, or the public would have me be. . . . When my songs come out, I have to be able to listen to them with out having to duck under the car seat."

Musically gifted as a child, Flack began taking piano lessons at the age of nine, and by thirteen had won second place in a state-wide piano contest for black students. Academically gifted as well, she skipped several grades in school, graduating at the age of fifteen. Entering Howard University on a piano scholarship, Flack eventually switched to music education, which required both vocal and instrumental training. It was then that her beautiful voice was recognized as first-rate classical material, but—self-conscious about her overweight, and eager to arouse in others the pleasure and excitement music stirred in her—Flack continued to pursue a career in education.

Eighteen years old and degree in hand, she took her first teaching post at a segregated school in Farmville, North Carolina, where many of the students were poor and regularly missed school to work in the fields; some of Flack's students were older than she was. Nonetheless, they were anxious to learn all their teacher put before them, and Flack became totally immersed in their lives: directing the school choir, supervising the

For the Record. . .

Born February 10, 1940, in Black Mountain, N.C., raised in Arlington, Va.; daughter of Zaron (a draftsman) and Irene (a domestic and cook) Flack; married Stephen Novosel (a jazz bassist), 1966 (divorced, 1972). *Education:* Howard University, B.A., 1958, postgraduate studies in music education; doctoral work at University of Massachusetts—Amherst.

Began piano lessons at age nine; later trained in operatic vocal technique; teacher of music, English, and math at segregated school in Farmville, N.C., for a year in the early 1960s; music teacher in three junior high schools in Washington, D.C., c. 1961-67; began playing piano and singing part-time in local clubs, mid-1960s; full-time performer, 1967—; recording artist, 1969—. Performances include concert tours, jazz festivals, television specials and motion-picture soundtracks (*Play Misty for Me, Bustin' Loose, If Ever I See You Again, Making Love*). Has scored for motion pictures and television, performed as a concert pianist, and conducted opera; engaged in music publishing and record producing; prepared a textbook for educators on understanding ghetto language.

Awards: Named female vocalist of the year by *down beat* magazine, 1971-73; Washington, D.C., celebrated Roberta Flack Human Kindness Day, April 22, 1972; Grammy Awards for record of the year, 1972, for "The First Time Ever I Saw Your Face," and 1973, for "Killing Me Softly With His Song"; Grammy Awards for best pop vocal performance by a duo (with Donny Hathaway), 1972, for "Where Is the Love?," and for best pop vocal performance by a female solo artist, 1973, for "Killing Me Softly."

Addresses: *Record company*—c/o Atlantic Records, 75 Rockefeller Plaza, New York, N.Y. 10019.

cheerleaders, creating special classes for the mentally and physically impaired.

For the next six years Flack taught music at three different junior high schools in Washington, D.C. In her spare time she directed church choirs, instructed voice students, and provided piano accompaniment for singers at local clubs; eventually it was she who was doing the singing. Before long she was a favorite pop vocalist at the fashionable clubs in the capital, her fans including such entertainers as Burt Bacharach, Woody Allen, and Bill Cosby. Jazz pianist Les McCann brought Flack to the attention of Atlantic Records, and the singer signed a recording contract in 1969. While *First Take* sold respectably, it was Flack's appearance on comedian Cosby's 1970 television special that brought her

national celebrity; captivating her audience, the vocalist sold more than one million copies of her next LP, *Chapter Two,* and of the subsequent album *Quiet Fire.* In 1971, *down beat* magazine named Flack female vocalist of the year, ending the nearly two-decade reign of jazz great Ella Fitzgerald.

In the summer of 1971 Flack and vocalist Hathaway cut the hit single "You've Got a Friend." Their joint gold album *Roberta Flack and Danny Hathaway* appeared a year later; the duo won a Grammy Award for their rendition of "Where Is the Love?" *Stereo Review* critic Phyl Garland deemed the collaborators "perfectly matched," sharing the same "sweetly flowing, honeyed texture" and "firm gospel tradition." (The two singers continued to perform together until Hathaway's apparent suicide in 1979.)

Flack earned a second Grammy in 1972 for "First Time Ever I Saw Your Face," a song originally appearing on her first album—and given new life on the soundtrack of the Clint Eastwood motion picture, *Play Misty for Me.* Reissued as a single, the song soared to number one on the charts (and Flack's debut LP belatedly went gold); it was even reported that U.S. astronauts took a copy of the dreamy ballad on their first moon mission to "calm their nerves." The next year brought Flack similar success, with two additional Grammies for another Number 1 hit, "Killing Me Softly with His Song." Her luck with smart, stylish singles continuing, "Feel Like Makin' Love" topped the charts in 1974.

By the mid-1970s Flack began to take over the creative aspects of her recording career, and, prey to her perfectionism, her records became less frequent. Other interests also claimed her attention: scoring for motion pictures and television, music publishing and record producing, doctoral work in education and linguistics. During the early 1980s the vocalist teamed with singer/songwriter Bryson for several successful duet recordings; their 1983 album *Born to Love* introduced the hit "Tonight, I Celebrate My Love." Garland observed that—where Hathaway shared Flack's earlier, gospel-rooted form—"Bryson is more in tune with Flack's current style, which is closer to middle-of-the-road pop modified by the smooth textures and lilting rhythms of Sixties soul music."

The critic added that "Flack's current mode sacrifices some of her previous depth for a broader, mass appeal, but she is still a serious artist operating on a high level, and she still has the same honey-ripened voice and velvety style." Reviewing the singer's 1988 album, *Oasis,* Garland noted further changes: "a lot of production," reflecting "Flack's decision to speak to a new generation in its own language." While finding the vocalist's gift for creating "a sense of intimacy" somewhat compromised here, Garland nonetheless concluded: "Flack's ability to communicate directly with the listener remains intact. In spite of the gaudier trappings, she is still a class act."

Selected discography

Albums

First Take, Atlantic, 1969.
Chapter Two, Atlantic, 1970.
Quiet Fire, Atlantic, 1971.
Killing Me Softly, Atlantic, 1973.
Feel Like Makin' Love, Atlantic, 1975.
Blue Lights in the Basement, Atlantic, 1977.
Roberta Flack, Atlantic, 1978.
Bustin' Loose (soundtrack), MCA, 1981.
Best of Roberta Flack, Atlantic, 1981.
I'm the One, Atlantic, 1982.
(With saxophonist Sadao Watanabe) *Rendezvous,* Elektra, 1984.
Oasis, Atlantic, 1988.

With Donny Hathaway

Roberta Flack and Donny Hathaway, Atlantic, 1972.
Roberta Flack Featuring Donny Hathaway, Atlantic, 1980.

With Peabo Bryson

Live and More, Atlantic, 1981.
Born to Love, Capitol, 1983.

Sources

Books

The New Rolling Stone Record Guide, edited by Dave Marsh and John Swenson, Random House, 1983.
Simon, George T., and others, *The Best of the Music Makers,* Doubleday, 1979.
Stambler, Irwin, *Encyclopedia of Pop, Rock and Soul,* revised edition, St. Martin's, 1989.

Periodicals

People, May 5, 1981; July 19, 1982; January 9, 1989.
Rolling Stone, March 9, 1989.
Stereo Review, July 1980; March 1982; October 1982; December 1983; April 1989.

—Nancy Pear

Fleetwood Mac

Pop/rock group

Although Fleetwood Mac is today recognized as one of the most successful pop/rock bands in contemporary music, they originally began as a strict blues outfit. Guitarist Peter Green, bassist John McVie, and drummer Mick Fleetwood were all alumni of Englishman John Mayall's Bluesbreakers when they first appeared on August 12, 1967, as Peter Green's Fleetwood Mac at the British National Jazz & Blues Festival. Jeremy Spencer added his Elmore James-flavored licks to the band which "in that early incarnation, evolved into a fantastic blues band—sharp-edged without rawness, steady in the Chicago blues mold, impressive and direct," according to *The Guitar: The Music, The History, The Players*.

The band signed with Mike Vernon's Blue Horizon label and were then known as Fleetwood Mac. Their first big hit came with "Black Magic Woman," from their debut LP, *Fleetwood Mac*, in 1968. The song, which remained on the charts for thirteen weeks, stretched their blues roots to include Latin percussions and weaving guitar lines. In late 1968 they added a third guitarist, Danny

For the Record. . .

Band formed in England in 1967 as Peter Green's Fleetwood Mac; original members included **Peter Green** (guitar; born October 29, 1946); **Mick Fleetwood** (drums; born June 24, 1942); and **John McVie** (bass; born November 26, 1945); **Danny Kirwan** (guitar) joined band in 1968, left band in 1973; Green left band in 1970, was replaced by **Jeremy Spencer** (born July 4, 1948); **Christine McVie** (originally performed under maiden name Christine Perfect; keyboards; born July 12, 1943) joined band in 1970; Spencer left band in 1971, replaced by **Bob Welch** (born July 31, 1946); Welch left band in 1975, replaced by **Lindsey Buckingham** (born October 3, 1947); **Stevie Nicks** (vocals; born May 26, 1948), joined group in 1975; during 1980s Buckingham launched a solo career and was replaced by **Billy Burnette** and **Rick Vito.**

Awards: Winner of *Rolling Stone* magazine's Critics' Awards for band of the year and for album of the year (*Rumours*), 1977; recipient of *Rolling Stone* magazine's Readers' Poll Awards for artist of the year, best album of the year (*Rumours*), best single ("Dreams"), and for band of the year, 1977.

Addresses: *Record company*—Warner Bros., 3300 Warner Blvd., Burbank, CA 91510.

Kirwan, as the band continued to slowly move away from their roots with a Number 1 U.K. single, "Albatross." "The BBC used it for some wildlife program and then someone put it on *Top of the Pops* and it was a hit," Fleetwood told *Rolling Stone.*

The band was still relatively obscure in America, however, and was billed as the opening act for a U.S. tour that included Jethro Tull and Joe Cocker. Green left the group temporarily in May of 1970 for religious reasons while the group scored a hit with his "Green Manalishi" soon after. The Mac broke into the U.S. market with their *Kiln House* LP later that year as McVie's wife, Christine Perfect (formerly of Chicken Shack), filled in on keyboards on the record and the ensuing tour.

The band struggled through more personnel changes as Spencer quit in February of 1971 to join a religious cult, Children of God. Green replaced him briefly (after quitting the second time Green was committed to a mental institution for giving his royalty money away) before a California singer/guitarist named Bob Welch joined. His work on *Future Games* and *Bare Trees* was instrumental in bringing the group recognition in the States as their U.K. popularity declined. In late 1972

Kirwan was booted from the band and Bob Weston and Dave Walker were hired for 1972's *Penguin* LP and the following year's *Mystery To Me.*

By now Fleetwood Mac was calling Los Angeles their home, but legal complications prevented them from working until late 1974. Their former manager, Clifford Davis, had formed a bogus Fleetwood Mac band, with no original members, and was gearing up for a U.S. tour. A court order finally blocked Davis' efforts but left the real band on hold until their *Heroes Are Hard To Find* LP. Mick Fleetwood and lawyer Michael Shapiro decided to run the band on their own after ditching Davis. "We probably would have broken up when there were problems," Fleetwood told *Rolling Stone* about the possibility of hiring an outside manager. "This band is like a highly tuned operation and wouldn't respond to some blunt instrument coming in. There's a trust between all of us that would make that a problem."

Fleetwood Mac's musical course took a financial upswing in 1975 when Welch left to form the band Paris and was replaced by the songwriting/performing team of Lindsey Buckingham and Stevie Nicks (who were, at the time, lovers). "When I joined [the band was] still hovering on the edge," Welch told *Rolling Stone.* "When I left, they'd done a complete switcharound to a slick, sophisticated, production kind of band." He later told *Guitar World,* "I agreed with the philosophy but I said, 'Naah, I don't really want to stay for another go-round.' Much to my dismay." While searching for a studio to record the band, Fleetwood overheard the duo's LP, *Buckingham/Nicks,* at Sound City Studios in Van Nuys, California. Nicks had previously sung with Buckingham in the band Fritz and their addition to Fleetwood Mac brought the group a new melodic sound that catapulted them to superstar status nearly overnight with the LP *Fleetwood Mac* in 1975.

With its folksy, lush vocals, the album "finally realized the apotheosis of that early-Sixties blues crusade to get back to the roots," wrote John Swenson in *Rolling Stone.* In concert, Nicks took on the persona of the mythological Welsh witch Rhiannon, swirling about on stage in a black cape and adding a new sexual element to the band's presence. Tunes like "Say You Love Me," "Over My Head," and "Monday Morning" pushed *Fleetwood Mac* to platinum status and became Warner Brothers' best-selling LP ever at the time (previous Mac albums sold around 200,000 copies each). Released in July of 1975, the LP reached the Top 20 and then sank to the Top 40 just before peaking at Number 3 right before Christmas. Of their success, Buckingham told *Guitar World,* "It wasn't a supergroup. They were selling no albums at all. They were broke for all practical purposes. . . . I'm not saying it was our doing, but it was all of our doing. It was the right chemistry."

Musically, the band members meshed perfectly, but their personal relationships were not as smooth. During the next eleven months they worked on their follow-up LP, *Rumours,* while trying to cope with the breakups of the McVies and Nicks and Buckingham. "Go Your Own Way" was typical of the album's tone and, as the band struggled with their relationship problems, their record flew up the charts to the Number 1 spot. "What makes the difference this time is knowing that, for all the problems we've encountered, we've got a huge album," Fleetwood told *Rolling Stone* during the recording of the LP. "It makes any bad things that happen seem not nearly as bad as if the last album had stifled."

The high recording expense paid off as *Rumours* eventually sold 16 million copies, more than any other album by a single group. With *Fleetwood Mac* and *Rumours,* the band had made pop history and defined the decade's musical characteristics. "Catchy but emotionally affecting pop rock for the late Seventies," was how John Rockwell described their music in *The Rolling Stone Illustrated History of Rock and Roll.* "The music was unabashedly pop, yet it touched on serious themes without being weighed down by them."

Buckingham took control on their next effort, the double-LP *Tusk,* from 1979. More folk than rock, nine of the tunes were penned by the guitarist. "Another series of saccharine-soaked melodies, guaranteed to stick to your cassette deck like a layer of crazy glue," stated Keith Sharp in *Rock Express.* "[Buckingham] recognizes the powerful Yuppie, Middle America market and he's orchestrated an album that will fill a huge void in the lazy summer months ahead. . . . Functional . . . but no longer fun. And with Lindsey Buckingham holding the reins, I'm surprised he hasn't renamed the band Buckingham Mac."

Other critics were not as harsh and some even compared *Tusk* to the finest work of the Beatles. No one could have possibly expected it to sell like their previous two LPs, and it didn't, but Buckingham told *Rolling Stone* about the pressures of trying to create Rumours Two. "Suddenly the phenomenon was the sales and not the work. And that's dangerous ground as far as I'm concerned."

During the 1980s, Fleetwood Mac released a live LP and two more studio albums while Nicks worked on a solo career for the Modern label and Buckingham recorded the exceptionally fine *Law and Order* on his own. After their *Mirage* LP in 1982, Mick Fleetwood declared bankruptcy and in 1987 called on Buckingham to take a break from his solo career to help out on the band's *Tango In the Night.* Fleetwood Mac was back in the spotlight thanks to the hit single "Seven Wonders" as Buckingham returned to his solo work while being replaced by two guitarists, Billy Burnette and Rick Vito.

In 1990 the band released their *Behind The Mask* LP and were, amazingly, still going strong after twenty-three years and eleven different lineups. "No rock band has had more excuses to break up. Or fewer inclinations to do so," wrote Edna Gundersen in the *Lansing State Journal.* "Fleetwood Mac has weathered soured romances, commercial slumps, drug addiction, alcoholism, bankruptcy and abrupt membership shuffles; any might have splintered a less resilient menage."

Selected discography

Fleetwood Mac, Blue Horizon, 1968.
Fleetwood Mac in Chicago, Blue Horizon, 1969.
Then Play On, Reprise, 1969.
English Rose, Epic, 1969.
Kiln House, Reprise, 1970.
Future Games, Reprise, 1971.
Bare Trees, Reprise, 1972.
Penguin, Reprise, 1972.
Mystery To Me, Reprise, 1973.
Heroes Are Hard To Find, Reprise, 1974.
Fleetwood Mac, Reprise, 1975.
Rumours, Warner Bros., 1977.
Tusk, Warner Bros., 1979.
Fleetwood Mac Live, Warner Bros., 1980.
Mirage, Warner Bros., 1982.
Tango In The Night, Warner Bros., 1987.
Behind The Mask, 1990.

Sources

Books

Christgau, Robert, *Christgau's Record Guide,* Ticknor & Fields, 1981.
Kozinn, Allan, Pete Welding, Dan Forte and Gene Santoro,*The Guitar: The Music, the History, the Players,* Quill, 1984.
Logan, Nick, and Bob Woffinden, *The Illustrated Encyclopedia of Rock,* Harmony, 1977.
The Rolling Stone Illustrated History of Rock & Roll, edited by Jim Miller, Random House/Rolling Stone Press, 1976.
The Rolling Stone Record Guide, edited by Dave Marsh with John Swenson, Random House/Rolling Stone Press, 1979.

Periodicals

Detroit Free Press, July 1, 1990.

Guitar Player, January 1977; January 1978.

Guitar World, January 1983; May 1987; December 1989.

Lansing State Journal, June 30, 1990.

Rock Express, May-June, 1987.

Rolling Stone, April 8, 1976; March 24, 1977; April 21, 1977; December 29, 1977; January 12, 1978; December 13, 1979; February 7, 1980; June 5, 1986; March 26, 1987; September 24, 1987.

—Calen D. Stone

The Grateful Dead

Rock band

The Grateful Dead is one of only a handful of rock bands that have been going at it for nearly two and a half decades. But, unlike their contemporaries, the Dead have built their reputation on noncommercial music dedicated to the art of improvisation. "I would never have thought I'd be interested in something for twenty-five years," band leader Jerry Garcia told *Rolling Stone*. "That's a long time for anything. But if we never get to that place, the process itself stays interesting, so the trip has been worth it."

The group began as an acoustic unit, Mother McCree's Uptown Jug Champions, with Bob Weir, Bob Matthews, Ron "Pigpen" McKernan, John Dawson and Garcia. Pigpen convinced the band to go electric and in 1964 they added Bill Kreutzmann on drums and bassist Phil Lesh, a classically trained trumpet player who had never before touched the four-stringed instrument. They were known briefly as the Warlocks before pulling the moniker Grateful Dead out of an Oxford dictionary. Based in the Haight-Ashbury district of San Francisco—the center of the peace-love-flower-power-drug

For the Record. . .

Band formed in San Francisco, Calif.; original members included guitarist-vocalist **Jerry Garcia** (full name, Jerome John Garcia; born August 1, 1942 in San Francisco, Calif.; father was a jazz musician); guitarist-vocalist **Bob Weir** (Full name, Robert Hall Weir; born October 16, 1947 in San Francisco, Calif.); bass guitarist **Phil Lesh** (born March 15, 1940 in Berkeley, Calif.); drummer **Bill Kreutzmann** (born June 7, 1946, in Palo Alto, Calif.); and vocalist-harmonica player **Ron "Pigpen" McKernan** (born September 8, 1946; died of a liver ailment, March 8, 1973). Drummer **Mickey Hart** (born in Long Island, New York) joined the band in 1967.

McKernan was replaced in 1974 by keyboardist **Keith Godchaux** (born July 19, 1948, in San Francisco, Calif.; killed in a car accident July 22, 1980; husband of band member Donna Godchaux) and vocalist **Donna Godchaux** (born August 22, 1947, in San Francisco, Calif.; wife of band member Keith Godchaux; left band shortly after husband's death in 1980); Keith Godchaux was replaced by keyboardist **Brent Mydland** (died July 26, 1990 of a morphine and cocaine overdose); Mydland was replaced in 1990 by **Vince Welnick**.

Addresses: *Office*—P.O. Box 1566, Main Office Station, Montclair, NJ 07043.

movement in the mid-1960s—the Dead became the house band for Ken Kesey and his Merry Pranksters' parties at the author's pad in La Honda (documented in Tom Wolfe's *The Electric Kool-Aid Acid Test* book).

The band's influences were not other musicians, but rather the Beat Generation writers, including Jack Kerouac and Allen Ginsberg, and the infamous LSD chemist Owsley Stanley, who encouraged the Dead to experiment freely with the then-legal drug and extremely loud volumes of music (at one point the Dead's arsenal included twenty-three tons of equipment!) "Garcia and company were the hippie band, playing music for getting stoned, seeing God, dancing, singing along, blowing bubbles, mellowing out, or whatever," wrote Jon Sievert in *Guitar Player,* "good-time music without rock star pretensions."

In 1967 they added a second drummer, Mickey Hart, and signed a record contract with Warner Bros. Their debut LP, *Grateful Dead,* was recorded in Los Angeles in a mere three days. Its hurried sound prompted the band to slow down and experiment with various studio techniques on their follow-up, *Anthem Of The Sun.* "We were thinking more in terms of a whole record, and we were also interested in doing something that was far out," Garcia said in *The Rolling Stone Interviews*. "For our own amusement—that thing of being able to do a record and really go away with it—really lose yourself." The Dead went a little overboard on their third album, *Aoxomoxoa,* which was, as Garcia continued in *Interviews,* "Too far out, really, for most people."

Their forte has been, and continues to be, live performances which free the band to explore and improvise on blues, jazz, rock and country genres in a very loose setting without the use of set lists. "They are essentially a 'live' band, the masters of the 'vibe,' the electrical flow between them and their audiences," stated *Rock 100*. "The Dead, it has been said 'play their audience,' and their performances are studies in synergy and the dynamics of sounds massing tension in titanic jams . . . until the ballroom seems ready to explode, and then cooling everything out at that breathtaking moment with a trickling steel guitar solo on a Merle Haggard shitkicker special."

The Dead encourage their fans, known affectionately as Deadheads, to freely record their concerts, which are of marathon length and sometimes include hourlong instrument tunings. "We have an audience which allows us to be formless. The Grateful Dead can go into any venue and play anything, and the audience will have experienced the Grateful Dead show," Garcia told *Rolling Stone's* Fred Goodman. "The audience has allowed us that luxury."

The Deadheads' allegiance is almost as phenomenal as the band itself. The club formed in 1971 and has grown to such large proportions that it now includes "The Deadhead Hour" radio show, the Golden Road fan magazine, and two 24-hour phone lines that constantly report concert dates. "I couldn't hold down a full-time job and do this," one Deadhead stated in *Rolling Stone*. "The Dead tour eight months out of the year." "I think our greatest appeal is to somebody who's a bright kid, in late high school or college," Dead lyricist John Barlow told *Rolling Stone*. "There aren't any initiations or requirements or membership tests or anything else to become a Deadhead; you just have to like it and feel like you're part of it, and then you're a brother to them all."

After 1970's *Live Dead,* which included the two Dead classics "Dark Star" and "St. Stephens," the band went back to their roots with an emphasis on vocals for a Crosby, Stills, Nash and Young-style folk flavor on *Workingman's Dead.* During the recording the group endured a sticky situation when Mickey Hart's father was fired for embezzlement of band funds. *American Beauty,* from the same year, was also vocal-oriented and recorded with very simple studio techniques. The LP included one of their signature tunes, "Truckin'," and was followed by their first gold LP, *The Grateful Dead,* in 1971. A year later they recorded the live three-record *Europe '72.*

The Dead lost one of their key members in 1973 when Ron "Pigpen" McKernan died of a liver ailment after a long history of substance abuse. The band issued a compilation LP in his honor, and then formed their own label and began working on *Wake Of The Flood* with new members Keith Godchaux and his wife Donna. Tragedy has continued to haunt the band's keyboardists: Keith himself was killed in a 1980 auto accident (Donna Godchaux left the band shortly after her husband's death) and *his* replacement, Brent Mydland, died as a result of a drug overdose in 1990. Mydland was replaced by former Tubes keyboardist Vince Welnick.

Weir played with both the Dead and Kingfish for the next few years and Garcia worked on various other projects as the band shifted directions for 1975's *Blues*

> *"The Grateful Dead can go into any venue and play* anything, *and the audience will have experienced the Grateful Dead show"*

For Allah. "I've always been happy with our albums but I've rarely listened to them after they're finished," Lesh said in *Rolling Stone.* "This one's different. It indicates a new point of departure for our music. We wanted to free ourselves from our own cliches, to search for new tonalities, new structures and modalities." They recorded one more LP on the Grateful Dead label before signing with Arista and releasing *Terrapin Station* and *Shakedown Street,* both of which smacked more of contemporary marketing than the usual Dead punch. *Shakedown Street* "was produced by twits and plumbers," Hart told *Rolling Stone,* "it was a shame and a travesty."

After 1980's *Go To Heaven,* the Dead took an eight-year hiatus from recording. Garcia delved heavily into cocaine and heroin in the meantime, resulting in an arrest in January of 1985. While performing in a backup band for Bob Dylan, Garcia collapsed into a diabetic coma following one of the shows and regained consciousness twenty-four hours later. By December 15, 1986, the Dead were back together and working on their highly acclaimed *In The Dark* LP. "The arrange-

ments are real," Garcia said in *Guitar World.* "The mix is my understanding about how Grateful Dead music works. . .There's real structure to it, there's real architecture to it and there's real conversation, like in a string quartet, to it."

The Dead scored their first Top 10 single, "Touch of Grey," which seemed to sum up Garcia's brush with death and the future of his band: "I will get by/I will survive." The Dead were suddenly being discovered by new audiences as their video *So Far* shot up the charts and they were trying to figure out ways to cope with their newfound success and popularity.

"I'm excited about it, and I have misgivings," said Robert Hunter, longtime Dead lyricist and Army pal of Garcia, in *Rolling Stone.* "I would like the world to know about the Grateful Dead; it's a phenomenal band. But I don't think the Grateful Dead is going to be as free a thing as it was. That's the devil we pay."

Selected discography

On Warner Bros. Records

Grateful Dead, 1967.
Anthem of the Sun, 1968.
Aoxomoxoa, 1969.
Live Dead, 1970.
Workingman's Dead, 1970.
American Beauty, 1970.
The Grateful Dead, 1971.
Europe '72, 1972.
Bear's Choice: History of the Grateful Dead, Volume 1, 1973.
Best of the Grateful Dead—Skeletons From the Closet, 1974.
What a Long Strange Trip It's Been: The Best of the Grateful Dead, 1977.

On Grateful Dead Records

Wake of the Flood, 1973.
From Mars Hotel, 1974.
Blues for Allah, 1975.
Steal Your Face, 1976.

On Arista Records

Terrapin Station, 1977.
Shakedown Street, 1978.
Go To Heaven, 1980.
Dead Set (live 2-record set), 1981.
Reckoning, 1986.
In The Dark, 1987.
The Dead Zone: The Grateful Dead CD Collection, 1977-1987 (available on compact disc only; six-CD set contains six

digitally remastered albums: *Terrapin Station, Shakedown Street, Go To Heaven, In the Dark, Reckoning,* and *Dead Set*), 1987.
Built To Last, 1989.
Without a Net, (double live album), 1990.

Sources

Periodicals

down beat, November 1987.
Guitar Player, November 1977; October 1978; August 1981; October 1987; July 1988; June 1989.
Guitar World, November 1985; December 1987.
Musician, September 1987.
Rolling Stone, November 6, 1975; February 26, 1976; May 6, 1976; June 16, 1977; October 6, 1977; April 20, 1978; March 8, 1979; August 28, 1986; July 16-30, 1987; August 13, 1987; November 30, 1989.
Rolling Stone's College Papers, Winter, 1980.

Books

Dalton, David, and Lenny Kaye, *Rock 100,* Grosset & Dunlap, 1977.
The Rolling Stone Illustrated History of Rock & Roll, edited by Jim Miller, Random House/Rolling Stone Press, 1976.
The Rolling Stone Interviews, 1967-1980, by the editors of Rolling Stone, St. Martin's Press/Rolling Stone Press, 1981.
The Rolling Stone Record Guide, edited by Dave Marsh with Jim Swenson, Random House/Rolling Stone Press, 1979.

—*Calen D. Stone*

M. C. Hammer

Rap singer

Hailed by *Entertainment Weekly* as "rap's most pervasive, persuasive ambassador," M. C. Hammer has a reputation for pursuing his goals with remarkable energy and tenacity. His first dream in life eluded his grasp, however; if he had achieved it, he would be a professional baseball player today. Instead, Hammer has had to settle for being the world's most successful rap artist.

Hammer was born Stanley Kirk Burrell in Oakland, California. He was the youngest of his parents' seven children. "We were definitely poor," he stated in describing his youth to *Rolling Stone* writer Jeffrey Ressner. "Welfare. Government-aided apartment building. Three bedrooms and six children living together at one time." Despite the rough neighborhood he grew up in, Hammer stayed out of trouble by immersing himself in his twin passions, baseball and music.

As a boy he'd be at the Oakland Coliseum to watch the Athletics play as often as possible. If he couldn't see the game, he'd hang around the parking lot hoping for a glimpse of one of his heroes, among them superstar pitcher Vida Blue. When the team was idle Hammer amused himself by copying the dance moves of James Brown, the O'Jays, and others. He showed the first glimmerings of his interest in business when he began writing commercial jingles for his favorite products.

One day his two interests collided in a way that would profoundly influence his life. He was dancing in the Coliseum's parking lot when the Athletics' owner, Charlie Finley, passed by. A comment by Finley on the young dancer's style led to a conversation, and eventually to a job working in the team clubhouse and going on the road as bat boy. Hammer quickly became a sort of mascot for the team. Finley even gave him the honorary title of executive vice-president, while the ballplayers began calling the former Stanley Burrell "Hammer" because of his striking resemblance to batting great Henry "Hammerin' Hank" Aaron.

After graduating from high school, Hammer tried to break into the world of professional baseball as a player, but to no avail. He briefly pursued a communications degree, but was unsuccessful in that field too. Dejected and at loose ends, Hammer considered getting involved in the lucrative drug trade thriving in his old neighborhood. "I was a sharp businessman and could have joined up with a top dealer," he told Ressner. "I had friends making $5000 to $6000 a week, easy. . . . I thought about that just like any other entrepreneur would." Hammer turned away from the fast money, however—making a moral choice that reverberates in his current image as a deeply religious, socially conscious performer—and joined the Navy for a three-year hitch, serving in Japan and California.

Real name, Stanley Kirk Burrell; born in Oakland, Calif.; youngest of seven children; married; wife's name, Stephanie; children: Akeiba Monique. *Education:* High school graduate; took undergraduate classes in communications.

Worked for the Oakland Athletics baseball team as a bat boy during high school years; served for three years in the U.S. Navy upon graduation from high school; formed first rap group, the Holy Ghost Boys, and founded music production company, Bust It Records; first debut single, "Ring 'Em," released in the mid-1980s; signed with Capitol Records, 1988. Performs in concerts worldwide.

Awards: Grammy Award (with co-composers Rick James and Alonzo Miller) for best rhythm and blues song, 1990, for "U Can't Touch This"; Grammy Award for best rap solo, 1990, for "U Can't Touch This"; Grammy Award for best music video (long form), 1990, for *Please Hammer Don't Hurt 'Em the Movie.*

Addresses: *Home*—Fremont Hills, CA.

When his stint with the military ended, Hammer applied the discipline he'd acquired in the service to launching a career in music. His first musical venture was a rap duo he dubbed the Holy Ghost Boys. Religious rap might seem to have limited commercial appeal, but Hammer talked two record companies into taking a chance on producing a Holy Ghost Boys album. He and his partner went their separate ways before the project could be completed, however.

Two of Hammer's friends from the Oakland A's helped him make his next move. Mike Davis and Dwayne Murphy each invested $20,000 in Bust It Records, Hammer's own company. He hawked his debut single, "Ring 'Em," on the streets. At the same time, he was auditioning and working with musicians, dancers, and his female backup trio, known as Oaktown's 3-5-7. Striving to put together a more sophisticated act, Hammer held rehearsals seven days a week, sometimes for fourteen hours at a time.

Shortly after the release of his second single, "Let's Get Started," Hammer teamed with Felton Pilate, a producer and musician from the group Con Funk Shun. The two worked long hours in Pilate's basement studio to bring out Hammer's first full-length album, *Feel My Power.* Produced on a shoestring budget and marketed without the tremendous resources of a major record

company, *Feel My Power* nevertheless sold a remarkable 60,000 copies.

Early in 1988 Hammer was catching an act at an Oakland music club when he was spotted by Joy Bailey, an executive at Capitol Records. She didn't know who he was, but his presence and attitude impressed her. She introduced herself and later arranged for him to meet with some of the company's top people at Capitol's Los Angeles headquarters. With his music, dancing, and keen business sense, Hammer convinced Capitol that he was the man who could lead the company successfully into the booming rap music market. He walked away from the meeting with a multi-album contract and a $750,000 advance. The record company didn't have to wait long for proof that they'd made the right decision; a reworked version of *Feel My Power,* titled *Let's Get It Started* climbed to sales of more than 1.5 million records.

Touring and appearing at hip hop shows around the nation in the company of well-established rap perform-

---

The Oakland A's ballplayers began calling the former Stanley Burrell "Hammer" because of his striking resemblance to batting great Henry "Hammerin' Hank" Aaron

---

ers Tone-Loc, N.W.A., and Heavy D and the Boyz didn't keep Hammer from working on his next album— he simply outfitted the back of his tour bus with recording equipment. Such methods enabled him to turn out the single "U Can't Touch This" for about $10,000, roughly the same cost of *Feel My Power.* He predicted to Capitol that the album would break all rap music sales records, and his boast was no idle one. Backed by a unique marketing campaign (which included sending cassettes to 100,000 children, along with personalized letters urging them to request Hammer's music on MTV), "U Can't Touch This" had already sold more than five million copies in late 1990, easily surpassing the record formerly held by the Beastie Boys' *Licensed to Ill.* The song also became the theme song for the Detroit Pistons basketball team during and after their second NBA championship campaign in 1990.

After the release of *Please Hammer Don't Hurt 'Em,* whose immensely popular "U Can't Touch This" was described by *Entertainment Weekly* as "shamelessly copp[ing] its propulsive riff from Rick James' 'Super Freak,'" James himself took legal action against Hammer. The two entertainers reached an out-of-court settlement, with Hammer paying James for "borrowing" James's early 1980s hit song. As reported in *Jet,* Hammer told James, "I felt good using music from a person I idolized. Ya'll used to come out and do a show. Then I'd do my thing at the club to *Super Freak."* According to *Jet,* the performers reconciled, with James telling Hammer, "Keep doing it."

Before each performance on his tour, Hammer leads his fifteen dancers, twelve backup singers, seven musicians, and two deejays in prayer, then puts on the most energetic show possible. His future ventures include an action-comedy film tentatively titled *Pressure,* an album to be produced by Prince, and a longform video for which 100,000 advance orders have already been placed. Furthermore, he has signed a contract uniting Bust It Records with Capitol in a $10 million joint-venture agreement. The rapper also makes commercial endorsements for Pepsi and British Knights athletic wear and a Saturday morning cartoon series focusing on the pre-Hammer childhood of Stanley Kirk Burrell. He hopes to someday break into a film career, telling *Rolling Stone's* Steve Hochman: "I'm not a singer-want-to-turn movie star. I've always been an actor."

For now, however, it looks like M. C. Hammer will endure in his present field. "I'm on a mission," Hammer told Ressner. "The music is in me, and I have to get it out." As *Entertainment Weekly* phrased it, "Hammer is cultural evolution in fast action, the rapper as wheeler-dealer and sleek entertainer—and the next logical step for a form of music that is quickly becoming part of the fabric of American life."

Selected discography

Singles

"Ring 'Em," Bust It Records.
"Let's Get Started," Bust It Records.

LPs

Feel My Power, Bust It Records (revised version released as *Let's Get It Started*), Capitol, 1989.
Please Hammer Don't Hurt 'Em, Capitol, 1990.

Sources

Ebony, January 1989.
Entertainment Weekly, December 28, 1990.
Jet, November 5, 1990.
New York Times, April 15, 1990.
Rolling Stone, May 17, 1990; July 12, 1990; September 6, 1990.

—Joan Goldsworthy

Stephen Hartke

Symphonic composer

Stephen Hartke is rapidly gaining prominence as one of the best young American symphonic composers of the late twentieth century. In an interview with *U.S. News and World Report,* Leonard Slatkin, conductor of the St. Louis Symphony and an avid supporter of contemporary music, maintained that Hartke numbers in the top three American composers of his era. Hartke has received numerous commissions and awards for his works, which have been featured in concerts and broadcasts throughout the United States, as well as in Europe, the Soviet Union, and South America. Reviewing a performance of Hartke's orchestral work *Pacific Rim* for the *Detroit News,* writer Lawrence B. Johnson described Hartke's music as reflecting an "eclectic style molded by keen originality, brilliant technique and a concern for reaching not just the ear and intellect but the heart as well."

In 1952 Hartke was born in Orange, New Jersey, to George and Priscilla Hartke. Stephen showed an early interest in music. At age 5 or 6 he could already identify the instruments of the orchestra. After the Hartke family moved to New York City, beginning at age 9, Stephen performed professionally as a boy soprano with the New York Pro Musica, the Metropolitan Opera, the Juilliard Opera, and with metropolitan area orchestras. Young Hartke was influenced to become a composer when the local parish choirmaster was cleaning and giving away 78 rpm records—Hartke ended up with a recording of Samuel Barber's *First Symphony.* It was a revelation to him that a living American was actually composing music that was not musical comedy.

Hartke began formal composition study age 14. He started his composition career composing atonal music, and even won a BMI Award at age 16 for a piece he wrote for string orchestra. He subsequently studied with James Drew at Yale University, where he earned his Bachelor of Arts degree in 1973. "[I] started out as an academic atonalist," Hartke told Kenneth LaFave, music editor for the *Kansas City Star.* "Then in the early 1970s I became dissatisfied. I wasn't loving every note I wrote. So I started cutting out the notes I didn't love and discovered that the more I cut out those notes, the more and more tonal the music became.

"A lot of the so-called neo-romantic tendencies have to do with nostalgia. But I didn't approach it that way. I just focused on the notes I like and the music came out tonal." But the more tonal Hartke's music became, the less it pleased academics and his works therefore received fewer and fewer performances. Hartke was firm in his conviction that his music was to be tonally based, however. To better his composition skills he studied composition at the University of Pennsylvania in Philadelphia with American composer George Rochberg, who believes that the expressive aspects of music need to balance the technical aspects or serialism could lead to a sterile and mechanical academicism.

After Hartke earned his Master of Arts degree in composition in 1976, he spent several years working in the advertising and educational areas of the music publishing industry. But he found such work hindered his composition efforts. "One of the worst ways to make any headway as a composer was to work in music publishing," he reflected to Richard S. Ginell of the *Los Angeles Daily News,* "because no one takes you seriously as an artist if you're inside the business." To further his career as a composer, in 1981 Hartke accepted a visiting lectureship in composition at the University of California (USC), Santa Barbara's College of Creative Studies and the following year earned his doctorate in composition at USC.

In 1984 Hartke was awarded a Fulbright professorship in composition at the Universidade de Sao Paulo, Escola de Comunicacoes e Artes in Sao Paulo, Brazil. While in Brazil Hartke composed a piece for two violins, *Oh Them Rats Is Mean in My Kitchen,* which he later orchestrated and retitled *Maltese Cat Blues.* The piece takes its original title from a song by Blind Lemon

Jefferson, a great blues singer and composer who died in 1929. "Years ago I heard a recording of Sleepy John Estes singing his own version of it, which begins 'Oh them rats is mean in my kitchen,'" Hartke explained in the concert program notes. "The melody has since faded from my mind, but the style of singing, with its energetic speech-song and wailing, typical of early blues, fixed itself in my memory. In 1985 . . . I underwent that sharpening of my sense of national identity which almost inevitably results from a prolonged stay abroad. That memory of Sleepy John's singing resurfaced and prompted me to compose a piece as an homage to the spirit of blues performance." Rather than attempting to reconstruct the tune, Hartke tried to distill and reflect the ingredients of the blues form, particularly the declamatory style of blues singing. *Maltese Cat Blues* and the original violin duo have been performed throughout the United States and in Europe, and *Maltese Cat Blues* won the Louisville Orchestra Prize in 1987.

In 1988 Hartke was appointed the first composer-in-residence of the Los Angeles Chamber Orchestra and commissioned to compose an orchestral piece to celebrate the ensemble's twentieth season. *Pacific Rim* was the result. "The work . . . is a virtuoso showpiece for the orchestra and is also a reflection of how certain aspects of Asian and Latin-American musics have filtered into my mind and become transformed and absorbed within in my compositional thought. The piece is in two linked

sections and may be simply described as a processional and fugue," Hartke explained in the program notes.

Hartke maintains that critics of his work overstress his interest in vernacular musics, such as jazz, because that seems to be a widespread bias in current criticism of contemporary music. "While I indeed draw on vernacular influences to my musical thought-processes," the composer told *Contemporary Musicians,* "I am in no way a re-packager of pop styles in some late twentieth-century guise; rather, I think I merely reflect my experience as a part of the audience, though I fear my tastes as an audience member do not necessarily fall in line with 'majority' opinion."

Compositions

Caoine, for solo violin, 1980.
Shetland Bridal Tunes, for violin duo, 1981.
Two Songs for an Uncertain Age, soprano and orchestra, 1981.
Cancoes modernistas, for high voice and instruments, 1982.
Iglesia abandonada, for soprano and violin, 1982.
Alvorada, for string orchestra, 1983.
Sonata Variations, for piano, 1984.
Oh Them Rats Is Mean in My Kitchen, two-violin version of *Maltese Cat Blues,* 1985.
Retumbante, for solo piano, 1985.
Template, for solo piano, 1985.
Maltese Cat Blues, for orchestra, 1986.
Precession, for thirteen instruments, 1986.
Sonata-Fantasia, for solo piano, 1987.
Pacific Rim, for orchestra, 1988.
The King of the Sun, for piano quartet, 1988.
Night Rubrics, for solo cello, 1990.
Symphony No. 2, 1990.

Selected discography

Caoine and *Iglesia abandonada,* Orion.
Oh Them Rats Is Mean In My Kitchen, New World Records.

Sources

Baltimore Sun, October 13, 1989.
Kansas City Star, October 30, 1988.
Los Angeles Daily News, September 23, 1988.
Los Angeles Times, March 10, 1983.
Musical America, February 1986.
Sun (Maryland), October 13, 1989.
U.S. News and World Report, November 27, 1989.

—Jeanne M. Lesinski

Herman's Hermits

Pop group

Perhaps best known for such light-hearted mid-sixties hits as "Mrs. Brown You've Got a Lovely Daughter," and "I'm Henry the VIII, I Am," as well as the gentle "There's a Kind of Hush," Herman's Hermits provided a bridge between the non-confrontational style of 1950s lyrics and the Mersey Sound brought to the world's attention by the Beatles. While their ultimate impact on the music industry was not as great as that of other members of the British Invasion (including the Beatles, the Animals, and the Moody Blues) the Hermits did enjoy their degree of success. Between 1965 and 1966 they placed nine songs in a row in the Top Ten—a feat even the Beatles could not claim.

Organized first as The Heartbeats in 1962 or 1963 (sources differ), the group featured 16-year-old vocalist and guitarist Peter Noone and included Keith Hopwood on guitar, Karl Greene also on guitar and harmonica, Derek Leckenby on guitar, too, and Barry Whitwam playing the drums. According to *Rock On,* the name change was inspired by Noone's supposed resemblance to the cartoon character Sherman in the

For the Record. . .

Band formed originally under the name the Heartbeats, in 1962 or 1963, in Manchester, England, by guitar player **Keith Hopwood** (born October 26, 1946, in Manchester, England); vocalist and guitarist **Peter Blair Denis Bernard "Herman" Noone** (born November 5, 1947, in Manchester, England); guitar and harmonica player **Karl Anthony Greene** (born July 31, 1946 or 1947, in Salford, England); guitarist **Derek "Lek" Leckenby** (born May 14, 1945 or 1946, in Leeds, England); and drummer **Barry Whitwam** (born July 21, 1946).

Toured, performed, and recorded after signing with record producer Mickie Most in 1964; released two Number 1 singles in 1965, "Mrs. Brown, You've Got a Lovely Daughter," and "I'm Henry VIII, I Am"; traveled to Los Angeles, Calif., in 1965 to make the film, *Where the Boys Meet the Girls*; after Noone's departure in 1971, dissolved; reformed for concerts in 1973, 1980, and 1986.

Addresses: *Record company*—ABKCO Records Inc., 1700 Broadway, New York, NY 10019.

television cartoon show, *Rocky and His Friends* (remember Mr. Peabody, Bullwinkle, Natasha, and Dudley Do-Right?). The nickname Herman stuck, and producer Mickie Most encouraged the group to adopt the name Herman's Hermits. After gaining a strong reputation in Manchester, the Hermits began their recording career in 1964. Their first hit came the same year with "I'm Into Something Good" by Carole King and Gerry Goffin. It would be the first of a string of hits that lasted nearly four years. In 1965, "Can't You Hear My Heartbeat" became their first smash hit, followed by "Silhouettes," and "Mrs. Brown You've Got a Lovely Daughter," the latter of which went on to become a gold single. Riding partly on the popularity of the Beatles and the youthful appeal of Noone, the group made a successful tour of the United States. Their music and film *When the Boys Meet the Girls* were well received by the younger set—especially after the Beatles began their slow metamorphosis away from the Fab Four Image. Other hits in 1965 included "Wonderful World" and the amusing gold single "I'm Henry the VIII, I Am." Remarkable in 1966 was "Dandy" and in 1967 the two-sided hit single "There's a Kind of Hush/No Milk Today." Despite a lack of new albums, the Hermits remained together until mid-1971, playing small clubs both in England and in the United States, where they had always been better recognized. Taking back his own name, Noone had already undertaken a solo ca-

reer, feeling the group had run its course. "I'm not ashamed of my past career as Herman," he commented. "Twenty-two hit singles and world sales of 40 million is nothing to be embarrassed about, but I've felt for some time that we have realized our potential as Herman's Hermits. I now need the freedom and broader scope of an individual." He was to pursue both musical and acting careers, resurrecting the Hermits for several rock revival shows and television shows, and finally reemerging in 1980 with a New Wave Los Angeles-based band called the Tremblers. Without Noone, the other Hermits reformed first in 1973 without much success and later in 1986 to tour with former members of other sixties acts the Monkees, the Grass Roots, and Gary Puckett. In Ontario, their 25-minute slot earned them a standing ovation, though, according to Kerry Doole for *Rock Express,* "These songs are better than the singers; it's a bit embarrassing hearing a 40-year-old sing about being taken home to meet his girlfriend's Dad."

Despite such criticism, it is worth noting that that tour was one of the hottest in North America for that year, well-attended by yesterday's teenyboppers as well as their kids. Something in the music survives and continues to entertain and touch the heart of the listener, and the band's continued success is a reminder of that fact. The appeal of the Hermits' brand of sweetness lives on; after all, what worked in 1965 and what works today is essentially the same. "Mum and dad used to (so they say)," was the wisdom of the Hermits' song "Mum and Dad." "Mum and dad used to every day. So why can't I and why can't you, begin to? Begin to fall in love." Some things don't change.

Selected discography

Herman's Hermits, Columbia and MGM, 1965.
The Best of Herman's Hermits, Columbia and MGM, 1965.
Introducing Herman's Hermits, MGM, 1965.
Herman's Hermits on Tour, MGM, 1965.
When the Boys Meet the Girls, MGM, 1965.
Both Sides of Herman's Hermits, Columbia and MGM, 1966.
Herman's Hermits Again, Columbia, 1966.
Lucky 13, Columbia, 1966.
Hold On (soundtrack), MGM, 1966.
Best of Herman's Hermits, Vol. 2, MGM, 1966.
There's a Kind of Hush, Columbia, 1967.
X15, Columbia, 1967.
Blaze, Columbia, 1967.
Mrs. Brown (soundtrack), Columbia, 1968.
Best of Herman's Hermits, Vol. 3, MGM, 1968.
The Best of UK, Columbia, 1969.
Very Best of Herman's Hermits, MFP, 1984.

Sources

Books

Nite, Norm N., *Rock On!,* Harper & Row, 1984.
Stambler, Irwin, *Encyclopedia of Pop, Rock and Soul,* St. Martin's
    Press, 1989.

Periodicals

High Fidelity, April 1988.
Rock Express, Number 106, 1986.
Rolling Stone, July 14, 1988 (British Invasion Supplement).

—Meg Mac Donald

Al Hirt

Trumpet player

Al Hirt is a favorite son of his native New Orleans, the town that gave America Dixieland Jazz. Known for years as the "Round Mound of Sound," the genial Hirt is the most popular working Dixieland musician in the country. His original fusion of jazz and rock elements helped to bring the music of New Orleans to the attention of a new generation in the 1960s; since then he and his trumpet have been closely associated with both the city and its signature sound.

Alois Maxwell Hirt was born in New Orleans late in 1922. The son of a police officer, he acquired his first trumpet from a pawnshop when he was six years old. He quickly mastered the instrument and became something of a prodigy with it, so much so that he headed the Sons of the Police Department Junior Police Band before he hit his teens. Hirt's first professional job came in 1939, when he was hired to call horses to the post at the Louisiana Fairgrounds. The weekly salary of 40 dollars was extravagant for a youth of 17, but the beginnings of a lifelong interest in betting on horse races absorbed some of the wages.

Deciding to pursue a career in music, Hirt enrolled at the Cincinnati Conservatory of Music in 1940 and attended classes there until he entered the Army in 1943. At the conservatory he studied classical trumpet and cornet, dabbling in jazz as a sideline. "I always aspired to be a legitimate player," Hirt told the *Richmond News Leader*. "That was my training. Now I'm a jazz player. People paid attention to trumpet always. It's an attractive instrument. It's got a great sound. Every kid in school wants to play the trumpet."

Hirt may have chosen a popular instrument, but he played it so well that he suffered little competition for high-paying work. After the war he played with a number of top-ranked big bands, touring America and Europe in grand style with Jimmy Dorsey, Tommy Dorsey, and Benny Goodman. In the early 1950s Hirt decided to form his own group. He settled down in New Orleans and fronted a Dixieland band that soon became the house outfit for Dan Levy's Pier 600 Club. The band quickly attracted a local following and within a few years it had gained a national reputation for its exuberant horn numbers.

Hirt became a national celebrity after he signed with RCA Records in 1960. Early albums *Greatest Horn, He's the King* and *Bourbon Street* sold very well and RCA began to release new material from the artist roughly every six months. At a time when rock 'n' roll seemed to hold a monopoly on the air waves, Hirt actually placed Dixieland-flavored band music on the charts with hits such as "Java" and "Cotton Candy." The rotund performer earned his nickname "Round

Mound of Sound" when he began appearing on television variety shows in the mid-1960s.

National prominence notwithstanding, Hirt never gave up his New Orleans roots. For years he owned his own club at 501 Bourbon Street; when he sold it, he moved to the J. B. Rivers Club along the Mississippi. He was a minority owner of the New Orleans Saints when the club moved to town and for many seasons played trumpet right behind the team bench at home games. Hirt has performed with a number of America's largest symphony orchestras as a guest soloist; in 1965 he gave a standing-room-only concert at New York City's Carnegie Hall.

Despite his popularity, reviewers have not always been kind to Hirt. Even at the height of his success, he was criticized for adding rock elements to his work and for watering down his personal ability to appeal to a mainstream audience. To this day Hirt bridles at such charges. "I couldn't care less what jazz purists say," he told the *Richmond News Leader.* "Who . . . is a jazz purist? Somebody who doesn't play an instrument."

Purists aside, the public still loves Hirt's playful sound. His affectionate nickname, however, no longer applies as a strict diet has reduced the jazz master's once legendary weight. Well into his sixties, Hirt plays dozens of concerts a year, both at home in New Orleans and across the country. His performances include not only Dixieland numbers, but Latin, pop, jazz, and classical works as well—though his finale remains the rousing "When the Saints Go Marching In." A grandfather nine times over, Hirt nonetheless has no plans to hang his trumpet on a peg. "It's always been fun for me," he confided to the *Richmond News Leader.* "I enjoy playing." He concluded: "There's more to playing than playing, though. You gotta be a nice person, too."

Selected discography

Al Hirt at Dan's Pier 600, Audio Fidelity.
Swingin' Dixie, two volumes, Audio Fidelity, 1960 and 1961.
Greatest Horn, RCA, 1961.
He's the King, RCA, 1961.
Bourbon Street, RCA, 1961.
Horn a Plenty, RCA, 1962.
Al Hirt at the Mardi Gras, RCA, 1962.
Trumpet and Strings, RCA, 1962.
Al Hirt in New Orleans, RCA, 1963.
Honey in the Horn, RCA, 1963.
Cotton Candy, RCA, 1964.
(With Ann-Margaret) *Beauty and the Beard,* RCA, 1964.
Honey Horn Hound, RCA, 1965.
Al Hirt at Carnegie Hall, RCA, 1965.
Sugar Lips, RCA, 1965.
Best of Al Hirt, RCA, 1966.
They're Playing Our Song, RCA, 1966.
Best of Al Hirt, Volume 2, RCA, 1966.
Happy Trumpet, RCA, 1966.
Horn Meets Hornet, RCA, 1966.
Music to Watch Girls By, RCA, 1967.
Latin in the Horn, RCA, 1967.
Struttin', RCA, 1967.
Soul in the Horn, RCA, 1967.
Hirt Plays Kaempfert, RCA, 1968.
Al Hirt, RCA, 1970.
This Is Al Hirt, RCA, 1970.
Al's Place, Camden, 1970.
Best of Al Hirt, with Pete Fountain, Ampex.
New Orleans by Night, 1986.
Blues Line (also contains Fountain's *Fountain of Youth*), 1987.
(With Fountain) *Super Jazz* (reissue), Monument, 1988.
All Time Greatest Hits, RCA, 1989.

Sources

Charlotte Observer, February 1, 1989.
Houston Post, March 27, 1988.
Richmond News Leader, July 7, 1988; July 18, 1988.

—Anne Janette Johnson

Holland-Dozier-Holland

Pop songwriting/producing team

Holland-Dozier-Holland (pictured below, with Diana Ross) were the ace songwriting and production team of the Motown Record Corporation in the 1960s. While many other writers and producers contributed to Motown's distinctive style, H-D-H songs became synonymous with the "Motown Sound" because of their hits of the 1963-1967 period. In those five years, they wrote twenty-five Top 10 pop records, twelve of which reached the Number 1 spot. In addition, they wrote twelve other songs that made the Top 10 on the rhythm and blues (r&b) chart, making a total of thirty-seven Top 10 hits.

H-D-H are considered pioneers in changing the sound of r&b to "crossover music" or pop/r&b. Their songs combined many influences, including soul, pop, country, and r&b. Their music appealed to both black and white audiences, thus "crossing over" from one market to the other. Hence, the "Motown Sound" was also billed as the "Sound of Young America" because of its wide appeal to young people of all races.

Eddie Holland had a moderately successful career as a

The Holland-Dozier-Holland songwriting and producing team consisted of **Eddie Holland** (born October 30, 1939, in Detroit, Mich.) **Lamont Dozier** (born June 16, 1941, in Detroit, Mich.), and **Brian Holland** (born February 15, 1941, in Detroit, Mich.). Eddie and Brian are brothers. While all three are talented composers, Eddie Holland was noted for his lyrics, Lamont Dozier for the melodies, and Brian Holland for production and engineering.

The team was formed at Berry Gordy's Motown Record Corporation in Detroit, Mich., in 1962. Depending on the source, their very first recorded collaboration was either Lamont Dozier's recording of "Dearest One" on the Melody label or the Marvelettes' recording of "Locking Up My Heart" on Tamla. Wrote and produced 25 Top 10 pop hits (12 of which reached Number 1) and an additional 12 songs that made the Top 10 on the r&b charts during career with Motown, 1963-67; left Motown in 1968 and formed own record companies, Hot Wax and Invictus, in Detroit.

Awards: Lamont Dozier awarded a Grammy, with Phil Collins, for best song written specifically for a motion picture or television, 1989, for "Two Hearts" from motion picture *Buster;* team inducted into the Rock and Roll Hall of Fame, 1990.

singer, charting such songs as "Jamie" and "Leaving Here" in the early 1960s. He was one of the first singers that Berry Gordy recorded as an independent producer in the late 1950s before Gordy formed Motown. Eddie's talent for writing lyrics led to his co-writing several songs for the Temptations with Norman Whitfield, and he wrote for other Motown artists and with other collaborators.

Brian Holland wrote and produced songs at Motown with Robert Bateman, Freddie Gorman, Lamont Dozier, and others before teaming up with his brother. Lamont Dozier had been singing with such groups as the Romeos and the Voice Masters in the late 1950s and as a soloist under the name Lamont Anthony. Lamont Dozier and Brian Holland formed a songwriting team at Motown with Freddie Gorman. When Gorman was replaced by Eddie Holland, the soon-to-become-famous Holland-Dozier-Holland team was born.

While many Motown artists recorded songs written and/or produced by H-D-H, they were most notably associated with the Supremes, Martha and the Vandellas, and the Four Tops. The Four Tops were virtually unknown after performing for nearly ten years, until they were teamed up with H-D-H and recorded such hits as "Baby, I Need Your Loving," "Bernadette," "I Can't Help Myself (Sugar Pie, Honey Bunch)," "It's The Same Old Song," "Reach Out I'll Be There," "7 Rooms Of Gloom," and "Standing In the Shadows of Love." "I Can't Help Myself" and "Reach Out I'll Be There" both went to Number 1 on the Billboard pop chart in 1965 and 1966, respectively.

The Supremes had joined Motown in 1962 and were hitless after releasing six singles, all produced by Berry Gordy or Smokey Robinson. The group didn't click with the record-buying public until their seventh single, released late in 1963. The song, "When The Lovelight Starts Shining Through His Eyes," was the group's first recording of a H-D-H composition. While the group reportedly didn't even like the song, they recorded it anyway. It reached a respectable Number 23 on the pop charts. The follow-up song, "Run Run Run," flopped; but it was to be followed by an amazing string of Number 1 pop hits that propelled the Supremes (and Diana Ross) into stardom.

H-D-H provided the Supremes with five consecutive Number 1 pop hits that began their reign over the pop charts for nearly four years, from 1964 through 1967. This first string of Number 1 hits began with "Where Did Our Love Go" in 1964, and was followed by "Baby Love," "Come See About Me," "Stop! In The Name Of Love," and "Back In My Arms Again." After the mid-1965 release, "Nothing But Heartaches," peaked at Number 11, the group added "I Hear A Symphony" to their list of Number 1 hits.

The Supremes began 1967 with two more H-D-H songs, "My World Is Empty Without You" and "Love Is Like An Itching In My Heart," both of which made the Top 10 on the pop charts. Then there were four more consecutive Number 1 hits, all written and produced by H-D-H, for 1966 and 1967: "You Can't Hurry Love," "You Keep Me Hanging On," "Love Is Here And Now You're Gone," and "The Happening." Two more Top 10 hits from the pen of H-D-H, "Reflections" and "In And Out Of Love," completed the year for the Supremes. The collaboration between H-D-H and the Supremes came to an end in 1968 when H-D-H left Motown in a dispute over royalties.

Martha and the Vandellas were another Motown group that found recording H-D-H songs a boost to their popularity. From 1963 through 1967, they recorded five Top 10 pop hits written and produced by H-D-H: "Heatwave," "Quicksand," "Nowhere To Run," "I'm Ready For Love," and "Jimmy Mack." H-D-H worked closely with the group and provided them with such songs as "Come And Get These Memories," "Live Wire," "In My Lonely Room," and "I'm Ready For Love."

Other Motown artists that recorded H-D-H compositions included Marvin Gaye ["Can I Get A Witness," "Little Darling (I Need You)," "How Sweet It Is (To Be Loved By You)," and "You're A Wonderful One"]; Kim Weston ["Take Me In Your Arms (Rock Me A Little While)"]; the Isley Brothers ["This Ole Heart Of Mine (Is Weak For You)"]; and even Smokey Robinson's Miracles ["Mickey's Monkey," "(Come 'Round Here) I'm The One You Need,"].

After H-D-H left Motown, they established their own labels in Detroit. Hot Wax and Invictus offered a talented roster of black artists doing infectious r&b that found favor with both black and white audiences. Topping the H-D-H list of artists were Chairmen of the Board ("Give Me Just A Little More Time"), Honey Cone ("Want Ads") and Freda Payne ("Band Of Gold"). While these songs all reached the Top 10 on the pop charts, none of the artists were able to string together the kind of hits that made H-D-H famous in the 1960s.

Holland-Dozier-Holland were inducted as a team into the Rock and Roll Hall of Fame in January 1990. They were also inducted into the Songwriting Hall of Fame the same year. Interestingly, they never received a Grammy for their compositions, but they received over 100 BMI awards for some 35 records that made the Top 10. In 1989, Lamont Dozier won his first Grammy for co-authoring "Two Hearts" with Phil Collins for the movie *Buster*.

Selected discography

Compositions released as singles by the Supremes

"When The Lovelight Starts Shining Through His Eyes," Motown, 1963.
"Where Did Our Love Go," Motown, 1964.
"Baby Love," Motown, 1964.
"Come See About Me," Motown, 1964.
"Stop! In The Name Of Love," Motown, 1965.
"Back In My Arms Again," Motown, 1965.
"Nothing But Heartaches," Motown, 1965.
"I Hear A Symphony," Motown, 1965.
"My World Is Empty Without You," Motown, 1965.
"Love Is Like An Itching In My Heart," Motown, 1966.
"You Can't Hurry Love," Motown, 1966.
"You Keep Me Hangin' On," Motown, 1966.
"Love Is Here And Now You're Gone," Motown, 1967.
"The Happening," Motown, 1967.
"Reflections," Motown, 1967.
"In And Out Of Love," Motown, 1967.

"Forever Came Today," Motown, 1968.

Compositions released on LP by the Supremes

Supremes Sing Holland-Dozier-Holland, Motown, 1967.

Compositions released as singles by the Four Tops

"Baby I Need Your Loving," Motown, 1964.
"I Can't Help Myself (Sugar Pie, Honey Bunch)," Motown, 1965.
"It's The Same Old Song," Motown, 1965.
"Something About You," Motown, 1965.
"Shake Me Wake Me (When It's Over)," Motown, 1966.
"Reach Out I'll Be There," Motown, 1966.
"Standing In The Shadows Of Love," Motown, 1966.
"Bernadette," Motown, 1967.
"7 Rooms Of Gloom," Motown, 1967.

Compositions released as singles by Martha & the Vandellas

"Come and Get These Memories," Gordy, 1963.
"Heatwave," Gordy, 1963.
"Quicksand," Gordy, 1963.
"Live Wire," Gordy, 1964.
"In My Lonely Room," Gordy, 1964.
"Nowhere To Run," Gordy, 1965.
"I'm Ready For Love," Gordy, 1966.
"Jimmy Mack," Gordy, 1967.

Compositions released as singles by Marvin Gaye

"Can I Get A Witness," Tamla, 1963.
"You're A Wonderful One," Tamla, 1964.
"How Sweet It Is (To Be Loved By You)," Tamla, 1964.
"Little Darling (I Need You)," Tamla, 1966.

Compositions released as singles by various artists

(By the Miracles) "Mickey's Monkey," Tamla, 1963.
(By Kim Weston) "Take Me In Your Arms (Rock Me A Little While)," Gordy, 1965.
(By the Miracles) "(Come 'Round Here) I'm The One You Need," Tamla, 1966.
(By the Isley Brothers) "This Old Heart Of Mine (Is Weak For You)," Tamla, 1966.

Sources

Bianco, David, *Heat Wave: The Motown Fact Book*, Pierian Press, 1988.

—David Bianco

Janis Ian

Singer, songwriter, guitarist, pianist

Disturbed by the problems and hypocrisies of modern society, singer/songwriter Janis Ian has made a career out of earnestly challenging the status quo. In 1966, at the tender age of 15, she addressed racial prejudice in her hit song "Society's Child," the poignant story of a white girl forced by parents, teachers, and others to forsake her black boyfriend. A decade later the performer touchingly conveyed the painful feelings of a plain adolescent girl in the award-winning "At Seventeen," indicting a society where female self-worth too often hinges on physical beauty. Ian's "Uncle Wonderful," written in the mid-eighties, looked at the secret world and indelible wounds of child molestation. "Janis Ian's intelligence and perception continue to shine through all that she does," observed Peter Reilly in a *Stereo Review* critique of the entertainer's 1979 album, *Night Rains*. "The title song . . . has vintage Ian lyrics, flushed with the kind of theatrical melodrama that only she can create . . . and it is performed with the pulsing, dark intensity that is her trademark." "No one ever accused songwriter Janis Ian of dodging life's difficult issues," *People* reporter Lois Armstrong agreed.

A musical child prodigy, Ian began classical piano training at the age of three and mastered the acoustic guitar a few years later. By age 12 she was writing songs and performing at school functions—music being her only solace as she moved from place to place repeatedly with her family. Her own musical tastes varied, with favorites like jazz vocalist Billie Holiday and folk singer Odetta; Ian's early compositions were largely stormy generation-gap pieces with folk song melodies that nonetheless contained some remarkably perceptive observations. By 16 she was singing and playing in Greenwich Village folk clubs and landed a recording contract with Verve.

Verve agreed to release Ian's daring "Society's Child," already rejected by twenty-two other recording companies. The year was 1966, and disc jockeys across the country were reluctant to air Ian's song of interracial love. But New York Philharmonic conductor Leonard Bernstein featured the young singer on his television special, and she became an instant celebrity—with "Society's Child" rising to Number 14 on the charts. Her debut album, *Janis Ian,* was a success; acclaimed as a female Bob Dylan, the performer embarked on a national concert tour. Yet her auspicious start proved impossible to sustain, disillusionment set in, and the entertainer's career began to flag. Turning to drugs and psychotherapy, Ian eventually settled in Los Angeles, where she could scarcely obtain a booking. "People were throwing bottles at me," she recounted to Armstrong. "It was all the dues I never paid when I was 15."

Ian announced her retirement—but could not stop

for years. Discussing "Under the Covers" in a review of the performer's 1981 album *Restless Eyes,* Reilly decided that "compared with the average pre-teen conversation these days, it's about as lewd as 'To a Skylark.'" "'Under the Covers' . . . is a typically fine piece of writing and performing by Ian," continued the critic. "Like all her work, it's distinguished by an earthy but romantic sensibility that expresses itself fearlessly regardless of social climate."

Compositions

Composer of numerous songs recorded by other artists, including Roberta Flack, Kenny Rogers, and Alabama; has collaborated with country songwriter Rhonda Kye Fleming. Has written songs for motion pictures, including *The Foxes* and *The Bell Jar.*

Selected discography

Singles

"Society's Child"/"Letter to Jon," 1967.
"Younger Generation Blues"/"I'll Give You a Stone If You'll Throw It," 1967.
"Insanity Comes Quietly to the Structured Kind"/"Sunflakes Pall, Snowrays Call," 1967.
"Song for All the Seasons of Your Mind"/"Lonely One," 1968.

LPs

Janis Ian, Verve/Forecast, 1967.
For All the Seasons of Your Mind, Verve, 1968.
The Secret Life of J. Eddy Fink, Verve, 1968.
Who Really Cares, Verve, 1969.
Present Company, Capitol, 1971.
Stars, Columbia, 1974.
Between the Lines, Columbia, 1975.
Aftertones, Columbia, 1975.
Miracle Row, Columbia, 1977.
Janis Ian, Columbia, 1978.
Night Rains, Columbia, 1979.
Best of Janis Ian, Columbia, 1980.
Restless Eyes, Columbia, 1981.

writing for long—she still had things to say. "I felt more mature, that I had more insight," she told Irwin Stambler in the *Encyclopedia of Pop, Rock, and Soul,* as she discussed her comeback efforts in the early 1970s. "The reasons I came back to the music field come down to this: I was writing songs I liked and I wanted to record them." While her next few albums brought disappointing results, Ian enjoyed moderate success with the 1974 LP *Stars.* Notable was the title song, Ian's cynical view of celebrity, as well as her version of "Jesse," a hit for vocalist Roberta Flack a year earlier (which helped rekindle Ian's reputation as a songwriter). Her comeback endeavors reached full flower a year later with the platinum album *Between the Lines,* containing the Grammy-winning single "At Seventeen." Critics found this new Ian less angry and grim, more thoughtful and assured.

Ian continued to write, record, and perform through the seventies and eighties, but never again approached the success of *Between the Lines.* Still, she remained uninhibited, addressing subjects that interested her. "Under the Covers," a 1981 song reflecting on the virtues of Latin men as lovers, was refused air play because its lyrics were deemed too risque; "Uncle Wonderful," which Ian performed in concert, was avoided by record companies in much the same way as "Society's Child" two decades before.

More than one critic has puzzled over the music industry's apparent wariness when it comes to Ian—ironic, given the provocative topics rock groups have dealt in

Sources

Books

Stambler, Irwin, *The Encyclopedia of Pop, Rock, and Soul,*
    revised edition, St. Martin's, 1989.

Periodicals

People, September 22, 1986.
Stereo Review, February 1980; October 1981.

—*Nancy Pear*

Jefferson Airplane/ Jefferson Starship/ Starship

Rock group

The Charlatans may have been the first band to emerge from the San Francisco drug culture in the mid-1960s, but it was the Jefferson Airplane, who formed almost immediately after, that came to be the voice of the hippie generation. Singer Marty Balin organized the Airplane in 1965 and their first exposure was at his nightclub, the Matrix. They signed a healthy contract with RCA that set off a tidal wave of music industry executives flocking to the Haight-Ashbury district of San Francisco to sign anyone that looked like they could play an instrument. The band sent out a musical call-to-arms with their debut LP, *Jefferson Airplane Takes Off!*, a folk-rock collection that marked the beginning of a recording history that has lasted well over twenty years and numerous personnel changes.

The first major move came with their second LP, *Surrealistic Pillow,* as one of the original vocalists, Signe Anderson (Balin shared microphone duties also), was replaced by Grace Slick. The soprano came from the band the Great Society and brought along with her two songs that threw her into the spotlight while

Jefferson Airplane formed in San Francisco, Calif., in 1965 by **Marty Balin** (vocalist; born January 30, 1943, in Cincinnati, Ohio) and **Paul Kantner** (guitar; born March 19, 1941, in San Francisco, Calif.); other original members included **Signe Anderson** (vocals), **Jorma Kaukonen** (lead guitar; born December 23, 1940, in Washington, D.C.), **Jack Casady** (bass; born April 13, 1944, in Washington, D.C.), and (Alexander) **Skip Spence** (drums). Spence left band in 1966 and was replaced by **Spencer Dryden** (drums; born April 7, 1943, in New York, N.Y.); Anderson left the band in 1967 and was replaced by **Grace Slick** (vocals; born October 30, 1943, in Chicago, Ill.; married to band member Kantner c. 1970-1978); Balin and Dryden left band in 1971.

Slick, Kantner, Balin, and **David Freiberg** (keyboards, bass; born August 24, 1938, in Boston, Mass.), **Pete Sears** (keyboards, bass; born May 27, 1948, in England), **Papa John Creach** (violin; born May, 1917) **Craig Chaquico** (lead guitar; born September 26, 1954, in Sacramento, Calif.), and **John Barbata** (drums) formed **Jefferson Starship** in 1974; Balin and Slick left band in 1978, were replaced by **Mickey Thomas** (lead vocals; born in Cairo, Ga.); band also added **Aynsley Dunbar** (drums); Slick rejoined band in 1981.

Starship was formed in 1984 when Freiberg, Kantner, and Sears left band and were replaced by **Donny Baldwin**. In 1989 Kantner, Balin, Slick, Casady, and Kaukonen renited for a reunion album.

Awards: *Rolling Stone* Music Award for album of the year, 1975, for *Red Octopus*, 1975.

unintentionally pushing Balin to the side, "White Rabbit" and "Somebody to Love."

Guitarist/songwriter Paul Kantner began to steer the group towards outer space with his science-fiction visions on their next two LPs. As *The Rolling Stone Record Guide* described *After Bathing At Baxters,* "the density of the album's production was truly staggering, but it was an attempt doomed to ultimate, even if heroic, failure. You can't record an LSD trip, so the album ends up sounding like a bizarre indulgence." While Kantner's weaving guitar lines have always been the glue that holds the group together, his futuristic lyrics, as on 1968's *Crown of Creation,* have also played a major role in defining the Airplane's direction.

The other side of the coin became their political rantings, as on *Volunteers,* which followed the live *Bless It's*

Pointed Little Head LP. "We Can Be Together," "Wooden Ships," and the title track, "Volunteers," were all anthems for a generation that was struggling to deal with the social changes that the Vietnam War era brought about. Their righteous stance also had another side, according to Charles Perry in *The Rolling Stone Illustrated History of Rock & Roll,* "Jefferson Airplane loved you, but they gave themselves plenty of room for psychic self-defense."

The Airplane's acid-rock light show extravaganza began to wear thin on bassist Jack Casady and lead guitarist Jorma Kaukonen by 1970 as the two started their own part-time, back-to-the-blues roots band, Hot Tuna, which began recording on Kantner's newly formed Grunt label. Balin was also beginning to feel unappreciated and was feuding with Casady and Kaukonen as the future of the Airplane was up in the air. Kantner meanwhile produced *Blows Against The Empire* under the moniker Paul Kantner and The Jefferson Starship, described by the *Illustrated Encyclopedia of Rock* as a "'space opera' of soap-opera standards, a mish-mash of hippie mysticism and platitudes which, whatever its intentions, represented a retreat from the outfront approach of *Volunteers."*

For the next few years the Jefferson Airplane continued to release albums while various members worked on other projects. The Airplane recruited ex-Turtles and Crosby, Stills, Nash & Young member John Barbata on drums and violinist Papa John Creach for 1971's *Bark.* By that time Balin had decided he could do better on his own and left the group. After *Long John Silver* in 1972 and the disappointing live effort *Thirty Seconds Over Winterland* a year later, the original Jefferson Airplane was officially gone.

Slick and Kantner had collaborated on *Sunfighter* in 1971 and *Baron Von Tollbooth and the Chrome Nun* in 1973, which also included David Freiberg, former bassist/keyboardist with Quicksilver Messenger Service. In 1974 Slick also released a solo effort titled *Manhole* as Kantner reorganized a new unit that featured a blistering young guitarist who had played on the latter three albums, Craig Chaquico. The Jefferson Starship released its official debut, *Dragon Fly,* in 1974 with the hit song "Caroline," written and sung by Balin, an unofficial member at the time. Behind the steady dual bass/keyboard work of Freiberg and studio ace Pete Sears, and the fine fretwork of Chaquico on cuts like "Ride the Tiger," the Jefferson Starship began to soar up the charts.

In 1974 they followed with *Red Octopus,* one of only four LPs in history to reach the Number 1 spot on *Billboard's* charts four separate times. Anyone who thought that the band was just a rehash of the Airplane was in for a big surprise. "Nostalgia, that's how they first started to sell us," Balin stated in *Rolling Stone.* "But we were a little better than just nostalgia. We were musical and something new, with lots of energy." Balin contributed a ballad with "Miracles" but still had not committed to the group and refused to sign any contracts. The Jefferson Starship stuck with the softer material on their next two LPs. Balin's "With Your Love" appeared on *Spitfire,* which Stephen Holden described in *Rolling Stone:* "While the music no longer has the explosive urgency of youth, it combines a rare stylistic breadth with awesomely controlled power."

Although the next album, *Earth,* went platinum, its use of strings and the willowy "Count on Me" caused Freiberg to refer to it as "the wimpy end of the stick," in *Guitar Player.* "I think it's a real good album for the times we're in," Kantner told *Rolling Stone.* "We're just passing out of the Seventies, which is like a big sleep after the Sixties. It's a light time, and the album feels real good to me on a light level—not the same way, but the good aspects, if you will, of disco. Just the feel ... the bubbling level. I don't think every album has to be serious and heavy."

Earth also signalled the departure of Balin from the group. "This formula that everybody thinks is so successful is death to me. I think it's death to the band. That's why it doesn't interest me," Balin told *Rolling Stone.* "The Starship is too limiting for me. There are eight million stories in this city. The Starship's only one of them."

Another story was Grace Slick's alcohol problem. After a riot in Germany's Lorelei Festival on June 17, 1978, destroyed most of the band's equipment and their spirit, she left the group, parting with Kantner, her husband of eight years, and hooking up with Starship roadie Skip Johnson. "No one would come out and say 'You're acting like a jerk.' So I had to fire myself," she told *College Papers.*

The band hired former Journey drummer Aynsley Dunbar and replaced both Slick and Balin with an unlikely choice, Mickey Thomas: a soulful singer from Elvin Bishop's band whom Kantner told *College Papers,* "could stand against the past." Chaquico took control of the band and turned up the heavy metal crunch for *Freedom At Point Zero.* "Without Grace Slick or Marty Balin, the Jefferson Starship is a hulk of a band, desperately in need of worthwhile material and marching inexorably toward oblivion," wrote Al Sperone in *Rolling Stone.*

Half the problem was solved in 1981 when Slick rejoined the band for *Modern Times* but it was just the end of another phase as Kantner split in 1984 and Freiberg

and Sears followed suit thereafter. Chaquico, Slick, and Thomas brought in Donny Baldwin (also formerly of the Elvin Bishop band) and sought the help of outside writers. The commercial appeal of *Knee Deep In The Hoopla* and *No Protection* brought a considerable amount of bad press from critics, but the group, now just named Starship, had three Number 1 hits in just eighteen months. "We Built This City," "Sara," and "Nothing's Gonna Stop Us Now" were guitar-driven vehicles that had the Starship ruling the charts once again.

In 1989 Kantner, Balin, Slick, Casady, and Kaukonen set aside their differences for a reunion LP, *Jefferson Airplane,* on Epic Records. "We visited Grace," Casady told *down beat.* "I said, 'If there's a possibility of us playing together again, you're going to be on stage playing piano like you used to. Paul's going to play his guitar; there'll be no surrounding instruments to cover up anything or to make it grander. . . . [We're] going to put our butts on the line.' That's what the original Airplane stood for."

Selected discography

Jefferson Airplane

Jefferson Airplane Takes Off, RCA, 1966.
Surrealistic Pillow, RCA, 1967.
After Bathing at Baxters, RCA, 1967.
Crown of Creation, RCA, 1968.
Bless It's Pointed Little Head, RCA, 1969.
Volunteers, RCA, 1969.
Worst of Jefferson Airplane, RCA, 1970.
Bark, Grunt, 1971.
Long John Silver, Grunt, 1972.
Thirty Seconds Over Winterland, Grunt, 1973.
Early Flight, Grunt/RCA, 1974.
Jefferson Airplane's Flight Log, 1966-1976, Grunt, 1977.
2400 Fulton Street—An Anthology, RCA, 1987.
Jefferson Airplane, Epic, 1989.

Jefferson Starship

Dragon Fly, Grunt, 1974.
Red Octopus, Grunt, 1975.
Spitfire, Grunt, 1976.
Earth, Grunt, 1978.
Gold, Grunt, 1979
Freedom at Point Zero, Grunt, 1979.
Modern Times, Grunt, 1981.

Starship

Knee Deep in the Hoopla, Grunt, 1985.
No Protection, Grunt, 1987.
Love Among the Cannibals, RCA, 1989.

Other

(Paul Kantner and the Jefferson Starship) *Blows Against the Empire,* RCA, 1970.
(Grace Slick and Paul Kantner) *Sunfighter,* Grunt, 1971.
(Kantner, Slick, and Freiberg) *Baron Von Tollbooth and the Chrome Nun,* Grunt, 1973.

Sources

Books

Christgau, Robert, *Christgau's Record Guide,* Ticknor & Fields, 1981.
Dalton, David, and Lenny Kaye, *Rock 100,* Grosset & Dunlap, 1977.

The Illustrated Encyclopedia of Rock, compiled by Nick Logan and Bob Woffinden, Harmony, 1977.
The Rolling Stone Illustrated History of Rock and Roll, edited by Jim Miller, Random House/Rolling Stone Press, 1976.
The Rolling Stone Interviews, 1967-1980, by the editors of *Rolling Stone,* Martin's Press/Rolling Stone Press, 1981.
The Rolling Stone Record Guide, edited by Dave Marsh with John Swenson, Random House/Rolling Stone Press, 1979.

Periodicals

down beat, June 1989.
Guitar Player, March 1976; June 1976; June 1977; October 1980; January 1982; June 1987; November 1989.
Guitar World, December 1987.
Rolling Stone, January 1, 1976; February 12, 1976; August 26, 1976; September 9, 1976; May 4, 1978; May 18, 1978; October 19, 1978; February 7, 1980; April 17, 1980; September 24, 1987.
Rolling Stone's College Papers, May-June 1980.

—*Calen D. Stone*

Spike Jones

Bandleader, drummer, music parodist

Spike Jones was "a man whose name was synonymous with laughter in America for more than a decade," Dr. Demento wrote in the forward to Jordan J. Young's profile, *Spike Jones and His City Slickers*. In the 1940s Jones and his City Slickers band became known across America as an outlandish group of musicians whose musical parody recordings, stage shows, and radio broadcasts frequently featured such "instruments" as the washboard, the cowbell, the auto horn, and the toilet seat, accompanied by the rhythmic punctuation of hiccups, Bronx cheers, and the sounds of various live animals. Jones and The City Slickers rose to prominence with the popularity of their hit "Der Fuehrer's Face," a World War II-era radio favorite that featured a blatant "raspberry" musical tribute to German dictator Adolf Hitler. George T. Simon commented in *Best of the Music Makers* on the special combination that brought Jones to fame in the early 1940s: "He created a blend of ricky-ticky Dixie and the soothing sounds of talent night in a lunatic asylum, and it added up to just the kind of spunky irreverence the nation needed in 1942."

Jones was born in Long Beach, California, and received the nickname "Spike" from his father's employment with the Southern Pacific Railroad. Jones played the drums in high school, during which he formed his first band. That group, The Five Tacks, eventually found itself on radio programs. Jones attended college for a time after high school, but left in 1931 to pursue jobs in music. Throughout the 1930s he played a variety of gigs in clubs around Southern California, eventually becoming a regular on Hollywood singer Bing Crosby's radio show. In the late 1930s Jones was active as a studio musician; he performed on recordings for Crosby and then-popular vocalists Judy Garland, Lena Horne, and Hoagy Carmichael. Not satisfied with the back-seat role of studio musician, however, Jones wanted more autonomy and exposure in his music career. One of his hobbies was collecting junk items that made interesting noises. In the late 1930s he joined a group of musicians similarly disenchanted with their music careers and began rehearsing novelty songs, experimenting with sounds and doing parodies of musical classics and standards of the day. The band eventually emerged in the early 1940s as The City Slickers, with Jones as the leader.

The City Slickers gained wide recognition in 1942 with their rendition of "Der Fuehrer's Face," a musical spoof that became a favorite of radio disc jockeys and soon after, a national hit. On the crest of the song's success, Jones and The City Slickers launched a nine-week "Meet the People" national tour in 1943, for which they added musicians and vaudeville performers to their lineup. "In addition to five or six shows a day," Young noted, "the band played for bond rallies, toured factories and otherwise made a spectacle of themselves." In 1944 The City Slickers traveled to Europe to entertain U.S. and Allied troops.

Among the band's favorite hit parody recordings at this time were "Cocktails for Two," which included a chorus of hiccupping, and "You Always Hurt the One You Love," which listed a series of "hurts" that included shootings, hangings, and poisonings. Jones was renowned as "The King of Corn" and in 1946 launched a two-hour stage extravaganza called "The Musical Depreciation Revue," which included jugglers, roller skaters, and other vaudeville acts. Throughout the 1940s Jones and The City Slickers were active making hit records, appearing on radio and in movies, and touring with their live act.

Young depicted the "sheer lunacy" of Jones's "Musical Depreciation Revue": "At the hub of the chaotic goings-on was Spike himself, manipulating an ensemble of homemade instruments he affectionately called 'the heap.' The contraption—which looked like nothing so much as the loot from a hardware store robbery—consisted of sleighbells, beer bottles, soup cans, a

Born Lindley Armstrong Jones, December 14, 1911, in Long Beach, Calif.; died of emphysema, May 1, 1965, in Trousdale Estates, Calif.; son of Lindley Murray (a railroad company depot agent) and Ada (a schoolteacher; maiden name, Armstrong) Jones; married Patricia Ann Middleton, September 7, 1935 (divorced, 1947); married Helen Greco (a singer; professional name, Helen Grayco), July 18, 1948; children: (first marriage) Linda Lee; (second marriage) Spike, Jr., Leslie Ann, Gina Marie. *Education:* Attended Chaffey College, Ontario, Calif.

Played drums in various club bands throughout the 1930s; studio drummer in late 1930s; formed comedy band The Feather Merchants in late 1930s, which evolved into The City Slickers; led The City Slickers, early 1940s-1965; City Slickers band members during the 1940s included Don Anderson (trumpet), Carl Grayson (violin), Frank Leithner (piano), Del Porter (clarinet), Luther Roundtree (banjo), John Stanley (trombone), and Country Washburne (tuba). Made numerous radio appearances in the 1940s and 1950s; had radio program *The Spike Jones Show,* CBS-Radio, 1949. Had four television series, all under the name *The Spike Jones Show,* airing on NBC-TV, 1954, and CBS-TV, 1957, 1960, and 1961; served as host of NBC-TV program *Club Oasis,* 1958; made numerous guest appearances on television in the 1950s and 1960s. Appeared in the film *Thank Your Lucky Stars,* 1942; music featured in other films in the 1940s.

telephone, a Greyhound bus horn, a locomotive whistle, a gong and other necessary props. . . . Jones, who sometimes accompanied his harpist on the *latrinophone*— a toilet seat strung with wire—got some of his best laughs by choosing the unlikeliest of batons. He conducted the band with a .38 caliber pistol, a mop, an umbrella, a nightstick, and frequently a toilet plunger."

Although the 1940s were the heyday of Jones and The City Slickers, they continued to work through the 1950s, and even into the 1960s. In 1954 *The Spike Jones Show* aired on NBC television on Saturday nights with several new band members. The show, which enjoyed moderate success, featured Jones's second wife, Helen Grayco, who had been a singer with the band since the late 1940s. In 1957 a reconfiguration of *The Spike Jones Show* aired on CBS television along with a new name for the Slickers: The Band That Plays for Fun.

Jones's recordings continue to maintain a dedicated following and several have become collector's items.

Simon commented on the lasting impression of Jones's talent: "His true genius had been revealed in his ability to make his countrymen smile when there wasn't much to smile at."

Selected discography

78s and 45s

Behind Those Swinging Doors, Bluebird, 1941.
Clink, Clink, Another Drink, Bluebird, 1942.
Der Fuehrer's Face, Bluebird, 1942.
Cocktails for Two, RCA Victor, 1945.
The Nutcracker Suite, RCA Victor, 1945.
You Always Hurt the One You Love, RCA Victor, 1945.
William Tell Overture, RCA Victor, 1948.
All I Want for Christmas Is My Two Front Teeth, RCA Victor, 1948.
I Saw Mommy Kissing Santa Claus, RCA Victor, 1952.

LPs

Spike Jones Plays the Charleston, RCA Victor, 1952.
Bottoms Up, RCA Victor, 1952.
Spike Jones Murders Carmen and Kids the Classics, RCA Victor, 1953.
Spike Jones Presents a Christmas Spectacular, Verve, 1956.
Dinner Music for People Who Aren't Very Hungry, Verve, 1956.
Mr. Banjo, Verve, 1956.
Hi-Fi Polka Party, Verve, 1957.
Spike Jones in Stereo, Warner Brothers, 1959.
Omnibust, Liberty, 1959.
The Submarine Officer, Kapp, 1960.
60 Years of Music America Hates Best, Liberty, 1960.
Washington Square, Liberty, 1963.
Spike Jones' New Band, Liberty, 1964.
My Man, Liberty, 1964.
The New Band of Spike Jones Plays Hank Williams Hits, Liberty, 1965.

Sources

Books

Simon, George T., *Best of the Music Makers,* Doubleday, 1979.
Young, Jordan R., *Spike Jones and His City Slickers,* foreword by Dr. Demento, discography by Ted Hering and Skip Craig, Disharmony Books, 1982.

Obituaries

Newsweek, May 10, 1965.
New York Times, May 2, 1965.
Time, May 7, 1965.

—*Michael E. Mueller*

Kentucky Headhunters

Country band

Nashville has hardly been the same since the Kentucky Headhunters took it by storm in 1990. A country act—in the loosest sense of the term—the Headhunters' hard-driving music ranges far afield into boogie, old-style rock 'n roll, and white-boy electric guitar blues. The result is as rowdy and woolly as the singers themselves—a guitar-charged stomping sound variously described as "psycha-billy" and "hillbilly speed metal."

Years ago the country music industry would have turned a deaf ear to the Headhunters, or at the very least trimmed their flowing hippy hairdos and outfitted them with cowboy hats. The pool of country is widening, however; many of the newest listeners were weaned on rock 'n' roll. Headhunter lead singer Ricky Phelps told *Rolling Stone:* "After [Southern rockers] Lynyrd Skynyrd met their fate [in a plane crash], their fans didn't have anything to listen to. They still had a hankering to hear something that's got a little kick in the ass to it. We filled that gap."

Three of the five Kentucky Headhunters were actually

born and raised in Kentucky—Greg Martin and brothers Fred and Richard Young. Martin met the Youngs in the late 1960s when he joined a blues and boogie band called the Itchy Brothers. Basically a standard 1970s bar band, the Itchy Brothers managed to work their way to New York where they were almost signed by the Swan Song label. When that deal fell through, however, the group disbanded. Martin found work backing singer Ronnie McDowell; Fred Young showed up in the movie *Sweet Dreams* as a drummer in a country band.

While with McDowell's group Martin met bass guitarist Doug Phelps, a native of Arkansas. Tired of the rigors of touring, Martin and Phelps decided to form their own band. They returned to Metcalfe County, Kentucky—Martin's home—and enlisted the services of the Young brothers. The group was rounded out when Phelps's brother Ricky joined. By late 1985 the Kentucky Headhunters were performing their hybrid country metal music in clubs throughout Kentucky and Tennessee. They managed to talk a local radio station into producing the live monthly *Chitlin' Show* that eventually brought them a wide base of support.

Remembering those early days, Richard Young told the *Akron Beacon Journal:* "We had people coming into the radio studio out of tobacco patches to see what was going on. They'd come in in their tobacco work clothes and say, 'What're you all doin' over here?'" The ques-

tion was not an easy one to answer. Martin and the Youngs had cut their teeth on rock and boogie, and the Phelps brothers were versed in bluegrass and country. What the men did as Headhunters was to fuse all their influences into a sound that would reach the legions of Dixie longhairs. The Kentucky Headhunters became a quintessential blue-collar bar band that seemed to play music just for the fun of it.

Eventually the Headhunters came to the attention of Harold Shedd, a Nashville producer who had worked with country acts Alabama and K. T. Oslin. Shedd signed the band to the Polygram label, and then—in a move almost unheard of for a fledgling group—he gave the Headhunters complete artistic license over their work. "Harold could tell we had a sound of our own," Martin told the *Lexington Herald-Leader.* "He knew the best way to get at that sound was to leave us alone. I think he stuck his head in the studio once for about five minutes to say hello. Once the whole thing was over, he listened to it and gave his approval. He's been very good to us."

The Headhunters released their debut album, *Pickin' on Nashville,* late in 1989. Within a few weeks they had placed a single on the country top forty charts, a wildfire version of the Bill Monroe song "Walk Softly on This Heart of Mine." To the astonishment of the Headhunters, the country music industry warmed to them immediately and opened every important avenue for their advancement.

Richard Young admitted that he was amazed at the support his group got from Nashville. "But the reason they were [supportive] is that they were just starved to death for good music with some soul in it of any kind because everything had been so one lane all the time." Young added: "Now all of a sudden this band comes along driving in five lanes. It was strange, but they liked it. I think we came at a time when the country music industry must have realized that they had to do something and change or they weren't gonna get a new market of people."

Pickin' on Nashville yielded two more hits, "Dumas Walker," and "Oh, Lonesome Me," both of which "cook up a foaming broth of guitar-based country rock, then serve it up steaming," to quote a reviewer in *Country America.* The raucous Headhunters were invited to tour with superstar Hank Williams, Jr., an opportunity that quickly brought their work to just the right audience. In a review of one of these joint concerts *Lexington Herald-Leader* correspondent Walter Tunis wrote: "There are no great revelations in the Headhunters' music. In fact, much of it seems rooted in very familiar late '60s and '70s boogie and blues, the same sort of material Williams toys with. But there [is] a humility and sense of fun throughout the band's performance that [proves] extremely refreshing.''

The *Country America* reviewer noted that in an age where music careers seem tailored with meticulous precision, ''the Headhunters provide a wonderfully untamed style of anything-goes back-porch picking.'' The group's members are elated with their sudden good fortune after so many years of struggle. Richard Young admitted that the Headhunters are one band who haven't gotten to the top on good looks—as he put it, ''We're ugly as spit, every one of us.'' What has worked for the Headhunters is energy, a spirit of good fun, and teamwork. ''There's a strong bond between all of us,'' Martin told the *Lexington Herald-Leader*. ''We're pretty much a family band. We argue and we fight like brothers would, but in the end, everyone sticks up for one another and makes each other play the best they can.''

The Kentucky Headhunters were named the best new vocal group of 1990 by the Academy of Country Music and were nominated for the same award by the Country Music Association. The future looks bright for the group as well. Richard Young told *Rolling Stone* that the Headhunters are ready to rip and roar. He said, ''We got 2000 songs we've written over the past twenty years.''

Selected discography

Pickin' on Nashville, Polygram, 1989.

Sources

Akron Beacon Journal, April 29, 1990.
Charlotte Observer, August 3, 1990.
Country America, May 1990.
Detroit Free Press, May 11, 1990.
Lexington Herald-Leader, October 29, 1989; March 18, 1990.
Post-Tribune (Gary, Indiana), May 11, 1990.
Rolling Stone, April 5, 1990.

—*Anne Janette Johnson*

Kid 'n Play

Rap duo

Rappers Kid 'n Play have been flirting with the mainstream since their first movie, *House Party,* filled theaters in 1990. Few performers are more instantly recognizable than Kid (born Christopher Reid), with his seven-inch vertical hairstyle and freckles, and Play (Christopher Martin), with his self-designed clothing and tidy mustache. The energetic Kid 'n Play have struck gold with their light, ironic, middle-class-oriented work, but their intentions are serious and their artistic goals substantial. *Rolling Stone* contributor David Wild called Kid 'n Play "two bright, young New Yorkers [who] want to be sure they're taken seriously"—even when they make comic records and films.

Like DJ Jazzy Jeff and the Fresh Prince and Salt-n-Pepa, Kid 'n Play have earned the approval of parents for their relatively clean act and comic capers. "It's clear Kid 'n Play are entertainers," wrote Jill Pearlman in *Vogue*. "Rather than shake a death rattle from the streets, they celebrate good times; they dance, mug, trade barbs and witticisms. They give the listener lots of big melodies, the ear candy that makes the charts. . . . All this, and they're still, entirely, totally hip. . . . Kid 'n Play are about acting out the craziness most kids are too cool (that is, too intimidated) to try, about being the odd man out and putting that individual style to work."

There is nothing particularly light or comic about the background of the two performers. Both were born in New York City and raised in its various boroughs. Both had unconventional families—Kid is the child of a black father and white mother; Play is the son of a former felon turned evangelical Christian minister. The latter's childhood included rough times at home and on the streets: He experimented with drugs, ran with a gang, and dropped out of school several times. Kid, on the other hand, was a model student who worked his way through college and was planning to go to law school while helping his father run a shelter for homeless men.

Kid and Play met while rapping for rival groups. Kid had worked with the Royal Masters, the Mighty Three, and the Turnout Brothers, and Play had sung and rapped with Solar Connection, Blue Velvet, Galaxy, and Quicksilver and the Superlovers. When they found that they lived in the same part of Queens, the young men became fast friends and tied their fortunes together. Play told *Vogue:* "When I met Kid, he had these thick prescription glasses, this Afro, freckles, one of those Texas ties, and he wore a jacket from Key Food grocery store, where he worked. I was amused by him; he was a refreshing change. I was hanging out with some real bad people, for peer appeal. But with Kid I could be myself, let my hair down."

While Kid attended Lehman College, Play buckled down and studied at Manhattan's School of Visual Arts. Both had chosen alternate careers, but both also hoped for success in rap. At first they used the name Fresh Force for their act, changing it to Kid Cool Out and MC Playboy. They finally shortened the name to Kid 'n Play, adding DJ the Wizard M.E. as their scratcher. On the strength of their raps—most of which are written by Kid—they signed with Select Records, a small specialty label. By 1989 they had released a string of hit singles, including "Gittin' Funky," "Rollin' with Kid 'n Play," and "2 Hype." Their first album, *2 Hype,* went gold.

Pearlman claimed that Kid 'n Play "ushered in a new school. It's rap that's evocative of teen life, full of playful, saucy, sly innocence—in a way, what Motown was to grittier soul." Innocent or not, the group found its niche among black listeners and cared little for the wealth to be reaped by appealing to pop audiences. Eventually, however, the sheer craziness of their act attracted the attention of Reginald Hudlin, a film producer. Hudlin cast the duo in *House Party,* the first movie to combine rap and comedy.

In *House Party* Kid sneaks out on his strict father in order to attend a wild bash at Play's home. He makes it to the party, romances a female guest—which leads to a hilarious "safe sex" scene—and eventually winds up cuts off the pop radio stations. Kid told *Rolling Stone:* "We didn't make a nice poppy, sappy record that pop stations jumped on before black stations, and we didn't make the kind of movie that white people liked before black people. They came to *us.*"

Nevertheless, it is likely that white, as well as black, audiences will continue to seek out Kid 'n Play, not because their work is less threatening, but because it is funny, daring, and ultimately optimistic. "All stories have to be told," Play said in *Vogue.* "We say you can be responsible without being corny and still wear the gold chains, still drive a car as good as your local drug dealer's, with a whole lot more security." Kid added: "We teach people not to be afraid to be themselves, even if you look different or act different. Run with it."

in jail, an object of interest to some large and nasty criminals. Critics loved the film and were quick to label Kid 'n Play the Abbott and Costello of rap. The performers, however, were dismayed by that characterization and were quick to respond. "We don't mind being comedians," Kid told *Rolling Stone,* "but we sure as hell aren't interested in being *clowns.* . . . We realize that pop success can be like the kiss of death to a rapper. Every time a rapper gains widespread pop appeal, black folks *hate* 'em. . . . Believe me, Play and I do *not* intend on messing things up."

That philosophy is reflected in the group's second album, *Kid 'n Play's Funhouse.* The work has a harder edge and some frank language, enough to keep its

Selected discography

2 Hype, Select, 1988.
Kid 'n Play's Funhouse, Select, 1990.

Also contributors to the film soundtrack *House Party,* 1990.

Sources

Philadelphia Inquirer, March 9, 1990.
Rolling Stone, May 17, 1990.
Vogue, July 1990.

—Anne Janette Johnson

Kiss

Rock band

Originally made up of four young men from New York City—Gene Simmons, Paul Stanley, Peter Criss and Ace Frehley—the group Kiss made a name for itself mainly by a dramatic stage show which featured band members in outrageous costumes and make-up. Boasting that they were the loudest rock and roll band in the world, Kiss would take to the stage dressed up as "fantasy characters" and give a high-energy, high-tech, highly theatrical show. With their appearance and raucous, crowd-pleasing concerts, the band soon became a popular success, especially with teenagers.

Their legions of fans joined the Kiss Army, worshiping the band that was never allowed to be photographed without their makeup. Comic books, movies and cartoons were released featuring the Kiss characters. The popularity of the band began to cool down in the early 1980s, around the time that it decided to perform without makeup. Ace Frehley and Peter Criss left the band, and some of the new replacements did not last long. Still, Kiss continued to give a wild stage show,

which attracted new fans, making them an enduring act in rock and roll history.

Paul Stanley and Gene Simmons were the founding force behind Kiss. They met in 1971, when Simmons transferred to Richmond College in Staten Island from an upstate, New York, school. The two formed a loosely organized group called Rainbow, playing music ranging from country to covers of the Beatles. In 1972 Rainbow broke up, but Simmons and Stanley stayed together. They made plans to form the kind of band that would launch them into stardom.

Using basic supply-and-demand philosophy, the two decided that what the rock world needed at the time was a group that could do a really wild, entertaining stage show. Bands that had been successful at that in the past—Alice Cooper, David Bowie, T Rex—had quit performing. Wanting to fill that gap, they decided to form a hard rock band with a theatrical theme. The two spent a lot of time in 1972 and 1973 researching their idea by seeing other groups. One, in particular, influenced them greatly, the New York Dolls. The Dolls were famed for dressing up in drag when they played.

Stanley and Simmons then went about trying to get a drummer and lead guitarist for the band. Peter Criss was found through an ad he had placed in *Rolling Stone*. Ace Frehley was recruited by an ad placed in the *Village Voice*. With all the elements in place, the group rehearsed in a Manhattan loft, named themselves Kiss and started experimenting with makeup and theatrics that would become the backbone of their stage show.

Deciding the drag look would not work for them, they hit upon the idea of getting made-up like fantasy characters. Their look, although not intentionally, was similar to Japanese Kabuki Theater. Simmons appeared as a monster with leather bat wings and scaly platform boots, characteristically wagging his 7-inch tongue in and out of his mouth for effect. Stanley was the lover, with pouty lips and a star over his right eye. Criss was a cat, and Frehley a spaceman with silver boots and a leather spacesuit. To add to the fantasy aspect, they decided none of the Kiss members would be photographed in public without their makeup.

Kiss began playing small clubs around New York, but all the members had their minds set on superstardom. They aggressively publicized the band, sending releases to many important record industry executives. Bill Aucoin, who was working as producer of a television music series, went to see the band play and was instantly impressed. Within a few weeks he had made a deal with Casablanca records to handle Kiss's records and publicity. Shortly after their signing with Casablanca, the group produced the album Kiss. Choreographer Sean Delaney was brought in to perfect the timing and effects of Kiss's already dramatic stage appearance. The band's first major show was on New Year's Eve, 1973, as an opening act. Kiss stole the show that evening, winning over the crowd with its performance.

In the years 1973 and 1974, Kiss worked hard on tour, playing in such out of the way places as Edmonton, Canada. Despite the group's popular appeal, critics generally lambasted their music. Steve Pond wrote in the *Detroit News* that "the music made by Kiss is overbearing, repetitive, simple-minded and derivative." His comments were indicative of many rock record reviews. Kiss's philosophy, however, was to give the fan a quality show no matter where it performed. And it was hard to dispute the fact that fans were thronging to their stage shows, entranced by the band's energy.

By 1975 Kiss was headlining in larger auditoriums around the country. They also released two popular albums, *Hotter Than Hell* and *Dressed to Kill*. The single "Rock & Roll All Nite" from the latter album became almost an anthem for the teenage crowd. In 1975, cash flow became a problem when Kiss's record company, Casablanca, split from Warner Brothers. Because Casablanca was having problems meeting royalty payments, Aucoin had to finance an entire Kiss tour on his American Express card. This situation turned around quickly in 1975 when the double album *Alive* was released. Recorded in small and medium-sized towns around the U.S., this album truly captured the energy and drive the group put into their live shows and was an instant success, ending the group's financial problems.

However other problems were to arise. There was backlash from concerned parents and the press that Kiss's stage show gave children dangerous ideas. For example, Simmons would breathe fire during one of the songs. Several teenagers tried this at home, and a few were seriously burned. There were accusations that the band was made up of devil worshippers and Kiss was actually an acronym for Knights in Satan's Service.

Despite this negative publicity, the years 1975-79 found Kiss's popularity with its fans at its peak. The band made a point of playing in small towns as well as larger markets, to build a grass roots following of loyal fans. The band was even invited to perform in Cadillac, Michigan, because the local high school football team had made Kiss their team mascot and broken their losing record. In a publicity coup, Kiss wowed the town

> The reason Kiss has been able to endure is precisely because they stuck to their original philosophy of giving fans what they wanted— high-energy, rock-solid shows in whatever arena they played.

and gained much press coverage by playing at Cadillac High School's prom. With stunts like this, it was not surprising that the band's fan club, named the Kiss Army, numbered over 100,000 members.

As further testimony to the band's popularity during the late 1970s, the Kiss characters also starred in comic books, and the band appeared in an NBC "Movie of the Week," *Kiss Meets the Phantom.* Kiss Halloween costumes were sold and a Christmas TV special aired. During this time the band also released the albums *Destroyer* (1976), *Kiss—the Originals* and *Rock and Roll Over* (1976), *Love Gun* and *Alive II* (1977), *Double Platinum* (1978), and *Dynasty* (1979). Although critics still generally disapproved of the group, Simmons commented in the *Detroit News*: "It's OK if *Rolling Stone* votes us 'Hype of the Year.' We still fill 20,000-seat halls every night. We'll take it."

In 1981, Peter Criss left the band, followed soon by Ace Frehley. Despite the turnover in these original group members, Stanley and Simmons kept a guiding hand on the strategy of the band. They recruited new players, kept releasing recordings and continued to give audiences outrageous stage shows. *Creatures of the Night* (1982), *Lick It Up* (1983) and *Animalize* (1984) hit the *Billboard* lists. *Asylum* (1985) and *Crazy Nights* (1987) also became hits. In 1983, the group decided to perform without their makeup, ending years of mystery about their real appearance. Simmons commented in the *Detroit News* that "When you've done everything you can with a form, it's time to change. I think it may have helped in keeping us a little more level-headed, that after 20 albums and 65 million records sold, we could stand in line and get a hamburger without being recognized."

Kiss's longevity is an amazing testimony to its popularity with fans. Even though the band has been around since the early 1970s, their music and live performances still win favor with legions of fans, continuing to attract new audiences in the U.S. and abroad. The reason Kiss has been able to endure is precisely because they stuck to their original philosophy of giving fans what they wanted—high-energy, rock-solid shows in whatever arena they played. They continue to revamp and change their stage show with each tour. Simmons commented in the *Detroit News:* "We don't like to rest on our laurels. . . . Rock 'n' roll by its very definition means excess. We do it this way because in truth, it's more fun. Why tour with the same show every year?"

Selected discography

Singles; on Casablanca

"Kissin' Time," 1974.
"Rock & Roll All Nite," 1975.
"Shout It Out Loud," 1976.
"Flaming Youth," 1976.
"Beth/Detroit Rock City," 1976.
"Hard Luck Woman," 1976.
"Calling Dr. Love," 1977.
"Christine Sixteen," 1977.
"Love Gun," 1977.
"Shout It Out Loud," 1978.
"Rocket Ride," 1978.
"I Was Made for Lovin' You," 1979.
"Sure Know Something," 1979.
"Kiss-Shandi," 1980.
"A World Without Heroes," 1981.

LPs; on Casablanca

Kiss, 1974.
Hotter Than Hell, 1974.
Dressed to Kill, 1975.
Alive, 1975.
Destroyer, 1976.
Kiss—The Originals, 1976.
Rock and Roll Over, 1976.
Love Gun, 1977.
Alive II, 1977.
Dynasty, 1979.
Kiss Unmasked, 1980.
Music from the Elder, 1981.
Creatures of the Night, 1982.

On Mercury

Lick It Up, 1983.
Animalize, 1984.
Asylum, 1985.

Crazy Nights, 1987.

Sources

Books

Swenson, John, *Headliners: Kiss,* Tempo Books, 1978.

Periodicals

Detroit News, December 13, 1985; April 16, 1976; January 23, 1977.
New York Times Magazine, June 19, 1977.
Rolling Stone, March 25, 1976.

—Nancy Rampson

Lenny Kravitz

Singer, songwriter

When Lenny Kravitz, an unknown, unsigned, and unrecorded musician began showing up in gossip columns in 1987 as the new husband of actress and *Cosby Show* beauty Lisa Bonet, celebrity watchers understandably scoffed with skepticism at his professional credibility. Here, they thought, was just another freeloader trying to advance his career by marrying somebody famous. As *People*'s Steve Dougherty wrote of Kravitz, "Better known for his mate than his music— detractors called him Mr. Bonet—he seemed just the sort of dreadlocked ring-through-the-nose hipster who would take a merciless needling from playful [*Cosby Show* character] Cliff Huxtable."

But that kind of sneering suddenly quieted in 1989 with the release of Kravitz's first album, *Let Love Rule,* a hard-rocking blend of soul and psychedelia that left critics and music fans comparing Kravitz to superstars like John Lennon and Prince. Ironically, at the same time, Bonet's career seemed on the wane—a nude photo in *Rolling Stone* and an X-rated love scene with actor Mickey Rourke in the film *Angel Heart* somewhat sullied her reputation—which forced her back to the relative safety of *The Cosby Show*. Suddenly, the dynamics of one of Hollywood's most glamorous young couples had done an about-face, leaving Kravitz as the partner most likely to succeed in the long term.

Although Kravitz's musical style is eclectic and ever-shifting, *Rolling Stone* reviewer Anthony DeCurtis aptly described it as symptomatic of an untested generation "trying to capture the sound of young America sifting through the fragments of postmodern culture and creating childlike musical collages of no particular point . . . as if the world were a kind of shopping mall in which this kind of music can be blended with that regardless of the inherent integrity of any particular genre. The consolation for living in a time when social problems are pushing our nation to the point of collapse . . . is the freedom to play aimlessly among the ruins." Kravitz's approach, DeCurtis continued, is one that "courts artistic disaster by continually evoking his betters. But what saves him, oddly enough, in this brave, new postmodern world, is a tried-and-true rock & roll virtue: This boy can ignite a groove."

If Kravitz relies more heavily on any one style of music above others, it is probably the psychedelic sounds of the late 1960s and early 1970s. If he is merely posing as a kind of throwback flower child of that era, however, he has certainly fooled critics like *Spin*'s Christian Wright, who speculated, "Maybe Lenny Kravitz is a new hippie with an old soul or maybe his neo-Bohemia is the supreme pretense. Either way he's convincing. He even uses crystals to cure his headache." The message that comes across in Kravitz's music, on songs

For the Record. . .

Born c. 1964 in New York, N.Y.; son of Sy Kravitz (television news producer) and Roxie Roker (actress); married Lisa Bonet (actress), 1987; children: Zoe.

Solo recording artist, 1989—.

Addresses: *Home*—New York, NY. *Record company*—Virgin Records, 75 Rockefeller Plaza, New York, NY 10019.

like "Flower Child," "My Precious Love," and "Let Love Rule" is so idealistic and upbeat that it almost sounds naive in an age run over by cynicism. "It *is* idealistic," Kravitz told *Spin,* "but you've got to try. I mean, why do the good things that you do? I believe in peace. I believe in getting along, all of us being as one, and looking at this place as a planet instead of separate little places. When you're up in a spaceship and look at the world, it's one place. . . . I'm into the world coming together, if that ever happens. Maybe it'll take a great tragedy first."

The only child of NBC television news producer Sy Kravitz and actress Roxie Roker, who played Helen Willis on the TV sitcom *The Jeffersons,* Kravitz lived an idyllic city life while growing up in Manhattan's rich cultural atmosphere. In 1974 Kravitz moved to Los Angeles with his parents. He got his first musical experience there as a member of the California Boys' Choir. He also studied musical instruments diligently during these years, teaching himself to play guitar, bass, keyboards, and drums. As a student at the exclusive Beverly Hills High School, Kravitz went through the identity crises typical of adolescence, assuming the role of rich preppie before shucking it in favor of first punk, then hippie, and finally settling briefly on a completely new persona—that of the free-wheeling, hard-partying Romeo Blue. The period "was a phony time for me," Kravitz told *Spin.* "So I know what posing feels like. That was when I was really into my [pop singer] David Bowie phase. I wanted to be David Bowie more than anything in the world."

But there was also a different, more idealistic side of Kravitz evolving at this time. When he was just 17, he told *Spin,* he helped a young prostitute escape her pimp and her dreary street life by actually hiding her in his house, under his bed, where he fed her, and kept the whole thing secret from his parents. "She was so pretty and so sweet and we were talking and she started crying. She told me the whole thing. I was that kind of guy. . . . My parents always said, 'You're always doing things for everybody except yourself.'"

Kravitz's involvement with Bonet began with a chance meeting backstage at a 1985 concert of the pop-soul group New Edition. Though both were seeing other people, they immediately became fast friends; the relationship slowly evolved into something more. Finally Kravitz's car broke down and he moved in with Bonet so that he could borrow hers. "If my car had been working during that time, I probably wouldn't be married to her," Kravitz told *Spin.* "It started to be this thing—every day, wake up, take her to work, pick her up. We'd have dinner and then I guess it was one day we realized like we couldn't be apart or something." They made a quick trip to Las Vegas to get married and before long their first child, Zoe, was born.

The couple then moved to Manhattan where Kravitz worked on his first album and Bonet continued taping *The Cosby Show. Let Love Rule* was recorded at Henry Hirsch's Hoboken, New Jersey, studio. Hirsch described the rather unique recording session for *People:* "Lisa was there almost every day, sometimes with the baby," while Kravitz "took the subway out every morning. It was very un-rock and roll." Even more singular was that Kravitz recorded all the instrumental *and* vocal tracks on *Let Love Rule* by himself—*a la* Prince—though for his first tour he recruited a band, the members of which lived at his home while they rehearsed. "It's like a commune. It's cool," Kravitz told *Spin,* adding that he tries to be as democratic as possible in leading other musicians. "Obviously there has to be a leader, a band leader, but I don't like that sort of—a lot of musicians get that tyranny attitude, you know, but it's really equal. When it comes to rehearsing music, obviously they're playing my music so it's got to be, but as far as living at home we're all equal." And judging by Kravitz's remarks to *People*'s Dougherty, he seems levelheaded enough to make it in music for the long haul. "I'm not in it for the stardom," he said. "I just want to continue to write great songs, make great records. This is only the beginning."

Selected discography

Let Love Rule, Virgin, 1989.

Sources

People, November 6, 1989.
Rolling Stone, September 7, 1989.
Spin, July 1990.

—David Collins

The Kronos Quartet

String quartet

Since its debut in 1973, the Kronos Quartet has carved out its own niche in the world of string quartets. In its self-proclaimed role as a champion of new music, the quartet exclusively plays works of twentieth-century composers, commissioning pieces by composers throughout the world. Initially music critics were skeptical of the group's musical ability. Yet the Kronos Quartet has over the years proven itself. It has played to full houses worldwide, attracting nontraditional audiences with a repertoire that ranges from the works of early twentieth-century Hungarian composer Bela Bartok to rock and roll guitarist Jimi Hendrix and jazz artist Ornette Coleman.

The quartet was founded in Seattle by David Harrington, who had then decided to discontinue his musical studies at the University of Washington. The name Kronos refers to a god in Greek mythology who devoured his own children and makes allusion to time, a necessary component of music, as *chronos* is the Greek root of the word chronology. While the group's personnel has varied over the years, in 1978 the ensemble settled on

its present membership: David Harrington and John Sherba, violins; Hank Dutt, viola; and Joan Dutcher Jeanrenaud, cello.

In 1977 the Kronos Quartet moved to New York, where it served two years as the quartet-in-residence at the State University of New York at Geneseo. The quartet later moved to the San Francisco Bay area, where for a while it was in residence at Mills College in Oakland, then at the University of Southern California. In its early years, the quartet often performed on campus and with grant sponsorship, gathering a steady following among young and old alike. By the late 1980s Kronos played concerts in major venues worldwide, at jazz festivals, and even in clubs, its sponsorship a mixture of public, corporate, and private funds. Unlike most members of string quartets, who teach or work other jobs to supplement their incomes, Kronos players make their livings solely through performing with the quartet.

Kronos's astounding success is in part due to its daring programing. The "old" pieces on any concert program might include works by Bartok, Dimitri Shostakovich, Aaron Copland, Alban Berg, or Anton Webern. Works by minimalist composers Terry Riley and Philip Glass and such jazz artists as Max Roach and Ornette Cole-

man are well represented in the group's repertoire. The quartet has commissioned more than 150 new works, and each year receives hundreds of unsolicited scores of new pieces from around the world. Kronos maintains 400 pieces in its active repertoire at any one time.

"We look for music that excites us," declared Harrington in an interview with the *Star-Ledger,* "that has a point of view, that's *real.* We see ourselves as involved in extending, developing and enriching a great tradition. We are seeking consciously and with perseverance to move the focus of this tradition out of the nineteenth century, out of Central Europe. We want to bring the vitality of the world's music into this tradition. We're examining the radical nature of the art form and continuing it. Some of the music being written for us is the best there is today. . . . If we didn't believe that, we wouldn't play it. I run into exciting music every day that's not in our repertoire. There's no end to the possibilities."

> *By the late 1980s Kronos played concerts in major venues worldwide, at jazz festivals, and even in clubs, its sponsorship a mixture of public, corporate, and private funds*

Kronos has avoided the often heavy-handed involvement of East Coast music managers by basing itself on the West Coast, hiring its own staff, and taking on many management responsibilities itself. Harrington acts as the artistic director and is responsible for public relations and repertory development. Dutt is the road manager and curator of the over 3,000 scores in the Kronos library. Sherba manages the group's library of recordings, and Jeanrenaud settles questions of attire. The quartet is run on the same principles as a small business (the Kronos Performing Arts Association) and has a board of directors that consists of the quartet members and several philanthropists from the San Francisco Bay area.

The members of most string quartets wear tuxedos to perform, but in this, as in other matters, the Kronos Quartet is nonconformist. Each year the group comes up with a new look, which has ranged from a squeaky clean appearance in the 1970s to a jaded worldly look in the 1990s. "We all came to the conclusion that it wasn't necessary for us to wear the same things that everybody wore, and I think that's just an outgrowth of our music. We're not approaching things the same way anyone else is," Jeanrenaud explained to *Musician* writer Joe Goldberg.

The Kronos Quartet maintains a hectic concert schedule of as many as 150 concerts a year, playing regular concert series in San Francisco, Los Angeles, Seattle, Chicago, and Minneapolis. It has been the subject of a Public Broadcasting Service (PBS) special and has produced a regular series, "Kronos Hour" on PBS radio, which features live performances by quartet members and discussions with composers.

To make the music more accessible to the public, Kronos might create a particular atmosphere using special costumes, theatrical lights, and even stage sets. Harrington told John von Rhein of the *Chicago Tribune*, "We have been experimenting for a long time with how a visual experience becomes a musical experience. For us the senses are linked. Every concert is partly a visual experience. I mean, we have always used body language as a way of demonstrating the music. String players play with a bow and that bow responds to body language. We're always looking for ways to graphically bring home the music. Costumes, lighting, and all the rest are another way for us to incorporate, let's say, new information into our performances."

Kronos has recorded with great success for such labels as Nonesuch, Gramavision, Landmark, and CRI. Many of its recordings have demonstrated enormous crossover appeal that reflects the quartet's diverse audience. The album *Kronos Quartet* spent more than forty weeks on the Top 20 on *Billboard*'s classical music chart.

Selected discography

Monk Suite, Landmark, 1985.
Music of Bill Evans, Landmark, 1986.
Steve Reich: *Different Trains; Electric Counterpoint*, Nonesuch, 1988.
Terry Reily: *Salome Dances for Peace* (two volumes).
White Man Sleeps, Elektra/Nonesuch.

Sources

Chicago Tribune, April 10, 1988.
Colorado Springs Gazette Telegraph, January 8, 1988.
Daily Camera (Boulder), January 27, 1989.
Desert News (Salt Lake City), April 10, 1988.
Milwaukee Journal, April 2, 1989.
Musician, May 1990.
Newsweek, November 19, 1984.
New York Times, November 17, 1985.
Peninsula Times-Tribune (Palo Alto), September 11, 1986.
San Jose Mercury News, October 24, 1986.
Seattle Times, April 20, 1989.
Star-Ledger (Newark), November 22, 1987.

—*Jeanne M. Lesinski*

Brenda Lee

Singer

Vocalist Brenda Lee was one of the most popular female singers of the 1950s and 1960s. She began as a child star, making musical guest appearances on television variety shows. A little later Lee won a recording contract and put out hits like "I'm Sorry," "Sweet Nothin's," and the holiday classic, "Rockin' Around the Christmas Tree." When her success in the pop genre began to dwindle, she returned to her country music roots to release songs such as "Big Four-Poster Bed" and "He's My Rock." As Brock Helander affirmed in his book, *The Rock Who's Who,* Lee has "a voice equally adept at mournful ballads and at hard-belting rock songs."

Lee was born Brenda Mae Tarpley on December 11, 1944, in or near Atlanta, Georgia. A precociously talented child, she was singing by the time she was four years old, and won first prize at a local spring festival for singing "Take Me Out to the Ball Game" when she was five or six. Lee's mother began taking her to talent auditions, and when she was seven, she became a regular on the Atlanta radio show "Starmaker's Revue." This opportunity led to yet another, that of frequent guest appearances on the local television show *TV Ranch.*

From there, Lee became acquainted with country star Red Foley, and shared his manager, Dub Albritten. She made concert appearances with Foley, and she soon came to the attention of the nationwide television variety shows; the likes of Steve Allen, Red Skelton, and Ed Sullivan invited her to sing on their programs. By 1956, record companies were competing to sign her, and Lee eventually settled with the Decca label. Her first big hit was the seasonal favorite, "Rocking Around the Christmas Tree"; around the same time, she also scored a minor success with "One Step at a Time." Just barely a teenager, young Lee began touring, facing huge audiences and meeting other stars, some of whom she was much in awe. She reminisced for a *Life* magazine reporter about her shyness around superstar Elvis Presley, whom she met when both sang for the Grand Ole Opry in 1957: "I don't know what it was. My heart just started pounding. No other performer did that to me."

More hits followed Lee's early efforts—her first non-holiday hit was 1960's humorous "Sweet Nothin's," sung from the point of view of a teenage girl on a porch swing with her boyfriend. In the same year, she also had a two-sided hit with the slow ballad of heartbreak "I'm Sorry," which was backed with the up-tempo "That's All You Gotta Do." In 1961, Lee made the charts with the hummable "Dum Dum" and the ballad "Fool Number One"; "Break It to Me Gently" and "All Alone

Am I" followed the next year. But then Lee's career began to slow down, like that of many other American musicians facing the onslaught of the "British Invasion" of the mid-to-late 1960s. Her last pop hits were "Too Many Rivers" and "Coming on Strong," in 1965 and 1966, respectively, though she did receive a Grammy nomination in 1969 for her recording of "Johnny One Time."

Undaunted, Lee began recording and performing the country music she had begun with in her childhood. Even her previous pop hits had been well received by country audiences, and they quickly welcomed her new efforts. Her first foray onto the exclusively country charts was 1971's "Is This Our Last Time." An even better year for Lee was 1974, when she had five country hits, including perhaps her biggest smash in the genre, the romantic "Big Four-Poster Bed." The next year, she scored again with "Bringing It Back" and "He's My Rock."

In the 1980s, Lee continued to make the country charts with "The Cowboy and the Dandy," "Broken Trust," and "Every Now and Then." With her strong vocals, even Lee's contributions to other artist's recordings get attention. She put her voice to work on "Honky Tonk Angels' Medley," a cut from country singer k.d. lang's *Shadowland* album; Alanna Nash of *Stereo Review* reported that Lee "almost steals the show."

Selected discography

Single releases

"Rockin' Around the Christmas Tree," Decca, c. 1956.
"One Step at a Time," Decca, 1957.
"Sweet Nothin's," Decca, 1960.
"I'm Sorry/That's All You Gotta Do," Decca, 1960.
"I Want to Be Wanted," Decca, 1960.
"Emotions," Decca, 1961.
"You Can Depend On Me," Decca, 1961.
"Dum Dum," Decca, 1961.
"Fool Number One," Decca, 1961.
"Break It to Me Gently," Decca, 1962.
"Everybody Loves Me But You," Decca, 1962.
"Heart in Hand," Decca, 1962.
"All Alone Am I," Decca, 1962.
"Losing You," Decca, 1963.
"The Grass Is Greener," Decca, 1963.
"As Usual," Decca, 1963.
"Is It True," Decca, 1964.
"Too Many Rivers," Decca, 1965.
"Coming on Strong," Decca, 1966.
"Johnny One Time," Decca, 1969.
"Is This Our Last Time," Decca, 1970.
"Nobody Wins," MCA, 1973.
"Sunday Sunrise," MCA, 1973.
"Wrong Ideas," MCA, 1974.
"Big Four-Poster Bed," MCA, 1974.
"Rock On, Baby," MCA, 1974.
"Bringing It Back," MCA, 1975.
"He's My Rock," MCA, 1975.
"Find Yourself Another Puppet," MCA, 1976.
"Takin' What I Can Get," MCA, 1976.
"Could It Be I Found Love Tonight"/"Leftover Love," Elektra, 1978.
"Tell Me What It's Like," MCA, 1979.
"The Cowboy and the Dandy," MCA, 1980.
"Don't Promise Me Anything," MCA, 1980.
"Broken Trust," MCA, 1980.
"Every Now and Then," MCA, 1981.
"Only When I Laugh," MCA, 1981.

Albums

Grandma, What Great Songs You Sang, Decca, 1959.
Brenda Lee, Decca, 1960.
This Is Brenda Lee, Decca, 1960.
Emotions, Decca, 1961.
All the Way, Decca, 1961.
Sincerely, Decca, 1962.
That's All, Brenda, Decca, 1962.
All Alone Am I, Decca, 1962.
Let Me Sing, Decca, 1963.
By Request, Decca, 1964.

Merry Christmas From Brenda Lee, Decca, 1964.
Top Teen Hits, Decca, 1965.
Versatile, Decca, 1965.
Too Many Rivers, Decca, 1965.
Bye Bye, Blues, Decca, 1966.
Ten Golden Years, Decca, 1966.
Coming on Strong, Decca, 1966.
Reflections in Blue, Decca, 1967.
Johnny One Time, Decca, 1969.
Memphis Portrait, Decca, 1970.
Brenda, MCA, 1973.
The Brenda Lee Story, MCA, 1973.
New Sunrise, MCA, 1974.
Now, MCA, 1975.
Sincerely, Brenda Lee, MCA, 1975.
L.A. Sessions, MCA, 1976.
Even Better, MCA, 1980.

Take Me Back, MCA, 1980.
Only When I Laugh, MCA, 1981.

Sources

Books

Helander, Brock, *The Rock Who's Who*, Schirmer Books, 1982.

Periodicals

Life, September 1987.
Stereo Review, September 1988.

—Elizabeth Wenning

L. L. Cool J.

Rap artist

"**L.** L. Cool J. (Ladies Love Cool James) is the hip hop prince of the rap revolution," stated Rhoda E. McKinney in *Ebony.* L.L., whose real name is James Todd Smith, is a self-assured, good-looking young rap artist, widely admired as one of the most gifted performers of his craft. But strutting shirtless in a show which includes his disc jockey, Cut Creator, and E-Love, his bodyguard valet, belies the private man. Leaving off the on-stage boasts when asked if he considers himself, as many do, the most articulate of rappers, Smith replied in *Interview,* "No, not really. I just consider myself one of the brothers who does what he gotta do."

Born and raised in Queens, New York, L.L. still lives in St. Albans, a black middle-class neighborhood, with his grandmother, Ellen Griffith. Her red brick house has been home to L.L. since he was three years old. His parents are separated. To encourage the boy's musical interest, his late grandfather, a professional jazz saxophonist, paid $2,000 for a couple of turntables, a mixer, and an amplifier when L.L. was eleven. "By the time I got that equipment, I was already a rapper," L.L. told Stephen Holden in the *New York Times Magazine.* "In this neighborhood, the kids grow up on rap. It's like speaking Spanish if you grow up in an all-Spanish house. I got into it when I was about nine, and since then all I wanted was to make a record and hear it on the radio."

In 1982, L.L. was performing with neighborhood rap groups at roller rink and block party gatherings. He told Holden, "Aspiring rappers like to challenge each other with disrespect. . . . Being the best in your neighborhood is what it's all about." When not performing, the thirteen-year-old was sending homemade tapes to various rap record companies. Rick Rubin and his partner Russell Simmons were just forming the production company, Def Jam, in 1984, when they received one of L.L.'s raps, "I Need A Beat," and decided to record the song for their first release. L.L. quit attending Andrew Jackson High School, where he played sports and got good grades (he still intends to finish), when his debut single sold over 100,000 copies. The number "I Want You" followed and did so well that L.L. was asked to participate in a national rapper's tour, the New York City Fresh Festival, in the summer of the following year.

Hailed as a rap landmark, the album *Radio* came next, changing the course of rap music in 1985, after Rubin instructed L.L. to arrange verses, choruses, and bridges in his raps, which keyed on simplicity. Rubin told *Rolling Stone,* "It was just making rap like songs."

Including two early rap ballads "I Want You" and "I Can Give You More" along with the dramatic "Rock the Bells!" and the B-boy anthem "I Can't Live Without My Radio," the album went platinum to good reviews.

Real name, James Todd Smith; born c. 1969 in Queens, N.Y.; grandson of Ellen Griffith. *Education:* Attended Andrew Jackson High School, Queens, N.Y. (left school in 1984).

Began performing with neighborhood rap groups at block parties, 1982; sent homemade tape of "I Need a Beat" to producers Rick Rubin and Russell Simmons just as they were forming Def Jam Productions, 1984; cut became Def Jam's first release, 1984; debut album, *Radio*, released, critically hailed as a rap landmark, 1985. Performs with rap group consisting of disc jockey Cut Creator and bodyguard E-Love.

Addresses: *Residence*—Queens, N.Y. *Record company*—Def Jam/Columbia, 51 West 52nd Street, New York, NY 10019.

Stephen Holden called "I Can't Live Without My Radio" a "quintessential rap in its directness, immediacy, and assertion of self: 'Walking down the street to the hard-core beat/While my JVC vibrates the concrete/I'm sorry if you can't understand/But I need a radio inside my hand/ Don't mean to offend other citizens/But I kick my volume way past 10.'" *Rolling Stone* pronounced *Radio* an early rap masterpiece "ushering in rap's blockbuster era and heralding the arrival of a superb rapper" who "because of his good looks and macho swagger" has become "one of rap's first heartthrobs."

"Sex and the hit single have taken a new twist" wrote Peter Goddard in *Chatelaine* when he reviewed "I Need Love" from L.L.'s second album, *Bigger and Deffer*. The song asked for nothing short-term or superficial in a relationship, which Goddard noted was a departure from a field of music, which, before L.L., had been "notoriously sexist." *Rolling Stone* called the song "the hippest bedroom monologue since Barry White's heyday," but Havelock Nelson in *High Fidelity* criticized the platinum follow-up album which featured the number for its "use of pilfered bits." He upbraided the use of "longer and more obvious samples and scratched passages" on the album, but still praised the witty narratives.

After *Bigger and Deffer* stayed on *Billboard*'s Top Ten for two months, L.L. Cool J. headlined the sold-out 70-city Def Jam tour. Featured on the tour with L.L., billed as "the Crown Prince of Rap," were Public Enemy, Eric

B. and Rakim, Stetsonic, Whodini, and Doug E. Fresh. Profiled in *Interview* by Fab 5 Freddy after the tour, L.L. disputed his macho public image. "I'm proud. If you see me smiling, standing straight up, gold around my neck, it's not because I'm conceited. It's because I'm proud of what I achieved. I made this. That's what all this is about."

L.L. continued to feature the balladry, bawdiness, and boasting from his second album, which set new standards for rap, in his third album *Walking With A Panther*, but the reception for this album was mixed in *Rolling Stone*. David Browne called the album "the best-sounding record of his career," but questioned L.L.'s limited repertoire. "That's all well and good, and *Walking With A Panther* bodes well for L.L.'s career as a rap autcur. But with so much happening outside of the recording studio and on the streets, is being the boaster with the mostest enough?"

When Fab 5 Freddy asked the "rap auteur," who had a cameo role in the rap movie *Krush Groove*, how he felt about the future of rap and of L.L. Cool J., L.L. replied, "First of all, I say as long as the individual stays creative and continues to come up with fresh new and exciting ideas, rap will be here. That's established. Simple. As far as what I want to do, I want to get busy, man. I want to rock 60,000 people. I want to rock the Superdome."

Selected discography

Radio (includes "I Want You," "I Can Give You More," "Rock the Bells!" and "I Can't Live Without My Radio"), Def Jam/Columbia, 1985.
Bigger and Deffer, (includes "I Need Love"), Def Jam/Columbia, 1987.
Walking With A Panther, Def Jam/Columbia, 1989.
Mama Said Knock You Out, Def Jam/Columbia, 1990.

Sources

Chatelaine, January 1988.
Ebony, January 1989.
High Fidelity, December 1987.
Interview, December 1987.
Rolling Stone, December 17, 1987; September 7, 1989; November 16, 1989.
New York Times Magazine, April 26, 1987.

—*Marjorie Burgess*

Patty Loveless

Singer, songwriter

P atty Loveless has been described as a "promising name in country music's new traditionalism." The petite and comely Loveless is yet another artist who has capitalized upon the public taste for old-style country music; her work—and her voice—have drawn comparisons with such country stalwarts as Loretta Lynn and Reba McEntire. Still, as Andrew Vaughan notes in *Who's Who in New Country Music,* Loveless is not merely another old-fashioned "girl singer." Instead, she "bridges the gap between pre-seventies country and progressive country with great finesse." Vaughan adds: "[Loveless's] band sounds up to the minute and her songs ring true with [modern] notions, but vocally she's reminiscent of the old-time sound. . . . Loveless brings a fresh voice to country music—traditional but always ready to rock 'n' roll."

Young and fresh as she seems, Loveless is no stranger to the rigors of the country circuit. She began singing professionally at the tender age of 12 and has never been far from a microphone since. Only on her third attempt did she break through into big time country music. Before that she was simply another opening act for more established stars, another of the legion of hopefuls who try their luck in Nashville.

Patty Loveless hails from Belcher Holler, Kentucky, a tiny community near the town of Pikeville. She was born there in 1957 into the large family of an ailing coal miner. Loveless's father suffered from both black lung and heart disease; the ten-member family subsisted on Social Security payments and occasional singing work by older siblings. When Patty was 10 her family moved to Louisville, where her father sought medical treatment for his condition. City life did not prove easy for young Patty—the children in Louisville made fun of her rural ways and drove her to seek friendship and solace within her immediate family.

Loveless decided upon a singing career at the age of eleven, after she saw her older sister perform in a USO show. Within a year she was singing onstage and even writing her own material. Her earliest performances most often took the form of duets with her brother Roger, who serves as her manager to this day.

In 1971, when she was only fourteen, Loveless set out for Nashville to seek her fortune. She and her brother managed to talk their way into a private meeting with Porter Wagoner, who was immediately impressed with Loveless's delivery and songwriting talent. Wagoner helped Loveless to make a master recording of several of her songs, and he also introduced her to his many friends in the business. One of these was his "girl singer," Dolly Parton.

"Dolly was just so warm and friendly, and we became

really good friends," Loveless told *Stereo Review*. "We ran around together a lot. She used to say, 'Keep up your writing.' And then when I was back in Louisville and she and Porter would pass through, they'd stop and call my house and say, 'Come over and eat with us.' It was sort of like a dream."

Loveless did indeed keep up her writing and her singing. In 1974 she and her brother were invited to open a package show in Louisville that included the Wilburn Brothers. The Wilburns were looking for an act to replace Loretta Lynn, who had recently left them to perform on her own, and they invited Loveless to audition for them. The day after she graduated from high school, Loveless travelled to Nashville once again, signed a publishing contract with the Wilburns' Sure Fire Music and began to tour with the group. Her success was not assured, however. After several months, the singers mutually agreed that Loveless was still too young to handle the heavy demands of touring. She "retired," married the Wilburns' drummer, Terry Lovelace, and moved to North Carolina.

Loveless's husband formed his own band, a rock and roll group, for which Patty provided vocals. The group hit the club circuit, performing in a variety of venues and occasionally opening for bands such as the Pure Prairie League. The perpetual motion began to take its toll on Loveless, as it had on many other performers. "I was taking a lot of uppers and downers, and it was nothing for me to finish a fifth of straight bourbon in a day," she told *Stereo Review*. "From about 1978 to 1982, I was just destroying myself. I looked twenty years older than

I really was. Finally, I took ahold of myself and said, 'I'm not letting this happen to me.'"

The real turning point came in 1984, when Loveless was engaged to perform country music at a small club. "It really felt good, and the audience went nuts over it— listening *and* dancing," she remembered. "Next thing I knew, I called my brother Roger and told him I felt like my life had come back together." Loveless and her brother returned to Nashville and made a five-song demo tape. On the strength of that work she was signed to the prestigious MCA label for recording and the Acuff-Rose company for music publishing. With her marriage ended in divorce, Loveless changed the spelling of her last name, principally because she did not want to be associated with the former pornographic film star, Linda Lovelace.

Loveless's debut album, *Patty Loveless*, was hailed as "traditional country with a little edge." Highest praise was reserved for "the power in the voice and the beauty of Patty's high lonesome mountain singing," to quote Vaughan. Actually the album contained a surprising variety of music, from a rocking version of Steve Earle's "Some Blue Moons Ago" to a Texas dance-hall number, "Lonely Days, Lonely Nights," to a torchy version of her original number, "I Did." The album sold well by Nashville standards, and Loveless found herself opening shows for headliners such as George Jones, Reba McEntire, and Randy Travis.

Today, with several more albums in print, Loveless is a headliner herself. Her "wild and wounded" delivery has found fans outside the traditional country arena, especially in England and on the West Coast of the United States. The new popularity of music videos has also proven profitable for the photogenic Loveless, who has spurned the sequined look for a more comfortable, down-to-earth appearance. Loveless told *Stereo Review* that her years of struggle have prepared her for success. "Somebody says, 'You're heading to be a star,'" she said. "And I say, 'But that's not really what I want to be.' Some people want to put you into a glamorous role. I just want to be known for my music, have people appreciate me for what I'm doing, and know that it makes people feel good inside. . . . I get off on that kind of thing."

Selected discography

Patty Loveless, MCA, 1986.
If My Heart Had Windows, MCA, 1987.
Honky Tonk Angels, MCA, 1988.
On Down the Line, MCA, 1990.

Sources

Books

Vaughan, Andrew, *Who's Who in New Country Music,* St. Martin's, 1989.

Periodicals

Stereo Review, November 1987.

—Anne Janette Johnson

Lyle Lovett

Singer, songwriter, guitarist

In 1988 a *Rolling Stone* reporter called Lyle Lovett "the best thing to come out of the country scene in years." Lovett combines the sounds of his native Texas with blues and folk to create a striking new music, welcome to fans of rock and country alike. At a time when many country artists are returning to their roots, Lovett seems unafraid to challenge boundaries. His cosmopolitan appearance and darkly humorous, sometimes violent lyrics mark him as an experimenter and a maverick. In *Who's Who in New Country Music,* Andrew Vaughan suggests that Lovett "is all set to take country music out of that mythical redneck ghetto and introduce the beauty and power of Texas music to a vast number of country and rock fans."

Artists who write all of their own songs are becoming quite rare in Nashville. Lovett is a standout in that respect; he creates all his own material, melody and lyrics. Vaughan notes that the musician "sees with a poet's eye and writes with a jaunty turn of phrase," and "he's just as happy with beat generation, finger-popping jazz as he is with dusty home-on-the-range Texas ballads. And what is most staggering is that he manages to blend his stylistic influences into an identifiable whole."

Lovett was born and raised in Klein, Texas, a community named for his great-great grandfather, a German immigrant. Klein is not exactly a small town—it has a population of some 40,000—but it had a rural feel when Lovett was a youngster. He grew up in a tight-knit extended family with parents who supported his adventurous tendencies. Lovett began playing the guitar when he was only seven and learned to love both country and rock music. His favorite artists were other blues-folk singer-songwriters, including Guy Clark, Townes Van Zandt, and especially Jerry Jeff Walker.

Lovett began to perform professionally while attending Texas A&M University, where he majored in journalism. From the first he gravitated to the coffee house circuit rather than the dance hall—his music has never lacked punch, but it is best appreciated by an attentive listener. He also began to write his own songs quite early in his career. He told Vaughan: "I started doing covers but I was never a good enough singer to do Merle Haggard tunes, so I realized that I had to do my own. If I'd been a better singer or player maybe I'd have never started writing."

Lovett took his singing and songwriting talents along with him when he went to do graduate study in Germany in the early 1980s. His performances there earned him an invitation to a country music festival in Luxembourg, where he worked as a between-sets filler. As Lovett recalled the time in *Rolling Stone,* he was more or less laying an egg with the crowd until one of the scheduled

For the Record. . .

Born ca. 1958 in Klein, Tex.; son of William and Bernell Lovett. *Education:* Texas A&M University, B.A. (journalism), 1980; also did graduate work.

Singer, songwriter, guitarist, 1980—. Signed with MCA Records, 1984, released first album, *Lyle Lovett,* 1985. Has performed live in the United States and Europe.

Awards: Grammy Award for best male country vocal performance, 1989, for album *Lyle Lovett and His Large Band.*

Addresses: *Record company*—MCA/Curb Records, 70 Universal City Plaza, Universal City, CA 91608.

bands, J. David Sloan and the Rogues, joined him onstage. Lovett struck up a friendship with the Rogues, a Phoenix-based ensemble, and when he earned a recording contract with MCA Records in 1984 he recruited the Rogues for his sessions.

Lovett's first album, *Lyle Lovett,* was released in 1985 and was quickly hailed as an "absolute must" by Steve Pond in *Rolling Stone.* The album contains more than one nod to Texas influences, but it also features jazz and even a cello accompaniment. Several of the songs found their way onto the country charts, with a best seller being "God Will," a frank but funny look at betrayal. Lovett followed his debut with another, bluesier album, *Pontiac,* released in 1988. Somewhat darker in its themes if not in its sound, *Pontiac* yielded another hit, "She's No Lady."

Pontiac confirmed the central tendencies in Lovett's work—the characters in his songs are hardly model citizens, and the course of true love never *ever* runs smooth. As David Wild puts it in *Rolling Stone,* Lovett's pieces "do contain an unusually high body count of casualties in the war between the sexes." Inevitably, Lovett has been accused of a streak of misogyny, a charge he denies vehemently. He told *People:* "A lot of times when I write, the female character is doing something to the male character. Frequently it's something that I have actually done in a relationship. And rather than point the finger at myself, it's a lot more fun to blame somebody else."

Antisocial though his creations may be, Lovett has not alienated his fans. His work is seen as a fresh direction for country—hip and modern but still pulsing with the bitter emotions that characterize rural music. Lovett has

never been afraid to challenge an audience. His music ranges through country, jazz, rock, blues, and R&B, his poetic lyrics call up a sea of troubles, and his intentionally avant-garde appearance breaks every rule for standard Nashville garb.

Lovett told *Rolling Stone* that he never worries about being misunderstood, even when he *is* misunderstood. "In some cases, I think people *get* the joke, but they just don't *like* the joke," he said. "I realize my sense of humor is tacky sometimes, but I hope it comes across in the shows that it's not malicious. Sure, I have psychopathic thoughts, but real psychopaths have nothing *but* those thoughts. And as for offending people, I've occasionally worried about hurting the feelings of the people I know that I write about. But it really hasn't been much of a problem."

Lovett makes some two hundred personal appearances each year, travelling across the country in a bus with his band. He is particularly popular as a live performer, achieving "remarkable intimacy with a voice that's weathered, comfortable and haunting," to quote Pond. The critic concludes that Lyle Lovett "writes songs whose lyrics are as flowing and musical as the tunes to which he sets them. He sings in the voice of a guy who disdains commitment, a ramblin' man who still rues the day some damn woman managed to tame him, and in the voice of the barroom cynic who'll occasionally give you a glimpse of his sensitive side." Still in his mid-thirties, Lovett seems poised to lead the way into a new era of experimental country.

Selected discography

Lyle Lovett, MCA/Curb, 1985.
Pontiac, MCA/Curb, 1988.
Lyle Lovett and His Large Band, MCA/Curb, 1989.

Sources

Books

Vaughan, Andrew, *Who's Who in New Country Music,* St. Martin's, 1989.

Periodicals

People, August 1, 1988.
Rolling Stone, March 24, 1988; July 14, 1988.
Stereo Review, January 1987; May 1988; May 1989.

—*Anne Janette Johnson*

Jeff Lynne

Singer, songwriter, guitarist, producer

British rock artist Jeff Lynne has been bringing music to fans in his home country and the United States for nearly two decades. He first came to real prominence as the leader of the Electric Light Orchestra—perhaps better known by its initials, ELO. With this band, he scored many hits throughout the 1970s, including "Can't Get It Out of My Head," "Livin' Thing," and "Don't Bring Me Down." After ELO's popularity died down somewhat during the 1980s, Lynne concentrated on production and songwriting work for fellow major stars, former Beatles Paul McCartney and George Harrison among them. Lynne resurfaced as a performer in 1988, when he became a member of the Traveling Wilburys.

Lynne's first small taste of success in the music world came with a group he fronted during the late 1960s called the Idle Race. The band had a sufficient following among British college students to merit recording an album on the Liberty label in 1969, *The Birthday Party.* A year later, Lynne was approached by Roy Wood of the underground rock group the Move; Wood wanted Lynne to join. The Move had recently undergone radical changes in personnel, and was down to two members, Wood and drummer Bev Bevan. Lynne consented, but not merely to become part of a more successful band. Rather, he was interested in what Brock Helander described in his book, *The Rock Who's Who,* as "Wood's conception of a fully electric rock band augmented by a classical string section."

The plan was that Wood and Lynne would develop this project, to be called the Electric Light Orchestra, at the same time as they worked on Move albums. The first album the group put out as ELO, *No Answer,* was well received in Great Britain, and scored a hit there with the single, "10538 Overture," in 1972. Ironically, however, Lynne's first success in the United States, as well as the Move's biggest record in that country, came with the 1973 single "Do Ya," from the Move's *Split Ends.* Lynne eventually included the number in ELO concert performances.

Split Ends proved to be the last album the Move released. And Wood had grown bored with ELO, leaving it in Lynne's control. As Helander reported, the latter "assumed the primary role as producer, arranger, composer, lead vocalist, and lead guitarist." To make the album *ELO II,* Lynne decided to put even greater emphasis on the blending of the rock and classical styles, and recruited keyboard player Richard Tandy (also a Move veteran), bassist Kelly Groucutt, cellists Melvyn Gale and Hugh McDowell, and violinist Mik Kaminsky. The latter three musicians had played previously with the London Symphony Orchestra. *ELO II* provided the remade band with a 1973 hit in the United

For the Record. . .

B orn December 30, 1947, in Birmingham, England. Member of group, the Idle Race, c. 1966-70; member of group, the Move, 1970-73; member of group, Electric Light Orchestra (ELO), 1972-83. Producer and songwriter for various other artists, 1983—. Member of group, The Traveling Wilburys, beginning 1988. Music (with ELO) featured in the 1980 film, *Xanadu*.

Awards: Co-recipient (with Bob Dylan, George Harrison, Roy Orbison, and Tom Petty; as group the Traveling Wilburys) of Grammy Award for best rock performance by a duo or group with vocal, 1989, for the *Traveling Wilburys, Volume I*.

Addresses: *Record company*—Reprise Records, 3300 Warner Blvd., Burbank, CA 91510.

States, a remake of rock pioneer Chuck Berry's "Roll Over, Beethoven" that featured excerpts from other rock classics.

Some critics felt that ELO's version of "Roll Over, Beethoven" was too much like a novelty record to presage further success for the group, but they were quickly proven wrong. *On the Third Day,* released later in 1973, provided ELO with a few more minor hits, and fueled audience appreciation for their U.S. concert tours. And *Eldorado,* released in 1974, launched ELO's first huge single success, "Can't Get It Out of My Head." In the following year, *Face the Music* included the smashes "Evil Woman" and "Strange Magic." As Helander phrased it, ELO had "secured [its] position in the forefront of so-called 'classical-rock.'"

Oddly enough, however, though Lynne and ELO occasionally charted in their native England, the band fared much, much better with fans in the United States. Their popularity in the latter country continued unabated through the late 1970s, and they saw songs like 1976's "Telephone Line" and "Livin' Thing," 1977's "Turn to Stone" and "Sweet Talkin' Woman," and 1979's "Shine a Little Love" and "Don't Bring Me Down" race up the U.S. record charts. The latter two singles came from the album *Discovery,* on which Lynne took the classical aspects of ELO further by backing them with a forty-two piece orchestra and a thirty-member all-male choir. In 1980, Lynne and ELO provided music for the soundtrack of the motion picture *Xanadu.*

Though ELO put out a few more albums during the early 1980s, Lynne's efforts turned increasingly to writing and producing for other stars. He has reportedly said that the major influences upon his songwriting style were John Lennon and Paul McCartney; fortunately his reputation has become such that he gained the opportunity to work for one of his idols, helping McCartney with an album. He has also produced for Dave Edmunds, and assisted Tom Petty and Randy Newman with recordings. And critics had high praise for his production work on George Harrison's 1987 album, *Cloud Nine.*

But the work that really brought Lynne back into the spotlight was getting together with his famous friends—Harrison, Petty, Bob Dylan, and the late Roy Orbison—and recording as the Traveling Wilburys. Apparently Lynne and friends got the idea while having dinner together in Los Angeles; they eventually decided to adopt the personas of the various Wilbury brothers to lend humor to the project. The result, the Grammy Award-winning *The Traveling Wilburys, Volume I,* proved popular with fans and critics alike. Lynne discussed the Wilburys' recording sessions with a *Rolling Stone* reporter: "We would arrive about twelve or one o'clock and have some coffee," he explained. "Somebody would say, 'What about this?' and start on a riff. Then we'd all join in, and it'd turn into something. We'd finish around midnight. . . . Then we'd come back the next day to work on another one. That's why the songs are so good and fresh—because they haven't been second-guessed and dissected and replaced."

Following the death of Orbison, the remaining Wilburys got together to record a follow-up album, released in 1990 under the title *Traveling Wilburys, Volume III* (in keeping with the lighthearted tone of the project they "skipped" Volume II, opting to follow Volume I with Volume III). Lynne also found time to put together a solo album for release in 1990, *Armchair Theatre.*

Selected discography

With the Move

Message From the Country, Capitol, 1971.
Split Ends (includes "Do Ya"), United Artists, 1973.

With the Electric Light Orchestra (ELO)

No Answer (includes "10538 Overture"), United Artists, 1972.
ELO II (includes "Roll Over, Beethoven"), United Artists, 1973.
On the Third Day, United Artists, 1973.
Eldorado (includes "Can't Get It Out of My Head"), United Artists, 1974.
Face the Music (includes "Evil Woman" and "Strange Magic"), United Artists, 1975.
Ole ELO, United Artists, 1976.
A New World Record (includes "Livin' Thing" and "Telephone Line"), United Artists, 1976.

Out of the Blue (includes "Turn to Stone," "Concerto for a Rainy Day," and "Sweet Talkin' Woman"), United Artists, 1977.
Discovery (includes "Shine a Little Love" and "Don't Bring Me Down"), Columbia, 1979.
Time, Columbia, 1981.
Secret Messages, Jet, 1983.

With the Traveling Wilburys

Traveling Wilburys, Volume I (includes "Handle With Care," "Rattled," and "End of the Line"), Warner Bros., 1988.
Traveling Wilburys, Volume III, Warner Bros., 1991.

Other

(With The Idle Race) *The Birthday Party,* Liberty, 1969.
(With ELO and Olivia Newton-John) *Xanadu* (soundtrack; includes "I'm Alive" and "All Over the World"), MCA, 1980.

(Solo) *Armchair Theater* (includes "Every Little Thing"), Reprise, 1990.

Sources

Books

Helander, Brock, *The Rock Who's Who,* Schirmer Books, 1982.

Periodicals

Rolling Stone, December 15, 1988; November 16, 1989.

—Elizabeth Wenning

Shelby Lynne

Singer, songwriter

In *USA Today* Shelby Lynne is listed as one of 1990's "hottest new country acts." The young, brooding Lynne has made a name for herself as a torch singer, a balladeer of heartbreak and disappointment who seems to feel what she sings. With her second album, *Tough All Over*, Lynne, 23, jumped into country's first rank and was praised by critics as a newcomer with great promise. Lynne is thrilled with the acclaim and eager to live up to her growing reputation. "I love being up on stage, and I don't mind travelling around," she told the *Philadelphia Inquirer*. "I like everything about it. . . . It really suits me."

Shelby Lynne is not terribly eager to discuss her childhood in print. She was born and raised in Jackson, Alabama, one of two daughters of a schoolteacher who also played and wrote country music. While Lynne was a teenager her parents separated amidst bitter quarrels. Late one night in 1986, her father returned to the home where Lynne and her sister were living with their mother. While the two girls waited inside, the parents argued in the driveway. The fight ended when Lynne's father pulled a gun, shot his estranged wife, and then shot himself.

Lynne would rather not dwell upon that tragedy, saying simply: "I don't think it has anything to do with my musical career. . . . It's not something that interests me right now." She did admit, however, that she has been putting some of her father's lyrics to music—one way in which her profession might help her to deal with the grief.

Lynne began auditioning for jobs at music theme parks in 1987. Although she did not make the cut at the Opryland USA park in Nashville, she did attract the attention of song publisher Bob Tubert, who offered her a chance to make a demo tape. That demo earned Lynne an appearance on *Nashville Now,* a nightly variety show aired on the Nashville Network.

Nashville can be a particularly daunting place for young, would-be singers—performers such as Patty Loveless and Tanya Tucker have both testified about the pressures of touring, the constant round of publicity, and the manipulation by producers and managers. Lynne seemed to take all the glitz in stride. "Real pressure," she once said, "is a fiddling convention when you have to win the solo voice competition because you need 25 dollars." At any rate, Lynne astounded the *Nashville Now* audience with her powerful vocal delivery and her composure—she was literally a standout on a show that features as many as twenty country acts each week.

The morning following her October 1987 appearance on *Nashville Now,* Lynne received offers from four major record labels. The one that seemed the most promising came from Billy Sherill, the producer who had engineered Tammy Wynette's successful career. Sherill helped Lynne to forge a deal with Columbia Records, and early in 1988, her debut album, *Sunrise,* was released.

Columbia also released a debut single, "If I Could Bottle This Up," featuring Lynne in duet with George Jones. That and a subsequent single only made a fair showing on the country charts, but Lynne quickly became a sought-after opening act for the likes of Jones, Willie Nelson, Ricky Van Shelton, and Randy Travis. In retrospect, executives at Columbia declared that *Sunrise* was "too down," with its smoldering melancholy and its sense of love gone south. Despite that assessment, however, the producers at Columbia allowed Lynne to turn in a similar work as her second release.

Tough All Over hit the stands in the summer of 1990, with much more satisfying sales. Two singles from the work made the country top twenty, "I'll Lie Myself to Sleep" and "Tough All Over"—both heartfelt torch songs that highlight Lynne's flame-thrower vocals. Music videos helped to widen Lynne's audience as

For the Record. . .

Born in 1968 in Jackson, Alabama; daughter of a school teacher. Country singer, 1987—. Signed with Columbia Records, 1987; released first album, *Sunrise,* 1988. Has appeared in numerous live concerts, opening for Randy Travis, Willie Nelson, George Jones, and Ricky Van Shelton; has also made numerous appearances on television show *Nashville Now.*

Addresses: *Record company*—Epic Records, 51 West 52nd Street, New York, NY 10019.

Lynne has had few days of leisure since beginning her career in 1987. She is on the road more than one hundred nights per year, still primarily serving as an opening act to more-established stars. Despite her youth, Lynne has a distinct philosophy under which she works—she concentrates on entertaining in a genuine style, without sugar-coating or shallow thrills. "I'm just here to do a job," she said, "just to sing and share music with people. . . . I just sing how I feel at the time and don't try to sound like anything I'm not. I put a lot of emotion in my music, and hopefully it comes out. I don't want people to think I'm up there acting or anything, because I'm not. I'm just a singer."

they provided the perfect atmosphere for her melancholy beauty and quiet dignity. While the sale of the album and its singles was not terribly brisk, the critical reaction to Lynne's singing was quite enthusiastic. Reviewers compared her to Wynette and even to the demi-goddess Patsy Cline, ranking *Tough All Over* as one of the best country releases of the year.

Philadelphia Inquirer correspondent Dan DeLuca wrote: "Whether the finely controlled pathos in Lynne's voice stems from some inner turmoil or is just a natural gift, it conveys a stunning sense of experience and pain for someone so young. The singer has an uncanny ease with her voice. Unlike many young powerhouses, she'd rather cajole and caress a song than bully it with show of vocal force." In at least one respect Lynne does rank with Patsy Cline—her bluesy numbers reach far beyond the boundaries of conventional country and are apt to find a mainstream audience someday soon.

Selected discography

Sunrise, Columbia, 1988.
Tough All Over, Columbia, 1990.

Sources

Books

Vaughan, Andrew, *Who's Who in New Country Music,* St. Martin's, 1989.

Periodicals

Philadelphia Inquirer, November 9, 1990.
USA Today Weekend, October 5-7, 1990.

—Anne Janette Johnson

Jimmy Martin

Singer, songwriter, guitarist

Jimmy Martin is a pioneer of bluegrass whose high tenor voice and ripping instrumental style continue to attract new fans to mountain music. Like his mentor Bill Monroe, Martin adheres to the traditional form of bluegrass, with its three- or four-voice harmonies and accelerated guitar, mandolin, and banjo runs. His band, the Sunny Mountain Boys, has been a training ground for some of the finest bluegrass musicians in the business, and Martin himself has contributed a number of classic songs to the bluegrass canon.

According to Bill C. Malone in *Country Music U.S.A.,* Martin is a "consistently loyal partisan of bluegrass music," keeping faith with the old-time sound even as others dabble with rock and jazz influences. Malone added: "At his best (which is most of the time) he has given the music he loves some of its greatest moments both as a singer and as a guitarist."

Jimmy Martin was born into the hard farming life of rural Tennessee. He grew up near Sneedville, singing in church and with friends from surrounding farms. When he was in his teens he bought a guitar. Martin told *The Big Book of Bluegrass:* "I learned the basic chords from an old hillbilly named Reuben Gibson, who lived in the

hills around Sneedville, and I taught myself how to play. I heard Lester Flatt and Charlie Monroe both play runs, but I didn't try to top them. I mostly just developed them how I felt, when it came natural for a song."

Early in his career Martin decided that he would try to sing with Bill Monroe. At the time—in the late 1940s—Monroe had a famous and ground-breaking band, the Blue Grass Boys. Almost on a whim, in 1949 Martin took a bus to Nashville and sought out his hero. In fact, Martin lived what must be every country musician's dream: He watched Monroe perform on the Grand Ole Opry and when the show was over went backstage unannounced and offered his services to the group. He auditioned in the dressing room and was hired on the spot.

Martin said: "I went backstage and got to sing [a song] with [Monroe] and one by myself, and he asked me if I wanted to go on the road with him. He said it would be hard traveling, and I said, 'Bill, it can't be no harder than plowing corn or digging a ditch or pulling a crosscut saw.' I think that's why we got along so well. We were both country boys, raised tough. We understood each other."

Martin's addition to the Blue Grass Boys helped to soften the blow Monroe received when he lost band members and later bluegrass legends Lester Flatt and Earl Scruggs. As Malone put it, "Martin's high, reedy voice, and subtle intonations complemented Monroe's singing extremely well, and his strong rhythm guitar playing, punctuated frequently with dynamic bass runs, gave the Blue Grass Boys a surging, supercharged sound that not even the Lester Flatt years had witnessed. . . . Martin and Monroe evoked images of that lonesome, rural life that had originally been the context for bluegrass music's emergence. It was 'white soul singing' at its best."

Martin played and sang with the Blue Grass Boys during the years 1950-51 and again from 1952-54; his contribution can be heard on such Decca Records classics as "Uncle Pen," "On the Old Kentucky Shore," and "The Little Girl and the Dreadful Snake." Martin's periods of absence from the group enabled him to forge professional relationships with other musicians, especially the Osborne Brothers. In 1951 Martin and Bobby Osborne formed a group, recruiting the teenage Sonny Osborne on banjo. Together they made a few recordings for small labels in the summer of 1951, but soon thereafter Bobby was inducted into the Marines. Martin returned to the Blue Grass Boys with Sonny Osborne and they both played with Monroe until Bobby was released from the service.

In 1954 the re-formed Martin-Osborne band found

For the Record. . .

B orn near Sneedville, Tenn., 1927; son of a farmer. Bluegrass singer, guitarist, and songwriter, 1949—. Joined Bill Monroe's Blue Grass Boys, 1950; formed band with Bobby, Sonny, and Louise Osborne and signed with King label, 1951; moved to Kitty label; rejoined the Blue Grass Boys, 1952-54; formed the Sunny Mountain Boys, 1955; performed on WJR Radio, Detroit, 1955-56, and on the *Louisiana Hayride*, 1956. Leader of the Sunny Mountain Boys, 1955—, recording principally with Decca Records. Other Sunny Mountain Boys have included J. D. Crowe, Vic Jordan, Bill Emerson, Allan Munde, Earl Taylor, Paul Williams, and Sam Hutchins.

Addresses: *Record company*—MCA Records, Inc., 70 Universal City Plaza, Universal City, CA 91608.

work at WJR Radio in Detroit. With the Osbornes and Casey Clark on fiddle, Martin finally had a group that could create its own style. The band signed a recording contract with RCA and one of its first singles, "20-20 Vision" was a Number-One hit on the country charts. The pay in Detroit was "good and steady," Martin remembered, but after making a series of recordings in Nashville, the Osbornes decided to go their own way. Martin remained in Detroit until 1956 and was then offered work on the *Louisiana Hayride,* a radio show that rivaled the Grand Ole Opry in popularity.

Later, Martin move to Shreveport, Louisiana, as the head of a new band, the Sunny Mountain Boys. While there he recorded with Decca, turning out "Hit Parade of Love," "Sophronie," and "Ocean of Diamonds." Success spawned success and soon the high-spirited Martin was attracting impressive young talent to his group. His recordings from this period feature the musicianship of J. D. Crowe, Paul Williams, and Bill Emerson. Recalling those days in *The Big Book of Bluegrass,* Martin said that hiring Williams and Crowe "brought my records out and got me on my feet more than any other musicians I've had in the Sunny Mountain Boys."

Martin has always been a disciplined and demanding artist, and the personnel changes in his band have been many. Despite the ever-changing round of musicians behind him, however, he managed to weather the lean years of the late 1950s and emerge in the 1960s as one of the few prosperous bluegrass performers. In 1972 Martin was invited to contribute to the Nitty Gritty Dirt Band album *Will the Circle Be Unbroken,* which featured the talents of giants Earl Scruggs, Doc Watson, Roy Acuff, and Maybelle Carter. In *The Big Book of Bluegrass* Herschel Freeman wrote that Martin's songs on *Will the Circle Be Unbroken* "brought Jimmy's talents full force to a whole new generation of acoustic listeners, many of whom were not yet born when Jimmy came to prominence."

Martin's hard-driving work is well represented in bluegrass anthologies, and his early recordings with the Osbornes and the Sunny Mountain Boys are collectors' items. Although well into his sixties, he still performs on the festival circuit and in Nashville, giving listeners a taste of bluegrass as it was performed in its earliest stages of development. "I love bluegrass," Martin told *The Big Book of Bluegrass.* "It's the only kind of music I ever will love. When I sing those songs it hits me deep, and when I'm at the microphone I give it all I've got. I want to see bluegrass stay up so bad, and do something for it however I can."

Selected discography

Jimmy Martin, MCA.
Big and Country Instrumentals, MCA.
Country Music Time, MCA.
Singing All Day and Dinner on the Ground, MCA.
Sunny Side of the Mountain, MCA.
This World Is Not My Home, MCA.
Jimmy Martin with the Sunny Mountain Boys, MCA.
Jimmy Martin and the Sunny Mountain Boys Sing, MCA.
Mr. Good 'n Country Music, MCA.
Mac Wiseman, Jimmy Martin, and the Stanley Brothers, Highland Music, 1987.

Also appeared on the Nitty Gritty Dirt Band album *Will the Circle Be Unbroken,* United Artists, 1972.

Sources

The Illustrated Encyclopedia of Country Music, Harmony, 1977.
Kochman, Marilyn, editor, *The Big Book of Bluegrass,* Morrow, 1984.
Malone, Bill C., *Country Music U.S.A.,* revised edition, University of Texas Press, 1985.

—Anne Janette Johnson

Kathy Mattea

Singer, songwriter

In some respects Kathy Mattea is country music's best-kept secret. Largely overlooked by the mainstream, Mattea is turning out some of the finest progressive country, folk, and blues of any performer—a fact not lost on country fans. Mattea's understated beauty and resonant alto are perfectly suited for acoustic-backed ballads; the singer has made several such songs number-one country hits during her long tenure as a Nashville recording artist.

Twice named Female Vocalist of the Year by the Country Music Association, Mattea seems poised to enter the 1990s as a versatile, thoughtful, and prominent performer. *St. Paul Pioneer Press* correspondent Bill Bell noted that the singer "has a knack for pretty, intelligent ballads that express sentiments that seem to go with rock-solid relationships in an uncertain world." Bell praised Mattea for her "deep, throaty, sincere voice and her easy-access image," concluding: "People in the industry have known about [her] for years, but it wasn't until 1988 that she really took off."

Mattea's voice is indeed earthy, a natural gift she has learned to use effectively. She has had little formal vocal training, perfecting her craft instead by singing a variety of folk, bluegrass, blues, and country. Mattea was born and raised in Cross Lanes, West Virginia, the daughter not of a coal miner but of a white-collar supervisor. She was an excellent student, enrolling at West Virginia University to study physics and chemistry.

While a student at WVU Mattea began singing with a bluegrass band. Realizing that she preferred performing to physics, she dropped out of college and headed to Nashville, hoping to find work as a folk singer. Mattea was in no way an overnight success, however. To support herself she took a job as a tour guide at the Country Music Hall of Fame, a position she learned to appreciate because it taught her poise in front of a crowd. What little singing she could find was usually back-up work and commercial jingles. "In the beginning there were some frustrating years," she told the *Chicago Tribune,* "when it just seemed like I was standing still. Other people were coming out of nowhere and being talked about, and I was kind of anonymous."

Even after she signed with Mercury Records in 1983 and released her debut album *Street Talk,* Mattea still struggled. *Street Talk* "faded pretty quickly," to quote Andrew Vaughan in *Who's Who in New Country Music.* Its middle-of-the-road sound failed to find an audience; Mattea's future at Mercury might have been brief had she not been invited to open for country star George Strait in many of his road concerts.

Two events saved Mattea's career: her touring with

Strait and her decision to reach for a more traditional folk style. In retrospect, she calls the years between 1983 and 1986 "a subtle gift." She told the *News and Sun-Sentinel* that on the road with Strait, "I was able to learn things without the magnifying glass of the public eye focused on me during my formative years—and learning how to be an artist, not just a singer, takes time." Mattea did take her time and eventually returned to music that properly showcased her sonorous voice. When in 1986 she finally managed to place a song at the top of the country charts—"Love at the Five and Dime"—Mattea was already a seasoned performer. "Looking back on it," Mattea told the *Chicago Tribune,* "I'm really glad it has happened the way it has, because it feels more solid somehow. I've gotten to the point where I really want to do it the way I want to do it—and if that doesn't work, I'll just go find something else to do."

There is little chance Mattea will have to "find something else to do." The late 1980s saw her blossom into a major country entertainer with a string of top-ten hits and best-selling albums. She won the 1988 Single of the Year award from the Country Music Association (CMA) for "Eighteen Wheels and a Dozen Roses," and walked off with the CMA's Female Vocalist of the Year award the following two years in a row. No longer an opening act, Mattea now headlines her shows and is becoming known to a wider audience through invitations to prime-time television variety shows. Recent Mattea hits include "Walk the Way the Wind Blows,"

"Untold Stories," "Goin', Gone," and "Battle Hymn of Love."

Mattea does not rest on formula work, no matter how tempting it might be. One of her biggest hits in 1990 was "Where've You Been," a song written by her husband, Jon Vezner. "Where've You Been"—a stark departure from standard country fare—is a plaintive work about a loving husband and wife placed on different floors in a nursing home after 60 happy years of marriage. Mattea called her recording of the song—and its somber but hauntingly beautiful video—a "gamble," though she added: "People usually don't want to rock the boat, . . . but I feel it's important to always remember to take a risk if it make sense."

At this point in her career, Mattea can afford to gamble. Like country singers K. T. Oslin and Anne Murray, she is a performer whose appeal is grounded in a down-to-earth, friendly approach that has little to do with appearances. "I don't feel like what I do is a sexual thing," she said. "I don't have big cleavage, and I don't flaunt that. It's just not part of my schtick. I don't even think in terms of gender very much. I mean, I think of myself as a human being first, and I'm singing to other human beings."

News and Sun-Sentinel contributor Holly Gleason allowed that Mattea's voice "has grown stronger from extensive touring." Mattea's is one of the finer vocal instruments in modern country music, especially as she applies it with restraint and never seems to compete with her back-up arrangements. The singer's subject matter is also strong, ranging as it does from genial love ballads to deeper, more challenging efforts. Gleason concluded that the best work of Kathy Mattea "goes far beyond country's drinkin', cheatin' and weepin' songs to celebrate the depth of emotions and the complexities of real lives. . . . Mattea [makes music] that is anything but obvious, even as it celebrates themes that are so common."

Selected discography

Street Talk, Mercury, 1983.
From the Heart, Mercury, 1985.
Walk the Way the Wind Blows, Mercury, 1986.
Untasted Honey, Mercury, 1987.
Willow in the Wind, Mercury, 1989.
A Collection of Hits, Mercury, 1990.

Sources

Books

Vaughan, Andrew, *Who's Who in New Country Music,* St. Martin's, 1989.

Periodicals

Chicago Tribune, October 1, 1989.
News and Sun-Sentinel, March 17, 1989.
Philadelphia Inquirer, October 8, 1990.
St. Paul Pioneer Press, October 9, 1990.
Washington Post, May 9, 1990.

—Anne Janette Johnson

Aaron Neville

Singer

Aaron Neville is one of the most gifted members of New Orleans's talented Neville clan. With his pure, sweet voice—an unlikely match for his formidable physical appearance—he earned the family its first national fame, as well as its most recent exposure through his duets with pop singer Linda Ronstadt on her album *Cry Like a Rainstorm, Howl Like the Wind.*

Neville and his brothers Cyril, Charles, and Art had made a name for themselves in New Orleans's rhythm and blues circles by the mid-1950s. Art had formed a band during high school called the Hawketts, who in 1954 had a big regional hit with their recording of the Carnival song "Mardi Gras Mambo." Aaron, a member of the Hawketts, assumed leadership of the group when Art joined the U.S. Navy in 1958. That same year, however, Aaron was arrested for car theft and sentenced to six months in prison. While incarcerated "there was nothing to do but sing and fight," he told *Playboy* contributor Steve Pond, so he honed his skills at both. Upon his release Neville promptly married and landed a record contract as a solo artist. His first success was "Over You," recorded for Minit Records; it went to the Number 21 spot on the rhythm and blues charts.

Throughout the 1960s Neville recorded intermittently for many labels, including Instant, Parlo, Bell, and Safari. In 1966 Parlo released the ballad "Tell It Like It Is," which became a national Number 1 rhythm and blues hit and a national Number 2 pop hit. Due to an exploitive contract, however, Neville never received any royalties for the recording. Such dealings were common during those days, he told Pond: "You got paid for the session, and that was about it. . . . I had to take care of the family. I had jobs like longshoreman, truck driver, house painter. You name it, I done it, and sang on the weekends. I figured we ought to be able to get a big record out, but we never really did—at least that's what the record company told us. Later, [Rolling Stones guitarist] Keith Richards told me, 'I've been listening to you since the early Sixties.' And I said, 'They told me my records weren't gettin' no further than Baton Rouge.'"

Backed by a three-man rhythm section, Art and Aaron played together through much of the 1960s as the Neville Sounds, but in 1967 producer Allen Toussaint broke up that alliance by hiring Art and the rhythm section to perform as his house band, the Meters. Toussaint also recorded some of Aaron's work, but most of it was released only on small regional labels, if at all. Shortly thereafter Aaron went through a low period plagued by drugs, crime, and few professional singing engagements.

In 1975 all four Neville brothers reunited to back up the

Wild Tchoupitoulas, a musical tribe of "black indians" in flamboyant Mardi Gras costumes, led by the Nevilles' uncle George "Big Chief Jolly" Landry. Their album, *The Wild Tchoupitoulas,* was released on Island in 1976. While touring to support the album, the siblings began performing whole sets as the Neville Brothers, singing four-part harmonies. This led to an album deal with Capitol; unfortunately, the brothers were marketed as a disco act and their album flopped. About that time, however, Bette Midler heard them and worked hard to further their success. She helped win the Nevilles another contract in 1978, which resulted in an album that featured Aaron's quivering voice on the standards "Mona Lisa" and "Ten Commandments of Love." Despite wide praise, the album was a commercial failure and another record contract was soon broken.

Although their recording career was foundering, the Nevilles were touring nationally, opening for popular acts like Huey Lewis and the News and the Rolling Stones. Those appearances were climaxed by the brothers' transformation into the Wild Tchoupitoulas. Aaron Neville was also undergoing a personal transformation, replacing his dependence on drugs with a deep religious faith. In the late 1980s he worked with Ronstadt on *Cry Like a Rainstorm, Howl Like the Wind,* singing four duets. The tremendous success of these efforts set the stage for the Neville Brothers' own album, *Yellow Moon,* which, according to Pond "brilliantly summarized the Neville Brothers' social concerns and musical strengths."

Despite a hard life, Aaron Neville has retained a child-like enthusiasm for singing. Pond quoted producer Daniel Lanois: "He just loves to sing. . . . Aaron sees music as 'Oh, I love this country song, and I like that Bob Dylan song, and I'll happily sing a syrupy ballad.' There doesn't seem to be a difference in his mind. He's still innocent."

Selected discography

Singles

"Over You," Minit, 1959.
"Tell It Like It Is," Parlo, 1966.

Albums

With the Neville Brothers

The Wild Tchoupitoulas, Island, 1976.
The Neville Brothers, Capitol, 1978.
Fiyo on the Bayou, A & M, 1981.
Treacherous: A History of the Neville Brothers, 1955-1985, Rhino, 1985. *Yellow Moon,* A & M, 1989.
Brother's Keeper, A & M, 1990.

Solo LPs

Orchid in the Storm (EP), Rhino, reissue, 1990.
Greatest Hits, Curb/CEMA, 1990.
Golden Classics Tell It Like It Is, Collectibles.
The Classic Aaron Neville: My Greatest Gift, Rounder Records, 1990.

Also appeared on Linda Ronstadt's album *Cry Like a Rainstorm, Howl Like the Wind.*

Sources

down beat, June 1989.
Musician, October 1990.
People, June 12, 1989.
Playboy, July 1990.
Rolling Stone, July 2, 1987; April 20, 1989; December 14, 1989; August 9, 1990.

—Joan Goldsworthy

Ric Ocasek

Singer, songwriter, guitarist

Singer-songwriter Ric Ocasek has been making hits since 1978. With the New Wave/rock group the Cars, he has been responsible for smashes such as "Just What I Needed," "My Best Friend's Girl," and "Shake It Up." In addition, Ocasek has released two successful solo albums; the latter, *This Side of Paradise,* included the hit single "Emotion in Motion." He has also appeared in films, such as director John Waters's *Hairspray.*

Ocasek, who keeps his age something of a secret, was born Richard Otcasek circa 1949 in Baltimore, Maryland. As a child, he loved the music of rock pioneer Buddy Holly, and he was encouraged in this by his grandmother, who presented him with a guitar when he was ten. Like many other children given similar presents, Ocasek took lessons on the instrument for a while, and then grew bored. As he told Lisa Robinson in *Interview* magazine, he had a relatively calm early adolescence in Baltimore, "with the crowd who were into electronics and good grades."

But when Ocasek was sixteen, his father got a job with the National Aeronautics and Space Administration (NASA) in Cleveland, Ohio, and at first the young man had a difficult time adjusting to the Midwest because of his strikingly different appearance. "I got punched in the face the very first day of school," he told Robinson. "Knocked on the floor. For nothing. Just because I had my hair dyed blond. . . . See, it was a trend in Baltimore to dye your hair blond in the front. . . . Anyway, people stared at me a lot because I was tall and skinny, but later on, it worked to my advantage."

But before Ocasek began to attract attention in the music world, he first tried college, attending both Bowling Green State University and Antioch College. By the late 1960s, however, he had had enough of higher education. As he explained to Jon Pareles in *Rolling Stone,* Ocasek returned to his efforts with the guitar, and in addition, he "started immediately writing; I thought that was the thing to do. . . . After I started writing songs I figured it would be good to start a band. Sometimes I'd put together a band just to hear my songs."

While Ocasek was rehearsing with one such band in Columbus, Ohio, he made the acquaintance of vocalist and bass player Ben Orr. The two hit it off, and Ocasek invited Orr to join his band. Together they enjoyed a small measure of local success, opening concerts in midwestern college towns for fading groups such as MC5 and the Stooges. Emboldened by such gigs, they decided to try their luck in New York City, but were largely unsuccessful. After a short return to the Midwest, Ocasek took off for Boston. When he had assessed that city's musical climate, he called Orr and told him that he should relocate there as well. Together

For the Record. . .

Name originally Richard Otcasek; born c. 1949 in Baltimore, Maryland; father was a computer analyst for NASA; currently married to Paulina Porizkova (a model and actress); *children:* (from former marriage(s)/liasons) several, including son, Christopher. *Education:* Attended Bowling Green State University and Antioch College.

Worked odd jobs, including steel mill worker, selling business forms, and selling clothing; played in various bands during the late 1960s and early 1970s, including Leatherwood, Milkwood, and Cap'n Swing; member of the Cars, c. 1976-1988; solo recording artist, 1982—. Has appeared in films, including *Hairspray* and *Made in Heaven.*

Awards: The Cars received a Grammy Award as best new group of the year in 1978.

Addresses: *Record company*—Geffen Records, 3300 Warner Blvd., Burbank, CA 91510.

they went through various bands, changing names and personnel with some frequency. At one time Ocasek and Orr constituted two-thirds of a folk trio called Milkwood, which was successful enough to release an album on Paramount in 1972. During roughly the same period, Ocasek also met fellow musician Greg Hawkes, who played with him and Orr very briefly before seeking out a better-paid band.

By 1976, Ocasek and Orr had started yet another band, this one called Cap'n Swing. For this vehicle they managed to discover, among others, lead guitarist Elliot Easton; with him, Ocasek and Orr felt confident enough to make another attempt on New York City. When they had failed yet again to attract the notice of record producers, they returned to Boston, where Ocasek fired everyone from Cap'n Swing except himself, Orr, and Easton. He managed to lure Hawkes back, and also recruited drummer David Robinson. At last, the Cars were formed.

The band made their professional debut at a New Year's Eve party in New Hampshire; by March of 1977 they were playing the better punk venues of Boston, notably the Rathskeller, and they received the opportunity to open a concert for rock artist Bob Seger. More opening opportunities followed, along with better club dates in the Boston area. Finally, a song from one of their demo tapes, "Just What I Needed," became so popular on two Boston radio stations that record companies began seeking them out. Ocasek and the Cars

had signed with Elektra by the time 1977 came to a close.

Their self-titled debut album was released in 1978, winning praise from fans and critics alike, and causing the Cars to capture that year's Grammy Award for best new group. Through the 1980s, other hits followed "Just What I Needed," including "My Best Friend's Girl," "Magic," "You Might Think," and "Drive," most of them written by Ocasek. He and the Cars also gained a reputation for making creative videos to accompany their hits, and these received a great deal of airplay on video channels such as MTV. After releasing the album *Door to Door,* which included the hit "You Are the Girl," the Cars broke up in 1988.

But Ocasek had already begun to turn his attention to solo projects long before. In 1982 he released *Beatitude,* which Mark Coleman described in *Rolling Stone* as "a set of arty oddities." Though the disc received some favorable critical comment, it did not sell well. Ocasek fared better with fans on his 1986 solo effort, *This Side of Paradise,* which featured the hit single, "Emotion in Motion." Ironically, some critics saw this album as insubstantial compared with Ocasek's previous work; Coleman complained that "where the Cars push their loves songs through cynical twists and sharp turns, Ocasek gets stuck in romantic glop." Robinson, however, praised both *Beatitude* and *This Side of Paradise* as "hauntingly beautiful."

Ocasek has also produced records for other groups and musicians, including the New Models and the Bad Brains, and he has enjoyed the small film roles he's had, including portraying an aging beatnik in *Hairspray* and a junkyard owner in *Made in Heaven.* He told Robinson that he doesn't "want to do that rock-star-turning actor bit," but that he'd "love to play some weird character things" in the future.

Selected discography

Albums with the Cars; on Elektra

The Cars (includes "Just What I Needed," "Good Times Roll," and "My Best Friend's Girl"), 1978.
Candy-O, 1979.
Panorama, 1980.
Shake It Up (includes "Shake It Up" and "Since You're Gone"), 1981.
Heartbeat City (includes "You Might Think" and "Magic"), 1984.
Door to Door (includes "You Are the Girl"), 1988.

Solo albums

Beatitude, Geffen, 1982.
This Side of Paradise (includes "Emotion in Motion"), Geffen, 1986.

Other

(With Milkwood) *Milkwood,* Paramount, 1972.

Sources

Interview, March 1987.
People, November 3, 1986.
Rolling Stone, January 25, 1979; November 20, 1986.
Stereo Review, February 1988.

—Elizabeth Wenning

Charlie Parker

Saxophonist, composer, arranger

Proclaimed the "Mozart of Jazz" by prominent jazz critic Barry Ulanov, Charles "Yardbird" Parker represents one of the most influential figures in the history of American music. Like the great classical composer, Parker was a musical genius who died in his mid-thirties without widespread acclaim or national recognition. Despite his lack of popular audience, Yardbird—or Bird as he was more affectionately called—was idolized by many musicians, intellectuals, and enthusiasts. It was from these elite circles of disciples that Parker ascended to the height of deification after his death. "Music is your own experience, if you don't live it, it won't come out of your horn," he lamented. Ironically, Parker's life became a struggle to balance his often reckless and self-destructive personal experiences with the gift of musical vision.

Charlie Parker was born on August 29, 1920, to Addie and Charles Parker in Kansas City, Kansas. At the age of seven he moved with his family to Kansas City, Missouri, a short distance from the nightclubs and dance halls where a new style of jazz was flourishing. Although Parker played baritone horn in the high school band, it wasn't until he was fifteen that he displayed a strong interest in music and passion for the alto saxophone. Not long afterward he joined the Deans of Swing led by pianist Lawrence Keyes.

Parker received his early musical tutelage in Kansas City nightclubs, listening to such saxophone giants as Lester Young, Johnny Hoges, and Leon "Chu" Berry. Around 1935 he decided to leave school in search of a full-time musical apprenticeship. In the year that followed, Parker faced humiliation at a jam session at the Reno Club, where Count Basie performed. After blowing a couple of faltering choruses, drummer Jo Jones signaled the end of the amateur performance by hurling his cymbal at Parker's feet. (This incident was vividly portrayed in the 1988 Warner Bros. film *Bird*.) It was also in this period that the young altoist began to experiment with drugs and alcohol. Commenting years later, Parker attributed his later heroin addiction to "being introduced too early to nightclub life."

Between the years 1936 and 1937, Parker traveled to the Ozarks to work with the bands of Ernie Daniels, George E. Lee and "Professor" Buster Smith. In the Ozarks, Parker spent long hours woodshedding—memorizing two saxophone solos of Lester Young from phonograph records. It was from Lee's rhythm guitarist, Efferge Ware, that he learned the cycle of fifths and advanced chord patterns.

Returning to Kansas City, Parker re-emerged a much more confident, or in his words, "coordinated" musician. In 1938, he joined pianist Jay McShann's band for a few months before his drug habit led to his dismissal.

A year later, he made his way to Chicago, where he astounded listeners with his fiery alto solos. At a club located on 55th Street, the bedraggled Parker sat in at a breakfast dance where Billy Eckstine was in attendance. "He blew so much," recalled Eckstine, "until he upset everybody in the place."

Parker's next destination was New York. Failing to find work with his horn, he washed dishes at Jimmy's Chicken Shack, where the brilliant pianist Art Tatum performed in the front room. He befriended guitarist Biddy Fleet, whose musical instruction expanded Parker's knowledge of harmonic theory. One evening while performing at the Chili House, he experienced a revelation. "I found by using high intervals of a chord as a melody line and backing them with appropriately related changes. I could play the thing I'd been hearing. I came alive."

Shortly after Parker returned to Kansas City to attend the funeral of his father, he joined Harlan Leonard's Rockets. During his five months with Leonard, he was introduced to the band's extremely talented pianist and arranger, Tadd Dameron. He rejoined McShann in 1939, and was put in charge of the reed section. While not performing with McShann's blues-based ensemble, Parker rehearsed and organized jam sessions. In his four years with McShann, he was a featured soloist on several recordings, including "Hootie Blues," "Sepian Bounce" and the 1941 rhythm-and-blues hit, "Confessin' the Blues." "Bird had crying soul," recalled McShann, who later designated the year's alto saxophonist as the "greatest blues player in the world."

While on tour with McShann in New York in 1942, Parker performed at jam sessions held at Monroe's and Minton's Playhouse in Harlem, where he attracted the notice of such modernists as trumpeter Dizzy Gillespie and pianist Thelonious Monk. That same year his worsening drug addiction led to his final break with McShann. In December, Parker began an eight-month stint blowing tenor with Earl Hines—providing him with the opportunity to appear with he progressive talents of Gillespie, Benny Harris and singer Sarah Vaughan. Although he greatly admired Parker's musicianship, Hines possessed little tolerance for his erratic lifestyle. "He was a fine boy and there was nothing wrong with him when it came to character," commented Hines, "all the harm he did he did to himself."

In 1944, Billy Eckstine brought together many of the veterans of the Hines ensemble to form one of the most innovative big bands of the period. Eckstine sent for Parker, who was in Chicago performing with Noble Sissle. Eckstine, like Hines, was astounded by Parker's genius for improvisation and "photographic memory" for learning arrangements. "Bird was so full of spontaneity," exclaimed Eckstine, "it just . . . Boom! . . . came out!" After his short stay with Eckstine, Parker performed at the Three Deuces on 52nd Street with Dizzy and saxophonist Ben Webber as well as a group including nineteen-year-old Miles Davis. According to Gillespie, the Dizzy-Parker collaboration was a "meeting of the minds." Their powerful unison work laid the foundation for modern jazz—or "be-bop" (a label that Parker greatly despised).

Throughout 1945 Parker recorded with Clyde Hart and guitarist Tiny Grimes. Leading his own group on the Savoy label, Parker also recorded the compositions "Billie's Bounce," "Thriving from a Riff," "Now's the Time" and the furiously executed "Ko Ko." A few weeks later, he appeared at Billy Berg's in Hollywood. Save for a few devoted followers, their be-bop invasion of the west received a harsh reception from patrons and critics. Parker's increasing absences prompted Gillespie to hire a replacement (Dizzy admitted years later that his decision did not effect his relationship with Parker).

Soon afterward, Parker toured with Norman Granz's

Jazz at the Philharmonic series—an engagement that put him on the same bandstand with Gillespie and Lester Young. In March 1946, Parker recorded for Ross Russel's newly founded Dial label, which included the arrangements "Yardbird Suite," "Ornithology," "Mouse the Mooche" and Gillespie's "Night in Tunisia." On the West Coast Parker's life took a serious downturn. Years of drug abuse, artistic disillusionment and failed marriages drove him to near-collapse. Following the session of "Lover Man," he suffered a nervous breakdown and was committed to Camarillo State Hospital, where he underwent psychiatric treatment for six months.

Returning east in 1947, Parker began his most innovative, or "classic" period. For the next few years he retained a level of stability—touring the U.S. and Europe with his own quintet (that most often included Miles Davis, bassist Tommy Potter, drummer Max Roach and pianist Duke Jordan). His unique sense of melody and rhythmic accents had a immense impact on all the instruments of modern jazz. Max Roach explained that he began using new variations on the drums to keep up

---

In his thirty-four years, Parker not only brought the art of improvisation to a new height, but helped found an entire modern school of jazz.

---

with Parker's breakneck tempos. Although critics still scoffed at him, Parker emerged in the late 1940s as the most influential jazz musician in the country.

Parker first traveled abroad in 1949 to perform at the Paris Jazz Festival, where he was hailed by crowds of enthusiastic followers. During the course of the year, he recorded "Bird with Strings"—an effort that fused his deep admiration for classical and modern composers with his blues and swing background. Although it became his biggest seller, it was not without its critics. "Some of my friends said . . . Bird is getting commercial. That wasn't it at all," asserted Parker, "I was looking for new sound combinations." Between 1948 and 1950, his artistic search for new forms of expression inspired him to record several Afro-Cuban sides with Machito's orchestra.

Parker's life, like his music, became unpredictable, often lacking the effusive spirit of his earlier work. In order to control his drug addiction he drank to excess—causing a severe ulcer attack that hospitalized him.

Disputes, debts, absences and inconsistent performances often forced club owners to hire him to play one show or a single set. In 1953, Parker led his last significant recording session, which contained "Chi Chi," "I Remember You," "Now's the Time" and "Confirmation."

Throughout the remainder of his career, Parker worked without a regular group—often performing with sidemen of varying talent as well as pick-up bands that often failed to provide him with adequate accompaniment. Following a disastrous performance with strings at Birdland (the club named in his honor) in 1954, he attempted suicide and was admitted to Bellevue Psychiatric Hospital. In October of that year, Parker recaptured a glimpse of his earlier prowess by performing brilliantly at the Town Hall Concert. In his final months, Parker lived in Greenwich Village, appearing occasionally at a club called the Open Door. Jazz writer Leonard Feather, who encountered Parker around this time, described him as "bloated" and "raggedly dressed," possessing "desperately sad eyes."

In his last public appearance, on March 4, 1955, Parker took the stage with Charles Mingus, Bud Powell, Kenny Dorham and Art Blakey. After a bitter verbal exchange with Powell, Parker got drunk and left the club. On Wednesday of the following week he died in the apartment of jazz disciple Baroness Pannonica "Nica" de Koenigswarter. In his thirty-four years, Parker not only brought the art of improvisation to a new height, but helped found an entire modern school of jazz. His life became a model for a postwar subculture that envisaged him as a god-like figure who broke with social and artistic tradition. "As with Mozart, the facts of Charlie Parker's life make little sense because they fail to explain his music," wrote Gary Giddings.

But Parker knew no boundaries in art or life—for Parker they were synonymous in his search for new avenues of expression and escape. His saxophone became the voice that delivered him from torment. "I was amazed how Bird changed the minute he put his horn in his mouth," observed Miles Davis. "He went from looking real down and out to having all this power and beauty just bursting out of him." Despite his personal travails, the power and beauty of his music remains.

Selected discography

(With Jay McShann) *First Recordings* (contains broadcast, private, and studio recordings, 1940-45), Xanadu ORI 221.
The Complete Savoy Sessions (studio recordings, 1944-48)), Savoy SJ5 5500.
Bird at the Royal Roost (recorded 1944), Savoy SJL-1108.

Charlie Parker on Dial, Vol. 1 (1946 studio recording), Spotlite.

Charlie Parker on Dial, Vol. 2 (1947 studio recording), Spotlite.

Bird: The Complete Charlie Parker on Verve (boxed set; contains 176 performances), Verve 837141-2.

The Verve Years, 1952-54, Verve VE-2-2523.

Bird with Strings, Columbia, 1951.

The Essential Charlie Parker, Verve V-6 8409.

Bird/The Savoy Recordings (master takes), Savoy SJ 2201.

Sources

Books

Bird: The Legend of Charlie Parker, edited by Robert Reisner, Da Capo Press, 1962.

Dance, Stanley, *The World of Earl Hines: An Oral History*, Scribner, 1977.

Davis, Miles, with Quincy Troupe, *The Autobiography of Miles Davis*, Simon and Schuster, 1989.

Feather, Leonard, *Inside Be-Bop* (second edition), Da Capo Press, 1980.

Feather, Leonard, *The Jazz Years: Eyewitness to an Era*, Da Capo Press, 1987.

Feather, Leonard, *The New Encyclopedia of Jazz*, Horizon Press, 1960.

Koch, Lawrence, *Yardbird Suite: A Compendium of the Music and Life of Charlie Parker*, Green State University Popular Press, 1988.

Giddins, Gary, *Celebrating Bird: The Triumph of Charlie Parker*, Beech Tree Books, 1987.

Gillespie, Dizzy, with Al Fraser, *To Be or Not to Bop: Memoirs*, Double.

Gitler, Ira, *Jazz Masters of the Forties*, Cullier Books, 1966.

Hear Me Talkin' to Ya: The Story of Jazz as Told By the Men Who Made It, edited by Nat Shapiro and Nat Hentoff, Dover, 1966.

Periodicals

down beat, April 20, 1953.

Liner Notes

The Essential Charlie Parker, written by Don Cerulli, Verve V6-8409.

—*John Cohassey*

Tom Paxton

Singer, songwriter, guitarist

Folk singer-songwriter Tom Paxton "belongs to that tradition of great American artists like [twentieth-century novelists] Sinclair Lewis and Sherwood Anderson who expose the flaws of [the United States] and its people through descriptions, not sermons," declared Loraine Alterman in the *New York Times*. In addition to satiric gems, ranging from "The Dogs of Alabama" to "I'm Changing My Name to Chrysler," Paxton has penned and recorded milder folk ballads, including "The Marvelous Toy," "Bottle of Wine," and "The Last Thing on My Mind." Though he has enjoyed a long, fruitful recording career in his own right, many of his compositions have reached wider audiences as performed by other artists, such as Dolly Parton, Judy Collins, John Denver, The Kingston Trio, and Neil Diamond.

Paxton was born on Halloween in 1937, in Chicago, Illinois. As a boy his primary interest was sports, but he credits his family's history with instilling the background he would later bring to his songwriting. According to an interview Paxton gave Mark Taylor in the *Guardian,* he is a descendant of one of the judges who condemned accused tyrant King Charles I of England to death. And as a boy in New Mexico, Paxton's father found an eagle feather that was later made into the pen that signed New Mexico into statehood. "That pen is now in the museum at Santa Fe," Paxton told Taylor. "Maybe this is what gave me my absorbing interest in history, particularly American history."

When Paxton was about eleven years old his family moved to Bristow, Oklahoma. By the time the youngster attended high school he had abandoned sports for the dream of becoming an actor. He also demonstrated musical talent, playing trumpet in the school band. When Paxton was sixteen, an aunt presented him with a guitar. Though he showed skill with the instrument, the guitar did not replace Paxton's desire to act, which led him to pursue a career in drama at the University of Oklahoma. While there, however, Paxton was introduced to the folk sounds of Pete Seeger, Burl Ives, Woody Guthrie, and Ed McCurdy through the records of his fellow students. Recalling the experience for Wayne Robins in *Newsday,* Paxton explained: "What attracted me to folk was that it wasn't like all the popular music on the radio. It had another dimension to it other than formula music." He began trying to play some of the things he heard, wrote his own material, and eventually performed for his friends. By the time he graduated and landed a lead role in a Colorado summer stock production, Paxton realized that he would rather be a folk singer than an actor.

After a brief stint in the U.S. Army, Paxton traveled to New York City's Greenwich Village in 1960 to become

For the Record. . .

Full name Thomas R. Paxton; born October 31, 1937, in Chicago, IL; son of George Burton Paxton and Esther Paxton; married Margaret Ann Cummings, August 5, 1963; children: Jennifer Ann, Katherine Claire. *Education:* University of Oklahoma, B.F.A., 1959.

Songwriter, performer, and recording artist, c. 1964—. Stage actor, c. 1959; performed in small clubs during the early 1960s. Appeared on television shows, including *Today, The Tonight Show,* and *60 Minutes.* Served in the U.S. Army, c. 1960.

Addresses: *Home*—East Hampton, Long Island, NY. *Record company*—Flying Fish Records, 1304 W. Schubert, Chicago, IL 60614.

part of its growing folk music scene. There he mingled with folk greats Joan Baez and Bob Dylan, and even shared an apartment with Paul Stookey of the famed trio Peter, Paul, and Mary. Like them, he performed in small clubs, including the Gaslight, which recorded his first album. During 1961 and 1962 Paxton toured folk clubs throughout the United States. Some of his songs were gaining reputations through recordings by major folk artists—Paxton's "Ramblin' Boy" became a hit for the Weavers, and "The Marvelous Toy" showed up in the repertoires of both the Chad Mitchell Trio and Peter, Paul, and Mary. Finally, Paxton himself landed a major contract with Elektra. He began releasing his own albums, including *Ramblin' Boy* in 1964 and *Ain't That News* in 1965.

Despite the decline in folk music's popularity during the late 1960s and 1970s, Paxton's output continued fairly steadily. He wrote and recorded songs about subjects such as the Vietnam War and Watergate, and composed Elizabethan-flavored love ballads like "My Lady's a Wild Flying Dove," which the *Guardian*'s Taylor lauded for possessing "all the lilt and cadences . . . that characterize the oldest folk songs." Paxton also penned tunes for children, including "Going to the Zoo" and "Jennifer's Rabbit." Capitalizing on a resurgence of the folk genre in England, Paxton moved there with his family for a few years during the 1970s and recorded for the Reprise label. Upon his return to the States, he signed with Vanguard. His 1977 release on Vanguard,

New Songs from the Briar Patch, discussed weighty topics such as strip mining and capital punishment, and included a song of requiem for the late president of Chile, Salvador Allende.

Heroes followed in 1978 with a lampoon of anti-gay protester Anita Bryant and a tribute to South African activist Stephen Biko. Paxton switched to Mountain Railroad Records to release *The Paxton Report* in 1980. He later published a children's book based on one of his songs, *Jennifer's Rabbit.*

Selected discography

Ramblin' Boy, Elcktra, 1964.
Ain't That News, Elektra, 1965.
Outward Bound, Elektra, 1966.
Morning Again, Elektra, 1968.
The Things I Notice Now, Elektra, 1969.
Number 6, Elektra, 1970.
The Compleat Tom Paxton, Elektra, 1971.
How Come the Sun, Reprise, 1971.
Peace Will Come, Reprise, 1972.
New Songs for Old Friends, Reprise, 1973.
Something in My Life, Private Stock, 1975.
New Songs from the Briar Patch (includes "Talking Watergate," "Bring Back the Chair," and "White Bones of Allende"), Vanguard, 1977.
Heroes (includes "Lucy, the Junk Dealer's Daughter"), Vanguard, 1978.
Up and Up, Mountain Railroad, 1980.
The Paxton Report (includes "We All Sound the Same," "All Clear in Harrisburg," "I'm Changing My Name to Chrysler," and "I Thought You Were an A-Rab"), Mountain Railroad, 1980.
One Million Lawyers . . . and Other Disasters, Flying Fish, 1986.
The Marvelous Toy and Other Gallimaufry, Flying Fish, 1987.
Even a Gray Day, Flying Fish.
And Loving You, Flying Fish, 1987.

Also released an album on Gaslight Club Records, c. 1961.

Sources

Guardian, February 5, 1966.
Newsday, August 14, 1981.
New York Times, October 24, 1971.

—Elizabeth Wenning

Pet Shop Boys

British pop duo

The Pet Shop Boys became world-recognized pop stars in 1986 with the huge success of their debut album *Please,* which featured the chart-topping dance hits "West End Girls" and "(Opportunities) Let's Make Lots of Money." Since then vocalist Neil Tennant and keyboardist Chris Lowe have maintained a steady stream of danceable hits, "crafting some splendidly catchy, intelligent pure pop records," wrote Kris Kirk in *Melody Maker.* The British duo has forged a unique brand of Euro-beat dance music, combining infectious synthesized melodies with intelligent lyrics that have been described as cynical and melancholic. Stephen Holden in the *New York Times* remarked on the "sophistication" of the Pet Shop Boys, "whose angular melodies and thoughtful lyrics transcend ordinary dance pop." Harold DeMuir in *Creem* called their sound "a curious blend of sincerity and archness . . . [which] manages to sound simultaneously effervescent and morose."

The Pet Shop Boys' popular music videos are styled appropriately to their world-weary musical tone; DeMuir explained that they "generally contain as little actual

physical movement as possible," which promotes a "dour, minimalist image." The reasoning behind the video concept, according to lead singer Tennant, is to avoid the "false enthusiasm" of other pop performances. "We're suspicious of all that rock tradition, and we don't want to fall into all the usual cliches," he told DeMuir. "We don't do that kind of recording you could mime a guitar solo to, or do a [now-defunct British pop duo] Wham! dance routine to. We're also a bit self-conscious, which is probably more important." Some critics have called the Pet Shop Boys the "perfect" pop group. "If we're talking elements, the Pet Shop Boys've got 'em," wrote Sylvie Simmons in *Creem*. "A group that manages to be naive and sophisticated, sincere and insincere, cheery and miserable all at the same time."

The Pet Shop Boys followed a somewhat unlikely path to pop music stardom. When Tennant and Lowe met in a Chelsea stereo shop in 1981, both were synthesizer hobbyists pursuing non-music careers. Tennant had been a book editor in London and was about to join the music magazine *Smash Hits;* Lowe was training at Liverpool University to become a professional architect. After discovering that they shared similar tastes in dance music, the two began writing songs together. Lowe says there was never a conscious effort to form a group. "I always used to spend a lot of time messing around on the piano at home, and Neil did the same on his guitar," he told DeMuir. "We were just interested in music, and it seemed to develop and take off by itself." Tennant, on the other hand, had always wanted to be a pop star or actor. As a youth he was involved in local theater and played in a band. Tennant grew up in a suburb of Newcastle, England, where, according to Michael Goldberg in *Rolling Stone,* he "saw both pop music and the theater as a way to escape the boredom of his life in suburbia—a theme that dominates *Please.*"

Tennant was in New York City in 1983 to interview pop singer Sting for *Smash Hits* when he met Bobby Orlando, a well-known disco music producer whom Tennant and Lowe admired. Orlando liked what he heard of the Pet Shop Boys—their name was coined by a pet shop employee friend—and soon both Tennant and Lowe were in New York recording a version of "West End Girls" for Orlando; the single would initially achieve only minor success in Europe. After a contract dispute with Orlando, the Boys signed with EMI in 1985 and began recording songs for *Please*. Their first release, "(Opportunities) Let's Make Lots of Money" flopped in England, thought it would later become a hit there. Undaunted, the duo decided to release "West End Girls" in the U.S. The recording took off this time; the Pet Shop Boys soon found they had a Number-One single on their hands and were famous on both sides of the Atlantic. "(Opportunities)" also reached Number One upon its re-release and the Pet Shop Boys have since produced a number of chart-topping dance records. Included among them are "What Have I Done to Deserve This," featuring British vocalist Dusty Springfield, and a neo-disco version of the Elvis Presley recording later made popular by country singer Willie Nelson, "You Were Always on My Mind."

Despite their success, and in fact, because of it, the Pet Shop Boys have had to contend with being called "calculated," a description owing to their respective career backgrounds. Tennant, sometimes referred to as another "pop-journalist-want-to-be-musician," has commented on this enduring misconception. He told Simmons: "There was some reviewer that described us as 'clever pop strategists,' whatever that means. People think that, because I was a journalist and all the rest of it—and because Chris was an architect—that we're very clever. Everything's very, very well thought out and planned down to the last detail, and we're quite cynical about it and have a clever mix of different kinds of music. . . . The truth of the matter is that we write songs that we like the sound of." Tennant also discounted the influence of his work as a music editor. "A lot of rock journalists—and I was exactly the same—often have a complete misunderstanding of what it's like for a group in the music business," he told Goldberg. "I didn't really learn anything on that score from being a rock journalist."

The Pet Shop Boys are very controlled about their image, however, and take pains to distinguish themselves from other music groups. Their first live tour—in

1989—came after years of planning and was a stage extravaganza that featured an emotionless Tennant and Lowe, in addition to a cast of dancers—some dressed as babies and pigs—elaborate costumes, and props including massive dolls. "We're doing it like this because it's what we want," Tennant was quoted in *Melody Maker* at the time of the show's premiere. "It's how we want Pet Shop Boys to be presented. We always try to present ourselves as being separate from everyone else." *This* measure of calculation seems to be essential Pet Shop Boys. A *Melody Maker* reviewer, commenting on their stage show, wrote: "Tennant's lexicon of taste is conspicuously critical; that's to say he's objective, distant, dry, he believes he knows what ought to be. Consequently nothing about the Pet Shop Boys live happens by accident, there's no spontaneity." The reviewer added, however: "Tennant . . . looked amazing, looked distant, looked liked he'd never met anyone. He wore a long, white fur coat, diamante broaches and a smile like Robert Morely in 'Theatre of Blood,' the very picture of privilege and depravity. He *was* the Pet Shop Boys."

Selected discography

"West End Girl" (single), Bobcat Records, 1984.
Please (includes "West End Girls," "(Opportunities) Let's Make Lots of Money," and "Love Comes Quickly"), EMI, 1986.
Actually (includes "It's a Sin" and "What Have I Done to Deserve This"), EMI, 1987.
Introspective (includes "Domino Dancing" and "You Were Always on My Mind"), EMI, 1988.
Behavior, EMI, 1990.

Sources

Creem, September 1986; January 1988.
Melody Maker, February 2, 1986; January 3, 1987; July 11, 1987; October 3, 1987; May 13, 1989; July 15, 1989; July 22, 1989.
New York Times, November 7, 1990.
Rolling Stone, October 23, 1986; December 18, 1986/January 1, 1987.

—*Michael E. Mueller*

Sam Phillips

Record company executive

There will always be debates as to who was the first rock and roller; Chuck Berry or Elvis Presley, Bill Haley or Bo Diddley, etc., etc. But the "Father" of the genre will always be recognized as Sam Phillips, the man whose Sun Records launched the careers of Presley, Jerry Lee Lewis, Carl Perkins, Roy Orbison, and a smattering of blues artists during the 1950s. "There can be little doubt that Sam Phillips played the crucial role of midwife in the birth of the new music," wrote Robert Palmer in *Rolling Stone*. Indeed, there can be no doubt about it.

Seemingly enough, Phillips's discovery of rock began with its very roots: blues. He was born in Alabama and raised on a plantation hearing black singers on radio station WDIA. He decided at an early age that the music would consume his life and worked toward giving back to its creators the recognition they deserved. Phillips worked at radio station WLAY during high school and after graduating from college was employed at WREC in Memphis in 1944 as an announcer. Bored with the type of music they featured, he saved enough money to start the Memphis Recording Services in a converted radiator shop located at 706 Union.

Phillips hand-built the studio that was so small he had to use a neighboring coffee shop for his office. The studio's motto was "We record anything—anywhere—anytime" but the bulk of their income came from a $2-per-side recording service and their wedding ceremony recordings. But Phillips's main ambition was the recording of black blues musicians who would otherwise have to travel to Chicago or New York to get on wax. He leased to Chess and Modern/RPM the aluminum masters of Howlin' Wolf, Walter Horton, Rufus Thomas, Little Milton, Elmore James, James Cotton and B.B. King among others. "When Leonard Chess came down here and promised him [Howlin' Wolf] the moon, it broke my heart. This was one of the things that made me want to start my own label," Phillips is quoted in *The Listener's Guide To The Blues*.

One of the big hits that enabled Phillips to quit his job at WREC was Jackie Brentson's "Rocket 88" (with Ike Turner's band backing) of 1951. With its theme of cars/girls and a big beat, it is cited by many as the first rock and roll tune ever. The tune is also probably the first recorded example of the distorted guitar sound popularized a decade later on the Rolling Stone's hit, "Satisfaction." On the way to the session one of the amplifiers fell off of Turner's car, rupturing the speaker cone. In an effort to save time, the ever-creative Phillips stuffed paper inside the box and carried on with the recording.

B.B. King's "Three O'Clock Blues" and Little Walter's "Juke" offered further proof that Phillips could make it with a legitimate label and thus Sun Records was formed in 1952. The first single, "Bear Cat," by WDIA disc jockey Rufus Thomas, went all the way to Number 3, and an ensuing lawsuit by Peacock Records for copyright infringement also helped to give Sun some notoriety. According to Robert Palmer in *Rolling Stone*, Phillips was fond of saying, "If you aren't doing something different, you aren't doing anything." Phillips was constantly searching for a unique sound which he felt was out there just waiting to be unleashed. "Over and over I remember Sam saying, 'If I could find a white man who had the Negro sound and the Negro feel, I could make a billion dollars,'" Marion Keisker, officer manager at Sun, told *The Rolling Stone Illustrated History of Rock & Roll*.

In the summer of 1953 a truck-driving teenager from Tupelo, Mississippi, named Elvis Presley entered the Sun studios and plopped down $3.98 to record two songs for his mother, "My Happiness" and "That's When Your Heartaches Begin." He left his name and number with Keisker in case they needed someone to sing sometime. She made a note about his voice and filed it away. "I'd run across a ballad written by a prisoner in the Tennessee State pen and I wanted a

For the Record...

Born in Florence, Alabama, January 5, 1923; married; wife's name, Becky; children: Knox, Jerry.

Created Memphis Recording Service in 1950, started Sun label in 1952; discovered and recorded some of rock music's earliest stars, including Elvis Presley, Roy Orbison, and Jerry Lee Lewis, as well as country stars Johnny Cash and Carl Perkins; sold Sun Records in 1969; an original shareholder in Holiday Inn chain; owns several radio stations.

crooner," Phillips said in *Rock 100*. And, according to *Rolling Stone*, Keisker offered, "What about that kid with the sideburns?" As Presley reported in *Honkers & Shouters*, Phillips phoned him and said, "'You want to make some blues?. . .' All I know is I hung up and ran fifteen blocks to Mr. Phillips's office before he'd gotten off the line—or so he tells me." "Elvis toyed around with it. I decided he needed a couple of good rhythm men back of him so I called Scotty [Moore] and Bill [Black] and still nothing happened," Phillips continued in *Rock 100*. "Then I got the notion of trying some of the old 'Big Boy' Cruddup material. Although it seemed incomprehensible to have a white man do those songs, I just got a notion and I called Elvis. . . . When we cut, things happened. I said right then, 'That's it.' I knew we had a hit."

History is clouded though, as Moore (who had been trying to get Phillips to record his Starlight Wranglers band) said "That's All Right" started out as some horsing around by Presley which prompted Moore and bassist Bill Black to jump in. The singer had been trying to cover "I Love You Because" in the style of the era's popular vocalist but it just wasn't working. Whether it was a calculated attempt or a fluke, "Phillips knew immediately that what another producer might have taken for a bit of lighthearted country clowning, a break from the serious work, was in fact one of the most serious cultural events of the 20th century," wrote Palmer in *Rolling Stone*.

WHBQ's Dewey Phillips played Presley's jumped-up Cruddup cover on his "Red, Hot and Blue" radio show and the reaction was phenomenal. At one point he played the song thirty times in one night. Between August 1954 and August 1955 Presley recorded 10 more sides for Sun, including "Good Rockin' Tonight," "Milkcow Blues Boogie," "Baby Let's Play House" and the flip side to "That's All Right," "Blue Moon of Kentucky." After listeners realized that Presley wasn't black, his popularity soared and brought a host of record

companies to Phillips's door wanting to sign the sensation.

In November of 1955 RCA's Steve Sholes bought Presley's contract and masters for $35,000 plus $5,000 in back royalties and Hill & Range Songs purchased publications of Hi-Lo Music (a Sun subsidiary) for $15,000 from Phillips. At the time it was an unprecedented amount for a relatively unproven newcomer, but in hindsight it seems like the steal of the century. Phillips, however, figured he could develop five more Presleys with the cash and set about to form his roster.

Carl Perkins joined the Sun lineup and released two singles in 1953 and 1954, "Turn Around" and "Let The Juke Box Keep On Playing," with mild success. But a year later Perkins and Phillips produced a major hit with "Blue Suede Shoes." Released on New Year's Day, the song soared to Number 5 on *Billboard*'s national charts while simultaneously scoring on the R & B and country charts as well (the first song to ever accomplish the feat). Perkins followed with more fine songs for Phillips

> *Phillips will be always be recognized as one of the innovators in the history of popular music*

with "Matchbox," "Boppin The Blues," "Dixie Fried"/ "I'm Sorry, I'm Not Sorry" and "Your True Love" before moving on to the Columbia label.

In 1956 Phillips purchased Roy Orbison's "Ooby Dooby"/ "Trying To Get You" from the Je-Wel label and soon it sold over a quarter of a million copies. Phillips tried to mold Orbison's sound like he had done with Presley and Perkins, but the singer/guitarist could not perform the rockabilly style. Orbison never really had another hit for Sun but was able to pen some fine tunes for others during the next three years even though Phillips failed to fully realize his vocal potential. Orbison left Sun for Monument records in 1960.

Johnny Cash joined Phillips's staff in 1955 with "Cry Cry Cry"/"Hey Porter" and followed it up the following year with the million-seller "I Walk The Line." Cash leaned more towards the country side of the blues as opposed to the still-young rock and roll end of the spectrum. Over the next three years Cash scored a half dozen more hits for Phillips before jumping to Columbia in 1958: "Orange Blossom Special," "Folsom Prison Blues," "Ballad of a Teenage Queen," "Home of the Blues,"

"Guess Things Happen That Way"/"Come in Stranger" and "The Ways of a Woman in Love." Up to that point Phillips's success relied on guitarists/vocalists who were all quite different from their contemporaries. "They were all free spirits, they were all uniques," stated publicist Bill Williams in *Feel Like Going Home*. "I think every one of them must have come in on the midnight train from nowhere. I mean, it was like they came from outer space."

Perhaps the most spaced-out of all was Jerry Lee Lewis, a brash, bragging, strutting, piano-stompin' shouter who staked out Phillips's Sun studios until they would give him a listen, claiming that he could play piano like Chet Atkins. Noting that Atkins was a guitar player, Sun engineer Jack Clement decided to see what this big shot was all about and let him in to record a few tunes (although Lewis claims it was a marathon session). Phillips liked what he heard and signed him on as a piano player until he heard Lewis singing "Crazy Arms" and decided to release him as a solo artist.

It was the beginning of one of Phillips's most lucrative ventures as Lewis countered in 1957 with "Whole Lotta Shakin' Goin' On," a Number 3 smash hit. The piano man's outrageous act made him a standout in rock and roll revues and his ensuing singles, featuring Phillips's trademark slap-back echo, were chartbusters to boot: "It'll Be Me," "High School Confidential," "Great Balls of Fire," "Breathless," and "Break Up"/"I'll Make It All Up To You." Phillips set up a tour of England but soon learned that Lewis had married his 13-year-old cousin. The star's career took a major nosedive and, although his "What'd I Say" Ray Charles cover in 1961 helped some, by 1963 one of Phillips's most promising artists had left Sun and appeared to be washed up. [An interesting footnote; in 1957 Presley, Perkins, Cash, and Lewis met at Phillips studio for an impromptu jam session of country and gospel classics, but the recordings would not be released until the 1980s as the *Million Dollar Quartet*.]

Although the Sun label continued to record artists like Charlie Rich, by 1958 Phillips had seemed to lose interest and was hanging on to it more or less as a hobby. Rather than compete with the big guns of the recording industry and their cutthroat tactics, Phillips sold the label in 1969 and shifted his concentration towards operating several radio stations.

Although only one of his first twenty-three recordings was by a non-black artist, Phillips was criticized for abandoning his original sources after Presley. "This is a regrettable thing on my part," he said in *The Listener's Guide to the Blues,* "but I saw what I was doing as not deserting the black man—God knows, there was no way I could do that—[but] I saw what I was trying to do with white men was to broaden the base."

Phillips will be always be recognized as one of the innovators in the history of popular music and his Sun recordings document the transition from blues to rock and roll. "My mission was to bring out of a person what was in him, to recognize that individual's unique quality and then to find the key to unlock it," he continued. "My greatest contribution, I think, was to open up an area of freedom within the artist himself, to help him to express what he believed his message to be."

Sources

Books

Dalton, David, and Lenny Kaye, *Rock 100,* Grosset & Dunlap, 1977.
Guralnick, Peter, *Feel Like Going Home,* Vintage, 1981.
Guralnick, *The Listener's Guide To The Blues,* Facts on File, 1982.
Guralnick, *Lost Highway,* Vintage, 1982.
The Illustrated Encyclopedia of Rock, compiled by Nick Logan and Bob Woffinden, Harmony, 1977.
The Rolling Stone Illustrated History of Rock & Roll, edited by Jim Miller, Random House/Rolling Stone Press, 1976.
Shaw, Arnold, *Honkers And Shouters,* Collier, 1978.

Periodicals

Guitar Player, November 1987.
Guitar World, May 1985.
Rolling Stone, September 22, 1977.

—*Calen D. Stone*

Eddie Rabbitt

Singer, songwriter

Country singer-songwriter Eddie Rabbitt has survived personal tragedy and a bout of professional obscurity to emerge as one of Nashville's favorite superstars. The lanky baritone scored a string of crossover hits in the late 1970s with songs such as "I Love a Rainy Night," "Step by Step," and "Someone Could Lose a Heart Tonight," but as the 1980s progressed he all but disappeared from the scene. The "new" Eddie Rabbitt returned to the limelight in 1988, saddened by the death of his oldest son but determined to let music ease his sorrow. His recent work shows the same country-soft rock fusion that proved so popular in his earlier songs.

In the *San Jose Mercury News,* Harry Sumrall suggested that Rabbitt is "like a hot corn dog: nothing fancy, nothing frilly. You know what you're getting and you like it." The critic added: "Never a country purist, Rabbitt nonetheless makes music that is plain and simple, with all of the virtues that make good country good. . . . [His songs] might be brisk, but they are also warm and familiar, like the breeze that wafts in over the fried artichokes."

Rabbitt first came to Nashville at a time when the industry was backing away from the traditional country sound in favor of a more pop-oriented product. Much of this crossover material was eminently forgettable, but Rabbitt's catchy songs were the exception. The artist produced a dozen top-selling albums and placed more than two dozen hits on the country and pop charts, ultimately becoming one of the most successful crossover acts in the country. Sumrall wrote: "Friendly, relaxed, good-natured and real down-home, [Rabbitt] seemed to symbolize all the good feelings that people have about themselves."

It is not terribly surprising that Rabbitt has never recorded pure country work. He is in fact a native of Brooklyn, New York, who spent most of his childhood in Newark, New Jersey. Rabbitt's parents were Irish immigrants who came to the United States in 1924. His father worked at an oil refinery by day and played fiddle and accordion in Manhattan dance halls by night, concentrating on traditional Irish music.

Rabbitt was born in 1941 and was christened Edward Thomas. He grew up in a home full of Irish influences and learned to love country music as well. "Country music is Irish music," Rabbitt told *People* magazine. "Appalachian music was brought over by the Scotch and Irish. I think the minor chords in my music give it that mystical feel." Rabbitt was so consumed by music that he had little interest in formal schooling. He dropped out of high school at sixteen and began to perform at clubs in New Jersey and New York.

For the Record. . .

Born Edward Thomas November 27, 1941, in Brooklyn, N.Y.; son of an oil refinery worker; married, November 27, 1976, wife's name Janine; children: Dimelza, Timmy (deceased), Tommy. *Education:* Earned high school equivalency diploma.

Country singer/songwriter, 1970—. Has also worked as a truck driver, fruit picker, and soda jerk. Signed with Elektra Records, c. 1974, and released a number of country-pop singles hits, 1975-79, including "I Love a Rainy Night," "Drivin' My Life Away," "Step by Step," and "Every Which Way but Loose."

Addresses: *Record company*—Capitol Records, 1750 N. Vine St., Hollywood, CA 90028.

Rabbitt told the *Akron Beacon Journal:* "I remember one night a long time ago—before anybody's really heard of me—I was playing this Jersey honky-tonk, and when I saw Eddie Rabbitt up there on the marquee, I have to admit that it looked more like the name of a magic act, or maybe a clown, than a singer. So I changed it to Eddie Martin—after the guitar I was using. But that didn't help. As a matter of fact, as Eddie Martin, I went from near obscurity to oblivion. So I switched back."

As Eddie Rabbitt the singer found his way to Nashville, where he worked as a truck driver, a fruit picker, and even a soda jerk while trying to peddle his original songs. His first sale was a number entitled "Working My Way up to the Bottom," which was recorded by Roy Drusky in 1968. Two years later Rabbitt's fortune was made when Elvis Presley bought one of his songs, "Kentucky Rain," and made it a million seller. "Kentucky Rain" showed the earmarks of future Rabbitt hits—it had country emotions interwoven with a pop melody—and it suggested the young songwriter might be a candidate for crossover success.

By 1975 Rabbitt had secured a contract with Elektra Records and was turning out solo albums at the rate of almost two per year. His gaunt good looks made him a favorite in live concert, where he drew legions of country and pop fans. Rabbitt's biggest hits included "Drivin' My Life Away," a tune based on his truck-driving experiences, "Step by Step," an optimistic love song, and the jazzy "I Love a Rainy Night." Rabbitt also provided the title song for the popular Clint Eastwood movie, *Every Which Way but Loose.* As the 1970s

ended, the songwriter from New Jersey was riding high in Nashville.

Rabbitt describes himself as an old-fashioned Irishman; home and family are very important to him. In 1983 his wife Janine gave birth to the couple's second child, a boy named Timmy. The child was born with a fatal liver disease that required constant hospitalization, so Rabbitt curtailed his touring and recording so he could visit the boy every day. The Rabbitt family spent long hours with their disabled child and mourned his loss after an unsuccessful liver transplant in 1985. "At that point, I sort of backed out of the business," Rabbitt told the *Wichita Eagle-Beacon.* "I put out albums that other people wrote, and I just kinda backed out. . . . It was a time to be with people I love—my wife and little girl. I didn't want to be out of the music business, but where I was was more important."

A year or so after Timmy's death Rabbitt resumed his career, finding solace in the music he performed. Since then he has had a number of country hits, most notably

> *It is not terribly surprising that Eddie Rabbitt has never recorded pure country work. He is in fact a native of Brooklyn, New York*

a remake of Dion's "The Wanderer" and an upbeat number, "I Wanna Dance with You." Rabbitt told *People* that his experience with his son's death has affected his songwriting, making him more sensitive to pain and suffering. Rather than write sad songs, though, he tends to view music as a comfort, a restorative when times get tough. "I don't like to write heavy downers," he told the *Wichita Eagle-Beacon.* "There are enough heavy downers in the world; you can turn on the news for them. I think music should sooth the wild beast in us. It should take people away from the hard stuff in life—the hard jobs, the bad times."

Rabbitt has returned to a full schedule, recording his albums with Capitol Records in Nashville. When not on the road he lives quietly with his wife, daughter Dimelza, and son Tommy, born in 1986. A new awareness of home and hearth informs Rabbitt's recent work—he has become a wholesome performer without sacrificing his popular offbeat sexiness. "I don't ever get down and dirty," he said. "I think the stage is no place for that. I think you have to be very careful as an entertainer about what you bring to the stage because some people try to think of you as more than human. I figure if we're going to be role models for people, we should at least try to be good role models."

Rabbitt is grateful that his fans still come to see him after so many years. He told the *Akron Beacon Journal* that he figures he is still successful because he enjoys his work so much. The singer concluded: "I absolutely love music and I don't know anything else I'd ever do."

Selected discography

Eddie Rabbitt, Elektra.
Rocky Mountain Music, Elektra.
I Wanna Dance with You, RCA.
Rabbitt Trax, RCA.
Best of Eddie Rabbitt, Warner Bros.
Best of Eddie Rabbitt, Volume 2, Warner Bros.

Greatest Hits of Eddie Rabbitt, RCA.
Greatest Hits of Eddie Rabbitt, Volume 2, Warner Bros.
#1's, Warner Bros.
Jersey Boy, Capitol.

Sources

Books

The Illustrated Encyclopedia of Country Music, Harmony, 1977.

Periodicals

Akron Beacon Journal, June 28, 1985; August 19, 1988.
People, April 17, 1989.
San Jose Mercury News, August 11, 1986.
Wichita Eagle-Beacon, March 27, 1987; February 19, 1988.

—*Anne Janette Johnson*

Otis Redding

Singer, songwriter

Otis Redding's recording history lasted a mere five years, from 1962 until 1967, but established him as perhaps the greatest soul singer of all time. His career was cut so short that he was never even able to enjoy the success of his most popular tune, 1968's "(Sittin' on) The Dock of the Bay," a song that Redding so perfectly transformed into a work of pop art that most artists still won't dare to attempt it.

Redding was born in Georgia and, like his fellow statesman Little Richard, was steeped in the gospel tradition of church singing. His solo career began quite by accident while working as the road manager-driver-occasional singer for Johnny Jenkins and the Pinetoppers of the southern college frat circuit fame. With about forty minutes left at the end of one of Jenkins Stax label recording sessions, Redding cut a song, "These Arms of Mine" backed with "Hey, Hey, Hey," on a whim. The unique mixture of Memphis gospel and soul went on to sell an amazing 800,000 copies and bolted the singer into prominence.

The cut broke the Hot 100 and earned Redding a contract with Volt Records whereupon he released his second single, "Pain in My Heart." Phil Walden, a high school pal of Redding's who had introduced the vocalist to Jenkins earlier, took over as his manager. With the backing of the Bar-Kays and Booker T. and the MG's (including Steve Cropper on guitar, who co-wrote many of Redding's songs, Duck Dunn on bass, and the Mar-Key horn section), Redding recorded his songs very quickly to capture the raw energy while somehow managing to retain a laid-back feel. "When I go into a studio to record a song, I only have a title and maybe a first verse," Redding is quoted in *Rock 100*. "The rest I make up as we're recording."

Redding soon outgrew the adolescent style of Little Richard but continued to expand on the style of another one of his idols, Sam Cooke, in an attempt to bring the feel of church music into the pop realm. "More than any other soul singer, Otis managed to communicate and intimate the encouraging, sustaining power of gospel and translate its fundamental faith into an international code," noted *Rock 100*. After Cooke died in 1964, Redding carried the torch and offered a tribute to the late artist with "Shake."

Redding's rough-edged but gentle approach garnered him a huge following overseas as he headlined the Stax-Volt European Tour of 1965. That same year he wrote and recorded "Respect," a soul charter that first established Redding's own unique style and later became a Number 1 hit in 1967 for Aretha Franklin. On the jacket of his *Live in Europe* LP from 1965, writer Deanie Parker stated, "Otis Redding has breathed new life into soul music and helped bring it to its current

Born September 9, 1941, in Dawson, Ga; raised in Macon, Ga; drowned following an airplane crash December 10, 1967, near Madison, Wis.

Singer, songwriter; signed with Volt Records and released first record, "These Arms of Mine," 1963; had numerous hit singles, including "Pain In My Heart," "Mr. Pitiful," "I've Been Loving You Too Long," "Respect," "Try a Little Tenderness," and "(Sittin' on) The Dock of the Bay."

Awards: Selected top male vocalist of 1967 by *Melody Maker* magazine.

---

prominence in the contemporary music world, where it is brightening hot charts the world over."

With his slow moaning pleas on ballads, Redding became known as Mr. Pitiful, but it was the uptempo tunes that were his forte and helped him become the first soul artist to break over into the white market. He covered the Rolling Stones' "Satisfaction" as a nod to the group who had covered his material on their *Out of Our Heads* LP. Redding's versions of "Satisfaction" and the Beatles' "Day Tripper" were instrumental in earning him pop radio airplay, a goal he had been trying to attain without sacrificing his roots within the black audience.

"Redding was not going to change his music," wrote Jon Landau in *The Rolling Stone Illustrated History of Rock & Roll.* "He loved it, had already received recognition for it, and was confident his turn would come. It's doubtful the idea of altering his style to boost record sales ever occurred to him. He had perfected his vocal syntax, his rapport with his sidemen, and his linear, totally committed music."

Redding's studio work—including songs like "Fa, Fa, Fa, Fa, Fa," "I've Been Loving You Too Long," "Mr. Pitiful," "Try a Little Tenderness," and "Shout Bamalama" (in tribute to Little Richard)—created a totally new sound soon to be known as the Memphis Sound, which soon attracted others like Aretha Franklin and Wilson Pickett to the Tennessee city in hopes of capturing its spirit. As fantastic as his records were, Redding's bread and butter was on stage, as evidenced from his stunning performance at the Monterey Pop Festival in 1967 (captured on film as *Monterey Pop*). A ball of energy, face grimacing with sweat and strutting in a shiny sharkskin suit, Redding controlled his audiences with precision. "Redding was a marvel: one of the great live showmen (*Live in Europe* is better than any other

live rock or soul album I can think of)," wrote Dave Marsh in *The Rolling Stone Record Guide,* "a masterful ballad singer and a true rocker in the spirit of his boyhood hero, Little Richard. Everything the man recorded. . .demands to be heard."

Redding's incredible career was brought to a sudden and tragic halt on December 10, 1967. While touring with the Bar-Kays (who had scored with the hit "Soul Finger"), Redding chartered a plane out of Cleveland to take him to the tour's next engagement. The twin-engine plane crashed into a fog-shrouded lake near Madison, Wisconsin, drowning Redding and taking the lives of four of the five members of his troupe.

Selected discography

Pain In My Heart, Atco, 1964.
Otis Blue, Volt/Atlantic, 1965.
Soul Ballads, Volt, 1965.
Dictionary Of Soul, Volt/Atlantic, 1966.
The Soul Album, Volt, 1966.
The Dock Of The Baby, Volt/Stax, 1967.
History of Otis Redding, Atco, 1967.
Otis Redding Live In Europe, Atco, 1967.
(With Carla Thomas) *King & Queen,* Volt/Stax, 1967.
The Immortal Otis Redding, Atco, 1968.
In Person At The Whiskey A Go-Go, Atco, 1968.
Love Man, Atco/Atlantic, 1969.
Tell The Truth, Atco, 1970.
Otis Redding/The Jimi Hendrix Experience: Historic Performances Recorded At The Monterey International Pop Festival, Reprise, 1970.
The Best Of Otis Redding, Atco, 1972.

Sources

Books

Christgau, Robert, *Christgau's Record Guide,* Ticknor & Fields, 1981.
Dalton, David, and Lenny Kaye, *Rock 100,* Grosset & Dunlap, 1977.
The Illustrated Encyclopedia of Rock, compiled by Nick Logan and Bob Woffinden, Harmony, 1977.
The Rolling Stone Record Guide, edited by Dave Marsh with John Swenson, Random House/Rolling Stone Press, 1979.
The Rolling Stone Illustrated History of Rock & Roll, edited by Jim Miller, Random House/Rolling Stone Press, 1976.
Shaw, Arnold, *Honkers And Shouters,* Collier, 1978.
Stambler, Irwin, *The Encyclopedia of Pop, Rock, and Soul,* revised edition, St. Martin's, 1989.

—Calen D. Stone

R.E.M.

Avant garde rock band

As southern regional bands like the B-52s began gaining national recognition in the late 1970s, four University of Georgia students decided to take the musical plunge and formed R.E.M. (for the term used by sleep researchers: rapid eye movement) in April of 1980. Drummer Bill Berry and bassist Mike Mills had already played in various Macon bands, but it would be guitarist Peter Buck's first group, which he described in *Rolling Stone* as "the acceptable edge of the unacceptable stuff." His simple chording allowed the band's rhythm section to stretch out and explore while Michael Stipe's vocals, according to Deborah Feingold in *Rolling Stone,* "combined vivid imagery with pithy telegraphic phrasing, sacrificing grammar for impact."

In 1981 R.E.M. released an independent single, "Radio Free Europe"/"Sitting Still," which immediately became a favorite of critics; the word on the band began to spread underground. They meanwhile gained valuable experience through grueling club work, playing mostly cover tunes. "We were playing five nights a week, usually three weeks out of the month, doing two

or three sets a night," said Buck in *Guitar Player*. "If anything, that's why we got to be an okay band. We learned to stand up in front of these guys who wanted to hear Allman Brothers, and made them understand it. " The band hooked up with Let's Active's Mitch Easter, who produced their five-song EP *Chronic Town* at his Drive-In Studios in Winston-Salem, North Carolina. "At the time, it wasn't a bigger project than anything else, but you could tell something was gonna happen with them," Easter said in *Musician*. "They had the now sound, and they seemed like stars."

But critics and Georgians seemed to be the only ones hip to R.E.M. until their September 1983 release, *Murmur*, recorded in Charlotte at Reflection Studios with Easter and Don Dixon producing. "We were dealing with a fragile sort of art concept and trying to bring in a little pop sensibility without beating it up," Dixon told *Rolling Stone*. The LP, which explored new studio ideas and odd overdubs, only made it to Number 136 on the charts but was voted best album of the year by *Rolling Stone's* critics, who also selected R.E.M. as band of the year. The magazine later recognized *Murmur* as the eighth-best LP of the 1980s. "We were conscious that we were making a record that really wasn't in step with the times," Buck stated in *Rolling Stone*. "It was an old-fashioned record that didn't sound too much like what you heard on the radio. We were expecting the record company to say 'Sorry, this isn't even a record, it's a demo tape. Go back and do it again.'"

Easter also produced their 1984 release, *Reckoning*, which broke the Top 30, but R.E.M. was still radically different from their contemporaries both musically and idealistically. "We could probably do all these multi-media things and be more successful right off the bat, but in the long run, if we keep plugging at it, we'll get to the level of popularity that we deserve," Buck said in *Guitar World*. "It may take longer but it'll be worth it."

Slowly the band's sales began to build momentum as

Fables of the Reconstruction became a big seller in 1985. David Fricke in *Rolling Stone* called it an "exploratory Smorgasbord," as the group continued on their own path and refused to become another commercial-oriented pop unit. "We made a contract with the world that says, 'We're going to be the best band in the world; you're going to be proud of us,'" Buck stated in *Rolling Stone*. "But we have to do it our way." R.E.M. conceded slightly on *Life's Rich Pageant* by recruiting John Cougar Mellancamp's producer, Don Gehrman, who added a rock punch to their sound with big drums, organs and pianos, but also incorporated banjos and accordions. The band, however, seemed to be caught between pleasing their loyal following and breaking into new audiences.

"Signing off both sides of an LP as rousing and raucous as *Life's Rich Pageant* with self-consciously hip jokes is an unfortunate waste," wrote Anthony DeCurtis in *Rolling Stone,* "an apparent effort to cling to insider status when every other aspect of the album is a lesson in how to assume the responsibilities of mass popularity without smoothing the subterranean edge. . . . As it is, it's a brilliant and groundbreaking, if modestly flawed, effort by an immensely valuable band whose most profound work is still to come."

After *Dead Letter Office,* an LP of studio outtakes, B-sides and covers, R.E.M. finally made their crossover statement in 1987: *Document*. They had aged seven years since their inception and their changing political and world views were evidenced on the album. They also had a hit single on their hands, "The One I Love," as the LP rose to Number 10 thanks to a back-to-basics approach that relied on a big beat and up-front guitars. R.E.M. had finally managed to reach a larger audience without compromising, their priorities still intact. "Without exception," stated Fricke in *Rolling Stone,* "their records combine a spirit of willful perversity with a healthy restlessness and a steadfast refusal to acknowledge either commercial or critical expectations."

With 1989's platinum-selling *Green,* the band solidified its reputation as progressive rock's reigning authority, while maintaining the delicate balance between artistic integrity and mass-market appeal. Testifying to this feat, Michael Azerrad wrote in *Rolling Stone:* "Having made the leap from a small label, I.R.S., to a monolithic major one, Warner Bros., R.E.M. hasn't sold out; rather, the band has taken the opportunity to crack open the shell it's been pecking at since it recorded its first album." *People* contributor Michael Small elaborated on R.E.M.'s method, explaining, "Not only does *Green* contain a heaping dose of appealing pop melodies, but each word stands out clearly and fits into phrases that actually make sense. 'It's high time I razed the walls that I've constructed,' sings Stipe in "World Leader Pretend," a pensive number that seems to signal his intention to drop some of the band's studied aloofness."

Rolling Stone featured Stipe and company on an April 1989 cover, dubbing them "America's Hippest Band." Inside, DeCurtis heralded R.E.M.'s full emergence from its shadowy status: "Once the darlings of the underground, they are now solicited by parents' groups to improve the social habits of the young. College-radio perennials, they have now graduated—into high schools. Having signed a five-record deal with Warner Bros. last year for a reported $10 million, the members of R.E.M. are approaching the status of—can it be?—superstars." Although the perhaps unfair, but unfortunately inevitable, cries of "sell-out" did eventually surface, R.E.M.'s members—still residents of Athens, Georgia—have tried to remain philosophical about their growing recognition. Buck told DeCurtis: "The influence that I'd like to think we have is that people saw that there's a way to go about doing this on your own terms. The thing is, you have to *not* worry about success."

Selected discography

Chronic Town (EP), IRS.
Murmur, IRS, 1983.
Reckoning, IRS, 1984.
Fables of the Reconstruction, IRS, 1985.
Life's Rich Pageant, IRS, 1986.
Dead Letter Office, IRS, 1987.
Document, IRS, 1987.
Eponymous (greatest hits compilation), IRS, 1988.
Green, Warner Bros., 1988.
Out of Time, Warner Bros., 1991.

Sources

Guitar Player, January 1985; June 1985.
Guitar World, July 1984.
Musician, August 1986; September 1986.
People, January 9, 1989.
Rolling Stone, November 7, 1985; August 28, 1986; July 2, 1987; October 22, 1987; January 12, 1989; April 20, 1989; November 16, 1989.

—Calen D. Stone

Carole Bayer Sager

Song lyricist, singer

"**A** much-repeated story in the music industry is that Carole Bayer Sager's lyrics have become such an important part of contemporary music that one record trade publication proclaimed a new album unique simply because it did not contain one Carole Bayer Sager song," wrote Linda Dozoretz in *BMI: Music World.* Throughout the 1970s and 1980s, Sager has been one of the most prolific and successful lyricists at work in the music industry. The list of stars who have recorded Sager's songs reads like a pantheon of popular music: Frank Sinatra, Dolly Parton, Dionne Warwick, Johnny Mathis, Barbra Streisand, Aretha Franklin, Roberta Flack, Carly Simon, Bette Midler, and Michael Jackson, to name only a few.

Likewise, a partial list of her song credits is enough to read like a hit parade: "A Groovy Kind of Love," "Heartbreaker," "Midnight Blue," "Nobody Does It Better," "Break It to Me Gently," "Arthur's Theme," and "That's What Friends Are For." Regarding the special appeal of Sager's songs, Dozoretz commented: "Love and joy have been the themes of much of Carole's music over the years. If one common denominator had to be found, it would be that her lyrics convey a strong sense of emotion, and people are touched by and remember her words."

Sager began writing songs as a teenager, while a student at New York's High School for Performing Arts where she studied piano and drama. She told Dozoretz that "songwriting has always been my most reliable means of communication." Her first song came when she was only fifteen, the 1966 hit "A Groovy Kind of Love," which was recorded by Wayne Fontana and the Mindbenders.

Nine years would pass, however, before her next hit, 1975's "Midnight Blue," co-written with and recorded by singer-composer Melissa Manchester. Sager described to Suzanne O'Malley in *Glamour* the perseverance that carried her through those early struggling years. "I kept writing, even though not with the greatest of confidence. If you hang in long enough—if you really love what you're doing and you're not on a time schedule that says 'if I don't have this done in three weeks, I'll go into shoe manufacturing'—it will happen."

In 1975, Sager met Oscar-winning composer Marvin Hamlisch (*A Chorus Line* and *The Sting*), with whom she formed a professional collaboration that developed into a personal relationship. One of their early successes was the hit song "Nobody Does It Better" from the film *The Spy Who Loved Me,* which earned Sager her first Academy Award nomination. But the pair's long-running Broadway musical, *They're Playing Our Song,*

For the Record. . .

Born March 8, 1944, in New York City; married Andrew Sager, 1970 (a record company executive; divorced, 1978); married Burt Bacharach (composer), 1982; children: Christopher Elton (second marriage). *Education:* High School of Performing Arts, New York City; graduated from New York University.

Song lyricist. Credits include "A Groovy Kind of Love," "Heartbreaker," "Our Night," "When I Need You," "Looking through the Eyes of Love" (music by Marvin Hamlisch), "I'd Rather Leave While I'm in Love" (music by Peter Allen), "Come In From the Rain" (with Melissa Manchester), "Nobody Does It Better" (music by Hamlisch), "Break It to Me Gently," "Heart Light" (music by Neil Diamond), "Don't Cry Out Loud" (with Manchester), "That's What Friends Are For" (music by Burt Bacharach), "On My Own" (music by Bacharach), and "Arthur's Theme (Best That You Can Do)" (with Bacharach and others). Lyricist for musicals, including *Georgy,* 1970 (music by George Fischoff), and *They're Playing Our Song,* 1979 (music by Hamlisch; play by Neil Simon). Lyrics for songs also included in plays, *All That Jazz* and *Dancin'.*

Awards: Academy Award nominations for best song, for "Looking Through the Eyes of Love" and "Nobody Does It Better"; Academy Award for best song and Golden Globe Award, both 1982, both for "Arthur's Theme (Best That You Can Do)"; Grammy Award for Song of the Year, 1986, for "That's What Friends Are For"; Golden Globe Award nomination, 1986, for "They Don't Make Them Like They Used To"; Humanitarian Award, American Foundation for AIDS Research, 1986; inducted into National Academy of Popular Music Songwriters Hall of Fame, 1987.

Addresses: *Home*—Bel Air, Calif.

was their greatest success and brought their songwriting/personal relationship into the public eye. Written by Neil Simon, with music by Hamlisch and lyrics by Sager, *They're Playing Our Song* portrays the mismatched relationship between Sonia Walsk, a lyricist, and Vernon Gersch, a composer. Loosely autobiographical, the show depicts the effects of a professional relationship that turns romantic. Opening on Broadway in 1979 with Robert Klein and Luci Arnaz in the starring roles, *They're Playing Our Song* went on for a successful three-year run.

The musical had a happy ending which did not, howev-er, necessarily parallel Hamlisch and Sager's own story; some time after the musical's opening, Hamlisch and Sager parted ways. In 1979, Sager began writing songs with composer Burt Bacharach, whom she later married in 1982. Ever open about personal and emotional aspects of her life, and how they merge with her work, Sager remarked to Gail Buchalter in *People:* "[*They're Playing Our Song*] is a romantic comedy. . . . Every night those people end up happy, kiss and take their curtain calls. But obviously, Marvin and I were not totally like those characters. . . . Marvin had a very fatherly way about him and liked to take care of me, but that brought out my childish qualities. Yet there was also an area within me that was fighting to be an adult. . . . With Burt, I do a lot of the taking care." Sager's collaborations with Bacharach marked new turning points in her songwriting career. In 1981, they were Oscar winners for the theme from the movie *Arthur,* and in 1986 received the song of the year Grammy for "That's What Friends Are For," which was recorded by Dionne Warwick, Elton John, Gladys Knight, and Stevie Wonder.

Sager's efforts on "That's What Friends Are For" were particularly gratifying for her. Both the artists and writer-

> *The list of stars who have recorded Sager's songs reads like a pantheon of popular music*

producers of the recording donated its earnings to AIDS research. "A song has the potential to touch the people," Sager commented to Dozoretz, "and this one lived up to its potential." The year's biggest hit, "That's What Friends Are For" earned nearly $1 million for the American Foundation for AIDS Research, which bestowed Sager and Bacharach with its Humanitarian Award. Sager received another honor in 1986 when she was inducted into the National Academy of Popular Music Songwriters Hall of Fame.

Although she divides her time today between songwriting, being a mother, and working for charitable organizations, music is still her primary desire. "I love music, and I love being able to share joy and emotion through songs," she told Dozoretz. "Besides, I still get excited every time I turn on the radio and hear one of my songs. How could I ever give that up?"

Writings

Extravagant Gestures (novel), Arbor House, 1985.

Selected discography

Carole Bayer Sager, Elektra, 1977.
Carole Bayer Sager . . . Too, Elektra, 1978.
Sometimes Late at Night, Boardwalk, 1981.

Sources

Books

Green, Stanley, *The World of Musical Comedy,* A. S. Barnes, 1980.

Periodicals

BMI: Music World, Number 1, 1987.
Glamour, June 1979.
People, April 16, 1979; June 1, 1981; September 30, 1985.

—Michael E. Mueller

Peter Schickele

Composer, conductor, pianist, musical humorist

In New York City in 1965 composer-musician Peter Schickele introduced the general public to his satiric creation, baroque composer P.D.Q. Bach. Billing himself as Professor Schickele, head of the department of Musical Pathology at the fictional University of Southern North Dakota at Hoople, the entertainer recounted his discovery of this "last but least" of Johann Sebastian Bach's twenty-odd children (earlier known only "from police records and tavern IOU's") while taking a tour of a castle in Bavaria.

He opened the program with P.D.Q. Bach's "Concerto for Horn and Hardart," a fifteen-minute spoof of eighteenth-century musical style and form played on a homemade "hardart"—an assemblage of toy instruments, household items, exploding balloons, and coin operated windows dispensing sandwiches and pastries. Following with other "long-lost" P.D.Q. Bach compositions, the professor vowed to continue the search for new pieces ("the lastest score can't possibly be as bad as the one before")—a pledge served faithfully for the next twenty-five years—much to the delight of his always sold-out audiences.

"His slapstick, pratfall sort of humor is often so terribly self-indulgent, outrageously sophomoric, and inexcusably bad that we find ourselves laughing not so much at the jokes themselves as at his nerve in trying to pull them off," wrote Lawrence Widdoes, assessing Schickele's enduring appeal in *High Fidelity*. "Thus, the hiss and the boo have become accepted responses at the concerts, ultimately eliciting a deliciously crummy comeback from Schickele." Admiring the entertainer's "ability to walk the fine line between humor and excess," UCLA musicologist Robert Winter told Alan Rich in *Smithsonian:* "It isn't only that [Schickele is] exposing sacred cows. He's spoofing things that most people don't even know, and yet he makes them feel like insiders."

Schickele's early interest in music was coupled with a flair for the dramatic; he first dreamed of becoming an actor, and he and brother David ran a theatre in their basement, performing movie serials and westerns. At age 10 Peter heard a recording of musical humorist Spike Jones, and was smitten by the King of Corn's use of outrageous instruments and sound effects—like car horns and goat bleats—to burlesque popular songs. A bassoonist with the local symphony orchestra while in high school, Schickele later made his mark as a serious composer at the Juilliard School, but still felt the pull between classical and popular music, his attraction to Elvis and Ray Charles as strong as his devotion to Bartok and Stravinsky.

Studying classical composition with the distinguished Vincent Persichetti and William Bergsma at Juilliard,

Born July 17, 1935, in Ames, Iowa; raised in Ames, Washington, D.C., and Fargo, N.D.; son of Rainer Wolfgang (an agricultural economist) and Elizabeth (Wilcox) Schickele; married Susan Sindell (a children's dance teacher), October 27, 1962; children: Karla, Matthew. *Education:* Studied music theory with conductor Sigvald Thompson; studied with composer Roy Harris, 1954; Swarthmore College, B.A., 1957; studied at Aspen Music School, 1959; Juilliard School, M.S., 1960, studied composition with Vincent Persichetti and William Bergsma.

Composer of classical music, mid-1950s—; created P.D.Q. Bach persona, 1953, P.D.Q. Bach music first performed at Juilliard concert, 1959; co-founded Composers Circle at Juilliard; composer-in-residence in Los Angeles public school system, 1960-61; teacher at Swarthmore College, 1961-62; teacher of extension courses at Juilliard, 1961-65; first P.D.Q. Bach commercial concert at Town Hall in New York City, 1965, P.D.Q. Bach recordings, 1965—; composer of film scores, mid-1960s—; performed and recorded with chamber-rock-jazz trio Open Window, 1967-71; composer and arranger for pop and folk vocalists, later 1960s—. Yearly nationwide P.D.Q. Bach concerts performed with local symphony orchestras or with Schickele's own New York Pick-Up Ensemble. Has performed frequently on television. Member of tAmerican Society of Composers, Authors and Publishers, American Federation of Musicians, Association for Classical Music, and American Music Center.

Awards: Gershwin Memorial Award, 1959; Ford Foundation grant, 1960-61; Elizabeth Tow Newman Contemporary Music Award, 1964; honorary doctorate, Swarthmore College, 1980; Grammy Award for best comedy recording, 1989, for *P.D.Q. Bach: 1712 Overture and Other Musical Assaults*, and 1990, for *P.D.Q. Bach: Oedipus Tex.*

Addresses: *Office*—c/o William Crawford, 237 East 72nd St., New York, N.Y. 10021.

Schickele earned a masters degree in 1960, returning there to teach. Yet, in an interview with *New York Times* writer Allan Kozinn, Schickele admitted that he spent much of his time composing, arriving for classes unprepared. Worse still, the teacher found himself chafing at the institution's restrictive attitude towards "quality" music; his *Serenade for Piano*—incorporating rock and roll in the final movement—was deemed unsuitable concert material when performed at Juilliard in 1961. Feeling that his serious music owed as much to jazz, folk, and rock as it did to traditional classical music, Schickele hatched in P.D.Q. Bach a good-humored way to challenge such musical myopia.

While an undergraduate student in 1953, Schickele—along with his brother and a musician friend—playfully overdubbed one of Bach's Brandenburg Concertos with a pair of tape recorders, making it sound "like mud wrestling." Further foolery yielded Schickele's "Sanka Cantata" (a take-off of Bach's "Coffee Cantata") and the first of forgotten composer P.D.Q. Bach's dubious masterworks. When asked to extend a Juilliard concert program six years later, Schickele obliged with *Concerto for Horn and Hardart*; thenceforth new P.D.Q. Bach pieces surfaced at annual concerts at the Aspen Music School in Colorado.

By April 1965 there was enough P.D.Q. material for a full-scale concert at New York's Town Hall—the Vanguard recording of it was as wildly successful as the live performance itself. Schickele told *Christian Science Monitor* reporter Jo Ann Levine that he chose to lampoon music from the era of Bach and Mozart both because he loved it, and because "eighteenth century

---

The creator of much non-P.D.Q. Bach music, Schickele has scored for film and television and written songs for musicals and popular recording artists.

---

music has a well-defined style, so you can depart from it."

Correspondingly, Widdoes noted that because baroque music "represents the epitome of periwigged musical dignity and sophistication" Schickele's satires are all the more striking; while acknowledging the professor's kinship to contemporary musical humorists Anna Russell and Victor Borge, the *High Fidelity* critic felt that Schickele lacked their cosmopolitan polish, using instead "unmistakably American," Spike Jonesian humor devices: "slipshod cadences, embarrassing country and western melodic fragments, blue notes, unexpected dissonant clusters, outdated scat phrases, . . . Guy Lombardo endings, and ridiculous-sounding homemade instruments."

Thus, P.D.Q. Bach's *Pervertimento* requires bagpipes, a bicycle, and balloons, and *Concerto for Piano vs.*

Orchestra culminates with an exploding piano bench; other Schickele/P.D.Q. irreverences include *Fanfare for the Common Cold,* the opera *Hansel and Gretel and Ted and Alice,* the dramatic oratorio *Oedipus Tex,* the *Unbegun Symphony,* and *The O.K. Chorale.* Taking his musical spoof one step further, the professor published the mock-scholarly *Definitive Biography of P.D.Q. Bach* in 1976, complete with tongue-in-cheek bibliography, glossary, and discography.

While cultivating thousands of fans with his musical wit, Schickele has also drawn praise for the consummate skill underlying his musical burlesques; in *High Fidelity* Michael Anthony felt that the entertainer's musical gags work so well only "because of Schickele's deep understanding of the eighteenth-century musical idiom." Former Juilliard student and minimalist composer Philip Glass admitted in *Smithsonian* that "Peter was, in all my class, the most gifted. . . . He could write synthetic Copeland, synthetic Stravinsky, and for that matter, synthetic Bach and Mozart. . . . He inspired us simply because he made music seem easy. He had no fear of the terrors of composition; he took the anxiety out of making music."

The creator of much non-P.D.Q. Bach music, Schickele has scored for film and television, and written songs for musicals and popular recording artists. From 1967 to 1971 he introduced a number of serious works while a member of the chamber-rock-jazz trio Open Window; later Schickele compositions include *Pentangle: Five Songs for Horn and Orchestra, String Quartet No. 1: American Dreams,* and *Spring Serenade, for Flute and Piano.* Reviewing the last of these for the *American Record Guide,* David W. Moore observed that the composer's "fondness for effective simplicity combines with a sensitive feeling for harmony and mood"; other critics have found in Schickele's serious works a mirror of the man himself: direct, individual, expert, and relaxed.

Selected discography

Diversions for Oboe, Clarinet and Bassoon, GC.
Windows, for Clarinet and Guitar, Protone.
Fantastic Garden: Three Views From the Open Window, Louisville Symphony/Vanguard, 1968.
The Open Window, Vanguard, 1969.
The Lowest Trees Have Tops, Grenadilla.
Pentangle: Five Songs for Horn and Orchestra, Louisville Symphony.

The Knight of the Burning Pestle: Songs: Aegies; Summer Trio, Vanguard.
Bestiary: Quartet for Clarinet, Violin, Cello and Piano.
Spring Serenade, for Flute and Piano, CRI.
String Quartet No 1: American Dreams, RCA.

P.D.Q. Bach albums; on Vanguard

An Evening with P.D.Q. Bach, 1965.
An Hysteric Return.
P.D.Q. Bach on the Air.
Addicted to P.D.Q. Bach and Professor Peter Schickele.
The Intimate P.D.Q. Bach.
Portrait of P.D.Q. Bach.
Black Forest Bluegrass.
The Wurst of P.D.Q. Bach, 1981.
Liebeslieder Polkas: Twelve Quite Heavenly Songs.
Music You Can't Get Out of Your Head.
A Little Nightmare Music.
1712 Overture and Other Musical Assaults.
P.D.Q. Bach: Oedipus Rex and Other Choral Calamities.

P.D.Q. Bach Videos

The Abduction of Figaro (three-act opera).

Compositions

In addition to numerous satiric pieces and serious compositions for orchestra, chamber ensemble, solo instruments, and voice, Schickele has scored television and nontheatrical films and the motion picture *Silent Running,* 1972; created music and lyrics for stage productions, including "Oh!Calcutta!"; and provided songs and musical arrangements for recording artists, including Joan Baez and Buffy Sainte-Marie.

Writings

The Definitive Biography of P.D.Q. Bach (1807-1742)?, Random House, 1976.

Sources

American Record Guide, Fall 1987.
Christian Science Monitor, August 16, 1976.
High Fidelity, April 1980; August 1984.
National Review, October 29, 1976.
New York Times, December 25, 1977.
Smithsonian, February 1990.

—*Nancy Pear*

The Sex Pistols

British punk rock band

The Sex Pistols' influence on rock and roll is far greater than one might surmise from their scant recorded output (only one album and single in the U.S., a few more singles in the U.K.) and their brief existence together as a group (just over 2 years from the time lead singer Johnny Rotten joined to the time he left). Yet, because they were involved in the punk rock explosion from the very beginning and in fact embodied that particular fashion at its height in London, they are the seminal punk rock band without whom the history of rock and roll would have been very different.

Their radical style of playing, the lyrical content of their songs, their attitude, their style of dress, and their behavior succeeded in changing the way rock was played. It brought a new and refreshing relationship to rock's audience and its performers. As British rock journalist Caroline Coon wrote about the Sex Pistols' live performances, "Participation is the operative word. The audience revels in the idea that any one of them could get up on stage and do just as well, if not better than the bands already up there." In fact, future pop

stars Billy Idol and Siouxsie Sioux (of Siouxsie and the Banshees) were among the most dedicated followers of the Sex Pistols, traveling along with a group of fans known as the Bromley Contingent to virtually every Pistols performance. The band had a direct influence on such punk rock bands as the Buzzcocks, the Clash, Chelsea, the Damned, Eater, Subway Sect, and Siouxsie and the Banshees.

The Sex Pistols represented a break with the past, a new way of performing rock and roll. Johnny Rotten was quoted as saying, "We're not trying to be commercial. We're doing exactly what we want to do—what we've always done." He also expressed a disdain for the rock of that time, denying any influences or idols. "I'd listen to rock 'n' roll, but I had no respect for it. It was redundant and had nothing to do with anything relevant." Rock was becoming quite decadent, with millionaire rock stars performing banal and trivial songs. Rock needed a change, and the Sex Pistols started it.

Upon seeing the band for the first time, Coon wrote: "What impressed me most . . . was their total disinterest in pleasing anybody except themselves. Instead, they engaged the audience, trying to provoke a reaction which forced people to express what they felt about the music. Quite apart from being very funny, their arro-

gance was a sure indication that they knew what they were doing and why." She noted that "their music had a new rhythm and an abrasive style expressing a hunger and need which was no longer satisfied by antiseptic r'n'b and art school burlesque."

If the rock scene was bad in England, it was worse in America. Disco was preeminent, and *Saturday Night Fever* represented the popular music of the time. When the Pistols toured America in early 1978, no one was ready for them. The punk rock movement that was so strong in London didn't yet make sense to America's rock fans. To Americans, the Pistols came and went before anyone realized the "new wave" was about to begin.

When the Pistols made their public performing debut in November 1975 at a dance at St. Martin's School of Art, someone pulled the plug on their equipment after a couple of songs. Whether or not they could play their instruments is a matter for disagreement. At some point in their brief career they actually played in tune and on time, according to noted rock guitarist Chris Spedding. Many other listeners would have disagreed. The Pistols' sound was basic and raw and played on cheap equipment. Defining the punk rock style, their music was played fast, the chords kept simple, and the songs rarely lasted more than three minutes.

By February 1976, the Pistols managed to land regular Tuesday night gigs at London's 100 Club, having been banned from other London clubs like the Nashville, the Marquee, and the Roundhouse for various acts of childish violence. As Coon noted, "The band's unprecedented commitment to raw energy and iconoclastic blasts at established idols and sacred cows, began attracting fiercely loyal fans." Their songs were more anti-social than political. Instead of writing protest songs, they were protest. Combining an anti-establishment style of music and dress, they sang anti-love songs, cynical songs about suburbia, and songs about hate and aggression.

By September 1976, the Pistols were able to command an audience of about 1,000 fans when they headlined The 100 Club Punk Rock Festival. Sharing the bill on the first of two nights with the Clash, Subway Sect, and Siouxsie and the Banshees, the Pistols had come a long way. As described by Coon, Glen Matlock (bass) and Paul Cook (drums) provided a "bed-rock of taut rhythmic structures." Steve Jones (lead guitarist), "once the brooding loner unsure of his sex appeal, is now exuding a magnetic confidence which guarantees a screen of exotic women around him." Johnny Rotten (lead singer), showed a new stage presence: "Lately, he rarely moves. He can be quite sickeningly still. This deathly, morgue-like stance sets skin crawling, and his lyrics are as suffocating as the world they describe." Without question, the Sex Pistols were the stars of this festival.

Their set at the 100 Club opened with "Anarchy in the U.K." and continued with such punk rock standards as "Seventeen," "I'm a Lazy Sod," "New York," "Pushing and A Shovin'," the Monkees' "Stepping Stone," "I Love You," "Sub-Mission," "Liar," "No Feelings," "Substitute," "Pretty Vacant," "Problems," and "No Fun." Most of their original songs are credited as group compositions, but Rotten wrote most of the lyrics to music provided by Matlock and Jones.

As a result of their performance at the 100 Club festival, the Pistols were signed by E.M.I. in October and quickly entered the studio to record their first single, "Anarchy in the U.K." The single was released in November and their first major British tour was planned for December. Unbeknownst to anyone involved, a series of unplanned events were about to propel the Sex Pistols into the public eye and make their name a household word, at least in Great Britain.

When British television contacted E.M.I. to request that the band Queen appear on the tea-time *Today* show hosted by Bill Grundy, they were unavailable. Instead, the Sex Pistols were sent as substitutes to promote their new single. The host, noted for his provocative manner of questioning, succeeded in provoking Rotten, Matlock, and Jones into uttering strings of nonstop four-letter obscenities. The next day, London's tabloids had a field day, with front-page headlines screaming about "The Filth and the Fury," "The Punk Rock Horror Show," and "TV Fury at Rock Cult Filth." Grundy was suspended for two weeks, but more significantly, nearly every date on the planned "Anarchy in the U.K." tour was canceled by the student unions at the colleges where the Pistols were to have played. By January, EMI had canceled the Pistols' contract for a cash settlement.

For the first six months of 1977, the Pistols only played three public performances. Matlock left the band in February to be replaced by Rotten's friend, Sid Vicious. Their second single, "God Save the Queen," was to have been released in England by A&M, but the record company mysteriously canceled the contract after pressing the record. The Pistols finally signed with Virgin in May. Virgin, a smaller record company at that time, had been interested in the Pistols all along, but had lost out in the bidding against the larger companies. Now, in the year of the Queen's Jubilee, celebrating 25 years of her reign, Virgin was probably the only record company willing to issue the Pistols' "God Save the Queen."

One of those three performances was for a record

release party aboard a chartered yacht named *Queen Elizabeth*. On June 15, Jubilee Day, the boat set sail on the Thames, only to be boarded by police and forced to dock. Arrests were made, and in subsequent months, various members of the band and management employees were seriously attacked and beaten. Unable to find places to play in England, the band went on a brief Scandinavian tour in August 1977, accompanied by many journalists. When they returned to the United Kingdom, they played a low-key tour under assumed names like Spots and Tax Exiles to avoid bans.

In October, they signed their only U.S. record deal with Warner Brothers, and later that month their first and only official album was released in the United Kingdom and in America. *Never Mind the Bollocks, Here's the Sex Pistols* raised a national furor in England, because "bollocks" is a slang obscenity there. Some record store owners were prosecuted under the 1889 Indecent Advertising Act. In England, advance orders of 125,000 copies assured the Pistols of a Number 1 spot on the British charts. In the United States, the Warner

---

The Sex Pistols represented a break with the past, a new way of performing rock and roll.

Brothers album never made the Hot 100, peaking at Number 107 in *Billboard*.

The Pistols' manager, Malcolm McLaren, began making arrangements around this time for a film about the band. Because of subsequent legal disputes between the band and their manager after the band broke up, Rotten was portrayed by an actor and never appeared in the film, which was released in 1980 as *The Great Rock 'n' Roll Swindle*. The soundtrack album contains only snippets of Rotten's vocals, with McLaren and others doing the lead vocals.

McLaren and Warner Brothers also were discussing the Pistols' American tour. Apparently, Warner wanted the Pistols to play large venues like New York's Madison Square Garden, albeit with a very low admission price in keeping with the band's image. McLaren felt the large auditorium/stadium format would reduce the band's intensity. When a compromise was finally reached, the American tour missed most of the major metropolitan cities in favor of several southern locations. It didn't matter much, though, because most

American fans didn't have a clue as to what the Sex Pistols were all about.

The Sex Pistols arrived in New York on January 4, 1978, where an appearance on *Saturday Night Live* was canceled at the last minute (Elvis Costello and the Attractions appeared instead). The U.S. tour began in Atlanta on January 5 and continued through Memphis, San Antonio, Baton Rouge, Dallas, and Tulsa. It ended January 16 with three nights at Winterland in San Francisco, where the show was opened by local punk rockers the Nuns and the Avengers. A 1979 film by Lech Kowalsky, *D.O.A.,* documents the Pistols' American tour and includes footage of other punk rock bands.

The final show at Winterland would be the band's last night together, with Johnny Rotten leaving and saying, "Ever get the feeling you've been cheated?" McLaren joined up with the remaining members of the band in Rio, where they recorded with the famous Great Train Robber, Ronald Biggs, singing lead and Sid Vicious doing the Sinatra tune, "My Way." While these were released as by the Sex Pistols, the Sex Pistols were in fact history.

Selected discography

Singles

"Anarchy in the UK," E.M.I., 1976 (United Kingdom).
"God Save the Queen," A&M, 1977 (United Kingdom, not released).
"God Save the Queen," Virgin, 1977 (United Kingdom).
"Pretty Vacant," Virgin, 1977 (United Kingdom).
"Holidays in the Sun," Virgin, 1977 (United Kingdom).
"Pretty Vacant," Warner Bros., 1978 (United States).
"No One Is Innocent" (with Ronald Biggs), Virgin, 1978 (United Kingdom)

Albums

Never Mind the Bollocks, Here's the Sex Pistols, Virgin, 1977 (United Kingdom) and Warner Bros., 1977 (United States).
The Great Rock 'n' Roll Swindle (movie soundtrack), Virgin, 1979 (United Kingdom).
Some Product Carrion (includes radio interviews and commercials), Virgin, 1979 (United Kingdom).
Flogging a Dead Horse (compiles singles releases), Virgin, 1980 (United Kingdom).
The Heyday (contains interviews only, cassette only), Factory, 1980 (United Kingdom).
(As by Various Artists) *Troublemakers* (contains two songs from the American tour), Warner Bros., 1980 (United States).

Sources

Books

Bianco, David, *Who's New Wave in Music: An Illustrated Encyclopedia, 1976-1982,* Pierian Press, 1985.
Coon, Caroline, *The New Wave Punk Rock Explosion,* Orbach and Chambers, 1977, Hawthorn Books, 1978.
Monk, Noel E., and Jimmy Guterman, *12 Days on the Road: The Sex Pistols and America,* William Morrow, 1990.
The Sex Pistols File, edited by Ray Stevenson, Omnibus, 1978.
The Sex Pistols File—Updated, edited by Ray Stevenson, Omnibus, 1980.
The Trouser Press Guide to New Wave Records, edited by Ira A. Robbins, Charles Scribner's Sons, 1983.
Vermorel, Fred, and Judy Vermorel, *The Sex Pistols,* Universal, 1978.

Periodicals

Goldmine, February 27, 1987.
Trouser Press, October 1977; May 1979; July 1981.

—*David Bianco*

Wayne Shorter

Saxophonist, composer

Wayne Shorter is considered one of modern jazz's most influential saxophonists and among its most original composers. Shorter, a tenor and soprano saxophonist, rose to prominence in the early 1960s when, as Mark Gilbert stated in *Jazz Journal International,* he introduced innovations to jazz which "were not piecemeal additions or alterations to mainstream tradition, but rather embodied a wholesale shift in perspective." Len Lyons and Don Perlo in *Jazz Portraits: The Lives and Music of the Jazz Masters* described Shorter's distinct contributions: "His compositions, characterized by unusual chord sequences and economical, impressionistic melodies . . . portray images and sounds of his youth, foreign cultures, and films. . . . [While] as a saxophonist, Shorter developed a flexible, vocalized articulation and tone."

Shorter's diverse musical career includes distinguished work as a free-lance musician, in addition to being a member of the Jazz Messengers, the Miles Davis Quintet, and Weather Report. Josef Woodard wrote in *Musician* that Shorter's "trademark approach, in which emotional fury is bound by a cool, linear economy, can be heard in altered or diluted form everywhere from James Newton to Branford Marsalis to George Howard."

Born into a family of non-musicians, Shorter grew up in Newark, New Jersey, and displayed an early fascination with sound, duplicating tracks of movies. He did not begin studying music, however, until the relatively late age of sixteen, when he took up the clarinet. Prior to his music studies, Shorter aspired to be a painter and sculptor, an ambition fueled after he won an art contest at a young age.

However, the "human interaction" of music swayed him away from art, and he became very interested in the bebop music he heard on the nightly New York City radio program, *Make Believe Ballroom*. "I loved the energy and life of the music," he told Scott Yanow in *down beat.* "I couldn't wait to go to New York to see Bop City, the Bandbox, the Latin bands and the Palladium and Birdland. It seemed like being part of this music would initiate a lot of what I'd like to get out of life—a good time! But a good time with deep roots and meaning." Shorter began studying the saxophone and progressed quickly as a musician, to the point that while still in high school, he was invited to sit in with saxophonist Sonny Stitt. He had established a reputation as a budding talent with a fresh and adventurous sound; local musicians referred to him as "that kid from Newark."

Shorter moved to New York City after high school and received a degree in music education from New York University, where he frustrated music teachers by his mixing of music composition styles. Shorter continued

Born August 25, 1933, in Newark, N.J.; wife's name, Anna Maria. *Education:* New York University, B.A., 1956.

Worked in a sewing machine factory prior to entering college; served in U.S. Army, 1956-58; saxophonist and musical director, Art Blakey's Jazz Messengers, 1959-63; saxophonist, Miles Davis Quintet, 1964-70; co-founded Weather Report with Joe Zawinul, 1970; saxophonist and co-leader, Weather Report, 1970-85; formed his own band in 1985. Appeared in the film *'Round Midnight.*

Awards: Numerous awards from *down beat,* 1970-77; Grammy nominations with Weather Report, 1972, 1981, and 1982; Grammy Award with Weather Report, 1979; named Best Soprano Sax by *down beat,* 1984 and 1985; Grammy Award, 1987, for best jazz instrumental composition.

Addresses: *Home*—Los Angeles, Calif. *Record company*—Columbia Records, 51 West 52nd St., New York, N.Y. 10019.

to play locally, establishing connections that would serve him well when he was drafted into the U.S. Army in 1956. Shorter did gigs while he was in the Army, and was once asked to play at New York's Cafe Bohemia alongside such jazz greats as Oscar Pettiford, Art Blakey, Max Roach, and Jackie McLean. Shorter recalled to Yanow the importance of the event: "I was standing at the bar by the door, and Max Roach, whom I'd never met, came up to me and said, 'Hey, you're the kid from Newark. . . . Come on up and play,' he said. I did what I could but wondered what kind of contribution I could be making with all of these giants up there. I started to leave the stand, but someone grabbed me by the back of the shirt—I think it was Max—and he told me to play more. It was a great night for me."

Shorter got his first big break after the Army, when Art Blakey asked him to be musical director of his be-bop group, The Jazz Messengers. Under Blakey, Shorter was encouraged to develop his unusual compositions, and obtained much recording and concert experience. He also traveled around the world with the band, gaining experiences that would later figure into his appearance in the 1986 jazz film *'Round Midnight.* Shorter played with the Miles Davis Quintet from 1964 to 1970, a period during which Lyons and Perlo stated he "reached maturity as a soloist." Throughout the 1960s, as Larry Kart reported in the *Chicago Tribune,* Shorter

was considered "one of the most dangerous players to ever pick up a horn—a man whose solos were described by various critics as 'quietly maniacal' and 'clinically precise,' full of 'abrupt changes of mood' and 'wild satanic humor.'"

In 1970, Shorter and pianist Joe Zawinul founded Weather Report, a jazz/fusion group with which Shorter would play for the next fifteen years. A number of jazz commentators note that this period in Shorter's career saw much of his musical talent underutilized; Lyons and Perlo commented that "Shorter assumed an ensemble, texture-oriented role here." Shorter composed less with Weather Report and his previously active freelancing career diminished. In 1985, however, he broke away to form his own group—a move which delighted music enthusiasts who felt that Shorter's talents deserved more exposure. Shorter commented to Yanow about the decision to break away: "I just said to myself that if I don't do it now, I never will. . . . I've decided that it's time for me to be more sociable as a musician and, with this new band, to get around more."

Shorter is known as an elusive conversationalist when talking about his career and music. Regarding the former, he told Yanow: "Describing music is very difficult. Eric Gravitt used to say that if he could describe how he played drums, he wouldn't need to play them. Music really has to be experienced. I used to try to explain to people what be-bop sounded like without playing a record. It can't be done. Members of our audience have called our music fresh, exhilarating, happy, hopeful, I even heard the word young—meaning enthusiastic."

A practicing Buddhist, Shorter is philosophical about the future direction of his music. Asked whether creativity is his primary guide, Shorter responded to Woodard: "The forces of the phantom navigator, to me, are a part of every human life. . . . Whether you're aware of it or not. It's a dormant part, but a very essential entity—the center of the entity of whatever life is. Whether we're alive or dead, there's this navigator which is not devoid of ourselves, but is actually us."

Selected discography

As Leader

Schizophrenia, Blue Note, 1968.
Supernova, Blue Note, 1970.
Native Dancer, Columbia, 1974.
Etcetera, Blue Note, 1981.
Juju, Blue Note, 1984.
Atlantis, Columbia, 1986.

Phantom Navigator, Columbia, 1987.
Adam's Apple, Blue Note, 1987.
Joy Ryder, Columbia, 1988.

With The Jazz Messengers

Roots & Herbs, Blue Note.
Indestructible, Blue Note.
Free for All, Blue Note.
Live Messengers, Blue Note.

With Miles Davis

E.S.P., Columbia, 1965.
Nefertiti, Columbia, 1968.
In a Silent Way, Columbia, 1969.
Bitches Brew, Columbia, 1970.
Live at the Plugged Nickel, Columbia, 1982.

With Weather Report

I Sing the Body Electric, Columbia, 1972.
Mysterious Traveler, Columbia, 1974.
Black Market, Columbia, 1976.

Heavy Weather, Columbia, 1977.
8:30, Columbia, 1979.
Night Passage, Columbia, 1980.
Weather Report, Columbia, 1982.

Sources

Books

Lyons, Len, and Don Perlo, *Jazz Portraits: The Lives and Music of the Jazz Masters,* Morrow, 1989.

Periodicals

Chicago Tribune, November 17, 1985.
down beat, April 1986.
Jazz Journal International, April 1986.
Musician, October 1987; September 1988.

—*Michael E. Mueller*

Beverly Sills

Operatic soprano

She may have retired a decade ago, but Beverly Sills remains one of the most famous opera stars in America. A coloratura soprano of the first magnitude, bearing the characteristic light, agile voice marked by elaborate embellishment, Sills achieved international fame after a long apprenticeship with the New York City Opera and other companies. For slightly more than a decade the effervescent and gracious Sills thrilled opera audiences worldwide with her passionate interpretations of opera's finest roles. *New York* magazine correspondent Peter G. Davis remembered that when Sills "reigned as America's Queen of Opera," her performances were distinguished by "her wonderful freshness, warmth, spontaneity, generosity of spirit, inner glow, and intuitive artistry."

Beverly Sills was born Belle Miriam Silverman in Brooklyn, New York, on May 25, 1929. Her parents were both immigrants from Eastern Europe. A nickname, "Bubbles," stuck with her from birth because she was literally born with a bubble in her mouth. Sills was in fact a bubbly and attractive child who showed musical talent from an incredibly early age. She was only three when she sang a song to win the "Miss Beautiful Baby of 1932" contest in Brooklyn; by the age of six she was performing regularly on New York City's WOR Radio.

Sills's parents had a small collection of opera recordings and the budding diva memorized the arias in phonetic Italian before she was seven. Her mother decided to give her private lessons with Estelle Liebling, one of New York's premier voice teachers. Liebling was impressed with the youngster's innate ability and encouraged her to pursue more radio work. While most girls her age were skipping rope, Sills was busy in the radio studio, first as a member of the *Major Bowes Capitol Family Hour* and then as a principle in the musical soap opera *Our Gal Sunday*. Her first love was opera, however, so she "retired" from radio at the age of 12 to study her primary interest.

Almost immediately after finishing high school in 1945, Sills landed a position as a member of a Gilbert and Sullivan national touring company. Sills quickly assumed principal roles in the company's operettas, including *Countess Maritza* and *The Merry Widow,* but the constant travel from city to city was exhausting. After less than two years she returned to New York and resumed her lessons with Liebling, determined to devote herself to grand opera.

Sills made her operatic debut with the Philadelphia Civic Opera in 1947, singing the part of Frasquita in Georges Bizet's *Carmen.* Although she received good notices, she was not an overnight success, and soon found herself back in Manhattan, singing at clubs to make ends meet. In 1951 and 1952 she toured the country again, this time with the Charles L. Wagner Opera Company. The pace was still rigorous—Sills sang Violetta in Giuseppe Verdi's *La Traviata* some 40 times and Micaela in *Carmen* more than 60 times in a single year. Her best notices from this period came for her San Francisco Opera performance as Helen of Troy in Arrigo Boito's *Mefistofele.*

Sills's greatest ambition was to sing with the New York City Opera; she auditioned for the company numerous times before finally earning a position in 1955. Her debut there, as Rosalinde in Johann Straus's *Die Fledermaus,* was an unqualified success; critics agreed that she showed great promise. Soon after, Sills married wealthy Cleveland newspaperman Peter Buckeley Greenough. In 1958 she earned the best notices of her career for her performance as Baby in the New York premier of Douglas Moore's *The Ballad of Baby Doe.*

Between 1958 and 1961 Sills commuted to New York from her homes in Cleveland and Boston in order to appear in a succession of important operas. She was forced to curtail her professional activities, however, when it became clear that her children—born in 1959 and 1961—had special needs that demanded her constant attention. Sills's daughter Meredith was discovered to have progressive deafness; her son Peter Jr. was diagnosed as autistic. Anguished, Sills decided to devote all her time to her children and did not return to the stage until the mid-1960s.

When she did return, in a Boston production of Mozart's *The Magic Flute,* she discovered that her work helped ease the anxiety about her children. She came back to the New York City Opera in 1966, just in time to open the company's new home in Lincoln Center with a performance as Cleopatra in George Frideric Handel's *Julius Caesar.* The performance was Sills's first major triumph; it assured her prima donna status with the company, but more importantly it endeared her to the demanding New York audiences.

By 1969 Sills had become one of the most important coloratura sopranos in the United States. *New Yorker* critic Winthrop Sargeant wrote of her: "If I were recommending the wonders of New York to a tourist, I would place Beverly Sills at the top of the list—way ahead of such things as the Statue of Liberty and the Empire State Building." Davis commented that Sills's performances in a number of operas in the late 1960s "are among my most cherished operatic experiences. I imagine they are also fondly remembered by many other New York operagoers who felt that something precious vanished soon after the birth of Supersills."

Sills was 40 when she reached opera's pinnacle of success, and she pushed her voice to the limit in order to record and perform as often as her audience demanded. She was still at the top of her powers throughout the 1970s, and her enduring beauty and flair for theater brought throngs of new fans to classical opera. At her long overdue Metropolitan Opera debut in 1975 she was greeted with an eighteen-minute ovation. In Italy she was known as "La Fenomena" (the phenomenon) and "Il Mostro" (the prodigy). Public television brought Sills into homes across America; she quickly achieved a height of fame exceedingly rare for stars of the stage—and almost unheard of for divas.

Davis noted, however, that age and a relentless professional pace began to take their toll on Sills's vocal ability. "Sills's depressing operatic performances during those final years of her career were worse than vocally disappointing," the critic wrote. "They had degenerated into little more than mechanical personal appearances by a self-absorbed media heroine." Sills herself was perfectionist enough to know that her work was suffering. In 1980 she retired from performing and accepted the challenge of running the company that had been her base for more than 20 years.

The task of managing the New York City Opera proved every bit as daunting as the most demanding vocal performance. When Sills took over in 1980 the company was five million dollars in debt. To make matters worse, the factory housing the company's costumes burned down and critics panned key productions. Sills was nevertheless able to reverse the fortunes of the Opera, principally by charming funds from corporate donors. Sills also managed to increase attendance at the company's productions by introducing supertitles—a screen with translations suspended over the stage. Today, wrote Kathleen Brady in *Working Woman*, "instead of being $5 million in the red, the company operates in the black with a $25 million budget and has eliminated the accumulated deficit."

Sills gave up her professional responsibilities in 1989. She is now truly retired, living quietly with her husband of 35 years. She has received a number of prestigious honors, most notably the Presidential Medal of Freedom bestowed upon her by Jimmy Carter in 1980. She expresses no regrets about retiring, however. "I've done everything I set out to do," she once said, "sung in every opera house I wanted to. . . . To go on past the point where I should, I think would break my heart. I think my voice has served me very well. I'd like to put it to bed so it would go quietly, with pride."

Writings

Bubbles: A Self-Portrait, Bobbs-Merrill, 1976.
Beverly, Bantam, 1987.

Selected discography

Julius Caesar, RCA Victor.

The Ballad of Baby Doe, Deutsche Grammophon.
Bellini and Donizetti Heroines (arias), Westminster.
Manon, Angel.
Lucia di Lammermoor, Angel.
The Tales of Hoffmann, Angel.
I Puritani, Angel.
The Art of Beverly Sills, Volume 1 (arias), Angel.
The Art of Beverly Sills, Volume 2 (arias), Angel.
A Beverly Sills Concert, Angel.
Scenes and Arias from French Opera, Angel.
Mad Scenes, Angel.
Welcome to Vienna, Angel.

Sources

Books

Current Biography Yearbook 1982, Wilson, 1983.
Sills, Beverly, *Bubbles: A Self-Portrait*, Bobbs-Merrill, 1976.
Sills, Beverly, *Beverly*, Bantam, 1987.

Periodicals

Esquire, September 1974.
High Fidelity, February 1969.
Life, January 17, 1969.
Newsweek, April 21, 1969; October 26, 1970; July 4, 1976; November 3, 1980.
New York, April 1, 1985; October 3, 1988.
New Yorker, March 1, 1969.
Opera News, September 19, 1970; April 19, 1975; October 1980.
Time, November 22, 1971; April 7, 1975.
Working Woman, June 1987.

—*Anne Janette Johnson*

Ricky Skaggs

Singer, songwriter, instrumentalist, producer

No single artist has done more since 1980 to shape the course of country music than Ricky Skaggs, the dynamic tenor from Kentucky. Skaggs's virtuoso musicianship and firm belief in the power of traditional mountain music brought Nashville's slide into country-pop to a screeching halt, paving the way to stardom for a new wave of young traditionalists in a score of styles. Today Skaggs rests comfortably at the pinnacle of country stardom and is revered in some circles as the savior of the genre.

"Without the pioneering work of Ricky Skaggs, there probably wouldn't be any new country or new traditionalist music," wrote Andrew Vaughan in *Who's Who in New Country*. "Before George Strait was popular, before Reba McEntire was a superstar, before The Judds captured hearts with their mountain harmonies, Skaggs was breaking through country music's lowest ebb. The late seventies and early eighties had seen country go pop. . . . But Skaggs re-introduced the backwoods sound and with an impeccably tight band and clear, snappy bluegrass-influenced productions, his records and live shows came like a breath of fresh air through a stagnant Nashville smog."

Skaggs was certainly the ideal candidate to rescue country from the brink of blandness. He was—and is—enormously talented *and* ambitious, with a youthful determination to make a name for himself without sacrificing his artistic ideals. "I'm as country as corn bread," he told *People* magazine. "I don't think I could go pop if I had a mouthful of firecrackers."

Ricky Skaggs was playing professionally at a time when most youngsters are learning to read. He was born and raised in Lawrence County, Kentucky, the son of amateur country and gospel musicians. By the time Skaggs was three he was singing with his parents at social gatherings in his home county, and by the tender age of five he could play mandolin well enough to do it onstage. Remembering those years, Skaggs told *The Big Book of Bluegrass:* "Me and my mom would do a lot of duets, and my dad would sing baritone or bass, so we would have lead and tenor and bass, and it would sound real haunting and neat. We used to work a lot of churches, and we played in high schools and at pie suppers and theaters and stuff."

Skaggs's heroes in the music business were the Stanley Brothers—Ralph and Carter—who were prominent bluegrass musicians. While still in his early teens, Skaggs perfected his singing and picking until it mirrored Carter Stanley's to an astonishing degree. He also learned to play other instruments, including the fiddle and guitar. The constant round of local engagements led to a friendship with another young would-be bluegrass musician, Keith Whitley. The two pickers formed their own trio (with Whitley's brother on banjo) and were soon playing radio shows on WLKS in West Liberty, Kentucky.

One night Skaggs and Whitley traveled to West Virginia to hear Ralph Stanley give a concert. Stanley was late for the engagement, so the owner of the club asked the two to perform until Stanley arrived. Skaggs remembered: "So we got up and entertained the crowd, and they were liking it—and in walks Ralph Stanley, my hero. We were singing 'Little Glass of Wine' or something like that. He set his banjo case down on the barstool and I glanced over at him out of the corner of my eye. He wasn't really smiling, he was looking off somewhere like he was reminiscing, in a way. It turned out that he was. Afterward he said, 'Boys, the first time I saw y'all it just brought back so many memories of me and Carter.'"

Stanley was so impressed with Skaggs and Whitley that he asked them to join his band, the Clinch Mountain Boys. Skaggs was fifteen at the time, so he had to restrict his work to holidays and summers, but he became a phenomenon nonetheless. Ralph Stanley recruited Skaggs initially because the youngster could play and sing so much like the late Carter Stanley, but as Skaggs learned the ropes of bluegrass musicianship, his own formidable talents began to surface. Skaggs played with the Clinch Mountain Boys for two years, from 1970 until 1972. "It was a good training ground," he said, "and I learned a lot of things about feel and music—I learned what *not* to play. . . . Those were really great days."

Unfortunately, the earnings for bluegrass musicians were meager, and in 1972 Skaggs "retired" and took a job as a boiler repairman for a Washington, D.C.-area power company. He hated the work, so he was only too glad to return to music as a member of the Country Gentlemen in 1973. In that bluegrass band he played fiddle and sang high tenor. By the time he quit the Country Gentlemen some two years later (around the time he turned twenty), Skaggs had a considerable reputation and was sought after by a number of groups. He cut a solo album for Rebel Records, *That's It,* and then joined another band, J. D. Crowe and the New South.

The New South was a progressive bluegrass band in which pickers were encouraged to experiment with any manner of jazz, rock, and country influences. If Skaggs needed any final polish on his talents—a debatable point—he found it in this eclectic group. After touring with the New South for a year, Skaggs formed his own group, Boone Creek. The band—which for a time included Vince Gill on bass—cut two albums before breaking up in 1978.

Skaggs had become friends with Emmylou Harris while he was still working with the Country Gentlemen and she was singing in bars in Washington, D.C. In 1978 Harris asked Skaggs to join her band and help her with her first album. Even though he was yearning to break through as a solo artist at the time, Skaggs offered his vocal and instrumental services to Harris and steered her toward the old-time sound that so suited her voice. Skaggs sang and played on several of Harris's early albums, most notably the Grammy-winning *Roses in the Snow.*

The network of friendships Skaggs had forged finally proved to be the catalyst for his successful solo career. In 1980 he released an acoustic album, *Sweet Temptation,* that earned favorable reviews, and in 1982 he earned his first major label contract with Epic Records. Skaggs's first album with Epic, *Waitin' for the Sun To*

Shine, was a breakthrough both for him and for bluegrass-influenced country music in general. The album yielded two number-one hits, "Crying My Heart Out Over You" and "I Don't Care," and on its strength, Skaggs was named best male vocalist of 1982 by the Country Music Association.

Skaggs's success was accomplished without stylistic compromise. His albums featured acoustic instruments and tight bluegrass harmonies, and he recorded such bluegrass classics as "Children Go Where I Send Thee" and "Uncle Pen." In his book *Country Music U.S.A.,* Bill C. Malone analyzed the many reasons for Skaggs's popularity. "Skaggs is blessed with the clearest and most expressive tenor voice that has been heard in country music since Ira Louvin, and his instrumental virtuosity is breathtaking," Malone observed. "Skaggs has been hailed as a traditionalist, and he still refers to his music as 'bluegrass' and openly speaks of building a repertory that will appeal to hard-core country fans. . . . But, of course, he is not purely a traditionalist, even though he does traditional material beautifully. His music is informed by the wide range of music that he and other young people have heard and played in today's world—and by the experiences of living in a society vastly different from that of their parents."

Instrumentalist, singer, songwriter, performer, and producer—Skaggs has filled all of these shoes for himself and other Nashville superstars. The extent of his success is doubly amazing in view of his age—he was born in 1954. The 1990s are likely to see further accomplishments from the affable Skaggs, who spends some 125 days a year touring in his custom-designed bus. In *Stereo Review,* Alanna Nash called Skaggs's resuscitation of the old-time style "a noble and striking effort, a tour de force of indomitable American musical spirit."

Ricky Skaggs was inducted into the Grand Ole Opry in 1982, the youngest performer ever to become a regular on the Opry.

Selected discography

Solo LPs

That's It, Rebel.
Sweet Temptation, Sugar Hill, 1980.
Waitin' for the Sun To Shine, Epic, 1982.
Highways and Heartaches, Epic, 1982.
Don't Cheat in Our Hometown, Epic, 1983.
Country Boy, Epic, 1984.
Ricky Skaggs Live in London, Epic, 1985.
Love's Gonna Get Ya, Epic, 1986.
Comin' Home To Stay, Epic, 1988.
Kentucky Thunder, Epic, 1990.
Family and Friends, Rounder.
Ricky Skaggs's Favorite Country Songs, Epic.

With Boone Creek

Boone Creek, Rounder.
One Way Track, Sugar Hill.

Other

(With Tony Rice) *Skaggs and Rice,* Sugar Hill.

Has also appeared as featured guest performer on recordings by other artists, including Boone Creek's *Boone Creek* and *One Way Track;* J. D. Crowe and the New South's *The New South;* and Emmylou Harris's *Pieces of the Sky, Blue Kentucky Girl,* and *Roses in the Snow.*

Sources

Books

Kochman, Marilyn, editor, *The Big Book of Bluegrass,* Morrow, 1984.
Malone, Bill C., *Country Music U.S.A.,* revised edition, University of Texas Press, 1985.
Vaughan, Andrew, *Who's Who in New Country Music,* St. Martin's, 1989.

Periodicals

Bluegrass Unlimited, January 1977.
Country America, May 1990.
People, October 25, 1982.
Pickin', February 1979.
Rolling Stone, November 22, 1984; March 13, 1986.
Stereo Review, February 1984.
Vogue, March 1984.

—Anne Janette Johnson

Squeeze

British pop/rock group

Squeeze, a British band whose songwriters Chris Difford and Glenn Tilbrook have been favorably compared to superstar composing team John Lennon and Paul McCartney, has been in existence since 1975. Though the group has garnered large amounts of critical favor for its new wave and pop sound almost ever since that time, it was only in 1987 that they scored their first Top 40 hit in the United States with "Hourglass," from the album *Babylon and On.* But popular success has not caused a reduction in the number of Squeeze's laudatory reviews. As Mark Coleman put it in *Rolling Stone,* "Squeeze [is] . . . the great white hope of thinking-people's pop."

Difford and Tilbrook began writing songs together in the early 1970s. After creating quite a few tunes, they looked for a band to back them up. In 1975 the duo, both of whom played guitar, formed a group with keyboardist Julian Holland, drummer Gilson Lavis, and bass player Harry Kakoulli. They initially called themselves U.K. Squeeze, and just over a year after the band's inception they had landed a recording contract

For the Record. . .

Formed in 1975, disbanded in 1982, reformed in 1985; originally called UK Squeeze; present members include: **Chris Difford** (born August 31, in the U.K.; lyricist, guitarist, and occasional vocals); **Glenn Tilbrook** (born November 4, in the U.K.; composer, guitarist, and vocalist); **Julian "Jools" Holland** (born in the U.K.; keyboardist); **Gilson Lavis** (born in the U.K., drummer); **Keith Wilkinson** (bass guitarist). Past members have included **Harry Kakoulli, Paul Carrack, John Bentley,** and **Don Snow.**

Recording artists and concert performers, 1976-82, 1985—.

Addresses: *Record company*—A&M, 1416 La Brea Ave., Los Angeles, CA 90028.

with A&M Records. Squeeze's debut album, *U.K. Squeeze,* immediately scored them a Top 10 hit in England with the cut "Take Me, I'm Yours," but even after the album and single were released in the United States in 1978, the band did not get much in the way of popular attention. Favorable critical attention, however, Squeeze received in plenty; reviewer's lauds only increased with the advent of the group's second and third albums, *Cool for Cats* and *Argy Bargy.* Noteworthy cuts from these efforts included "Up the Junction" and "Slap and Tickle" from the former, and "Pulling Mussels" and "If I Didn't Love You" from the latter.

Squeeze's U.S. exposure was increased when the band was befriended by popular new wave musician Elvis Costello; he featured Squeeze as his warm-up act for his 1981 concerts in the United States. But at about the same time, Squeeze was experiencing important personnel changes. Kakoulli had left the band two years before to be replaced by John Bentley; Julian Holland left to be replaced by Paul Carrack. Carrack's vocals were featured in Squeeze's 1981 hit "Tempted," which, although it did not make a Top 40 position on the U.S. pop charts, was nevertheless an important breakthrough in gaining the band an audience in that country.

"Tempted" was only one of many critically acclaimed tracks on Squeeze's 1981 album, *East Side Story;* the group's 1982 effort, *Sweets From a Stranger,* produced another near hit in the United States—the thoughtful "Black Coffee in Bed." But on *Sweets From a Stranger* Carrack had already been replaced by yet another keyboard player, Don Snow. As Tilbrook told Coleman in *Rolling Stone,* "Snow was a brilliant pianist, but we'd just had one change too many at that point. The whole

internal structure of the band was falling apart." Thus, in 1982, Squeeze announced that they were disbanding, several of its members citing the difficulties of working together with the other strong individuals who made up the group.

Difford and Tilbrook continued to compose and record together. Lavis found work as a cab driver, and Holland had become the host of a popular British television show featuring music videos. In 1984 Difford and Tilbrook habitually told reporters that they were completely finished with Squeeze, but in 1985 they were in search of backup musicians for a charity performance. In addition to Keith Wilkinson, who had served as bass player for the duo during their post-Squeeze period, they came up with Lavis and Holland. Tilbrook explained to Coleman: "When we did that charity gig, it was so obvious that we should get back together, I felt embarrassed. It took a couple of days of hesitant phone calls to establish that everyone felt the same way I did."

The four former members, plus Wilkinson, reconstituted Squeeze. The band's first comeback album was titled *Cosi Fan Tutti Frutti,* symbolizing the fact that its musical influences range from classical composer Wolfgang Amadeus Mozart to 1950s pioneer rocker Little Richard. Though critics welcomed Squeeze's return, most agreed that *Cosi Fan Tutti Frutti* seemed artificial and stilted compared to the group's previous work. *Babylon and On,* released in 1987, fared much better. "Comeback albums aren't supposed to eclipse a band's original work, but Squeeze's 'Babylon and On' comes pretty close," a *Stereo Review* critic applauded. Eric Levin of *People* joyfully exclaimed: "Squeeze, it is a big thrill to report, is still inimitably, immutably, incorrigibly Squeeze." In addition to the many rave reviews, however, the band finally broke the U.S. Top 40 with the bouncy hit single "Hourglass."

Still together in 1990, Squeeze continued its winning ways with the album *Frank.* Michael Small of *People* labeled it "fine," and singled out cuts like "Slaughtered, Gutted, and Heartbroken" and "Love Circles" for special praise.

Selected discography

U.K. Squeeze (includes "Take Me, I'm Yours"), A&M, 1978.
Cool for Cats (includes "Cool for Cats," "Up the Junction," and "Slap and Tickle"), A&M, 1979.
Argy Bargy (includes "Pulling Mussels" and "If I Didn't Love You"), A&M, 1980.
East Side Story (includes "Tempted," "Labeled With Love," "Heaven," and "Vanity Fair"), A&M, 1981.
Sweets From a Stranger (includes "Black Coffee in Bed"), 1982.

Singles—45's and Under, A&M, 1982.
Cosi Fan Tutti Frutti, A&M, 1985.
Babylon and On (includes "Hourglass," "Footprints," "Tough Love," "The Prisoner," and "Trust Me to Open My Mouth"), A&M, 1987.
Frank (includes "Slaughtered, Gutted, and Heartbroken" and "Love Circles"), A&M, 1990.

Sources

People, November 2, 1987; January 8, 1990.
Rolling Stone, December 3, 1987; November 16, 1989.
Stereo Review, February, 1988.

—Elizabeth Wenning

Ralph Stanley

Bluegrass singer, songwriter, and banjo player

Ralph Stanley is one of the patriarchs of bluegrass, a banjo player, singer, and songwriter whose work harks back to the very genesis of the bluegrass style. Stanley made his name singing with his brother Carter and their group, the Clinch Mountain Boys, in the late 1940s. Ever since that time—and despite Carter's sudden death in 1966—Ralph Stanley has been a headliner on the country-folk circuit. As Douglas Gordon put it in *The Big Book of Bluegrass*, Stanley's "sky-reaching tenor voice and the simple, bright clarity of his banjo are sounds dear to the ears of thousands of loyal fans."

Ralph and Carter Stanley were born and raised in Virginia's Clinch Mountains, a fertile ground for string-band musicians. Their parents both played musical instruments, and their mother often entertained with the banjo, playing it in the old clawhammer style. Ralph took up the banjo when he was barely ten and soon could pick in both his mother's style and a finger-and-thumb style that he learned from a mountain musician. Carter gravitated to the guitar, and soon the brothers were singing and picking together.

Atlantic contributor Robert Cantwell noted that the Stanley Brothers' style was "strangely steeped in an ancient mountain modality which persisted even after they had acquired the habits of bluegrass." The brothers actually began performing professionally even before the music known as "bluegrass" was born. In the early 1940s—when both were still teens—they could be heard on WNVA in Norton, Virginia. They moved to the larger WCYB in Bristol, on the Virginia/Tennessee border, in 1946.

Just at the same time, a banjoist named Earl Scruggs was introducing a new picking style as a member of Bill Monroe and the Blue Grass Boys. Ralph Stanley was quick to incorporate the new style into his own playing. By 1947 the Stanley Brothers had gained wide popularity by playing music similar to Bill Monroe's. They could therefore lay claim to the distinction of being perhaps the second or third bluegrass band in the country. At any rate, the Stanley Brothers' *Farm and Fun Time* show became a favorite radio broadcast on WCYB, and the group was in high demand for live shows as well.

"Now that was one happy time," Ralph Stanley told Gordon. "We started playing five, six, seven nights a week. And everywhere we'd go we'd pack [the house] one or two times. I know for a time in '47 we was booked as high as 90 days ahead. Those were some real happy days." The Stanley Brothers signed with a Bristol recording label, Rich-R-Tone, and cut their first bluegrass side, "Molly and Tenbrooks," in 1948. The following year they moved to the larger Columbia label, where they turned out some of bluegrass music's classic recordings.

The Stanley Brothers did not achieve fame clinging to any other artist's coat tails. In fact they carved a unique style, greatly in debt to the simple, mournful, and often eerie music of their Clinch Mountain home. Ralph wrote a number of enduring songs, including "Rank Stranger," "White Dove," "The Fields have Turned Brown," and "Clinch Mountain Backstep," a spirited banjo tune that made advances on the Scruggs picking style. The brothers made fine vocal harmony together, too, with Ralph taking tenor and Carter taking lead. The band was rounded out by a variety of sidemen on mandolin, fiddle, and bass.

Ralph Stanley told Gordon that the Stanley Brothers endured some very lean years in the mid-1950s. "This rock and roll trend, with Elvis Presley, changed everything around," he said. "Flatt and Scruggs, Don Reno and Red Smiley, Bill Monroe, and the Stanley Brothers were the only bands I know who survived that. . . . We wasn't makin' a livin' at it then, but we survived." The Stanley Brothers not only survived, they actually thrived

For the Record. . .

Full name, Ralph Edmond Stanley; born February 25, 1927, in Stratton, Va.; son of country musicians.

Banjo player and vocalist, 1938—. With brother, Carter Stanley (guitarist/vocalist; born August 27, 1925, died December 1, 1966), began playing and singing professionally for station WNVA, Norton, Va., ca. 1942; moved to WCYB, Bristol, Tenn., 1946. Member of the Stanley Brothers and the Clinch Mountain Boys, 1946-66; currently plays as Ralph Stanley and the Clinch Mountain Boys. Other Clinch Mountain Boys have included Pee Wee Lambert (mandolin), George Shuffler (mandolin), Curly Cline (fiddle), Ricky Skaggs (mandolin, fiddle), Keith Whitley (guitar), Ricky Lee, and Jack Cooke.

Signed with Rich-R-Tone Records (Bristol, Va.), 1948; moved to Columbia Records, 1949; also recorded with Mercury, Starday, and King labels. Group has toured widely in the United States, Europe, and Canada and has appeared at the Newport Folk Festival and at the Albert Hall in London.

Addresses: *Record company*—Rebel Records, Box 3057, Roanoke, VA 24015.

artistically, and thus they were well poised to take advantage of the new interest in bluegrass brought about by the folk revival of the early 1960s.

Between 1960 and 1966, the popularity of the Stanley Brothers soared. They played all over the United States and in such unlikely venues as Switzerland, Germany, Sweden, and Denmark. A highlight of their career came in March of 1966 when they performed at London's Albert Hall. Later that same year they were featured entertainers at the prestigious Bean Blossom bluegrass festival in Bean Blossom, Indiana. And then, quite suddenly, Carter Stanley died on December 1, 1966.

Unlike some musicians who work with their siblings, the Stanley brothers were very close. For years after Carter's death Ralph paid homage to his brother in every show he did. More significantly, Ralph recruited musicians who played and sang just like his deceased brother. Cantwell wrote in 1972 that to hear Ralph Stanley and the Clinch Mountain Boys "is to feel that Carter has been reincarnated. . . . To hear the whole group . . . is to hear not only Ralph and Carter Stanley but also a kind of geological record of their career,

collapsed into some of the most hair-raising and beautiful harmonies in any music."

Ralph may have intended to preserve his brother's memory, but what he also preserved was the sound of the very roots of bluegrass. Throughout the 1980s he continued to perform with the Clinch Mountain Boys and also lent his talents to such avant-garde groups as the O'Kanes. The Stanley Brothers have proven enormously influential in the course of country music—Ricky Skaggs, for instance, is a former Clinch Mountain Boy, and a number of virtuoso banjoists list Ralph as a mentor.

"If Bill Monroe's voice sounds like the wind," Cantwell wrote, "Ralph Stanley's sounds like the woods. . . . Ralph's voice is not perfect; there is a slight quaver in it, and a laurel twig. But it can stir up matter at the primitive floor of the soul with as much authority as a Navajo chant." Ralph Stanley was awarded an honorary Doctor of Arts degree from Lincoln Memorial University in 1976. He lives in McClure, Virginia, a town not far from his Clinch Mountain birthplace.

Selected discography

Solo Albums

Ralph Stanley: A Man and His Music, Rebel.
Hills of Home, King.

With the Clinch Mountain Boys

A Cry from the Cross, Rebel.
Old Home Place, Rebel.
The Stanley Sound Around the World, King.
Ralph Stanley Plays Requests, Rebel.
Ralph Stanley With the Clinch Mountain Boys, Rebel.
I Want To Preach the Gospel, Rebel.
Let Me Rest on Peaceful Mountain, Rebel.
Old Country Church, Rebel.
Ralph Stanley and the Clinch Mountain Boys Live in Japan, Rebel.
Lonesome and Blue, Rebel.

With Carter Stanley and the Clinch Mountain Boys

That Little Old Country Church House, County.
Long Journey Home, County.
The Legendary Stanley Brothers Recorded Live, Volume 1, Rebel.
The Legendary Stanley Brothers Recorded Live, Volume 2, Rebel.
Folk Concert, Starday.
Jacob's Vision, Starday.
Mountain Music Sounds, Starday.

Hymns of the Cross, King.
Good Old Camp Meeting Songs, Starday.
The Best of the Stanley Brothers, Starday.
For the Good People, King.
The Stanley Brothers' First Album, Melodeon.
The Stanley Brothers, Mercury.
The Stanley Brothers Together for the Last Time, Rebel.
The Stanley Brothers on the Air, Wangol.
Banjo in the Hills, Starday.
Sing the Songs I Like Best, King.
The Stanley Brothers in Person, Power Pak.
Bluegrass, Volume 1, Rounder.
Bluegrass, Volume 2, Rounder.
The Stanley Brothers' Sixteen Greatest Hits, Starday.
Mountain Boys, King.
Mountain Song Favorites, Nashville.

Sources

Books

The Illustrated Encyclopedia of Country Music, Harmony, 1977.
Kochman, Marilyn, editor, *The Big Book of Bluegrass*, Morrow, 1984.
Malone, Bill C., *Country Music U.S.A.*, revised edition, University of Texas Press, 1985.

Periodicals

Atlantic, March 1972.

—*Anne Janette Johnson*

Steely Dan

Pop/rock duo

In an eight-year recording history stretching from 1972 to 1980, Steely Dan earned a reputation as perfectionists. Each of their seven albums is like a highly polished diamond, created by a thinking man's band, with finely crafted compositions that weave back and forth between jazz and rock, and lyrics loaded with irony and cynicism. This unique approach has won them admirers and yet also turned off many a listener who felt their approach too cold and calculating. "Think of the Dan as the first post-boogie band: the beat swings more than it blasts or blisters, the chord changes defy our primitive subconscious expectations, and the lyrics underline their own difficulty—as well as the difficulty to which they refer—with arbitrary personal allusions, most of which are ruses," explained Robert Christgau in *Christgau's Record Guide*.

The nucleus of the group, or rather the duo, is Walter Becker and Donald Fagen, two musicians who met at Bard College in upstate New York in 1967. The two played in amateur bands (with names like Bad Rock Group) during school and afterwards hit the road as

172

backup musicians for Jay and the Americans from 1970 to 1971. In the meantime they enjoyed little success in pedaling their own tunes to various labels; the most notable being "I Mean to Shine" which found its way onto a Barbara Streisand LP.

While touring with the Americans, Becker and Fagen befriended Gary Katz, who had recently joined the staff at ABC Records in California. The two relocated to Los Angeles at the insistence of Katz and were soon working at ABC themselves rewriting songs. They recorded their own compositions when studio time was available and ran the product by their bosses. "We had zero expectations," Becker told *Rolling Stone.* "In fact, we were amazed that ABC bought the album at all. It was like a dream come true." 1972's *Can't Buy A Thrill* yielded two substantial hits for the duo, "Do It Again" and "F_elin' In The Years." Katz produced the LP, while Jeff Baxter and Denny Diaz played guitars and Jim Hodder handled the drumming. Lead singer David Palmer soon left the group and Fagen took over on vocals the following year for their second album, *Countdown to Ecstasy.*

That album relied heavily on extended soloing and studio techniques but produced the fine cut entitled "My Old School" with slide guitar courtesy of Rick Derringer. Steely Dan (named after a female sex tool from William S. Burroughs's novel, *The Naked Lunch*) was pushed into a touring blitz by then-manager Joel Cohen to support their records. But that would only last one more album for Becker and Fagen were not enticed by the road or any of its cliches. The band played their last live show in 1974 after the release of *Pretzel Logic,*

which included another hit, "Rikki Don't Lose That Number." The two leaders decided to devote their energies solely toward producing excellent albums, while the other band members, who still wanted to tour, moved on.

"It was 1974 and the mystique of rock was starting to fade, certainly as a cultural item," Fagen told Robert Palmer in *Rolling Stone.* "The concert scene seemed sleazy to us, and we weren't satisfied with the way the band was clicking. It was taking a tremendous psychic and physical toll on us. Basically, we couldn't hack it; we just didn't want to live that way anymore." Jeff Baxter and keyboardist Michael McDonald quit to join the Doobie Brothers and Becker and Fagen decided to dip into the rich pool of studio musicians to create their songs. Fagen said in *Rolling Stone,* "If we can't find a studio musician who's comfortable with a particular feel, then we'll haul out our instruments." Becker added, "It wouldn't bother me at all not to play on my own album."

Apparently it didn't as their next LP, 1975's *Katy Lied,* relied on studio veterans Larry Carlton, Hugh McCracken, Chuck Rainey, Jeff Porcaro and David Paich, as did their follow-up, The *Royal Scam,* which included four excellent tracks, "Kid Charlemagne," "Don't Take Me Alive," "The Royal Scam," and "The Fez." Diaz was the only original member left by *Katy Lied,* and after that Carlton took over and produced guitar solos that influenced a whole generation of six-stringers who sought to duplicate his sound.

Becker and Fagen had found a vehicle for creating and ignored critics who found their music formulaic. "We've real charts and everything," Becker countered in *Rolling Stone.* "It's more productive. The musicians enjoy getting asked to do something that's challenging. We like working with an overview, too. It's difficult, but it's fun. It's not stupid music." As for their employees, Fagen told the same publication, "That cold stigma about studio hacks is nonsense. You can get studio musicians to sound exactly like a rock and roll band."

In 1977 Steely Dan released their first album to break into the Top 5, *Aja,* "a particular favorite of fanatics who savor Becker's and Fagen's Gordian Knot of oblique losers, dopers, ravaged lovers and doomed optimistics," wrote Cameron Crowe in *Rolling Stone.* Of their lyrics, Becker said to *Stone's* Richard Cromelin, "We're writing about people who are more or less at the end of their proverbial tethers. There's nothing more boring than affluence and a stable, effortless existence. There's not much to say about that anyway. That's Paul Simon. We'd be walking into his dangling conversation."

Once again expert sidemen were utilized, like Wayne

Shorter, Victor Feldman, Bernard Purdie, and Lee Ritenour, to name but a few. The LP contained only seven cuts, which may or may not have been beneficial, according to one's taste. "Whole songs like 'Josie' and 'Aja' are structured around solos by sidemen," wrote Ken Tucker in the *Rolling Stone Illustrated History of Rock & Roll.* "For all the technical complexity, every tune is inevitable after the first chorus." Becker and Fagen *were* relying on the players more and more, but their audience didn't seem to mind. Steely Dan scored a major hit in 1978 with "FM (No Static At All)" for their new manager, Irving Azoff, and his motion picture, *FM.*

A greatest hits album was released in 1978 and shortly after, ABC was absorbed by MCA. The band had already decided to switch to Warner Brothers but owed one more album under their contract. Shooting immediately into the Top 20 in 1980 was *Gaucho,* which Ariel Swartley in *Rolling Stone* described as having "perfected the aesthetic of the tease. Their sound is as slippery as their irony." Guitar virtuosos Mark Knopfler (now of Dire Straits), Rick Derringer, and Hiram Bullock were called in for duty this time around. Bullock described to Tad Lathrop in *Guitar Player* the process that occurs in the recording of a Steely Dan record. "They are as meticulous as everyone says. I think we worked a week on one song. At one point we worked nine hours on one fourbar insert. You know, you just do it. They wanted perfectionism, and I could understand what they were doing . . . they have these sort of crystalline compositions, like little jewels. They don't want you to imprint your personality over their music; they want you to get inside their music and use your talent to bring their song to life."

Steely Dan, for all their popularity, still may have been ahead of their time. Artists like Sting and Sade shined during the 1980s with music crafted in very much the same vein where Becker and Fagen left off. Maybe the vast majority of contemporary music fans finally grew up and favored a sound that broke out of the three-chord syndrome. Style and taste were things Steely Dan exuded but sometimes felt they had to hold back. "I think a lot of people in the audience are unaware that anything unusual is happening harmonically, and so much the better, because there are people who are offended by that sort of thing, who think it's Ed Sullivan pop. Broadway show music," Becker explained to *Rolling Stone.* "For the benefit of that portion of the audience, we try to make these things work so that they don't stick out."

Selected discography

Can't Buy A Thrill, ABC, 1972.
Countdown to Ecstacy, ABC, 1973.
Pretzel Logic, ABC, 1974.
Katy Lied, ABC, 1975.
The Royal Scam, ABC, 1976.
Aja, ABC, 1977.
Greatest Hits, ABC, 1978.
Gaucho, MCA, 1980.

Sources

Books

Christgau, Robert, *Christgau's Record Guide,* Ticknor and Fields, 1981.
The Rolling Stone Illustrated History of Rock and Roll, edited by Jim Miller, Random House/Rolling Stone Press, 1976.
The Rolling Stone Record Guide, edited by Dave Marsh with John Swenson, Random House/Rolling Stone Press, 1979.

Periodicals

Guitar Player, November 1976; December 1980; January 1987; September 1988.
Rolling Stone, June 17, 1976; December 29, 1977; February 5, 1981.

—Calen D. Stone

Stephen Stills

Rock guitarist, singer-songwriter

Singer-songwriter Stephen Stills has influenced rock music in many different guises. He first gained fame as a member of the 1960s group Buffalo Springfield, whose biggest hit was Stills's composition, "For What It's Worth." After that band dissolved, Stills came together first with David Crosby and Graham Nash, later with Neil Young, to form the group responsible for folk-rock classics such as "Suite: Judy Blue Eyes" and "Wooden Ships." He has had success as a solo artist as well, particularly with his 1971 hit, "Love the One You're With."

Stills was born January 3, 1945, in Dallas, Texas. His family moved around quite a bit, staying mostly in the southern United States, with the exception of a brief sojourn to Central America. They stayed the longest in New Orleans, Louisiana. Stills displayed an interest in music throughout his childhood, and by the time he reached adolescence he had learned to play several instruments, including drums, guitar, and tambourine. He continued to practice both during his stints as a racetrack stable boy and while he attended the University of Florida studying political science.

As with most good musicians, the lure of Stills's art overcame his academic will, and he left college. He traveled to New York City, attracted by its burgeoning folk music scene. After brief apprenticeships with several bands, he settled with the Au Go Go Singers, a folk group that got dates in the eastern United States and Canada. While with them, Stills made the acquaintance of Richie Furay and Neil Young, with whom he would later found Buffalo Springfield. Before he did so, however, he and Furay grew more interested in the rock scene; Stills left the Au Go Gos and moved to Los Angeles, California, in pursuit of this interest.

While in Los Angeles, Stills tried out for the created-for-television pop group, the Monkees. As Geoffrey Stokes revealed in the book *Rock of Ages: The Rolling Stone History of Rock and Roll,* however, he was "passed over because of imperfect teeth and incipient baldness." Undaunted, Stills called Furay and urged him to follow him to California shortly afterwards. They were in the process of working up songs together when they met up with Young, coincidentally visiting from his native Canada. With the addition of Bruce Palmer and Dewey Martin, Buffalo Springfield was born.

Los Angeles-area gigs quickly led to a recording contract for Stills and Springfield, but their reputation spread before they could release records. They were recruited to provide the opening act for the Byrds; at this time Stills met Byrds member David Crosby. When Buffalo Springfield's records were released, they scored a quick regional hit with "Nowadays Clancy Can't Even

Sing," but this was soon overshadowed by a song Stills wrote about the Sunset Strip riots in Los Angeles in 1966, "For What It's Worth." Stokes hailed it as "the first explicit document of an unbridgeable generational chasm," and it became one of the anthems of the late 1960s youth movement, reaching Number 7 on the charts.

Though Stokes emphasized that "Buffalo Springfield was anything but a one-hit wonder," the group broke up after about a year because of the strong, independent creativity of its members, who wished to pursue individual projects. Soon afterwards, Stills found himself in the middle of a jam session with his friend Crosby, and fellow musician Graham Nash of the British group the Hollies. The three were so delighted with the harmonies they created that they decided to form a band, overcoming many difficulties with their respective record companies and negotiating Nash's release from the Hollies to do so.

By 1969 the trio was able to release their first album on Atlantic Records, *Crosby, Stills, and Nash.* One of the most successful singles from it was Stills's composition to his then-lover, singer Judy Collins, "Suite: Judy Blue Eyes." In addition to Nash's "Marrakesh Express," the album also included Stills's "Helplessly Hoping" and his collaboration with Crosby, "Wooden Ships." Despite the individuals' various commitments, Stills managed to get together with his fellow band members to tour successfully three months after *Crosby, Stills, and Nash* was released. Just in time for these appearances, they also recruited Young. He was a large factor in the success of their second album, *Deja Vu,* which also included a popular version of songwriter Joni Mitchell's

"Woodstock," and the hits "Teach Your Children" and "Our House." Stills contributed the cut "4 and 20."

As with Buffalo Springfield, however, Crosby, Stills, Nash, and Young was composed of strong individuals who often wished to work on separate projects. In 1971, Stills released his first solo album on Atlantic, aptly titled *Stephen Stills.* This included his energetic hit, "Love the One You're With." He followed up with *Stephen Stills II,* but while the album sold well, none of the singles were quite as successful as his first solo hit. In 1972, Stills took a new direction and formed a more country-flavored group called Manassas. Though many critics panned them, they did well with fans and their two albums, *Manassas* and *Down the Road,* spawned the moderate hits "Rock'n'Roll Crazies" and "Isn't It About Time."

After recording two more solo albums, Stills reunited with Crosby and Nash for a 1977 effort, again titled *Crosby, Stills, and Nash.* The trio had a hit with "Just a Song Before I Go" and with Stills's composition, "Dark Star." Stills continued to work on his own projects during the late 1970s and 1980s, occasionally coming together with Crosby, Nash, and Young for concerts. All four released the album *American Dream* in 1989. Though critic David Browne in *High Fidelity* panned the comeback album, concluding that the four musicians had performed better when they first joined, Susan Borey in *Audio* praised Stills's composition "Got it Made" as "a gem." She described it further as "soulful, full of irony . . . a perfect vehicle for a voice that's become *more* buttery and resonant."

Selected discography

Albums; with Buffalo Springfield

Buffalo Springfield, Atlantic, 1966.
Buffalo Springfield Again, Atlantic, 1967.
Last Time Around, Atlantic, 1968.

Albums; with Crosby and Nash, or with Crosby, Nash, and Young

Crosby, Stills, and Nash (includes "Suite: Judy Blue Eyes," "Marrakesh Express," "Helplessly Hoping," and "Wooden Ships"), Atlantic, 1969.
Deja Vu (includes "Woodstock," "Teach Your Children," "Our House," and "4 and 20"), Atlantic, 1970.
Four Way Street, Atlantic, 1971.
So Far, Atlantic, 1974.
Crosby, Stills, and Nash (includes "Just a Song Before I Go" and "Dark Star"), Atlantic, 1977.
American Dream (includes "American Dream,""Got It Made," "Compass," and "Nighttime for the Generals"), Atlantic, 1989.

Albums; with Manassas

Manassas (includes "Rock'n'Roll Crazies"), Atlantic, 1972.
Down the Road (includes "Isn't It About Time"), Atlantic, 1973.

Selected solo albums

Stephen Stills (includes "Love the One You're With"), Atlantic, 1970.
Stephen Stills II (includes "Change Partners," "Marianne," "Sit Yourself Down," and "It Doesn't Matter"), Atlantic, 1971.
Stephen Stills, Columbia, 1975.
Illegal Stills, Columbia, 1976.

Sources

Books

Helander, Brock, *The Rock Who's Who,* Schirmer Books, 1982.
Ward, Ed, Geoffrey Stokes, and Ken Tucker, *Rock of Ages: The Rolling Stone History of Rock and Roll,* Summit Books, 1986.

Periodicals

Audio, March 1989.
High Fidelity, March 1989.

—*Elizabeth Wenning*

George Strait

Singer, songwriter

A vocalist blessed with good looks and a vibrant personality, George Strait has dominated the country music scene since the early 1980s. Strait was on the verge of quitting the entertainment business in favor of a job in agriculture when he managed to wrangle a contract with MCA Records. Since then he has arguably been MCA's biggest pure country performer, with almost a dozen gold albums to his credit.

Strait's work is classic country and honky tonk—the kind of fiddle and pedal steel guitar-laced music that has been called "country" since the days of Hank Williams and Ernest Tubb. To quote Montgomery Brower in *People* magazine, Strait's "throwback blend of lilting guitar licks, keening fiddles, plaintive pedaled steel and taut, lonesome cowboy vocals has put him in the vanguard of country music's counterrevolutionaries, those performers who have refused to abandon old-time simplicity for Nashville slick." Strait has never—and probably *will* never—set his sights on a crossover hit. According to Andrew Vaughan in *Who's Who in New Country Music,* the clean-cut Strait has proved "that country roots [are] still preferable, even in the age of compact disc."

George Strait was born and raised in Pearsall, Texas, the second of three children of a high school math teacher. His childhood on a small Texas ranch was rather conventional, and like most teenagers in the 1960s he gravitated to rock music and thought little of country. After high school Strait tried college, but he dropped out, married his high school sweetheart, and joined the Army. Only then did he begin to respond to the music of the artists who have become his idols—George Jones, Merle Haggard, and Hank Williams.

Strait was stationed at the Schofield Barracks in Hawaii in 1973 as part of his military service. While there he auditioned for an Army-sponsored country and western band, and was made lead singer. The band entertained at Army functions, presenting hours of Jones and Haggard songs, and gradually Strait's style began to echo his favorite country stars. When he was discharged from the Army, Strait formed his own band in Texas and continued to perform. The singer told Vaughan that he never really tried to be original when he did club work. "When you're a local act, and you're doing Merle Haggard and George Jones songs, people want you to sound like the records. So that's what you do; you sing like Merle or George and pretty soon that's just the way you sing."

The prospects did not seem brilliant for Strait and his band, despite their popularity in Texas. Several trips to Nashville in pursuit of a recording contract came to nothing, so Strait returned to college and earned a degree in agriculture. He was just on the verge of

Born in 1952 in Pearsall, Tex.; son of a high school math teacher; married, wife's name, Norma; children: Jennifer, George, Jr. *Education:* B.S. in agriculture, Southwest Texas State University, 1978.

Country singer, 1973—; began singing with a U.S. Army band during military service in Hawaii, continued fronting a band after discharge in 1975. Signed with MCA Records, 1981; had first top-ten country hit, "Unwound," 1981.

Awards: Recipient of numerous awards and honors from the country music industry, including male vocalist of the year and album of the year, both 1985, and male vocalist of the year, 1989, from Country Music Association. Has recorded more than ten gold albums.

Addresses: *Record company*—MCA Records, 70 Universal City Plaza, Universal City, CA 91608.

accepting a job with a firm that manufactured ranch equipment when his wife persuaded him to give Nashville one more try. With the help of a former MCA promotions man, Erv Woolsey, Strait managed to arrange a recording session with the MCA label. One of the songs from that first session, "Unwound," went to Number 4 on the country charts. MCA was quick to sign Strait after that, and Woolsey became his manager.

Hardly a month has passed since 1981 in which a George Strait song has not appeared somewhere on the country Top 100. Indeed, Brower suggested that Strait "has ridden the . . . country singles chart like a broncobuster with Krazy Glue on his jeans." Typically his albums have shipped gold and have hit Number 1 in the first week of release. His best-known work to date is probably *Does Fort Worth Ever Cross Your Mind?,* the album which won him 1985 entertainer of the year honors from the Country Music Association.

In the days when "crossover hit" was on everyone's lips in Nashville, Strait had the courage to resist the glitz. He stuck to his strengths—honky tonk and heartache—and won fans with his impeccable appearance and pine-fresh voice. Some critics scoffed, calling him a "yuppie-billy," but Strait made no apologies for his style. "If you start messing around with changing yourself," he told *People,* "you'll end up screwing up." By the mid-1980s Strait was playing more than 250 live appearances per year. He told *Newsweek:* "Everywhere I go, people tell me, 'Keep it country—don't change it.'"

Strait has also not succumbed to the Nashville tendency to make a star's life an open book. Offstage he is intensely private, living on a secluded ranch with his wife and two children. Strait does not describe himself as a talented songwriter, although he has written a few original compositions. Instead he is able to find songs that are right for him and a core of backup musicians who play with him exclusively. In *People,* Brower described Strait's sound as "hot as a fresh-baked cathead biscuit."

Strait's greatest ambition is to see himself enshrined one day in the Country Music Hall of Fame. The new interest in country traditionalism has given him a good chance of achieving that goal. Vaughan wrote that when the history of country music is written, "Strait's albums will rank alongside Haggard, Patsy Cline and George Jones. His voice is pure old-time country, the band, rough and rural but as good as any hand-picked Nashville session band, and Strait himself may just be the finest country music performer since Hank Williams."

Selected discography

Strait Country, MCA.
Strait From the Heart, MCA.
Right or Wrong, MCA.
Does Fort Worth Ever Cross Your Mind?, MCA, 1984.
George Strait's Greatest Hits, MCA, 1985.
Something Special, MCA, 1986.
Number 7, MCA, 1986.
Merry Christmas Strait to You, MCA, 1986.
Ocean Front Property, MCA, 1987.
George Strait's Greatest Hits, Volume 2, MCA, 1987.
If You Ain't Lovin', You Ain't Livin', MCA, 1988.
Beyond the Blue Neon, MCA, 1989.
Livin' It Up, MCA, 1990.

Sources

Books

Vaughan, Andrew, *Who's Who in New Country Music,* St. Martin's, 1989.

Periodicals

Newsweek, January 9, 1984.
People, June 3, 1985.

—Anne Janette Johnson

Sun Ra

Keyboard player, bandleader, composer

The eccentric Sun Ra has exerted a profound influence over modern jazz for more than four decades. As a solo performer and also as leader of the Sun Ra Arkestra, the musician has blazed new trails in the development of improvisational, or "free," jazz. Sun Ra was the first American musician to make use of African percussion and electronic instruments in a jazz setting. Through his Arkestra, he proved that a larger band could play the footloose styles of free-form jazz supposedly exclusive to tiny ensembles. *Philadelphia Inquirer* contributor Francis Davis called Sun Ra "an innovative force in jazz for more than 30 years as a keyboard player, bandleader and composer . . . one of America's most venerable avant-gardists."

Sun Ra was the recipient of high praise in the work *Black Music* by Amiri Baraka (published under Baraka's given name, LeRoi Jones). Baraka was a fan of the Arkestra during the early 1960s, when Sun Ra was playing in New York City. In *Black Music,* Baraka wrote: "All the [musical] concepts that seemed vague and unrealized in the late 50's have come together in the mature and profound music and compositions of this philosopher-musician. . . . Sun-Ra wants a music that will reflect a life-sense lost in the West, a music full of

Africa." Baraka stated further that the Arkestra is "the first big band of the New Black Music. . . . Sun-Ra's Arkestra is really a black family. The leader keeps fourteen or fifteen musicians playing with him who are convinced that music is a priestly concern and a vitally significant aspect of black culture."

It is indeed impossible to separate Sun Ra's music from its spiritual foundations. The musician himself has fostered an otherworldly persona, often speaking quite seriously of extraterrestrial travel and a state of higher consciousness once enjoyed by the black race. Little is known about the artist's earthly origins—most sources trace his birth to May, 1914, in Birmingham, Alabama. He learned to play piano by ear as a child and was a fine enough musician by his teens to win a full scholarship to Alabama A. & M. University. There he majored in education and directed the student band.

Sun Ra told the *Philadelphia Inquirer* that, after leaving the university, he was kidnapped by extraterrestrials who took him to Saturn. These space aliens, he said, convinced him that his music would bring order to a chaotic world and meaning to the lives of the confused. It is hardly surprising, therefore, that he earned the nickname "Moon Man" when he surfaced in Chicago as a jazz keyboardist in the late 1940s. By that time Sun Ra was already developing pure sound pieces similar to the work of John Coltrane and Ornette Coleman. He told the *Inquirer* that his fellow musicians "didn't understand what I was doing, but they were fascinated by it."

The nucleus of the Sun-Ra Myth-Science Arkestra formed in the early 1950s in Chicago and began to turn out albums on small jazz labels. Sun Ra experimented constantly, adding African drums to his growing band and dressing himself in traditional African garb—a habit that he kept in the ensuing years. By the time the Arkestra moved to New York City in 1961 it had a considerable following among enthusiasts of avant-garde jazz. The Arkestra pieces of this period seem like a veritable wall of sound, challenging all earthly limits with every beat. As Baraka described it, the music took up "all available sound space. . . . Sun-Ra's music creates the arbitrary sounds of the natural world."

This style inevitably led to the misconception that Sun Ra's dissonant sound was a matter of pure improvisation by individual Arkestra members. Such spontaneity was welcomed, but it was not considered a chance occurrence. In fact Sun Ra has always composed pieces, incredibly complex though they may be, and has merely made dissonance an element of his style. In the decades since 1970 he has returned to a more mainstream jazz approach, offering arrangements of pop standards and even Walt Disney songs in live performances or on albums. Still, he tries to infuse all his work with a sense of spiritual definition and a suggestion of unfulfilled possibilities.

Davis noted that Sun Ra "gives the impression that he has been withholding his most visionary music from a species not yet prepared for it"—or a species that has fallen from grace. Sun Ra himself told the *Inquirer:* "The black races were in touch with the real creators of the universe at one time, in perfect communication with them, but they lost it. So they go to church, take dope, do all sort of things to try to regain that state. The white man never had it." Ra suggests that he has felt that perfect communication in moments in his own life and could eventually render that state of perfection in his music.

In the meantime, Sun Ra and his Arkestra play and record their unique music from a base in Philadelphia, a city Sun Ra calls "death's headquarters." The musician, at 76 or so, continues his quest to "save the planet" through his music. Baraka wrote: "Sun-Ra is spiritually oriented. He understands 'the future' as an ever widening comprehension of what space is, even to the 'physical' travel between the planets as we do anyway in the long human chain of progress. . . . It is science-fact that Sun-Ra is interested in, not science-fiction. It is evolution itself, and its fruits. God as evolution. The flow of *is.* . . . And the mortal seeking, the human knowing spiritual, and willing the evolution. Which is the Wisdom Religion."

Selected discography

The Heliocentric World of Sun-Ra, ESP, c. 1968.
Walt Dickerson and Sun Ra, Steeplechase, 1979.
(With Others) *Stay Awake,* Hal Wilner Recordings, 1987.
Reflections in Blue, Black Saint, 1987.
Blue Delight, 1989.

Also recorded *Sun Ra Live at Montreaux, Atlantis,* and over 200 privately published albums.

Sources

Books

Jones, LeRoi, *Black Music,* Morrow, 1968.

Periodicals

Philadelphia Inquirer, February 16, 1990.

—Anne Janette Johnson

Technotronic

House band

The success of the Belgium-based group Technotronic was the surprise story of 1990. Technotronic's blend of rap vocals and electronic house music seemed a far cry from pop fare until the group's debut album, *Pump Up the Jam: The Album,* went gold in sales. Now, thanks to the work of Technotronic's Jo Bogaert, Ya Kid K, and MC Eric, house music has found its way out of the dance clubs and onto the radio, where some critics say it may pave the way for a whole new era in pop.

House music had its genesis in Chicago in the mid-1980s and spread quickly to other American cities and into Europe. Its sound is more mechanized than melodic, with emphasis on a dance beat and spare vocals. Essentially an electronic creation—tracks from previous recordings, drum machines, synthesizers, and sequencers—house music is unique in its interchangeability of personnel. This aspect of the music gives the members of Technotronic a great deal of independence—they can work as solo performers, or with other groups, while Technotronic continues to make records.

Technotronic's creator, Jo Bogaert, told the *Detroit Free Press* that he sees the band as an open project. "I want it to be open, to get new people involved, to make it a platform for people to try out things," he said. "I think the whole underground movement in dance music is where things are happening now. I don't hear that many new things in rock or new wave or whatever. But I do hear a lot of experimentation going on in hip-hop and house. It's nice to be there with it."

Bogaert is a former philosophy teacher who moved from the United States to Belgium in order to work as a record producer. His specialty was "new beat," an amalgam of hip hop and house music that has since been retitled hip house. In 1989 Bogaert began a project called "Pump Up the Jam," an effort to make a house song that also included elements of rap. "I really wanted to get away from that computerized, electronic, heavy beat and go into something that had more soul in it, another groove to it," Bogaert said. "To do that, the most important thing was to get a few people involved to do rap and vocals. I wanted to get everything in there together."

Although rappers are not terribly common in Belgium, Bogaert was able to recruit two, Ya Kid K, a young woman born in Zaire, and MC Eric. Bogaert sent his tapes to the vocalists, and they topped them with rap. That might have been the end of it, as far as everyone was concerned, but the resulting album proved uncommonly successful. Before she knew it, Ya Kid K saw a music video of her Technotronic song "Pump Up the Jam" with a *model* lip-syncing the rap. Ya Kid K promptly engaged an agent who saw to it that she was accorded her rightful place in future videos. However, the album cover still featured the comely model, Felly, causing further confusion.

As *Pump Up the Jam,* the album, made its way up the charts, however, the confusion disappeared. Ya Kid K and MC Eric began to tour as Technotronic, opening for bands such as D. J. Jazzy Jeff and the Fresh Prince and Madonna. Before long the individuals who had "tossed together" an album for the dance halls found themselves identified as a group—and not just as *any* group, but as a pioneering act that was bringing house music out of the clubs and onto the air waves.

Bogaert told the *Detroit Free Press:* "This is the biggest surprise of my life. The only thing I was sure about with 'Pump Up the Jam' was it was going to take off in the clubs. To cross over to radio stations and large audiences, I didn't expect that at all. I think it's a big surprise for everyone involved in house music, and I just hope it's going to open the doors wide for everybody."

A Detroit disc jockey described Technotronic's sound as "pretty accessible. . . . The music is melodic and has a nice beat to it. It doesn't make the pretense of being art. It's like a regular pop record." Pretense or no pretense, the Technotronic work is more than just prepackaged, easy-come-easy-go pop music. It is computerized and synthesized, but the vocals give it an intimate touch, and the beat shows distinct evolution from the overwrought rhythms of disco.

Other house artists have also discovered the human touch and are blending rhythm & blues, rock, soul, and funk with the dance tracks. Fans in larger English and American cities can even hear "acid house," a sound influenced by the psychedelic era. Bogaert told the *Philadelphia Inquirer:* "Dance music is often looked on as second-rate. But I think if you go digging, you can find interesting things. There's lots of experimentation

that's been lost in rock music. The pioneer spirit has been lost."

Technotronic's future may rest entirely with Bogaert. Both MC Eric and Ya Kid K plan to record solo albums; they may or may not associate themselves with Bogaert at a later date. The defection of its two vocalists will most likely have little effect on Technotronic—a successful enterprise always attracts talent. In the meantime, Bogaert is enjoying the fruits of his newfound fame. "House music took [a long time] to become popular," he told the *Philadelphia Inquirer,* "but it's becoming more and more mainstream. The best years are happening now. Afterward, I don't know—it may be around for a long time, like soul."

Selected discography

Pump Up the Jam: The Album, SBK, 1989.

Sources

Akron Beacon Journal, December 20, 1989.
Detroit Free Press, March 16, 1990.
Philadelphia Inquirer, March 22, 1990.
Rolling Stone, June 28, 1990.

—Anne Janette Johnson

Three Dog Night

Pop/rock group

Just what is a three dog night? Australian aboriginal custom has one sleep with his dogs for warmth when the temperature dips. The colder the night, the more dogs. A three dog night, then, is a very cold one. The group Three Dog Night, however, was anything but cold. On the contrary, they were one of the hottest acts of the 1970s, utilizing an electric rock format and featuring a strong vocal trio that belted out such rock classics as "Joy to the World," "Black and White," and, from the musical *Hair,* "Easy to Be Hard."

The group was organized in 1968 by Danny Hutton, a young singer-songwriter, producer, and vocalist who had had minor success with the song "Rises and Rainbows" in 1965. Hutton recruited Cory Wells, formerly of the Enemies, and Chuck Negron to form the tightly harmonized core of what would prove to be both a unique and highly successful rock group. A backup band was assembled out of various musicians in the Los Angeles area and remained a stable unit for nearly five years. Earning early successes on the West Coast club circuit and playing a long-term engagement at the

Original band members included **Cory Julius Wells** (vocals; born February 5, 1942, in Buffalo, N.Y.); **Charles "Chuck" Negron** (vocals; born June 8, 1942, in Bronx, N.Y.); **Daniel "Danny" Anthony Hutton** (vocals; born September 10, 1942 [some sources say 1946], in Buncrana, Ireland); **James "Jimmy" Boyd Greenspoon** (keyboards; born February 7, 1948, in Los Angeles, Calif.); **Michael Rand Allsup** (guitar; born March 8, 1947, in Modesto, Calif.); **Floyd Chester Sneed** (drums; born November 22, 1943, in Calgary, Alberta, Canada); **Joseph "Joe" Schermie** (bass; born February 12, 1948, in Madison, Wis.).

James "Smitty" Smith replaced Allsup in 1975. **Skip Konto** (keyboardist) was added to the group in 1974, and in 1973 **Jack Ryland** (bass; born June 7, 1949) replaced Schermie. In 1973 **Dennis Belfield** replaced Ryland on bass and in 1975 **Mickey McMeel** replaced Sneed on drums.

The group was organized in 1968 by Danny Hutton; recorded first LP in 1969, with Dunhill Records; toured beginning in 1969; achieved six gold records. Disbanded in 1976.

Addresses: *Record company*—MCA Records, Inc., 70 Universal City Plaza, Universal City, CA 91608.

Whisky-A-Go-Go, the group was soon offered a recording contract with ABC/Dunhill.

The Dogs' self-titled debut album appeared in 1969, launching them into a tremendously successful career. *Three Dog Night—One* went gold and yielded three singles: "Nobody," "Try a Little Tenderness," and the Number 1 hit "One," written by Harry Nilsson. The LP established the group as powerful performers capable of taking the compositions of others (Hoyt Axton, Paul Williams, and Laura Nyro, for instance) and turning them into hits. In the same prodigious year, as the group became an increasingly popular live act, their second album, *Suitable for Framing,* produced three major hits in "Celebrate," "Eli's Coming," and the heart-wrenching ballad "Easy to Be Hard" from the rock opera *Hair.* Over a relatively short period of time, the group achieved a number of best-selling albums including *Seven Separate Fools, Cyan, Coming Down Your Way,* and *American Pastime,* attained twelve consecutive certified gold albums, and scored major hits

with such songs as "Out In the Country"(from *It Ain't Easy,* 1970), "Joy to the World" (from *Naturally,* 1970), "An Old-Fashioned Love Song" (from *Harmony,* 1971), "Pieces of April," and what would become something of a children's national anthem in "Black and White" (from *Seven Separate Fools,* 1972). Even as their popularity waned on the East and West Coasts, the group continued to play to record crowds in sports stadiums in such places as Dallas, Texas, and Atlanta, Georgia.

The band's later history was dotted with changes in personnel until percussionist Floyd Sneed, bass player Jack Ryland, and lead guitarist Mike Allsup all left in 1975 to form S. S. Fools. The Dogs disbanded in 1976, and member Cory Wells went on to pursue a solo career in 1978. Throughout the Dogs' career, critics made few comments aside from the fact that the group did not write the songs they were fashioning into hits— a major no-no after the whirlwind success of such song masters as the Beatles' John Lennon and Paul McCartney. According to John Wasserman in his 1972 article for *Saturday Review,* "The problem seems to be that nobody takes them seriously." He indicated that the group's music was not terribly innovative, nor was the group itself raunchy, ethnically rich, or in trouble with the law. They were, he contended, "accomplished professionals, excellent entertainers, and clearly able to reach vast audiences." Writing the music, according to this commentator, was not nearly as important as delivering it successfully. On this count, the Dogs made good.

Selected discography

Three Dog Night, Dunhill, 1969.
Suitable for Framing, Dunhill, 1969.
Captured Live at the Forum, Dunhill, 1969.
It Ain't Easy, Dunhill, 1970.
Naturally, Dunhill, 1970.
Golden Biscuits, Dunhill, 1971.
Harmony, Dunhill, 1971.
Seven Separate Fools, Dunhill, 1972.
Around the World With Three Dog Night, Dunhill, 1973.
Cyan, Dunhill, 1973.
Hard Labor, Dunhill, 1974.
Joy to the World—Their Greatest Hits, MCA, 1974.
Dog Style, Dunhill, 1974.
Coming Down, Dunhill, 1974.
Coming Down Your Way, ABC, 1976.
American Pastime, ABC, 1976.
It's a Jungle, Teldec, 1984.

Sources

Books

Nite, Norm N., *Rock On,* Harper, 1978.
Stambler, Irwin, *Encyclopedia of Pop, Rock, and Soul,* St. Martin's, 1974.

Periodicals

Saturday Review, October 7, 1972.

—*Meg Mac Donald*

Steve Vai

Guitarist, songwriter

Steve Vai is two musicians—a virtuoso guitarist who approaches his art with deep reverence and mysticism, and a heavy metal rocker willing and able to share arena stages with the likes of David Lee Roth and Whitesnake. His fascination with all types of music manifested itself at an early age, and his parents encouraged it by sending him to accordion lessons. At the age of twelve he announced his preference for the guitar and bought himself one at a garage sale. Although his parents initially dismissed this as an adolescent phase, they bought him a good instrument when they realized that he was serious about switching. Soon noted rock guitarist Joe Satriani, who lived near the Vais, had become Steve's tutor.

At the age of fourteen, Vai began to have extremely vivid dream experiences relating to music. He described them to Joe Gore in *Guitar Player:* "I saw myself playing the guitar, but I handled it in ways that made totally abnormal sounds. I would touch it a certain way, and it would make a squeak, or I'd scream into it. There were no barriers—even my movements were beyond gracefulness. . . . That event was the beginning of my realization that I had an identity on the instrument, and it was the single most important event in my musical career. . . . It's where I got most of my musicality from, I believe, or at least that's how I discovered it."

Working in a home studio, nineteen-year-old Vai wrote, performed, and produced a wildly experimental recording called *Flex-Able.* He undertook the project simply to teach himself more about music and studio techniques, but it was eventually released by Relativity and sold some 250,000 copies with no promotion whatsoever. After attending the Berklee College of Music in Boston, Vai joined Frank Zappa's band. This was a dream-come-true for him, because Zappa had been his hero ever since he'd taken up guitar. Zappa's music, full of high-level technical and theoretical eccentricities, was both challenging and satisfying for the young guitar prodigy. He played on many albums and went through many tours with the group.

Despite his success, Vai found himself sliding into emotional problems. He told Matt Resnicoff in *Musician:* "I was hanging out with Zappa, and he's an extremely cynical character. . . . I had an identity crisis and I started to take on Frank's cynicism and his disgust for the world. . . . I entered this really deep depression, for about a year-and-a-half, where it was just complete anxiety. . . . I couldn't smile, I couldn't laugh. And I just started deteriorating . . . physically and mentally, spiritually." Eventually, this downward spiral was broken when "mysteriously this book appeared in the mail, and it was called *The Magic in Your Mind* by U.S. Anderson. It was a pretty simple book—it

For the Record. . .

Born in 1961 in New York; son of Johnny (a liquor salesman) and Theresa Vai; married, wife's name, Pia; children: Julian Angel. *Education:* Attended Berklee College of Music.

Lead guitarist. Has performed and recorded with Frank Zappa, Alcatrazz, Public Image, Ltd., David Lee Roth, and Whitesnake. Contributed "Martian Love Secrets" to *Guitar Player*, February-August, 1989. Appeared in the film *Crossroads*, Columbia, 1986.

Addresses: *Record company*—Relativity Records, c/o 18707 Henderson Ave., Hollis, NY 11423.

just talked about the ego and certain beliefs—and I started to connect with things in the book that filled the yearning in my heart. I decided I had to change my life, because I had hit rock bottom. I became a vegetarian, I quit smoking and basically I cleaned up a whole lot."

Eventually Vai moved on to a gig that was diametrically opposed to Zappa's intellectual satire: he became the lead guitarist for David Lee Roth's solo revue. Hard-rock fans used to seeing Roth perform with hot-shot guitarist Eddie Van Halen were surprised to find that Vai was more than capable of filling in. He even toyed with audiences' expectations by cockily reproducing some of Van Halen's best known solos—and adding a little extra flash by playing them with his teeth. While touring with Roth, Vai worked up some stunning solo turns, such as "Sunspots," which Resnicoff called "six gripping minutes where [Vai] sailed over a spacey groove, eventually laying the instrument on its back and continuing to play as he sprawled on his stomach behind it and pushed across the stage, finally slumping over it, drained, in a corner as the last strangled notes echoed into the hall. It was incredible."

When the time came to part with Roth, Vai set to work on a musical project based on the visionary dreams of his adolescence. He told Resnicoff: "I locked myself into a room and said, 'To hell with everything—I'm doing this and it's a complete expression of what I am. I'm not concerned about singles, I'm not concerned about mega-platinum success, I'm not concerned about record companies.'" To prepare for one track, entitled "For the Love of God," he stopped playing the guitar altogether for several weeks and fasted to purify himself for the performance. When he finally picked up his instrument to lay down the track, his "fingers were totally out of shape, and they got trashed—they all had blood clots under the skin," he reminisced to Gore. "It was extremely painful to touch anything. . . . I needed to be in that state of mind to record this song."

Gore stated that the completed album, *Passion and Warfare,* is "likely to set new technical, compositional, and expressive standards for the instrumental rock guitar LP. [It] captures all the paradoxes that have made Steve's playing so beguiling. . . . Grand, yet funny; flashy, yet substantial; spiritual, yet dirt-earthy; it's music to satisfy the head, heart, and crotch." Soon after completing this deep spiritual statement, Vai received a distress call from the band Whitesnake. Guitarist Adrian Vandenberg had been indefinitely sidelined with an injured wrist, and Vai was the band's first choice for his replacement. He readily accepted the offer, going on to tour and record with the band.

Switching gears from art to metal left Vai quite unruffled. He explained to Resnicoff: "I'm still at a young age where I like to go out and play in big arenas and run around and exert that kind of rock 'n' roll attitude and energy. . . . There's a certain energy and a certain experience you feel when you're on a big stage with a singer like Coverdale screaming. I enjoy that feeling, and I enjoy not having the pressure of being the one whose up front all the time. . . . There will be a time when I'll sit back and be the total musician, but right now it's a lot of fun to run around and play simple rock songs on stage."

Selected discography

Flex-Able, Akashic/Relativity.
Passion and Warfare, Relativity, 1990.

With Frank Zappa; on Barking Pumpkin

Shut Up 'N' Play Yer Guitar, 1986.
Shut Up 'N' Play Yer Guitar Some More.
Son of Shut Up 'N' Play Yer Guitar.
Ship Arriving Too Late to Save a Drowning Witch.
The Man from Utopia.
Them or Us.
You Are What You Is.
Tinsel Town Rebellion, 1990.

With David Lee Roth

Eat 'Em and Smile, Warner Brothers, 1987.
Skyscraper, Warner Brothers, 1988.

With Others

(With Alcatrazz) *Disturbing the Peace,* Capitol.
(With Shankar) *The Epidemics,* ECM.
(With Whitesnake) *A Slip of the Tongue.*

Sources

Guitar Player, February 1983; October 1984; October 1986; May
   1988; May 1990.
Musician, September 1990.

—*Joan Goldsworthy*

Ricky Van Shelton

Country singer, songwriter

Fans of traditional country music have found a new hero in Ricky Van Shelton, a singer who took Nashville by storm in 1987. Since his debut album, *Wild-Eyed Dream,* went gold, Van Shelton has ranked among the most popular—and most visible—entertainers in the country field. His soothing voice and down-home good looks have won him numerous female admirers, helping to assure a wide audience for his repertoire of conventional country and honky tonk songs. *Detroit Free Press* columnist Gary Graff called Van Shelton "the hottest new male singer in country music," a performer who was "a success from the get-go."

It might surprise Ricky Van Shelton to hear himself described as an overnight success. In fact he struggled for years to establish himself in Nashville, although he never lost faith in his talent. Van Shelton is in his late 30s, and he has been a country singer since his teens—his stardom has been a matter of a lucky break after years of anonymity. Having found a record label for his work and a producer he respects, Van Shelton is reluctant to tamper with the formula that has brought him almost a dozen Number 1 country hits. "I'm not one to gamble on success," he told the *Detroit Free Press.* "I *am* singing traditional country music, and I've had phenomenal success, which I'm not about to mess with."

Van Shelton was born in tiny Grit, Virginia, in the early 1950s. His parents were deeply religious people who forbade any music in their home. Van Shelton learned to sing at the area Pentecostal Holiness Church, where he and his two brothers and two sisters were on the church choir. His parents' demands notwithstanding, Van Shelton found ways to listen to secular music. Friends at school introduced him to rock and roll and rhythm and blues, and he became a big fan of the Beatles and the Rolling Stones. Like many teens in the 1960s, Van Shelton held country music in contempt—that is, until he heard it performed live.

One night Van Shelton was asked to sing with his brother's bluegrass band for the evening. The experience energized the young man, and he began to listen to country, honky tonk, and rockabilly with a new respect. While he worked as a pipe fitter and a tobacco picker in rural Virginia, he began to dream of a career as a country musician. Weekends would find him on any stage that he could find, playing guitar and singing for the sheer joy of it.

Van Shelton found constant encouragement from his then-fiancee, Bettye. In 1984 (the couple was married in 1986) she urged him to move to Nashville, where she supported him while he peddled his talents. In fact, it was Bettye who assured Van Shelton's fame when she persuaded a co-worker to give one of Van Shelton's

For the Record. . .

Born c. 1952 in Grit, Va.; son of Jenks (a factory worker) and Eloise Van Shelton; married Bettye Witt, 1986.

Country singer and songwriter, 1984—. Also worked as a pipe fitter and tobacco puller in Virginia. Signed with Columbia Records, 1986; released debut album, *Wild-Eyed Dream*, 1987; had numerous Number 1 country singles, including "Wild-Eyed Dream," "Crime of Passion," "Somebody Lied," and "Hole in My Pocket." Live performer at concerts in the United States and Canada, and on the Grand Ole Opry, in Nashville; subject of documentary, *Ricky Van Shelton: From Grit to Gold*, on the Nashville Network, 1990.

Addresses: *Record company*—Columbia/CBS Records, 51 W. 52nd St., New York, NY 10019.

tapes to her husband, an influential Nashville newspaper columnist. Within two weeks Van Shelton had a contract with Columbia Records and was in the studio cutting his first album. Released in 1987, *Wild-Eyed Dream* sold a phenomenal one million copies and produced three Number 1 singles.

Wild-Eyed Dream is composed primarily of classic numbers by Harlan Howard, Merle Haggard, and Buck Owens. Van Shelton is very comfortable mining the vein of classic country, although when he writes songs himself he produces everything from rock to bluegrass numbers. Success has come with the traditional music, however, and Van Shelton is only one of several new stars who recall country's roots with almost every note. As the singer put it in *People,* "I think the audience was really hungry for pure country music."

"Pure country music" is the essence of Ricky Van Shelton's style. His backup band includes wailing fiddles and steel guitars, although the up-tempo numbers may have a rockabilly beat. Ed Morris, *Billboard*'s representative in Nashville, told the *Detroit Free Press* that Van Shelton "sounds like a latter-day Conway Twitty. So many of his songs are just simple, unadorned

laments of some sort or another. They're not sophisticated. They just have an emotional tug that the big country audience really goes for." Van Shelton himself put it another way in *People.* Whenever he's around a microphone, he said, "I just start cryin' out loud."

Van Shelton has a fine voice with an exceptional range, but it is his stage presence—his good looks and easy but sincere charm—that have made him a star. Female fans have been known to riot around his tour bus, and he is regularly pelted with lingerie at his live shows. Still, the singer credits his success to the depth of emotion he can bring to his material, rather than the way he looks when he sings. "I'm happy and alive when I walk up on that stage," he told *People.*

By 1990 Ricky Van Shelton had earned a shelf full of awards from the country music industry and had watched three albums sell over a million copies. Asked to reflect on his stardom, he told the *Detroit Free Press:* "I'm not surprised. If I was surprised, it would mean I didn't have faith in myself, wouldn't it? I've always had faith in myself. . . . With these three albums, it's been wonderful. If it ends tomorrow, I would just walk away with a smile on my face."

Selected discography

Wild-Eyed Dream, Columbia, 1987.
Living Proof, Columbia, 1988.
Ricky Van Shelton Sings Christmas, Columbia, 1989.
RVS III, Columbia, 1990.

Sources

Books

Vaughan, Andrew, *Who's Who in New Country Music*, St. Martin's, 1989.

Periodicals

Detroit Free Press, May 11, 1990.
People, June 26, 1989.

—Anne Janette Johnson

T-Bone Walker

Jazz, blues guitarist, songwriter

A rguably the first musician to employ an electric guitar, T-Bone Walker is without doubt the one who laid the foundation for what is known as modern urban blues. Walker's sophisticated playing in the 1930s and 1940s bridged the gap between jazz and blues and created a style which has influenced every electric guitarist since. "He has a touch that nobody has been able to duplicate," stated B.B. King in *Guitar Player*. "I knew I just had to go out and get an electric guitar." In Sheldon Harris's *Blues Who's Who* a list of artists Walker has influenced contains nearly every major blues (and quite a few rock) guitarists in the last four decades.

Walker's meal ticket was his ability to play single string, hornphrased solos that brought the guitar out of its role as an accompanying, rhythm-oriented instrument. He was one of the first musicians who proved that a guitar could go head-to-head with brass, pianos, and woodwinds as a legitimate solo instrument.

Walker was obviously musically gifted, but electricity helped to bring that out and let him rise above his contemporaries. "It took Walker to exploit electricity," wrote Robert Palmer in the *Rolling Stone Illustrated History of Rock & Roll*. "By using his amplifier's volume control to sustain pitches, and combining this technique with the single string-bending and finger vibrato practiced by traditional bluesmen, Walker in effect invented a new instrument."

He was born Aaron Thibeaux Walker (the nickname T-Bone is a slang version of his middle name) in 1910 in Linden, Texas, and was raised in Dallas after 1912. Walker was born into a musical family with both his parents working as musicians. He took up the guitar at age 13 but played various other stringed instruments as well. Walker's earliest influences were Lonnie Johnson, Scrapper Blackwell, Leroy Carr, and Blind Lemon Jefferson—all advanced stylists at the time. In his early years, Walker worked as "lead boy" for Jefferson, leading the blind guitarist around the city to play for crowds and pass the hat. By the time he was 16, Walker was making enough money on his own in Dallas to become a professional, working various dances and carnivals.

In 1929 he recorded two singles for Columbia Records, "Trinity River Blues" and "Witchita Falls Blues," as Oak Cliff T-Bone (Walker lived in the Dallas suburb of Oak Cliff). He continued playing with a 16-piece band formed during his school days with Lawson Brooks until 1934, when he quit and moved to Los Angeles. Walker turned his job over to another guitarist who went on to become as important and equally influential, Charlie Christian. The two had at one time performed a street act together that combined guitar and bass playing with some fancy footwork. Christian later rose to stardom in the late 1930s as a featured soloist with the Benny Goodman Orchestra, but his brilliant career was cut short by tuberculosis in 1941.

Walker made his living on the West Coast playing with various small combos in the thriving jazz clubs of Los Angeles. In 1939 he joined Les Hite's Cotton Club Orchestra as a singer, guitarist, and composer. It's hard to say who was the first electric guitarist at this point, but Walker, Christian, Eddie Durham, and Floyd Smith were all beginning to see the advantages an amplified guitar's volume had in a club setting when competing with the full horn section of a big band. "I was out there four or five years on my own before they all started playing amplified," Walker stated in the liner notes of *T-Bone Walker: Classics of Modern Blues*. "I recorded my 'T-Bone Blues' with Les Hite in 1939, but I'd been playing amplified guitar a long time before that."

Regardless of who was first, it was Walker's playing that made him great. "[He has] striking originality and expressive power," wrote Pete Welding in *Guitar World*.

For the Record...

Full name, Aaron Thibeaux Walker; born May 28, 1910, in Linden, Tex.; son of Rance Walker (a musician) and Movelia Jimerson (a musician); married Vida Lee in 1935; children: three; died of pneumonia March 16, 1975.

Worked as a professional musician at dances and carnivals in Dallas with such groups as the Cab Calloway Band, the Coley Jones Dallas String Band, and the Lawson Brooks Band, c. 1926-34; recorded two singles for Columbia Records, 1929, and recorded with many other bands in the 1940s; moved to the West Coast and performed at the Little Harlem Club, the Trocadero, and other clubs, 1934-40; moved to the East Coast and worked with the Les Hite Orchestra, 1940; formed and appeared with his own touring band, 1940-1975; traveled with the band in England, 1965, and throughout Europe, 1966, 1968, and 1969.

Awards: Grammy for best ethnic or traditional recording, for *Good Feelin'*, 1971; Lifetime Achievement Award, *Guitar Player*, 1985.

Addresses: *Record company*—Fantasy/Prestige/Milestone, 10th and Parker, Berkeley, CA 94710.

"[His playing is] fleet, supercharged, harmonically resourceful, rhythmically adroit and, above all, immensely exciting." Walker was a consummate showman to boot. He played a large Gibson hollowbody guitar, held straight out from his chest and parallel to the floor (which contributed in part to his unique tone) but would cut loose and play behind his back, between his legs or do the splits in an effort to get the crowd going. He had, as Dan Forte stated in *Guitar Player*, "the uncanny ability to burn and stay cool at the same time."

By the 1940s Walker had made a name for himself and embarked on a solo career. He combined blues, shuffles, and jump tunes into his act and eventually scored a hit with "Mean Old World" in the mid-40s. However, it was in 1947 that Walker produced his most famous tune, "Stormy Monday," which is probably the all-time blues standard. "It's just like a national anthem; it tells the truth," said vocalist Jimmy Witherspoon in *The Guitar Player Book*. "It tells the strife of working people getting paid on Friday, Saturday they go out and have a ball." Walker later played on Witherspoon's *Evenin'* LP and obviously had a profound impact on the singer. "He's one of the few people who put dignity into the blues," continued Witherspoon. "He's the Charlie Park-er of guitars when it comes to blues. . . . No one else can touch T-Bone."

Walker may have been the one to elevate the status of the blues, but the lifestyle it demanded certainly took its toll on him. He stayed in southern California during the 1950s and toured endlessly into the following decade. The stress of travel combined with heavy drinking, gambling, and bad business dealings, took their toll on him. On March 16, 1975, T-Bone Walker succumbed to pneumonia, bringing an end to one of the most spectacular and innovative musical careers ever.

Pete Welding wrote in the liner notes of the excellent and wide-ranging anthology, *T-Bone Walker: Classics of Modern Blues,* "In length of service, adaptability and continuous creative activity, perhaps only Coleman Hawkins or Duke Ellington [has] matched him."

Selected discography

Singles for Columbia Records; as Oak Cliff T-Bone

"Trinity River Blues," 1929.
"Witchita Falls Blues," 1929.

LPs; with Jimmy Witherspoon

T-Bone Blues, Atlantic, 1956.
The Truth, Brunswick, 1968.
T-Bone Walker: Classics of Modern Blues, Blue Note, 1976.
T-Bone Jumps Again, Charly, 1980.
Evenin' Blues, Prestige, 1988.

Sources

Books

The Guitar Player Book, editors of *Guitar Player,* Grove Press, Inc., 1979.
Guralnick, Peter, *The Listener's Guide to the Blues,* Facts on File, 1982.
Harris, Sheldon, *Blues Who's Who,* Da Capo, 1979.
Kozinn, Allan, Pete Welding, Dan Forte, and Gene Santoro, *The Guitar—The History The Music The Players,* Quill, 1984.
Miller, Jim, editor, *The Rolling Stone Illustrated History of Rock & Roll,* Random House/Rolling Stone Press, 1976.

Periodicals

Guitar Player, March 1977; December 1985; January 1987; December 1987; February 1988.
Guitar World, December 1987.

—*Calen D. Stone*

Joe Walsh

Guitarist, singer, songwriter

Joe Walsh's reputation as one of rock's premiere guitar craftsmen is highly understandable when one looks at the volume of studio work he has done over the past twenty years. From B.B. King to Dan Fogelberg, from Rod Stewart to Graham Nash, countless artists have called upon Walsh's melodic playing to enhance their records. But Walsh's fame has not come primarily through the work of others. His three-year stint with the James Gang marked the beginning of a fruitful career that has seen nine solo LPs as well as three more with the Eagles in their final and most successful phase.

Born in Wichita, Kansas, in 1947, Walsh grew up in Ohio where he eventually learned to play bass guitar, performing in high school bands like the Nomads. He enrolled as a full-time student at Kent State University for three quarters before switching to part-time studies. Walsh began to work seriously on his guitar playing while at college and complemented this with courses in electronics, enabling him to perform Dr. Frankenstein-like experiments on his equipment.

Walsh joined the James Gang in 1969 (replacing Glen Schwartz), the same year the group (with Walsh handling vocals and guitar chores, Jimmy Fox on drums and Dale Peters on bass) released *Yer' Album* and established themselves as "the most significant post-Cream power-trio strategy," according to John Swenson in *The Rolling Stone Record Guide.*

The James Gang followed up their successful debut the next year with *Rides Again,* a Top 10 LP that included "Tend My Garden" and "Fun #49," a Walsh tour de force. In support of the record, the trio toured Europe in 1970 with the Who, a band whose members had a profound impact on the young guitarist. "Peter's [Townshend] my guru. He taught me how to play lead-rhythm, and Keith Moon taught me how to break things," Walsh told *Guitar World.* The influence of Pete Townshend's style on Walsh's is quite evident in the thick power chords of tunes like "Walk Away" from the James Gang's third LP, *Thirds.* Keith Moon's insanity would take slightly longer to show in Walsh's character, but it would become an equally identifiable trademark of the guitarist in the near future.

In 1971 the James Gang released *Live in Concert,* compiled from their foreign dates with the Who. Walsh capitalized on Townshend's style but found himself painted into a corner creatively. "I saw myself being stereotyped almost into a heavy metal guitarist about 10 years before heavy metal came out, and I didn't like that," Walsh told Matt Resnicoff in *Guitar World.* "I got extremely frustrated being the only melodic instrument."

His dissatisfaction, coupled with his distaste for the

tactics involved in the record business, led to his departure from the James Gang and a move to Colorado. There he hooked up with bassist Kenny Passarelli and drummer Joe Vitale for 1972's *Barnstorm* and *The Smoker You Drink, the Player You Get* in 1973. The latter produced a Walsh classic, "Rocky Mountain Way," a stomping good-time rocker that featured an odd musical device called the "talk box," which transforms the human voice into a synthesized-sounding musical instrument. Rocke Grace and Joe Lala were added on keyboards and percussion for the album.

Walsh's heavy sustain and nasty slide work may have seemed groundbreaking, but were actually just a natural progression. "I'm a third-generation blues studier, and that's why I sound like I do," Walsh told *Guitar World.* "I studied the blues through white English guys!" However, unlike his mentors Eric Clapton, Peter Green, and Mick Taylor, Walsh was not restricted to just the guitar. "I hear a lot of tones and textures and such," he told Jas Obrecht in *Guitar Player.* "I know I'm known mostly for my guitar work, but in terms of being a musician, there are other vehicles that I am quite capable of playing, and sometimes that ain't guitar. The song tells me what to play."

Soon Walsh's talented ear and tasteful playing were popping up on other musicians' work, making him one of the most in-demand non-studio players. In later years his searing guitar would be heard on Steve Winwood's "Split Decision" and Richard Marx's "Don't Mean Nothin'," both top hits thanks to Walsh's creative slide. "I like to accept the energy involved in that first

pass," Walsh said in *Guitar World* of his recording technique, "that's really where the magic is."

With a successful solo career well at hand, and enough choice studio dates to keep any musician rich and happy, Walsh was recruited by the Eagles to replace guitarist Bernie Leadon in 1976. "I got asked to join the Eagles as a specialist, because they wanted some humor," he told *Guitar World.* "They were taking everything too seriously. . . . My job was to keep everybody laughing, or at least keep the band from breaking up." Walsh accomplished more than that at first for the Eagles. His initial flight with the band, the Grammy-winning album *Hotel California,* soared up the charts in 1976 to the Number 1 spot. The title track featured an incredible guitar jam, while "Life in the Fast Lane" and "New Kid in Town" were hot-selling singles.

Walsh continued his solo recordings with the live *You Can't Argue With a Sick Mind* in 1976 and *But Seriously Folks* in 1978, which included "Life's Been Good," a Number 12 single that struck right to the heart of the rock and roll lifestyle. "I think it might have been a little too close to the truth," Walsh confessed in *Guitar World,* "and I didn't want to overextend my sense of humor to the public." The zany guitarist even took a shot at running for president after the song became so popular.

In 1979 Walsh was back in the studio with the Eagles working on *The Long Run,* an impressive LP that featured a fine title track and the funky "Those Shoes." The inner turmoil of the group and the usual music corporation hassles eventually led to the breakup of the Eagles following the release of a live album a short while later. Even if Walsh couldn't keep the band from folding, he inspired them to record some of their finest, and certainly their most successful, music. "We were a damn good band for a while," Walsh stated in *Guitar Player.* "I'm proud of having been a part of that and *Hotel California.* Besides the royalties and everything, just the fact that was a special album for a lot of people on the planet. I feel that I was part of a true band, and that we made a very valid musical statement for the generation that we represent."

Walsh went back to a three-piece format with Joe Vitale on an LP by John Entwistle, bassist for the Who. In 1985 he released *Confessor,* "the apologia of a strictly raised mid-western episcopalian after living in rock and roll sin for 'Fifteen Years' on the road," wrote Bruce Malamut in *Guitar World.* "The balance . . . is a sober retrospective from rock's own Harpo Marx."

Selected discography

With the James Gang

Yer' Album, ABC, 1969.
James Gang Rides Again, MCA, 1970.
Thirds, ABC, 1971.
Live In Concert, ABC, 1971.
16 Greatest Hits, ABC, 1974.
Best of the James Gang Featuring Joe Walsh, MCA, 1981.

Solo LPs

Barnstorm, ABC/Dunhill, 1972.
The Smoker You Drink, The Player You Get, MCA, 1973.
So What, ABC/Dunhill, 1974.
You Can't Argue With A Sick Mind, MCA, 1976.
But Seriously Folks, Asylum, 1978.
There Goes the Neighborhood, Asylum, 1981.
The Best of Joe Walsh, MCA, 1981.
You Bought It, You Name It, Full Moon, 1983.
The Confessor, Full Moon, 1985.
Got Any Gum?, Warner Bros., 1987.

With the Eagles

Hotel California, Asylum, 1976.
The Long Run, Asylum, 1979.
Eagles Live, Asylum, 1980.
Eagles Greatest Hits, Volume 2, Asylum, 1982.

Has appeared as a featured guest performer on numerous albums by other artists, including B.B. King's *Indianola Mississip-pi Seeds, LA Midnight*, and *The Best of B.B. King;* Jay Ferguson's *All Alone in the End Zone, Thunder Island, Real Life Ain't This Way, Term & Conditions*, and *White Noise;* Dan Fogelberg's *Souvenirs* and *Netherlands;* John Entwistle's *Too Late The Hero;* Rick Derringer's *All American Boy;* Keith Moon's *Two Sides Of The Moon;* Graham Nash's *Earth and Sky;* Rod Stewart's *A Night On The Town;* Bill Wyman's *Stone Alone;* Randy Newman's *Little Criminals;* Emerson, Lake & Palmer's *Works;* Warren Zevon's *Bad Luck Streak in Dancing School;* Steve Winwood's *Back in the High Life;* Jimmy Davis & Junction's *Kick The Wall;* Richard Marx's *Richard Marx;* and Albert Collins & Etta James's *Jump The Blues Away.*

Sources

Books

The Illustrated Encyclopedia of Rock, compiled by Nick Loban and Bob Woffinden, Harmony, 1977.
The Rolling Stone Record Guide, edited by Dave Marsh with John Swenson, Random House/Rolling Stone Press, 1979.

Periodicals

Guitar Player, February 1988; April 1988.
Guitar World, November 1985; January 1988.

—Calen D. Stone

Dinah Washington

Blues singer

Vocalist Dinah Washington "was not just a creature of the blues," according to Betty De Ramus and Leslie Gourse in *Ebony*. "She could strut through jazz, slide through pop and break your heart with ballads." After singing with jazz great Lionel Hampton's band, she began a successful solo career in the late 1940s that lasted until her untimely death in 1963. Washington's hits include "I Only Know," "Time Out for Tears," and her greatest smash, "What a Difference a Day Makes." As De Ramus and Gourse elaborated, "Dinah Washington could work magic with a song, taking it apart and stitching it back together in her own quirky and moving way."

Washington began her life as Ruth Jones; she was born August 29, 1924, in Tuscaloosa, Alabama. When she was 3 or 4 years old, her family moved to Chicago, Illinois. By this time, Washington was already telling her mother she wanted to be a show girl, though her primary exposure to music was through church. When she was 8, her voice was strong enough to sing harmony with her mother, and she was learning to play the piano. Washington soon joined the church choir, and about the time she graduated from high school, she started serving as its director.

Meanwhile, Washington was learning more about secular music. She loved big bands, and for high school shows she often performed popular romantic ballads. Her mother disapproved of this interest, and frowned on the idea of Washington singing in local nightclubs; the young vocalist resolved this when, while still in her late teens, she married the first of her many husbands, John Young. After the wedding, she and Young lived with *his* parents, and she could fulfill singing engagements without her mother's approval. Wanting to maintain family ties, however, Washington often shared money from these early performances with her relatives without divulging her source of income.

For a short time Washington returned professionally to her gospel roots, singing with Sallie Martin's gospel group. But in 1943 she auditioned for Lionel Hampton's band and won a place. When she joined Hampton, she changed her name to Dinah Washington for professional reasons. While with Hampton's band, her musical efforts won her popularity among jazz fans, and by the late 1940s Washington had decided to pursue a solo career. Having already recorded with Hampton's band, she easily won a contract with Mercury Records.

Beginning in 1950, Washington was constantly topping the rhythm and blues charts. In that year she had several hits, including "I Only Know," "I Wanna Be Loved," "I'll Never Be Free," "It Isn't Fair," and "Time Out for Tears." Though she followed this feat with yet

Name originally Ruth Jones; born August 29, 1924, in Tuscaloosa, Ala.; died September 14, 1963, in Detroit, Mich., of an accidental overdose of diet pills; daughter of Alice Jones (a pianist and choir director); married at least seven times: husbands included John M. Young; Eddie Chamblee (a saxophone player); and Dick Lane (a professional football player); children: George Jenkins, Bobby Grayson.

Served as a church choir director in her teens; sang in local nightclubs in Chicago, Ill., during the early 1940s; sang with Sallie Martin's gospel group in the early 1940s; performed with Lionel Hampton's band c. 1943, when she changed her name to Dinah Washington; solo recording artist and concert performer, late 1940s-1963.

more success during the early 1950s, and was the best-selling female artist in the rhythm and blues genre at that time, her music did not cross over to white audiences. Washington had the frustrating experience of watching white artists have bigger pop hits with cover versions of songs she had recorded first—such as Kay Starr's rendition of "Wheel of Fortune," which had afforded Washington a hit in 1952. Washington's other rhythm and blues chartmakers of the period include "Trouble in Mind," "Fat Daddy," and "Teach Me Tonight."

Washington's recording career fell off somewhat during the mid-1950s, but she came back in a big way with 1959's "What a Difference a Day Makes." On this bluesy ballad, Washington broke racial barriers to ascend to the Top 10 of the pop charts. She followed "What a Difference" with a popular rendition of the standard "Unforgettable." In 1960 Washington got together with burgeoning singing success Brook Benton to record the album *The Two of Us,* which contained the pop hits "Baby, You've Got What It Takes" and "A Rockin' Good Way." She continued to have rhythm and blues hits in the early 1960s as well, such as "This Bitter Earth." Washington switched to Roulette Records in 1962, scoring a Top 40 pop hit with "Where Are You." As early as 1955 the vocalist had begun appearing in films—that year's *Rock and Roll Revue* and 1960's *Jazz on a Summer's Day* being notable among them.

In addition to having an affecting voice, Washington also possessed a forceful personality. She was not shy about calling herself "the Queen of the Blues." A friend recounted for *Ebony*'s De Ramus and Gourse a time when she was speaking to Washington on the phone

while watching singer Lou Rawls on television. Noticing her friend's attention wandering, Washington rebuked her: "She's telling me she watchin' Lou Rawls and she talkin' to the Queen. Are you crazy for real?" Washington also had a tendency to call other women that she worked with "bitches." Nevertheless, she reportedly possessed a kind heart. Eddie Chamblee, one of Washington's husbands, told De Ramus and Gourse that "she would curse you out or she would curse out a club owner and then put a girl in the hospital for her to have a baby and pay all the expenses."

But Washington also had trouble controlling her use of diet pills. According to one of her pianists, quoted in *Essence,* the singer often gained weight and didn't know how to lose it again without the aid of pills. Chamblee explained further to De Ramus and Gourse: "Dinah would take pills, drink and forget she had taken her pills." He stressed, however, as have most other sources, that "her death was a pure and simple accident." Though she was not suicidal, Washington died of an overdose of diet pills on December 14, 1963.

Selected discography

Selected singles; on Mercury Records, except where noted

"I Only Know," 1950.
"I Wanna Be Loved," 1950.
"I'll Never Be Free," 1950.
"It Isn't Fair," 1950.
"Time Out for Tears," 1950.
"I Won't Cry Anymore," 1951.
"New Blowtop Blues," 1952.
"Trouble in Mind," 1952.
"Wheel of Fortune," 1952.
"Fat Daddy," 1953.
"TV Is the Thing," 1953.
"I Don't Hurt Anymore," 1954.
"Teach Me Tonight," 1954.
"That's All I Want From You," 1955.
"What a Difference a Day Makes," 1959.
"Unforgettable," 1959.
"This Bitter Earth," 1960.
(With Brook Benton) "Baby, You've Got What It Takes," 1960.
(With Benton) "A Rockin' Good Way," 1960.
"September in the Rain," 1961.
"Where Are You," Roulette, 1962.

Selected albums; on Mercury Records and subsidiaries

Best of the Blues, 1957.
Dinah Washington Sings Bessie Smith, 1958.

What a Difference a Day Makes, 1959.
Unforgettable, 1959.
(With Benton) *The Two of Us*, 1960.
For Lonely Lovers, 1961.
September in the Rain, 1961.
This Is My Story, 1963.
Late, Late Show, 1963.
Dinah Washington Sings Fats Waller, 1964.
(With Quincy Jones) *Queen and Quincy*, 1965.
Discovered, 1967.

Also recorded albums on Roulette Records, including *Back to the Blues, Best of Dinah Washington, Dinah '62, Dinah '63, Dinah Washington, Drinking Again, In Love and Tribute, Strangers on Earth, World of Dinah Washington,* and *Dinah Washington Years.*

Sources

Books

Haskins, James, *Queen of the Blues: A Biography of Dinah Washington,* Morrow, 1987.
Stambler, Irwin, *Encyclopedia of Pop, Rock, and Soul,* St. Martin's, 1989.

Periodicals

down beat, May 1988.
Essence, May 1983.

—*Elizabeth Wenning*

Grover Washington, Jr.

Saxophonist, composer

Robert Palmer of *Rolling Stone* called Grover Washington, Jr., "the most popular saxophonist working in a jazz-fusion idiom." And because of Washington's great success some critics have downgraded his music, calling it bland, too commercial, and not real jazz. However, Washington is an obviously talented musician who always surrounds himself with other top-notch musicians and who has had the good fortune to string together a long procession of hit albums. As Albert De Genova wrote in *down beat,* "Grover Washington Jr. has found his niche, and though some are offended by his commercial ventures, no one can deny his musical abilities (or those of the musicians behind him). He creates mood music, soothing and pastoral, tinged with urban funk, done with taste and quality."

Washington was born in Buffalo, New York, on December 12, 1943. He came from a musical family; his father played tenor saxophone, his mother sang in a choir, one brother was an organist in church choirs, and his youngest brother, Darryl, became a drummer (who would later also join the professional ranks). Like his father, Washington soon took up the saxophone. "I started playing at around age ten," he told Julie Coryell and Laura Friedman in *Jazz-Rock Fusion: The People, The Music,* "and my first love was really classical music." He took lessons at the Wurlitzer School of Music and studied a variety of instruments. "My early lessons were on the saxophone, then it was the piano, the drum and percussion family, and the bass guitar." Asked how he found the time for all these instruments, he said, "It was basically what I wanted to do at a very early age, so I had the time. I could really get into all of them on the basic level." Washington also loved basketball as a child but quickly realized that music would be his future. "I stopped growing at 5′ 8-1/2″," he told *People.*

Washington played in his high school and for two years was a baritone saxophonist with the all-city high school band. He also studied chord progressions with Elvin Shepherd. At the age of 16, Washington finished high school and left Buffalo to become a professional musician, joining the Four Clefs. Based in Columbus, Ohio, the band was on the road much of the time. The Four Clefs split up in 1963 and Washington joined organist Keith McAllister's band. Two years later, in 1965, Washington was drafted into the U.S. Army. Stationed at Fort Dix, New Jersey, he was headed for Vietnam until, according to Joy Wansley of *People,* "he talked his way into the base band." Besides playing with the 19th Army Band, he also played in Philadelphia during his free time, working with a variety of organ trios and rock groups. In addition, he played in New York City with jazz drummer Billy Cobham.

For the Record. . .

Born December 12, 1943, in Buffalo, N.Y.; father was a saxophonist, mother was a singer in a choir; married, 1967, wife's name, Christine; children: Grover III, Shana. *Education:* Attended Wurlitzer School of Music and Temple University School of Music.

Saxophonist in musical group the Four Clefs, 1960-63; played with Keith McAllister, 1963-65; following induction into the U.S. Army became member of 19th Army Band, also appeared with numerous musicians and musical groups in the Philadelphia/New York City area, including Billy Cobham, 1965-67; played with Don Gardner's Sonotones, 1967-68; worked for a record distributor, Philadelphia, 1969-70; with Charles Earland's band, 1971; recording artist, featured and solo performer, 1971—. President of G.W. Jr. Music, Inc. (music publishing company) and of G-Man Productions, Inc. (production company).

Awards: Grammy Award for best jazz fusion performance, vocal or instrumental, 1981, for *Winelight;* winner of 1983 outstanding achievement in the arts award at the Pitt Jazz Seminar, University of Pittsburgh; holder of one platinum and six gold albums.

Addresses: Office—c/o Lloyd Z. Remick, 700 Three Penn Center, Philadelphia, PA 19102; and 1515 Market St., Suite 700, Philadelphia, PA 19102. *Agent*—ABC, 1995 Broadway, New York, NY 10023.

It was at one of his off-post gigs that Washington met his future wife, Christine, who was then an editorial assistant. Christine told *People,* "We met on a Saturday and he moved in on Thursday." They were married in 1967. Washington was discharged from the service that same year. Washington and his new wife then moved to Philadelphia. From 1967 to 1968 he played with Don Gardner's Sonotones. In 1969 he took his first full-time job out of the musical arena, working for a local record distributor. "I was totally immersed in jazz at the time," he told Coryell and Friedman, "and this taught me another side of music. I got to check out people like Jimi Hendrix, Jethro Tull, and John Mayall." In 1971, he returned to music, playing with Charles Earland's band. He also began recording as a sideman with various musicians such as Joe Jones, Leon Spencer, and Johnny Hammond.

His first big musical break came quite by accident. Commercially-minded record producer Creed Taylor had put together a set of pop-funk tunes for alto saxophonist Hank Crawford. On the eve of the recording date, Crawford was arrested "on a two-year-old driving charge," Washington told *Rolling Stone.* Taylor then called in the little-known Washington as a last-minute replacement and had him play the alto parts. The album, *Inner City Blues,* was released in 1971 under Washington's name. It became a hit—an album, Palmer wrote in the *New York Times,* "that sold hundreds of thousands of copies and did much to break down barriers between jazz and pop." As Washington admitted to Wansley, "My big break was blind luck."

He continued to record as a sideman with Randy Weston, Don Sebesky, Bob James, and others, as well as record his own albums. In 1972 he released *All the King's Horses,* followed by *Soul Box* in 1973. It was his next album, *Mister Magic,* released in 1974, that established Washington as a major jazz star. It was the first of several of his albums to reach number one on the jazz charts and go gold. Succeeding best-sellers included *Feels So Good, Live at the Bijou,* and *Reed Seed.*

Washington developed what is called a jazz-pop or jazz-rock fusion musical style. It consists of jazz improvisation over a pep or rock beat. Although he came from a jazz background, influenced by such artists as John Coltrane, Joe Henderson, and Oliver Nelson, Washington's wife got him interested in pop music. "I encouraged him to listen to more pop," Christine told *Rolling Stone.* "His intent was to play jazz, but he started listening to both, and at one point he told me he just wanted to play what he felt, without giving it a label." Recognizing that Washington is unrestrained by labels and tradition, Joachim Berendt wrote in *The Jazz Book: From New Orleans to Rock and Free Jazz* that he plays contemporary music "not worrying about styles and schools." A versatile musician, Washington plays tenor, alto, soprano, and baritone saxophones, plus clarinet, electric bass, and piano. He also composes some of his own material.

The popularity of Washington's brand of jazz-pop helped make jazz-pop music a success. Keyboardist Bob James told Wansley, "Grover was one of the main people to make this crossover movement happen. We had people intrigued by jazz, but a lot of it was so complex they didn't relate to it. Grover maintained a very high level of musicianship and yet his playing was very melodic and direct."

Critics had mixed reactions to Washington's music, some praise and some pans. The "commercialism" of his music was what usually earned the pans. In a review of his 1979 album *Skylarkin',* Frank-John Hadley of down beat said that "were commercial jazz saxophonists exalted to monarchic positions, Grover Washington Jr. would be the sovereign." Hadley added that Washington's "credo might read: Let my music reach out and spread love. Alas, his past recordings . . . have been as superficial, contrived and dishonest as a Harlequin romance." The *Skylarkin'* album, on the other hand, received high marks from Hadley because of the emotion of Washington's playing. "Now and then his phrases are predictable, tremolos as cliches, but there's enough unrehearsed excitement and compassion in his playing to permanently exile the affected waxings of any dozen commercial jazz pretenders."

Respected critic Ron Welbum noted in *Radio Free Jazz* that "Grover is perhaps the strongest young fusion reedman in the tradition of Hal Singer, Gatortail Jackson, and Junior Walker. That which is predictable about his music can be excused because of the power and . . . sincerity of his projections." Although some writers considered his music "fuzak," Palmer, in *Rolling Stone,* stated: "Powerful live performances make it clear that, whatever his commercial proclivities, Washington knows his soprano, alto, tenor and baritone saxophones thoroughly. On soprano and alto especially, his sound is attractively personal; he combines liquid grace with an understated residue of R&B grit."

Even some fellow jazz musicians knocked Washington's music. Wansley reported that bassist Percy Heath accused Washington of "bastardizing" jazz. But he defended himself against the barbs: "My music is for the everyday person—people music. There's no pretense. It's honest. It transmits feelings and moods. That's about all you can hope to achieve."

In 1980, Washington released his most successful album ever—*Winelight.* And from that album came a smash hit single—"Just the Two of Us," with vocalist Bill Withers. Both the album and the single had wide appeal. As *People* noted, the two recordings were "simultaneously among the top five sellers on five record charts: soul singles and LPs, pop singles and LPs, and jazz LPs." The popular jazz saxophonist achieved even broader popularity. The album eventually went platinum and the single went gold. Remarked the *New York Times,* "[Washington's] commercial success is unusual for a contemporary jazz instrumentalist."

Ever since he moved to Philadelphia, Washington had been a big fan of the Philadelphia 76ers professional basketball team. His love for the 76ers, and particularly their star player, went public with the *Winelight* album. One of the tracks on the record is called "Let It Flow ("For Dr. J")," dedicated to the team's Julius "Dr. J"

Erving. Around the same time, Washington approached the team and began playing the national anthem occasionally before games. "Why not?" he said to Lisa Twyman of *Sports Illustrated.* "I was at the games anyway."

Also in 1980, Washington applied for a doctoral program in music composition at Temple University. He explained to Wansley that he "was told he had to audition. 'The next day,' he smiles, 'I came back with a stack of my albums and told them to listen and let me know if they thought I could play.' He was admitted."

Washington's next albums carried on his familiar mellow sound and the critics continued their mixed reactions. In a 1982 review of his recording *Come Morning,* De Genova said: "Commercial? Yes. Trite? No. Appropriately titled, this album sets a 'cool summer morning, grass still wet with dew, lover laying next to you' mood." He added that "Grover's sincerity and his natural, almost whimsical saxophone interpretations make his refreshingly lyrical phrasing a pleasure to listen to." However, De Genova maintained, "Some may call this music vinyl Valium, and depending on personal taste, the album may become monotonous. Similarities in mood, texture, and tonality often make some of the tunes seem to blend together."

In addition to producing some of his own albums, Washington has also worked as a producer for the group Pieces of a Dream. In a review of their 1982 recording *We Are One,* Robert Henschen of *down beat* proclaimed, "With Grover Washington in a producer's role, you know the final mix is going to have a light, enjoyable touch. It does." Washington also had a featured solo on one of the songs and his playing, Henschen said, was "as sweet as ever." Reviewing Washington's 1983 album, *The Best Is Yet To Come, People* suggested that he definitely is capable of better. This album "is more pop than jazz, taking wing only in occasional bursts from Washington that break out of a staid set of arrangements." Better things did happen to him when he attended the annual Pitt Jazz Seminar at the University of Pittsburgh and was presented with the year's Outstanding Achievement in the Arts award.

In 1984 Washington released the album *Inside Moves.* Robert Hiltbrand of *People* remarked that "Grover's jazz is accessible to listeners of all musical tastes. Turn him loose on choice material, as on *Inside Moves,* and his fluid and graceful style is incomparable." Describing some of the cuts, Hiltbrand said, "'Dawn Song' moves from soft and dreamy to sharp and funky. The title cut undergoes a similar change, with Washington blending alto, tenor and baritone saxes over the sweet opening and then pulling out all the stops on top of a bass-percussive riff that is reminiscent of the pioneer fusion ensemble Weather Report."

The next year saw Washington collaborate on an album with jazz guitarist Kenny Burrell. A review by Ralph Novak of *People* stated that "Even those people who find Washington's popular solo-saxophone albums too bland and unchallenging don't question his sense of melody and tone. This LP lets him unleash those talents with a passionate vengeance." Burrell and Washington mesh well together according to Novak. "There are few more enjoyable moments in jazz than when two imaginative soloists mix and match with each other's moods, and this album is full of such moments."

Washington will undoubtedly continue to create his smooth, melodic saxophone sounds for years to come. And if he follows the advice of Hadley, he will also "continue his present policy, the policy of circulating warmth."

Selected discography

Inner City Blues, Kudu, 1971.
All the King's Horses, Kudu, 1972.
Soul Box, Kudu, 1973.
Mister Magic, Kudu, 1974.
Feels So Good, Kudu, 1975.
Secret Place, Kudu, 1976.
Soul Box, Volume 2, Kudu, 1976.
Live At the Bijou, Kudu, 1978.
Reed Seed, Motown, 1978.
Paradise, Elektra, 1979.
Skylarkin', Motown, 1979.
Winelight, Elektra, 1980.
Baddest, Motown, 1981.
Come Morning, Elektra, 1981.
The Best Is Yet to Come, Elektra, 1982.
Inside Moves, Elektra, 1984.

Anthology Of, Elektra, 1985.
Strawberry Moon, Columbia, 1987.
Then and Now, Columbia, 1988.
Greatest Performances, Motown.
Anthology, Motown.
At His Best, Motown.

Has also recorded as a sideman or featured artist with numerous musicians, including Eric Gale, Bob James, Ralph MacDonald, Don Sebesky, Randy Weston, and Bill Withers.

Also producer of and occasional guest performer on albums by musical group Pieces of a Dream, including *We Are One,* 1982; has also produced Jean Carne.

Sources

Books

Berendt, Joachim, *The Jazz Book: From New Orleans to Rock and Free Jazz,* translation by Dan Morgenstern, Barbara Bredigkeit, and Helmut Bredigkeit, Lawrence Hill & Co., 1975.
Coryell, Julie, and Laura Friedman, *Jazz-Rock Fusion: The People, The Music,* Dell, 1978.
Feather, Leonard, and Ira Gitler, *The Encyclopedia of Jazz in the Seventies,* Horizon Press, 1976.
Pareles, Jon, and Patricia Romanowski, *The Rolling Stone Encyclopedia of Rock & Roll,* Rolling Stone Press, 1983.

Periodicals

down beat, October 1980; June 1982; December 1982; February 1983.
New York Times, April 24, 1981.
People, May 18, 1981; February 7,1983; October 29, 1984; April 22, 1985.
Rolling Stone, October 18, 1979.
Sports Illustrated, July 11, 1983.

—Greg Mazurkiewicz

Whitesnake

Heavy metal band

B ritish heavy metal group Whitesnake has become one of the best-selling acts of the late 1980s and early 1990s. Their self-titled 1987 U.S. breakthrough album sold over six million copies, making critics who called them "derivative"—including David Hiltbrand of *People*—look rather out of touch with the heavy metal audience. Featuring lead singer David Coverdale, guitar players John Sykes, Adrian Vandenberg, and Steve Vai, and drummer Aynsley Dunbar, Whitesnake also did well with the 1990 effort *Slip of the Tongue,* though reviewers continued to express their dismay.

After Coverdale left his former band, Deep Purple, he helped form Whitesnake in 1976. Whitesnake steadily built up a following in Great Britain and Europe, but did not really begin to gain attention in the United States until it recorded *Slide It In* in 1984. Perhaps the band's eventual star status would have followed shortly after if Coverdale had not been sidelined with what he assured Steve Dougherty of *People* was a "non-drug-related" deviated septum that prevented him from singing. Coverdale further explained to Dougherty that surgery

For the Record. . .

Group formed in 1976 by **David Coverdale** (lead vocalist; born c. 1947, in Saltburn-by-the-Sea, Yorkshire, England), **Adrian Vandenburg** (guitarist), **John Sykes** (guitarist), **Aynsley Dunbar** (drummer). **Steve Vai** temporarily replaced Vandenburg in 1990; subsequently joined the band.

Recording and live performance artists, 1976—.

Address: *Record company*—Geffen Records, 75 Rockefeller Plaza, New York, NY 10010; 9130 Sunset Boulevard, Los Angeles, CA 90069.

to correct this problem delayed the production and subsequent release of *Whitesnake* for a year.

When *Whitesnake* did hit the record stores in 1987, it began racing up the charts. But critical opinion at best was mixed. Some favorably compared Whitesnake to Led Zeppelin, but others maligned them for copying not only Zeppelin's style but those of other groups, including the Scorpions and Foreigner. The album produced a hit single in "Still of the Night," however, which *High Fidelity* reviewer Ken Richardson hailed as "top-notch," and J.D. Considine of *Rolling Stone* also praised. The latter, noting the Zeppelin influence, called "Still of the Night" "a guilty pleasure," explaining that "Coverdale isn't simply stealing licks; he and . . . Sykes understand the structure, pacing and drama of the old Led Zeppelin sound." Other noteworthy tracks from *Whitesnake,* according to *Rolling Stone* critic Kim Neely, were "Crying in the Rain" and "Is This Love?" Following this album, Whitesnake obtained even more exposure to U.S. audiences by touring with fellow heavy metal group Motley Crue.

Whitesnake's 1990 disc, *Slip of the Tongue* featured the addition of guitarist Steve Vai, who formerly played with David Lee Roth's band. Vai temporarily replaced Adrian Vandenberg, who was unable to play due to a hand injury. After Vandenberg's recovery, both guitarists performed in Whitesnake's tour appearances. But though Hiltbrand conceded that "you have to marvel at Vai's technique" on *Slip of the Tongue,* it did not prevent him and other critics from panning the album, which Hiltbrand added was devoted "to rock's dumbest myth: the nymphomaniac, stiletto-heeled succubus." Neely lamented that *Slip of the Tongue* was "not passionate enough to evoke pleasure" and "not rude enough to spark contempt." Like Hiltbrand, she welcomed Vai's addition to the band, but complained that his talent was "buried under a mishmash of sappy string arrangements and declawed power chords."

According to Dougherty, however, Whitesnake—or Coverdale, at least—is not bothered by negative reviews. "The critics love to get out their knives and dine on Coverdale," the lead singer told the reporter. "But the worse the criticism gets, the more successful I become."

Selected discography

Slide It In, Geffen, 1984.
Whitesnake (includes "Still of the Night," "Bad Boys," "Straight for the Heart," "Children of the Night," "Is This Love?" and "Crying in the Rain"), Geffen, 1987.
Slip of the Tongue (includes "Now You're Gone," "Slow Poke Music," and "Kittens Got Claws"), Geffen, 1990.

Sources

High Fidelity, September, 1987.
People, October 5, 1987; February 5, 1990.
Rolling Stone, June 18, 1987; December 31, 1987; February 8, 1990.
Stereo Review, April, 1990.

—Elizabeth Wenning

Paul Williams

Singer, songwriter, actor

Multitalented songwriter, singer, and actor Paul Williams is perhaps best known for scoring the 1976 film *A Star Is Born,* and collaborating with super-star Barbra Streisand to write the extremely popular love theme from that film, "Evergreen." He earned several awards for that work, as well as many award nominations for his efforts on other film scores, including *Cinderella Liberty* and *The Muppet Movie.* In addition, Williams has provided music fans with many sweet-sounding ballads over the years, including "We've Only Just Begun" and "Just an Old-Fashioned Love Song."

Williams was born September 19, 1940, in Omaha, Nebraska. His father was an architectural engineer who pursued various construction projects throughout the Midwest, so the future entertainer traveled a great deal as a child. In addition to the usual social misfortunes that go with always being new at school, Williams also had to deal with the stigma associated with his shorter stature—he described the other children's attitude towards him thus to Tony Kornheiser in the *Washington Post:* "New kid. Smaller—hey, let's whack him."

When Williams was 13, his father was killed in an automobile accident, and he went to live with an aunt and uncle in Long Beach, California, where he spent the remainder of his adolescence. On the way to his new home, however, he had the opportunity to see a show in Las Vegas, Nevada; this experience solidified his desire—perhaps first sparked by childhood competition in local talent shows—to become an entertainer. While attending a Long Beach high school, he developed an interest in drama, appeared in many school plays, and was vice-president of the institution's Thespian Club. After graduating, Williams wandered for a while and eventually came to rest in Albuquerque, New Mexico, where he became a featured member of the community theater. He appeared in plays such as *A Thousand Clowns* and William Shakespeare's *A Midsummer Night's Dream.*

By 1960, however, Williams had come back to Long Beach, where he joined the slightly more prestigious repertory company Studio 58. During some of his performances with them, such as one in *Under the Sycamore Tree,* he received favorable attention from critics in Los Angeles, California, and this encouraged him to go to Hollywood in pursuit of a film career. He did find one, but it was small—he received only minor roles during the 1960s and 1970s, in pictures that were generally panned by the critics. As Williams began to despair of becoming a respected actor, however, he turned to other forms of expression. Comedian Mort Sahl hired him to write skits for a local television program; through this job, he met Biff Rose, a composer who needed a lyricist.

Williams began collaborating with Rose, and the result

For the Record. . .

Full name, Paul Hamilton Williams; born September 19, 1940, in Omaha Neb.; son of Paul Hamilton (an architectural engineer) and Bertha Mae (Burnside) Williams; married wife, Katie (marriage ended); children: Christopher Cole.

Actor, 1958—; comedy writer during the late 1960s; songwriter, beginning in the late 1960s; recording artist and concert performer, c. 1971—. Screenwriter, beginning c. 1981—. Appeared in films, including *The Loved One*, 1965, *The Chase*, 1966, *Watermelon Man*, 1970, *Battle for the Planet of the Apes*, 1973, *Phantom of the Paradise*, 1974, *Smokey and the Bandit*, 1977, *The Cheap Detective*, 1978, *The Muppet Movie*, 1979, *Smokey and the Bandit II*, 1980, *Smokey and the Bandit III*, c. 1983, and *The Doors*, 1991. Appeared in plays, including *Under the Sycamore Tree* at the Magnolia Theater in California, 1961, and *Tru* on Broadway, in New York City, 1989. Appeared on television shows, including *The Tonight Show*, *The Odd Couple*, *Wild, Wild West Revisited*, *Hawaii 5-0*, *The Love Boat*, *Fantasy Island*, *The Fall Guy*, and *Midnight Special*. Scored and/or composed songs for films, including *The Getaway*, 1972, *The Man Who Loved Cat Dancing*, 1972, *Cinderella Liberty*, 1973, *Phantom of the Paradise*, 1974, *The Day of the Locust*, 1975, *Malone*, 1976, *A Star Is Born*, 1976, *One on One*, 1977, *The End*, 1978, *Agatha*, 1979, *The Muppet Movie*, 1979, and *The Secret of NIMH*, 1982. Scored or wrote music for television shows, including *The Love Boat*, *The McLean Stevenson Show*, *It Takes Two*, *Sugar Time!* and *Emmet Otter's Jug Band Christmas*.

Awards: Academy Award nomination for best song, for "Nice to Be Around," from the film *Cinderella Liberty*, 1973, and Academy Award nomination for best score, for the film *Phantom of the Paradise*, 1974; Academy Award, Grammy Award, and Golden Globe Award for best song, for "Evergreen," from the film *A Star Is Born*, 1976, and a Golden Globe Award for best score, for the film *A Star Is Born*, 1976; and Academy Award nomination and Grammy nomination for the score of *The Muppet Movie*, 1979.

Addresses: *Record company*—A&M, 1416 La Brea Ave., Los Angeles, CA 90028.

and its parent company Warner Brothers—believed in Williams, however, and he released a solo effort in 1970 called *Someday Man*. This disc, too, was met with silence from music audiences.

Soon afterwards, however, Williams signed on as a songwriter for A&M Records. With composer Roger Nichols, he started writing songs for other artists, including Johnny Mathis and Claudine Longet. Then they started racking up hits. Their first huge success was the song "Out in the Country," which scored a hit when recorded by Three Dog Night. Their "Rainy Days and Mondays," recorded by the Carpenters, became quite popular as well. Williams and Nichols were also contracted to compose music for a bank commercial advertising their special services for newlyweds. Williams explained to Henry Edwards in *After Dark:* "Since I am an incurable romantic, I fell in love with the idea of making a sugary commercial about a young couple getting married." Apparently, audiences responded to William's inspiration so favorably that he and Nichols decided to expand the jingle into a full-length song. The result, "We've Only Just Begun," became a massive hit for the Carpenters, and has since become a ballad standard, recorded by many other artists.

Encouraged by his success, Williams began recording his own albums for the A&M label, starting with *An Old-Fashioned Love Song*. This, along with follow-up efforts such as 1972's *Life Goes On* and 1974's *A Little Bit of Love* and *Here Comes Inspiration*, fared much better with fans than did Williams's earlier recordings. He began performing on variety shows and in the better nightclubs, and while many dismissed his songs as too sentimental, most conceded along with *Los Angeles Times* reviewer Terry Atkinson that Williams was a very good musical entertainer in person, "with an appealing blend of unpretentiousness and effective dramatic sense."

In 1974 Williams was invited by film director Brian De Palma to score much of his musical update of *The Phantom of the Opera*, entitled *Phantom of the Paradise*. Williams also acted in the film, but received the most notice for his work on the music, earning an Academy Award nomination. In 1976 he had even greater success with his work on the film *A Star Is Born*. With various other composers, Williams wrote the lyrics to the motion picture's songs "Watch Closely Now," "The Woman in the Moon," "With One More Look at You," "Everything," and the now-classic love theme "Evergreen." He garnered a Golden Globe Award for the film's score, another for "Evergreen," and a Grammy and an Academy Award for "Evergreen." Other films Williams has written music for include *Cinderella Liberty, The End,* and *The Muppet Movie*.

During the 1970s and early 1980s, Williams found

was "Fill Your Heart," a ballad that eventually found itself on the B-side of novelty singer Tiny Tim's hit, "Tiptoe Through the Tulips." Tiny Tim's producer suggested that Williams, who had previously learned to play the guitar, form his own band. He did, called it Holy Mackerel, and released an album on Reprise Records that attracted virtually no attention from fans. Reprise—

himself in demand for character roles in many motion pictures, including the *Smokey and the Bandit* movies and playwright Neil Simon's *The Cheap Detective*. He also released more albums, including *Ordinary Fools, Classics,* and *Crazy for Loving You.* Many of these efforts featured his music from films. He also wrote both scripts and music for television programs. In 1989, Williams appeared on the Broadway stage in the title role of the play *Tru,* a one-man show about the late author Truman Capote. Before he performed, he told Richard Leivenberg in *Harper's Bazaar:* "I am *not* simply going to put on a hat and mince around. I want to crawl inside the man and have people be moved by him, so by the end of the evening they will miss his presence as much as I do."

Selected discography

(With Holy Mackerel) *Holy Mackerel,* Reprise, c. 1969.

Someday Man, Warner Bros., 1970.
An Old-Fashioned Love Song, A&M, c. 1971.
Life Goes On, A&M, 1972.
A Little Bit of Love, A&M, 1974.
Here Comes Inspiration, A&M, 1974.
Ordinary Fools, A&M, 1975.
Classics, A&M, 1977.
A Little on the Windy Side, Portrait, 1979.
Crazy for Loving You, Firstline, 1981.

Sources

After Dark, June 1972.
Harper's Bazaar, September 1989.
Los Angeles Times, December 20, 1977.
Washington Post, June 30, 1980.

—Elizabeth Wenning

Ransom Wilson

Flutist

Ransom Wilson has carved a niche for himself as both a solo flutist and chamber music conductor. He is acclaimed as a flutist, having performed widely as a recitalist and as a soloist with the world's leading chamber orchestras. In recital, Wilson has appeared regularly in major concert series in Los Angeles, Boston, New York, Dallas, Seattle, and San Francisco and has collaborated with such celebrated soloists as flutists Jean-Pierre Rampal and James Galway, mezzo-soprano Frederica von Stade, soprano Jessye Norman, and harpist Nancy Allen, among others. He is also the founder, music director, and principal conductor of the Solisti New York Chamber Orchestra and holds guest conducting positions with several other orchestras.

Born and raised and Tuscaloosa, Alabama, Wilson early discovered his interest in music. At age 14 he studied at North Carolina's School of the Arts and later he attended the Juilliard School of Music in New York City. While at Juilliard, Wilson chaffed at his training to become an orchestral musician, for a desire to perform solo literature consumed him. Yet while still a student he performed with orchestras on a freelance basis, as well as appearing as a soloist in recital.

Wilson pursued post-graduate studies as an Atlantique Scholar (the equivalent of a the U.S. Fulbright scholar program) in France, particularly so that he could study with celebrated flutist Jean-Pierre Rampal, who is generally credited with the flute's emergence as a solo instrument to rival the piano on concert stages worldwide.

In the early 1970s Wilson made several recordings for the Orin and Musical Heritage Society labels. After his mentor, Rampal, invited him to record an album of flute duets in 1974 and later glowingly endorsed Wilson's work, the young flutist's solo career was launched. In 1978 the fledgling musician was offered an exclusive contract with EMI/Angel. Since then Wilson has made more than ten solo recordings, including two Grammy-nominated albums.

In about 1980 Wilson became interested in conducting and began studying conducting formally with Roger Nierenberg, James Dixon, and Otto-Werner Mueller. "I began conducting because I had to," Wilson told Allan Kozinn in an interview for *Ovation*. "I just had to. I felt I had reached the end of the flute repertoire. Not that there aren't new pieces being written—there are, of course, and I look forward with relish to each one. But there are few flute works that can claim any real depth. Why hadn't I noticed this earlier? I was having a lot of fun. I had been turned on by the flute in a very visceral way. It was—and still is, for me—a sensual experience to play it. It gives me a satisfaction that I get from

For the Record. . .

Born 1951, Tuscaloosa, Ala. *Education:* Attended the North Carolina School of the Arts; The Juilliard School in New York City, 1969-73; pursued post-graduate studies as an Atlantique Scholar in France with Jean-Pierre Rampal; studied conducting with Roger Neirenberg, James Dixon, and Otto-Werner Mueller.

Solo flutist; founder, music director, and principal conductor of Solisti New York, 1981—. Artistic director of the OK Mozart Festival in Barlesville, Oklahoma; music director of the Tuscaloosa Symphony Orchestra.

Awards: Alabama Prize, 1988; National Public Radio award for best performance by a small ensemble on a national broadcast (with pianist Christopher O'Riley), 1989.

Addresses: *Record company*—EMI/Angel, 1750 N. Vine St., Hollywood, CA 90028. *Manager*—ICM Artists, Ltd., 40 West 57th St., New York, NY 10019.

nothing else. You're pouring your insides into this little pipe, and somehow it becomes more than that."

Wilson wasted little time in finding a podium. In 1980 he gathered a group of about thirty musicians to form Solisti New York, a chamber orchestra. The group worked together several more times over the next few years—including a tour of the Midwest—and in May 1983 it made its "official" New York debut at Lincoln Center. While the orchestra's repertoire contains some fairly standard pieces for chamber orchestra, such as works by Bach, Handel, Mozart, and Vivaldi, it also includes twentieth-century pieces by Samuel Barber, Aaron Copeland, Ralph Vaughan Williams, Francis Poulenc, and Zoltan Kodaly, among others.

An advocate of contemporary music, Wilson has commissioned works by a number of composers, including Peter Schickele, Joseph Schwanter, Jean-Michel Damase, Carlos Surinach, and Deborah Drattel. Wilson has especially brought to the podium his interest in minimalism, a style of twentieth-century music in which a minimum of material is repeated to the maximum effect. Solisti New York has performed and recorded works by minimalist composers Steve Reich and John Adams in what have been billed as "Meet the Minimalists" concerts.

While many instrumentalists in the 1980s have been harshly and often justly criticized for their conducting efforts, reviews of Wilson's work have generally been favorable. Wilson prefers to separate his conducting from solo performing for he is uncomfortable assuming both responsibilities simultaneously as was often done by the principal violin players of the eighteenth century. In addition to his formal training, Wilson credits much of his success with his ability as an instrumentalist to work well with the musicians under his baton. "I think of my role up here on the podium as akin to that of a great movie director, which is to work with an extra-ordinarily talented group of people, and to help them be seen in the best possible light," he explained to Kozinn. "That's a bit different from the way an autocratic conductor sees his job; but coming form the standpoint that I do, I think I have a lot more respect for the musicians than many conductors do. I prefer my time with the orchestra to be more relaxed, friendly, and productive." Wilson welcomes orchestra members' suggestions on tempos, dynamics, and other musical matters.

Not only does Wilson conduct, he assumes the responsibilities of management for Solisti New York, at times even supporting it financially. Wilson also serves as artistic director of the OK Mozart Festival in Bartlesville, Oklahoma, where Solisti New York is in residence each June, and as music director of the Tuscaloosa Symphony Orchestra. As his conducting activities have increased, Wilson has reduced the number of flute engagements, which at one time numbered more than one hundred per year.

Selected discography

John Adams: *Grand Pianola Music;* Steve Reich: *Eight Lines; Vermont Counterpoint,* Ransom Wilson conducting Solisti New York Chamber Orchestra, EMI/Angel.

Bach: *Brandenburg Concertos; Suite in B Minor,* EMI/Angel.

Bach: *Partita in A Minor,* Orion Records.

Bach: *Partita in A Minor;* Marais: *Variations on "Les Folles d'Espagne";* Telemann: *Fantasias;* Blavet: *Minuet,* Orion Records.

C.P.E. Bach: *Sonata in E Major;* Corrette: *Sonata in D Major;* Clementi: *Sonata in G Major;* Mozart: *Sonata K. 12, 14,* Orion Records.

Bach and Telemann Suites, EMI/Angel.

Impressions for Flute with Nancy Allen (harp), works by Ravel, Faure, Satie, and others, EMI/Angel.

Four Vivaldi Concertos, EMI/Angel.

Mozart: *Mozart Horn Concerti,* with David Jolley (horn), Ransom Wilson conducting the Solisti New York Chamber Orchestra, Sine Qua Non Records.

Mozart: *Piano Concerto No. 23;* Haydn: *Piano Concerto in D Major,* Steven Lubin (piano), Ransom Wilson conducting the Mozartean Players, Arabesque Records.

Steve Reich: *Vermont Counterpoint;* Philip Glass: *Facades;* Frank

Becker: *Stonehenge*; Debussy: *Syrinx*; Jolivet: *Asceses (I)*,
   EMI/Angel.
Ransom Wilson: *Baroque Concerts for Flute* (Blavet, Devienne,
   Tartini), EMI/Angel.
Ransom Wilson: *Pleasure Songs for Flute*, EMI/Angel.

Sources

Horizon, January/February 1986.
Houston Post, July 10, 1988.
Indianapolis Star, October 2, 1988.
New York Times, December 11, 1988.
Ovation, August 1984.
Rocky Mountain News (Denver), February 4, 1988.

—Jeanne M. Lesinski

Wilson Phillips

Pop singing trio

Pop trio Wilson Phillips has quickly found fame with the release of its first album in 1990. The self-titled effort has earned the group a smash hit with the single, "Hold On." Wilson Phillips, with its name taken from the last names of its members—Chynna Phillips and sisters Carnie and Wendy Wilson—specializes in harmony, and "sound[s] quite pleasant," according to *People* critic Ralph Novak.

As many reviewers and reporters have noted, the members of Wilson Phillips have music in their blood. Phillips is the daughter of John and Michelle Phillips, veterans of the folk group the Mamas and the Papas, and the Wilson sisters are the daughters of Beach Boy member Brian Wilson. Though all three young women were very much exposed to music during their childhood, and Carnie and Wendy made appearances on some of their father's recordings, none was really that interested in the art except for enjoying the music of such groups as Fleetwood Mac and the Eagles. During their adolescences, Chynna and Carnie were more interested in acting, and Wendy wanted to be a writer and a model.

But in 1986, after such examples as Band Aid, Farm Aid, and U.S.A. for Africa, Phillips—a longtime friend of the young Wilsons—thought it would be a good idea to get some children of famous musicians together to make a record for charity. Though Moon Zappa, daughter of Frank Zappa, and actress Ione Skye, daughter of 1960s folk singer Donovan, were considered for the project, it fell through.

Nevertheless, Chynna, Carnie, and Wendy were too pleased with the results of their own practice to abandon the idea of becoming recording artists. Wendy Wilson recalled for *Rolling Stone*'s David Wild: "Our three-part harmony just felt so natural. My sister naturally goes low, I naturally go high, and Chynna just fit right into the middle. And we realized that we didn't want to do just one charity record. We wanted to form a group." There was also talk of including the late Mamas and Papas member Cass Elliot's daughter Owen, but as Phillips confided to Wild, "we decided it would be best just to have three."

The young women soon announced their ambitions to producer Richard Perry, who worked with them for a few years to find the right sound for them. After they had enlisted the help of songwriter Glen Ballard, whose experience included helping Michael Jackson write "Man in the Mirror," the trio was overwhelmed with offers from record companies. Eventually they signed with song publisher Charles Koppelman's fledgling SBK label.

The singers tossed many different possible group names around, and, according to Wild, "considered calling themselves Leda and titling their first album *Chasing Swans*," but, of course, settled on Wilson Phillips. They do not believe, however, that their famous parents' names have helped them with their fans. "The funny thing," Phillips explained to Wild, "is that most kids today have *no idea* what those names mean. You ask a kid on the street and they may know some of the songs and maybe they've heard of the Beach Boys. But they don't know who Brian Wilson or John Phillips are. If you say Phillips to a kid today, they'd think 'screwdriver' or 'milk of magnesia.'"

Despite some negative reviews, *Wilson Phillips* has sold well and "Hold On" has received much airplay both from radio and music video stations. While Novak had some criticisms for the young women, he conceded that "they have lots of time to develop, and this album suggests they have the talent" to do so, and he praised the songs "A Reason to Believe," "Next to You," and "Eyes Like Twins." SBK head Koppelman concluded for Wild: "People *should* hear them. Their sound, their perspective on life at twenty years old, their ideas, their freshness is just a smile. And I think we're all ready for a smile."

Selected discography

Wilson Phillips (includes "Hold On," "A Reason to Believe," "Next to You," and "Eyes Like Twins"), SBK Records, 1990.

Sources

People, May 7, 1990; June 4, 1990.
Rolling Stone, May 17, 1990.

—Elizabeth Wenning

Johnny Winter

Guitarist

In 1968 an article in *Rolling Stone,* written by Larry Sepulvado and John Burks, entitled "Texas" stated, "Imagine a 130-pound cross-eyed albino bluesman with long fleecy hair playing some of the gutsiest blues guitar you have ever heard." By 1969 Johnny Winter had signed with Columbia Records for a reported $300,000 and soon released his incredible self-titled debut LP. "He played the blues, real driving blues that had the heaviness of Chicago pumping underneath it and his darting lines dancing melodically over it," wrote Gene Santoro in *The Guitar: The History, The Music, The Players.* "Like Bloomfield's band and the Blues Project, he pulled blues classics, like 'Mean Mistreater' and 'When You Got A Good Friend,' back into the mainstream of rock music and forced rock guitarists once again to pay attention to their musical heritage and draw from it."

Winter's own musical legacy began as a 5-year-old playing clarinet in Beaumont, Texas. He continued on the instrument for four years but had to quit when an orthodontist informed the youth that he had a serious overbite. Winter switched to ukelele but that only lasted until rock and roll came out. His father advised him to switch to guitar because there weren't too many famous ukulele players that came to his mind. A local disc jockey named Clarence Garlow turned Winter on to the blues through his Bon Ton Show on radio station KJET. The two soon became friends as Winter began to build up an impressive record collection that allowed him to study the blues masters and cop their licks. "I would learn how to play a record note-for-note," Winter told Don Menn in *The Guitar Player Book.* "After I kind of got the feel of what was supposed to be going on, I just took what I heard and assimilated it, and I guess it would come out part mine and part everybody else's . . . I tried to make it my own after I got the basic things down."

He also learned country licks from Luther Nalley, a Beaumont music store employee, as well as the current rock tunes of the late 1950s. Winter and his brother Edgar played together in various teenage bands and the two albino brothers made quite an impression in their hometown. At 15 Winter won a talent contest for "School Day Blues" and, after recording the tune on Pappy Dailey's Dart label, it immediately shot to Number 8 in Beaumont.

Although Edgar appeared on Johnny's first two LPs, he was featured more on the latter in an effort to bring the younger sibling a share of the spotlight. Edgar's style, however, was much more jazz-based than blues, though he scored a monster hit with "Frankenstein" later down the road.

Johnny moved on to record for the Jin, KRCO, Pacemaker, and Diamond labels under various titles: Texas

Guitar Slim, Black Plague, and Johnny and the Jammers. These first cuts were later released after Winter became famous and are considered collector's items today. "Winter's early recordings now stand as a testament to his youthful range and prowess, offering examples of blues, soul, rock, pop, and psychedelia far superior to many highly touted recent reissues by more obscure artists," wrote Larry Birnbaum in *down beat*. "Had he not become a celebrity, he would still have been a legend." It was during this period that Winter began jamming with black blues artists at a local club called the Raven, until problems began to surface. "The old stuff, blues, just went out," he recalled in *The Guitar Player Book*. "The black people were ashamed of it, and white people didn't like it yet. So there was just nobody to hear until the young English guys started picking up on it."

Winter dropped out of Lamar State College and headed north to Chicago to join his friend Dennis Drugan's band, the Gents, but by 1963 he was back in Texas. He recorded the single "Eternity" for the Ritter label who then leased it to Atlantic. It became a big regional hit and Winter found himself opening for major acts. In 1964 he toured the south with the Crystalliers and It & Them before stopping in Houston to record with the Traits on the Universal label in 1967.

He then teamed up with drummer Tommy Shannon (who later played with another Texas guitar virtuoso, the late Stevie Ray Vaughan) and drummer Uncle John Turner to tour the Lone Star state. When the British kids began to make blues fashionable, Winter headed to England with a demo tape recorded on Sonobeat in hopes of making a name for himself overseas. With little success in the U.K., he returned to the states to realize that the aforementioned *Rolling Stone* article had come out singing his praises.

Steve Paul, owner of New York's The Scene nightclub, signed the hot ticket to a management contract and shuffled him off to Nashville to record his first LP with the help of Jimi Hendrix's engineer, Eddie Kramer. In addition to Turner and Shannon, blues stalwarts Willie Dixon and Shakey Horton also appeared on the album in which Winter quickly established himself as an authentic bluesician. Confusion arose when Winter's Sonobeat demo was issued as *Progressive Blues Experience* at the same time as Columbia's release. Winter quickly began to experience hype and overkill as he was touted as the new sensation while touring to support the LP. "I had always thought of myself as a singer who backed himself up with a guitar," he told *Guitar World*. "But once I realized that people were thinking of me more as a guitar player than a singer, I gradually changed in my head the way I thought of myself."

On Winter's third release he recruited guitarist Rick Derringer and his McCoys (of "Hang On Sloopy" fame) to back him up. Derringer produced *Johnny Winter And* while also penning the raunchy "Rock and Roll Hoochie Coo." Winter capitalized on the hot lineup with *Johnny Winter And: Live,* but realized that the further he strayed from his blues roots with rock and roll renditions, the harder it became to please people. "I got really freaked out, once I had 'made it'," he told *Guitar World*. "Before that, everybody wanted you to play everything. Once you made it, they wanted to figure out which category to put you in, and they'd never let you do anything that was out of the ordinary." Winter's desire to delve into his R&B, Cajun, hillbilly, and rock roots created outside pressure on the artist. In addition, a wretched case of heroin addiction forced him to drop out of action for the next two years.

He recovered in a New Orleans hospital and came back with the scorching, aptly-titled *Still Alive And Well* in 1973. After jumping over to Steve Paul's Blue Sky label, his next few albums proved that he was stronger than ever in all musical styles. He teamed with his brother in 1976 on *Johnny And Edgar Winter: Together* as the two blasted through a set of their favorite oldies like "Jailhouse Rock," "Soul Man," and "Baby Watcha Want Me To Do." "That was just a lot of fun," Winter said in *Guitar World*, "just a lot of old rock 'n' roll songs that we had done together over the years in clubs. I guess it pretty much represents what we have in common, musically."

As Winter had made rock guitarists look at their roots in the late 1960s, he would also re-evaluate his music in 1977 after convincing his label to sign blues legend Muddy Waters. Winter produced and played guitar on four brilliant Waters LPs and was largely responsible for bringing the master back to his throne. "That really helped me immensely because it got me back into doing blues," Winter told *down beat*. "I kind of rededicated myself to the blues after the Muddy Waters thing."

The effect was reflected on his own albums also with *White Hot And Blue* ("An effective balance between force and polish," wrote John Milward in *Rolling Stone)* and *Nothin' But The Blues,* a predominantly acoustic blues outing featuring many of the same musicians used on Waters's *Hard Again* Grammy winner. "Winter simply has never recorded in as vital a blues context," stated John Swenson in *Rolling Stone,* "effectively [bridging] the gap between hard rock and the blues in a way that only great stylists like Jimi Hendrix and Eric Clapton have been able to, thus proving himself as one of our greatest musical resources." Winter's fingerpicking on the dobro slide guitar brought back memories of one of his main influences, the late Robert Johnson. After 1978's *Raisin' Cain,* Winter would have to wait a few years before signing with a small Chicago-based label run by Bruce Igualer named Alligator. Winter's first chore there was to work with Sonny Terry on his fine *Whoopin'* LP. "The Muddy Waters records and the one with Sonny Terry were so much fun," stated Winter in *Guitar Player*. "For me, they are some of the things that make playing worthwhile. When you play with guys who have been doing it that much longer, you feel like you're playing with a part of history."

Winter released his own *Guitar Slinger* in 1984 with the assistance of labelmate Albert Collins's Icebreakers band. He recreated older R&B gems with horn backing, but the guitar playing was pure, over-the-edge Winter all the way. "If he were paid on a per-note basis, just about any of these tracks would send him up a tax bracket," wrote Jas Obrecht in *Guitar Player*. Winter borrowed the Icebreaker's rhythm section for *Serious Business* but dropped the horns in favor of a more stripped-down approach. He was reunited with his old mates, Tommy Shannon and Uncle John Turner, on 1986's *Third Degree*. "It's almost as if his two previous Alligator LPs were detox stops, letting him gradually rediscover the leaner, hungrier sounds he burst out of Texas with some 20 years ago," stated Gene Santoro in *Guitar World*.

With a wild dragon tattoo adorning his chest and wielding a futuristic Lazer guitar, Johnny Winter is still a one-of-a-kind, easily distinguishable from any of his contemporaries by both sight and sound. He's stayed right on top of the market, recruiting ZZ Top's ace producer, Terry Manning, for his *The Winter of '88* LP. His live shows likewise highlight a fabulous mixed bag but his roots are definitely well-preserved. "As long as I can do blues, I don't mind rock & roll, but I wouldn't do just rock & roll and no blues," he said in *down beat*. "I like rock & roll, too, but I love the blues more."

Selected discography

Early career recordings released after signing with Columbia in 1969

First Winter, CBS, 1970.
About Blues, Janus, 1971.
Early Times, Janus, 1971.
Austin Texas, United Artists, 1976.
The Progressive Blues Experiment, Liberty, 1969.
The Johnny Winter Story, released in Great Britain by Blue Sky, 1980.

Albums

Johnny Winter, Columbia, 1969.
First Winter, CBS, 1970.
Second Winter, Columbia, 1970.
Johnny Winter And, Columbia, 1970.
Johnny Winter And: Live, Columbia, 1971.
Still Alive And Well, Columbia, 1973.
Saints And Sinners, Columbia, 1974.
John Dawson Winter III, Blue Sky, 1976.
Johnny and Edgar Winter: Together, Blue Sky, 1976.
White Hot and Blue, Blue Sky, 1978.
Nothin' But The Blues, Blue Sky.
Raisin' Cain, Blue Sky, 1978.
Guitar Slinger, Alligator, 1984.
Serious Business, Alligator, 1985.
Third Degree, Alligator, 1986.
The Winter of '88, Voyager/MCA, 1988.

With Lonnie Brooks

Wound Up Tight, Alligator, 1986.

With Sonny Terry

Whoopin', Alligator, 1980.

With Muddy Waters; produced and played guitar

Hard Again, Blue Sky, 1977.
I'm Ready, Blue Sky, 1978.
Muddy "Mississippi" Waters Live, Blue Sky, 1979.
King Bee, Blue Sky, 1981.

Sources

Books

Christgau, Robert, *Christgau's Record Guide,* Ticknor & Fields, 1981.

Evans, Tom and Mary Anne Evans, *Guitars: From The Renaissance To Rock,* Facts on File, 1977.

The Guitar Player Book, by the editors of *Guitar Player,* Guitar Player Books/Grove Press, 1979.

Kozinn, Allan, Pete Welding, Dan Forte and Gene Santoro, *The Guitar: The History, The Music, The Players,* Quill, 1984.

Logan, Nick, and Bob Woffinden, compilers, *The Illustrated Encyclopedia of Rock,* Harmony, 1977.

Marsh, Dave, editor, with John Swenson, *The Rolling Stone Record Guide,* Random House/Rolling Stone Press, 1979.

Periodicals

down beat, September 1984; October 1984; February 1986; May 1987.

Guitar Player, June 1984; November 1986.

Guitar World, November 1985; March 1987; March 1989.

Rolling Stone, August 25, 1977; November 2, 1978.

—Calen D. Stone

Bobby Womack

Singer, songwriter

Bobby Womack is one of the most respected artists in black music, with a long and distinguished career in rhythm & blues and soul. Like many other black singer/songwriters, Womack began performing gospel music in church settings as a youngster and then moved into the secular field as a composer, guitarist, and singer. Although so-called "mainstream" success has always eluded him, Womack is immensely popular among black American listeners and a veritable superstar in Europe, where his albums often sell in the millions. In the *Encyclopedia of Pop, Rock & Soul,* Irwin Stambler notes that, through his many stylistic incarnations, Womack has "provided a body of work ranking among the finest in modern pop music."

Bobby Womack was born in Cleveland, Ohio, one of five sons of a steelworker. He and his brothers—Cecil, Curtis, Friendly, and Harris—began singing gospel as the Womack Brothers while Bobby was still a youngster. The group travelled throughout the Midwest and performed in shows with other gospel ensembles. Looking back on those days in the *Philadelphia Inquirer,* Womack said: "We were so sincere we thought singing anything else was the way to hell." Despite his deep faith, Womack felt something else stirring in the mid- to late-1950s—the nascent soul music movement that provided money and fame far beyond the bounds of the gospel circuit.

Womack became fast friends with another gospel singer, Sam Cooke, who had decided to move into secular music. Cooke offered Womack a job as backup guitarist in his first rhythm & blues band, and in 1960 Womack accepted, dropping out of school. Womack told the *Philadelphia Inquirer* that his father warned him he would face eternal damnation if he joined Cooke. "Sam got me thinking," he said. "I remember telling my father, '[God] blessed you with this voice and look at you—$100 a week in the steel mill.' So I started to think, 'I hope the Lord understands that I can sing a different kind of music and do good deeds as well.'"

The move proved fruitful for both Cooke and Womack. By 1962 Cooke had convinced the other Womacks to go secular as well, and the brothers formed a group called the Valentinos. Within two years the Valentinos were filling halls on the R&B circuit, led by Bobby's smooth vocals and steadily sharpening songwriting talents. Their biggest hit came in 1964, when Bobby's "It's All Over Now" sold four hundred thousand copies. The song was also picked up by a white group—none other than the Rolling Stones, who made it their second American hit. Another Womack song, "Looking for a Love," later became a major hit for the J. Geils Band.

Womack has always been ambivalent about the fact that white artists have been able to make bigger hits of

For the Record. . .

Born March 4, 1944, in Cleveland, Ohio; son of a steel-worker; children: Vincent.

Singer, songwriter, guitarist, 1955—. With brothers Cecil, Curtis, Friendly, and Harris formed gospel group the Womack Brothers; changed group name to the Valentinos, 1960. Solo performer, 1964—; has cut albums with R&B, Minit, United Artists, CBS, and MCA, among others. Major R&B singles hits include "Looking for Love," 1962, "Fly Me to the Moon," 1967, "Check It Out," 1975, "If You Think You're Lonely," 1982, and "I Wish He Didn't Trust Me So Much," 1985.

Awards: Named the best male vocalist, best songwriter, and best live performer by Britain's *Blues & Soul,* 1984.

Addresses: *Record company*—Epic, 51 West 52nd St., New York, NY 10019.

his music than he could himself. "I like the fact that people sang my songs," he told the *Philadelphia Inquirer,* "because there was a blockage for me because I was black. So I appreciated the fact that they could take the message a lot further than me. But then, after 30 years, you've got to ask yourself: 'Can I say something myself now?'"

In effect, Womack has been asking himself that question all along. He went solo shortly after Sam Cooke's violent death in 1964 and steadily worked his way to prominence in the soul field. Womack has earned Top 40 hits in three decades while providing material and backup work to artists as varied as Aretha Franklin, Joe Tex, Ray Charles, Janis Joplin, and jazzman Gabor Szabo. He has also maintained close ties with the Rolling Stones, contributing instrumentals and even vocals to more than one Stones album.

Womack's solo career has had peaks and valleys, the lowest ebbs coming when he has tried to write and sing for the middle-of-the-road audience. In the late 1960s and early 1970s he had an array of soul hits with United Artists, including "A Woman's Got To Have It," "Daylight," "Check It Out," and a remake of "Looking for a Love." In 1976, however, he moved to Columbia Records, where a crossover consciousness and an overloaded roster of stars virtually buried him. In *The Death of Rhythm & Blues,* Nelson George writes: "With his gutsy voice echoing Cooke's gospel recordings, Womack should have remained a vital force in R&B throughout the decade. Instead, his career was lost in the flood of black CBS releases. By 1978 Womack was gone from CBS and, after a failing album at Arista, ended the seventies a nonentity in R&B."

Womack rebounded quickly as the 1980s began, producing one of his best-known albums, *The Poet.* That work rose into the Top 10 on *Billboard's* soul chart and even made it into the Top 30 on the pop chart. A single, "If You Think You're Lonely," peaked in the Top 20 on the soul chart in early 1982. After a painful hiatus caused by the shooting death of his brother, Womack returned to work in 1984, releasing *The Poet II* the same year. That album sold even better than its predecessor, especially in Europe, bringing Womack his first platinum recording. The artist had two Top 10 singles from *The Poet II,* "Let Me Kiss It Where It Hurts," and "I Wish He Didn't Trust Me So Much."

In the early 1990s, Bobby Womack is assured of a devoted audience both in America and abroad. His 1986 duet with Mick Jagger, "Harlem Shuffle," introduced him to MTV viewers, while his albums *Womagic* and *The Last Soul Man* endeared him to his many black fans. Womack's continuing success is no mystery—as *Philadelphia Inquirer* contributor John Milward puts it, the artist "knows what it takes to write a sexy song." Womack also knows what it takes to infuse a song with emotion. "People will buy the news if it's got a melody," he said. "The news is cold and hard. But put a melody onto it, and people take it with a smile."

Womack's releases *So Many Rivers* (1985) and *Save the Children* (1990) are works with a social theme that confront the singer's own problems with drug abuse as well as his concerns for his friends and his son. "In my music, I have . . . tried to tell the truth," Womack told *Blues & Soul.* "I've never been afraid to do so because the truth never dies. It lives on beyond the person. Look, I'm not ashamed to tell you that I was hooked on drugs. Everybody around me always used to tell me not to talk about it but . . . it's the truth. . . . Man, I'll tell you—I'm just glad to even be here today to talk to you about it. It could easily have been me up there on the night shift with Marvin Gaye."

Milward calls Womack a "soul survivor" who can "give you a firsthand account of the connection between the sanctuary and the street." Milward adds that the performer "operates on the . . . notion that the best songs are rooted in common experience. Womack learned from a master [Sam Cooke], and years later continues to keep that faith. He knows that whether it's in church or in the recording studio, the most profound music comes from a singular place: the soul." Womack has come to terms with his roots and is proud to be simply a soul man, making music for his people. He told *Blues & Soul:* "You know, a . . . big problem today is that blacks no longer want to be soul singers anymore. Have you noticed how they all want to be crossover artists these days? Me? I'm not ashamed. People like Otis [Redding], Sam [Cooke], and James Brown have laid down a tradition and I'm proud to say that I want to continue in that tradition. I want to be one of the true survivors."

Selected discography

Fly Me to the Moon, Minit, 1968.
California Dreaming, Minit, 1968.
How I Miss You, Baby, Minit, 1969.
More Than I Can Stand, Minit, 1970.
That's The Way I Feel about You, United Artists, 1971.
Communication, United Artists, 1971.
Understanding, United Artists, 1972.
A Woman's Got To Have It, United Artists, 1972.
Sweet Caroline, United Artists, 1972.
Harry Hippie, United Artists, 1972.
Facts of Life, United Artists, 1973.
Across 110th Street (film soundtrack), United Artists, 1973.
Nobody Wants You When You're Down and Out, United Artists, 1973.
Lookin' for a Love, United Artists, 1974.
Bobby Womack's Greatest Hits, United Artists, 1974.
You're Welcome, Stop on By, United Artists, 1974.
Check It Out, United Artists, 1975.
BW Goes CW, United Artists, 1976.
Safety Zone, United Artists, 1976.
Home Is Where the Heart Is, CBS, 1976.
Pieces, CBS, 1977.
Roads of Life, Arista, 1979.

The Poet, Beverly Glen, 1981.
The Poet II, MCA, 1984.
Bobby Womack and the Valentinos, Beverly Glen, 1984.
So Many Rivers, MCA, 1985.
Womagic, MCA, 1986.
Soul Survivor, EMI America, 1987.
The Last Soul Man, MCA, 1988.
Greatest Hits of Bobby Womack, Liberty, 1989.
Save the Children, Epic, 1990.

Also recorded *Facts of Live* and *I Don't Know What the World Is Coming To* with United Artists.

Sources

Books

George, Nelson, *The Death of Rhythm & Blues,* Pantheon, 1988.
Given, Dave, *Dave Given Rock 'n' Roll Stars Handbook,* Exposition Press, 1980.
Illustrated Encyclopedia of Black Music, Harmony, 1985.
Nite, Norm N., *Rock On: The Illustrated Encyclopedia of Rock 'n' Roll,* Volume II, Crowell, 1978.
Stambler, Irwin, *Encyclopedia of Pop, Rock & Soul,* St. Martin's, 1989.

Periodicals

Blues & Soul, October 1985.
Philadelphia Inquirer, January 25, 1990.

—*Anne Janette Johnson*

Udo Zimmerman

Opera composer

Some opera buffs are wondering if there is a new wave in operatic aesthetics coming largely from Germany. Udo Zimmerman's *Die Weisse Rose* (which means "The White Rose") has enjoyed tremendous international acclaim since its 1986 premiere in Hamburg. Within its first four years, the opera was performed nearly one hundred times in countries all over the world and hailed as "full of raw power" by Alan Glasser of *Musical America*. Indeed, no opera more aptly fits this description than *Die Weisse Rose,* with its story of a brother and sister's resistance to Hitler. Alan Rich summed it up in the *Los Angeles Herald Examiner:* "To these dark, passionate texts, some of them no more than an outcry of pure anguish, Zimmerman has brought a score that, to put it modestly, tears at your heart." Remarkably, in an era when many believe that melody is a rare commodity in opera, it is exactly the consonance of Zimmerman's melodies that fuels *Die Weisse Rose's* dramatic power.

Zimmerman was born in Dresden in 1943. During much of his childhood he sang in the Dresdner Kreuzchor boys choir. At the age of 19 he began six years of studies at the Dresden Hochschule fur Musik, including composition with Johannes Paul Thilman. He later attended Gunther Kochan's master classes at the German Academy of Arts in Berlin. At 27 years of age he became composer-in-residence and producer for the Dresden Staatsoper, a position he held for fifteen years. During his tenure with the Staatsoper, however, he also maintained an active composing career of non-operatic works. These include several large orchestral works, a few chamber and instrumental pieces, and a large number of vocal and choral works. Zimmerman also made time during these same years to found and direct the "Neue Musik" Studios in Dresden and to hold a professorship in composition at the Hochschule fur Musik. In 1986 he became the director of the Dresden Center for Contemporary Music.

Zimmerman first came to the attention of the American public in 1988, following the American premiere of his now famous opera *Die Weisse Rose.* The work, which originally premiered in 1986 in Hamburg, was first performed in the United States by Opera/Omaha in September of 1988 and by the Long Beach Opera in California in November of that same year. The opera performed in the United States is a second version of an opera based on the same story composed by Zimmerman in 1967. The original version was the first of the composer's six operas.

Based on a libretto by his brother, Ingo Zimmerman, the original opera was a relatively conventional one, with realistic action portrayed by nine soloists and a full orchestra. The plot revolved around the fate of real-life personages Hans and Sophie Scholl, who participated in the resistance movement against Hitler known under the code name of "White Rose" during World War II. The brother and sister team was caught distributing anti-Nazi leaflets and subsequently condemned to death. In *The Rise and Fall of the Third Reich,* William L. Shirer reports that during her trial Sophie Scholl said: "We haven't done anything special. We only did the natural thing: to be human, to stay human in a time when humanity no longer counts for anything."

When Hamburg State Opera officials decided they wanted to revive the opera in the mid-1980s, Zimmerman decided the subject needed a fresh presentation and set to work on an entirely new opera. He even discarded his brother's libretto in favor of a new text by Wolfgang Willaschek. The format of the new opera is completely different from that of the 1967 version. The new work is a one-act opera, consisting of a set of sixteen scenes, each a coherent musical unit, adding up to a total of seventy minutes. There are only two roles in the new opera, those of Hans and Sophie, and the "orchestra" is reduced to fifteen instrumentalists. The revised account is composed of letters, diary entries, and

Born October 6, 1943, in Dresden, Germany. *Education:* Hochschule fur Musik, Dresden, 1962-68; attended Gunther Kochan's master class at German Academy of Arts in Berlin, Germany.

Composer, dramturg with Dresden Staatsoper, 1970-85; founder and director of the "Neue Musik" Studios, 1974—; professor at the Hochschule fur Musik, Dresden, in composition, 1976—; director of Dresden Center for Contemporary Music, 1986—.

Awards: Three-time winner of the German Democratic Republic's Mendelssohn Scholarship; Hanns Eisler Prize of East German Radio, 1972-73; Martin-Anderson-Nexo-Kunstpreis (Dresden), 1974; DDR Nationalpreis, 1975.

---

poems that depict the Scholls' thoughts as their fate draws near.

With the new presentation of the subject, some say Zimmerman has created a much more powerful and universal work. As it is aptly put in the Spring 1989 issue of *MadAmina!:* "Although the Zimmerman/Willaschek team chose the real-life Scholls as their protagonists, their collaboration has produced, through words and music but with minimal stage trappings, a flow of ideas and emotions that are as fundamental as they are timeless. Wherever the sanctity of life, the preciousness of freedom, the terror of aloneness, the inevitability of death are put into focus, this spectacle may find valid application and the ill-fated Scholl pair becomes a parable." One interpretation of the opera went so far as to examine the threat of acquired immune deficiency syndrome (AIDS) and depicted the characters in their struggle against this fatal disease. In creating *Die Weisse Rose*, Zimmerman was clearly concerned with truth and honesty. In an interview for *MadAmina!* he stated, "Truth was defined by Sophie and Hans Scholl's conduct. . . . It's not only about political resistance. It's about inner resistance, a resistance for the cause of love, of life, of the spirit."

Not only the subject matter, but the melodiousness of Zimmerman's music appeals to audiences worldwide. Zimmerman is a master of melody making, yet he also uses silence with unexpected effectiveness. He infuses new life into some old methods of organizing musical materials, always paying his debt to past composers. Although Zimmerman's earlier operas have not enjoyed

the international attention given *Die Wiesse Rose,* they have been performed frequently in what was formerly East Germany, as well as occasionally in what was once West Germany and neighboring countries. Two of them, *Levins Muhle* and *Der Schuhu und die fliegende Prinzessin,* have been recorded on what were East German labels. *Die Weisse Rose* is available on the Orfeo label with the composer conducting.

Selected compositions

Operas

Die Wiesse Rose (first version), 1967-68.
Die zweite Entscheidung, 1969 70.
Levins Muhle, 1971-72.
Der Schuhu und die fliegende Prinzenssin, 1974-75.
Die Weisse Rose (second version), 1986.

Orchestral works

Dramatische Impression auf den Tod von J.F. Kennedy, 1963.
Borchert-Orchester-Gesange, 1965.
Musik fur Streicher, 1967.
L'honime, after E. Guillevic, 1970.
Siehe meine Augen . . . (Reflexionen uber Ernst Barlach), 1972.
Choreographien nach Degas (Die Tanzerinnen), 1972.
Cantiones, 1973.
Mutazione, 1973.
Musik, after Hans Arp, 2, 1974.
Sinfonia come un grande lamento, 1977.

Chamber and instrumental works

Kontraste, 1964.
Movimenti caratteristici, 1965.
String Quartet, 1974.

Vocal works

Neruda-Lieder, 1965.
Sonetti amorosi, 1967.
Der Mensch, 1970.
Ode an das Leben, 1972.
Ein Zeuge der Liebe, die besiegt den Tod, 1972.
Bobrowski-Lieder, 1974.
Psalm der Nacht, 1977.

Selected discography

Die Wiesse Rose, Orfeo.
Levins Muhle, Bestell.
Der Schuhu und die fliegende Prinzessin, Bestell.

Sources

Books

Sturzbecher, Ursula, *Komponisten in der DDR: 17 Gesprache,* Hildescheim, 1979.

Udo Zimmerman Opern, VEB Deutscher Verlag fur Musik, Leipzig.

Periodicals

MadAmina!, Spring 1989.

Musical America, February 1989.

Musical Opinion, June 1989.

Musik und Gesellschaft, May 1987; October 1988; February 1989.

Neue Zeitschrift fur Musik, November 1988; June 1989.

Opera (England), September 1987; January 1989; February 1989.

Opera News, September 1988.

Opernwelt, June 1988; January 1989; April 1989; February 1990.

Orchester, February 1987; March 1990.

—*Margaret Escobar and Jeanne M. Lesinski*

Subject Index

Volume numbers appear in **bold**.

Wynette, Tammy **2**
Yoakam, Dwight **1**

Country Jazz
Asleep at the Wheel **5**
Crowe, J.D. **5**
Haggard, Merle **2**
The Judds **2**
Rich, Charlie **3**

Disco
Abdul, Paula **3**
The Bee Gees **3**
Fox, Samantha **3**
Richie, Lionel **2**
Stewart, Rod **2**

Dixieland
Hirt, Al **5**

Dobro
Auldridge, Mike **4**
Burch, Curtis
    See New Grass Revival **4**
Knopfler, Mark **3**

Drums
See **Percussion**

Dulcimer
Ritchie, Jean **4**

Feminist Music
Near, Holly **1**

Fiddle
See **Violin**

Film Scores
Anka, Paul **2**
Bacharach, Burt **1**
Bernstein, Leonard **2**
Cafferty, John
    See the Beaver Brown Band **3**
Copland, Aaron **2**
Ellington, Duke **2**
Guaraldi, Vince **3**
Hamlisch, Marvin **1**
Harrison, George **2**
Hedges, Michael **3**
Jones, Quincy **2**
Knopfler, Mark **3**
Lennon, John
    See the Beatles **2**
Mancini, Henry **1**
McCartney, Paul
    See the Beatles **2**
Metheny, Pat **2**
Richie, Lionel **2**
Robertson, Robbie **2**
Sager, Carole Bayer **5**
Schickele, Peter **5**
Waits, Tom **1**
Williams, Paul **5**
Young, Noil **2**

Flamenco
de Lucia, Paco **1**

Flute
Galway, James **3**
Wilson, Ransom **5**

Folk
Armatrading, Joan **4**
Baez, Joan **1**
The Carter Family **3**
Chapman, Tracy **4**
Childs, Toni **2**

Cohen, Leonard **3**
Collins, Judy **4**
Crosby, David **3**
Denver, John **1**
Dylan, Bob **3**
Elliot, Cass **5**
Galway, James **3**
Garfunkel, Art **4**
Griffith, Nanci **3**
Guthrie, Woodie **2**
Hartford, John **1**
Ian, Janis **5**
Indigo Girls **3**
Lightfoot, Gordon **3**
Mitchell, Joni **2**
Morrison, Van **3**
Near, Holly **1**
O'Connor, Sinead **3**
Paxton, Tom **5**
Penn, Michael **4**
Peter, Paul & Mary **4**
Redpath, Jean **1**
Ritchie, Jean, **4**
Rodgers, Jimmie **3**
Rogers, Kenny **1**
Seals & Crofts **3**
Seeger, Pete **4**
Simon, Paul **1**
Snow, Pheobe **4**
Vega, Suzanne **3**
Watson, Doc **2**
Young, Neil **2**

French Horn
Ohanian, David
        See Canadian Brass **4**

Funk
Abdul, Paula **3**
Brown, Bobby **4**
Brown, James **2**
Jackson, Freddie **3**
Jackson, Janet **3**
James, Rick **2**
Reid, Vernon **2**
Richie, Lionel **2**
Sheila E. **3**

Fusion
Clarke, Stanley **3**
Coleman, Ornette **5**
Davis, Miles **1**
Jarreau, Al **1**
Metheny, Pat **2**
O'Connor, Mark **1**
Shorter, Wayne **5**
Summers, Andy **3**
Washington, Grover, Jr. **5**

Gospel
Brown, James **2**
The Carter Family **3**
Charles, Ray **1**
Cleveland, James **1**
Cooke, Sam **1**
Ford, Tennessee Ernie **3**
Franklin, Aretha **2**
Knight, Gladys **1**
Little Richard **1**
Oak Ridge Boys **4**
Presley, Elvis **1**
Redding, Otis **5**
Watson, Doc **2**
Williams, Deniece **1**
Womack, Bobby **5**

Guitar
Ackerman, Will **3**
Adams, Bryan **2**

Allsup, Michael Rand
    See Three Dog Night **5**
Armatrading, Joan **4**
Atkins, Chet **5**
Auldridge, Mike **4**
    Also see the Seldom Scene **4**
Baez, Joan **1**
Barrere, Paul
    See Little Feat **4**
Barrett, (Roger) Syd
    See Pink Floyd **2**
Baxter, Jeff
    See the Doobie Brothers **3**
Beck, Jeff **4**
Belew, Adrian **5**
Berry, Chuck **1**
Benson, Ray
    See Asleep at the Wheel **5**
Black, Clint **5**
Bono
    See U2 **2**
Browne, Jackson **3**
Buck, Peter
    See R.E.M. **5**
Buck, Robert
    See 10,000 Maniacs **3**
Buckingham, Lindsey
    See Fleetwood Mac **5**
Buffett, Jimmy **4**
Burch, Curtis
    See New Grass Revival **4**
Burnette, Billy
    See Fleetwood Mac **5**
Bush, Sam
    See New Grass Revival **4**
Byrne, David
    See Talking Heads **3**
Cafferty, John
    See the Beaver Brown Band **3**
Campbell, Ali
    See UB40 **4**
Campbell, Glen **2**
Campbell, Robin
    See UB40 **4**
Cash, Johnny **1**
Chapman, Tracy **4**
Chaquico, Craig
    See Jefferson Starship **5**
Clapton, Eric **1**
Clark, Roy **1**
Clark, Steve
    See Def Leppard **3**
Cohen, Leonard **3**
Collin, Phil
    See Def Leppard **3**
Collins, Albert **4**
Collins, Judy **4**
Cooder, Ry **2**
Cook, Jeff
    See Alabama **1**
Costello, Elvis **2**
Cougar, John(ny)
    See Mellencamp, John "Cougar" **2**
Crenshaw, Marshall **5**
Croce, Jim **3**
Crofts, Dash
    See Seals & Crofts **3**
Crosby, David **3**
Dacus, Donnie
    See Chicago **3**
Daniels, Jack
    See Highway 101 **4**
Davies, Ray **5**
de Lucia, Paco **1**
Denver, John **1**
Diamond, Neil **1**
Diddley, Bo **3**
Difford, Chris
    See Squeeze **5**

See Stryper **2**
Taylor, Roger
　See Duran Duran **4**
Timmins, Peter
　See Cowboy Junkies **4**
Watts, Charlie
　See the Rolling Stones **3**
Weaver, Louie
　See Petra **3**
Whitwam, Barry
　See Herman's Hermits **5**
Williams, Boris
　See The Cure **3**
Wilson, Cindy
　See B-52s **4**
Wilson, Dennis
　See the Beach Boys **1**
Wright, Simon
　See AC/DC **4**
Young, Fred
　See Kentucky Headhunters **5**

Performance Art
Anderson, Laurie **1**

Piano
Arrau, Claudio **1**
Bacharach, Burt **1**
Basie, Count **2**
Browne, Jackson **3**
Bush, Kate **4**
Charles, Ray **1**
Clayderman, Richard **1**
Cleveland, James **1**
Cole, Nat King **3**
Collins, Judy **4**
Collins, Phil **2**
　Also see Genesis **4**
Connick, Harry Jr. **4**
Cotoia, Robert
　See the Beaver Brown Band **3**
Crofts, Dash
　See Seals & Crofts **3**
Domino, Fats
Drew, Dennis
　See 10,000 Maniacs **3**
Ellington, Duke **2**
Flack, Roberta **5**
Frey, Glenn **3**
Gibb, Maurice
　See the Bee Gees **3**
Glass, Philip **1**
Guaraldi, Vince **3**
Hamlisch, Marvin **1**
Hornsby, Bruce **3**
Horowitz, Vladimir **1**
Jackson, Joe **4**
Jarrett, Keith **1**
Joel, Billy **2**
John, Elton **3**
Lamm, Robert
　See Chicago **3**
Lennon, John
　See the Beatles **2**
Lewis, Jerry Lee **2**
Little Richard **1**
Manilow, Barry **2**
McCartney, Paul **4**
　Also see the Beatles **2**
McDonald, Michael
　See the Doobie Brothers **3**
McVie, Christine
　See Fleetwood Mac **5**
Milsap, Ronnie **2**
Mitchell, Joni **2**
Newman, Randy **4**
Payne, Bill
　See Little Feat **4**
Rich, Charlie **3**

Schickele, Peter **5**
Sedaka, Neil **4**
Simon, Carly **4**
Solal, Martial **4**
Stevens, Cat **3**
Stewart, Ian
　See the Rolling Stones **3**
Story, Liz **2**
Waits, Tom **1**
Winwood, Steve **2**
Wonder, Stevie **2**
Wright, Rick
　See Pink Floyd **2**

Piccolo
Galway, James **3**

Pop
Abdul, Paula **3**
Adams, Bryan **2**
Aerosmith **3**
Armatrading, Joan **4**
Armstrong, Louis **4**
Astley, Rick **5**
Atkins, Chet **5**
Avalon, Frankie **5**
B-52s **4**
Bacharach, Burt **1**
Bailey, Pearl **5**
Basia **5**
The Beach Boys **1**
The Beatles **2**
The Beaver Brown Band **3**
The Bee Gees **3**
Bennett, Tony **2**
Berry, Chuck **1**
The Blues Brothers **3**
BoDeans **3**
Bolton, Michael **4**
Bowie, David **1**
Branigan, Laura **2**
Brickell, Edie **3**
Brown, Bobby **4**
Browne, Jackson **3**
Buffett, Jimmy **4**
Campbell, Glen **2**
Carnes, Kim **4**
Cash, Johnny **1**
Chapman, Tracy **4**
Charles, Ray **1**
Cher **1**
Cherry, Neneh **4**
Chicago **3**
Clapton, Eric **1**
Clark, Dick **2**
Clark, Roy **1**
Clayderman, Richard **1**
Cline, Patsy **5**
The Coasters **5**
Cocker, Joe **4**
Cohen, Leonard **3**
Cole, Nat King **3**
Cole, Natalie **1**
Collins, Judy **4**
Collins, Phil **2**
Connick, Harry Jr. **4**
Cooder, Ry **2**
Cooke, Sam **1**
Costello, Elvis **2**
Crenshaw, Marshall **5**
Croce, Jim **3**
Crosby, David **3**
Daltrey, Roger **3**
　Also see The Who **3**
D'Arby, Terence Trent **3**
Darin, Bobby **4**
Davies, Ray **5**
Davis, Sammy Jr. **4**
Dayne, Taylor **4**

Denver, John **1**
Depeche Mode **5**
Diamond, Neil **1**
Dion **4**
Domino, Fats **2**
The Doobie Brothers **3**
The Doors **4**
Duran Duran **4**
Dylan, Bob **3**
The Eagles **3**
Easton, Sheena **2**
Elliot, Cass **5**
Estefan, Gloria **2**
The Everly Brothers **2**
Exposé **4**
Fabian **5**
Ferry, Bryan **1**
Fitzgerald, Ella **1**
Flack, Roberta **5**
Fleetwood Mac **5**
Fogelberg, Dan **4**
Ford, Tennessee Ernie **3**
Fox, Samantha **3**
Frampton, Peter **3**
Franklin, Aretha **2**
Frey, Glenn **3**
　Also see the Eagles **3**
Galway, James **3**
Garfunkel, Art **4**
Gaye, Marvin **4**
Gayle, Crystal **1**
Genesis **4**
Gibson, Debbie **1**
Gift, Roland **3**
Goodman, Benny **4**
Grebenshikov, Boris **3**
Griffith, Nanci **3**
Hammer, M.C. **5**
Harris, Emmylou **4**
Harrison, George **2**
　Also see the Beatles **2**
Harry, Deborah **4**
Hartford, John **1**
Healey, Jeff **4**
Henley, Don **3**
　Also see the Eagles **3**
Herman's Hermits **5**
Hirt, Al **5**
Holland-Dozier-Holland **5**
Holly, Buddy **1**
Hornsby, Bruce **3**
Ian, Janis **5**
Idol, Billy **3**
Iglesias, Julio **2**
Indigo Girls **3**
Jackson, Janet **3**
Jackson, Joe **4**
Jackson, Michael **1**
James, Rick **2**
Jarreau, Al **1**
Jefferson Airplane **5**
Joel, Billy **2**
John, Elton **3**
Jones, Quincy **2**
Jones, Rickie Lee **4**
Jones, Spike **5**
Joplin, Janis **3**
Kiss **5**
Knight, Gladys **1**
Knopfler, Mark **3**
Kristofferson, Kris **4**
Lee, Brenda **5**
Lennon, Julian **2**
Lightfoot, Gordon **3**
Lindley, David **2**
Little Richard **1**
Loggins, Kenny **3**
Lovett, Lyle **5**
Lynne, Jeff **5**

Collins, Phil **2**
Cooder, Ry **2**
Cooke, Sam **1**
Costello, Elvis **2**
Cougar, John(ny)
    See Mellencamp, John "Cougar" **2**
Crenshaw, Marshall **5**
Crosby, David **3**
The Cure **3**
Curry, Tim **3**
Daltrey, Roger **3**
    Also see The Who **3**
D'Arby, Terence Trent **3**
Darin, Bobby **4**
Davies, Ray **5**
Dayne, Taylor **4**
Def Leppard **3**
Depeche Mode **5**
Diddley, Bo **3**
Dion **4**
Domino, Fats **2**
The Doobie Brothers **3**
The Doors **4**
Duran Duran **4**
Dylan, Bob **3**
The Eagles **3**
Easton, Sheena **2**
Elliot, Cass **5**
Emerson, Lake & Palmer/Powell **5**
Etheridge, Melissa **4**
The Everly Brothers **2**
Ferry, Bryan **1**
Fleetwood Mac **5**
Fogelberg, Dan **4**
Fogerty, John **2**
Fox, Samantha **3**
Frampton, Peter **3**
Frey, Glenn **3**
    Also see The Eagles **3**
Gabriel, Peter **2**
Garcia, Jerry **4**
Genesis **4**
Gift, Roland **3**
Grateful Dead **5**
Grebenshikov, Boris **3**
Guns n' Roses **2**
Harrison, George **2**
    Also see The Beatles **2**
Harry, Deborah **4**
Healey, Jeff **4**
Hendrix, Jimi **2**
Henley, Don **3**
    Also see The Eagles **3**
Holland-Dozier-Holland **5**
Holly, Buddy **1**
Idol, Billy **3**
INXS **2**
Jackson, Joe **4**
James, Rick **2**
Jefferson Airplane **5**
Jett, Joan **3**
Joel, Billy **2**
John, Elton **3**
Joplin, Janis **3**
Kiss **5**
Knopfler, Mark **3**
Kravitz, Lenny **5**
Kristofferson, Kris **4**
Led Zeppelin **1**
Lee, Brenda **5**
Lennon, Julian **2**
Lewis, Jerry Lee **2**
Lindley, Dave **2**
Little Feat **4**
Little Richard **1**
Loggins, Kenny **3**
Los Lobos **2**
Lynne, Jeff **5**
Marx, Richard **3**

McCartney, Paul **4**
    Also see the Beatles **2**
Mellencamp, John "Cougar" **2**
Miller, Steve **2**
Morrison, Jim **3**
    Also see the Doors **4**
Morrison, Van **3**
Mötley Crüe **1**
Myles, Alannah **4**
Nelson, Rick **2**
Newman, Randy **4**
Nicks, Stevie **2**
Nugent, Ted **2**
Ocasek, Ric **5**
O'Connor, Sinead **3**
Orbison, Roy **2**
Osbourne, Ozzy **3**
Page, Jimmy **4**
    Also see Led Zeppelin **1**
Palmer, Robert **2**
Paul, Les **2**
Phillips, Sam **5**
Pink Floyd **2**
Plant, Robert **2**
    Also see Led Zeppelin **1**
Pop, Iggy **1**
Presley, Elvis **1**
Prince **1**
Raitt, Bonnie **3**
Reed, Lou **1**
Reid, Vernon **2**
R.E.M. **5**
Rich, Charlie **3**
Robertson, Robbie **2**
Rogers, Kenny **1**
The Rolling Stones **3**
Roth, David Lee **1**
Satriani, Joe **4**
Sedaka, Neil **4**
The Sex Pistols **5**
Sheila E. **3**
Shocked, Michelle **4**
Simon, Carly **4**
Simon, Paul **1**
Smith, Patti **1**
The Smiths **3**
Spector, Phil **4**
Squeeze **5**
Steely Dan **5**
Stevens, Cat **3**
Stewart, Rod **2**
Stills, Stephen **5**
Sting **2**
Stryper **2**
Summers, Andy **3**
10,000 Maniacs **3**
Three Dog Night **5**
Timbuk 3 **3**
Tosh, Peter **3**
Townshend, Pete **1**
    Also see The Who **3**
Turner, Tina **1**
UB40 **4**
U2 **2**
Vai, Steve **5**
Vaughan, Stevie Ray **1**
Walsh, Joe **5**
    Also see the Eagles **5**
Whitesnake **5**
The Who **3**
Wilson, Jackie **3**
Winter, Johnny **5**
Winwood, Steve **2**
Young, Neil **2**
Zappa, Frank **1**
ZZ Top **2**

Rockabilly
Holly, Buddy **1**

Nelson, Rick **2**
Presley, Elvis **1**
Robillard, Duke **2**
Watson, Doc **2**

Salsa
Blades, Ruben **2**
Jackson, Joe **4**

Saxophone
Antunes, Michael
    See the Beaver Brown Band **3**
Astro
    See UB40 **4**
Berlin, Steve
    See Los Lobos **2**
Carter, Benny **3**
Coleman, Ornette **5**
Coltrane, John **4**
Love, Mike
    See the Beach Boys **1**
Neville, Charles
    See the Neville Brothers **4**
Parazaider, Walter
    See Chicago **3**
Parker, Charlie **5**
Pengilly, Kirk
    See INXS **2**
Sanborn, David **1**
Shorter, Wayne **5**
Travers, Brian
    See UB40 **4**
Washington, Grover, Jr. **5**

Songwriters
Ackerman, Will **3**
Acuff, Roy **2**
Adams, Bryan **2**
Anderson, John **5**
Anka, Paul **2**
Armatrading, Joan **4**
Astley, Rick **5**
Atkins, Chet **5**
Augustyniak, Jerry
    See 10,000 Maniacs **3**
Bacharach, Burt **1**
Baez, Joan **1**
Balin, Marty
    See Jefferson Airplane **5**
Banks, Tony
    See Genesis **4**
Barrett, (Roger) Syd
    See Pink Floyd **2**
Basia **5**
Basie, Count **2**
Beard, Frank
    See ZZ Top **2**
Becker, Walter
    See Steely Dan **5**
Belew, Adrian **5**
Berry, Bill
    See R.E.M. **5**
Berry, Chuck **1**
Black, Clint **5**
Blades, Ruben **2**
Bogaert, Jo
    See Technotronic **5**
Bolton, Michael **4**
Bono
    See U2 **2**
Brickell, Edie **3**
Brown, Bobby **4**
Brown, James **2**
Browne, Jackson **3**
Buck, Peter **5**
Buck, Robert **3**
Buckingham, Lindsey
    See Fleetwood Mac **5**
Buckley, Betty **1**

Buffett, Jimmy **4**
Bush, Kate **4**
Cafferty, John
See the Beaver Brown Band **3**
Carlson, Paulette
See Highway 101 **4**
Carnes, Kim **4**
Cash, Johnny **1**
Cash, Rosanne **2**
Cetera, Peter
See Chicago **3**
Chapman, Tracy **4**
Charles, Ray **1**
Childs, Toni **2**
Clapton, Eric **1**
Clark, Steve
Def Leppard **3**
Clayton, Adam
See U2 **2**
Cleveland, James **1**
Coe, David Allan **4**
Cohen, Leonard **3**
Cole, Nat King **3**
Collins, Albert **4**
Collins, Judy **4**
Collins, Phil **2**
Cooder, Ry **2**
Cooke, Sam **1**
Costello, Elvis **2**
Cougar, John(ny)
See Mellencamp, John "Cougar" **2**
Crenshaw, Marshall **5**
Croce, Jim **3**
Crofts, Dash
See Seals & Crofts **3**
Crosby, David **3**
Crowe, J.D. **5**
Darin, Bobby **4**
Davies, Ray **5**
Dayne, Taylor **4**
Densmore, John
See the Doors **4**
Denver, John **1**
Diamond, Neil **1**
Diddley, Bo **3**
Difford, Chris
See Squeeze **5**
Dion **4**
Domino, Fats **2**
Dozier, Lamont
See Holland-Dozier-Holland **5**
Drew, Dennis
See 10,000 Maniacs **3**
Dylan, Bob **3**
The Edge
See U2 **2**
Ellington, Duke **2**
Elliot, Joe
See Def Leppard **3**
Emerson, Keith
See Emerson, Lake & Palmer/Powell **5**
Etheridge, Melissa **4**
Everly, Don
See the Everly Brothers **2**
Everly, Phil
See the Everly Brothers **2**
Fagen, Don
See Stelly Dan **5**
Farriss, Andrew
See INXS **2**
Felder, Don
See the Eagles **3**
Ferry, Bryan **1**
Flack, Roberta **5**
Flatt, Lester **3**
Fogelberg, Dan **4**
Fogerty, John **2**
Frampton, Peter **3**
Franklin, Aretha **2**

Frey, Glenn **3**
Also see The Eagles **3**
Gabriel, Peter **2**
Garcia, Jerry **4**
Garfunkel, Art **4**
Gaye, Marvin **4**
George, Lowell
See Little Feat **4**
Gibb, Barry
See the Bee Gees **3**
Gibb, Maurice
See the Bee Gees **3**
Gibb, Robin
See the Bee Gees **3**
Gibbons, Billy
See ZZ Top **2**
Gibson, Debbie **1**
Gift, Roland **3**
Gilmour, David
See Pink Floyd **2**
Goodman, Benny **4**
Grebenshikov, Boris **3**
Green, Peter
See Fleetwood Mac **5**
Griffith, Nanci **3**
Guthrie, Woodie **2**
Guy, Buddy **4**
Haggard, Merle **2**
Hall, Tom T. **4**
Hamlisch, Marvin **1**
Hammer, M.C. **5**
Harris, Emmylou **4**
Harrison, George **2**
Also see The Beatles **2**
Harry, Deborah **4**
Hartford, John **1**
Hartman, Bob
See Petra **3**
Headon, Topper
See the Clash **4**
Healey, Jeff **4**
Hedges, Michael **3**
Hendrix, Jimi **2**
Henley, Don **3**
Also see The Eagles **3**
Hidalgo, David
See Los Lobos **2**
Hill, Dusty
See ZZ Top **2**
Hillman, Chris **4**
Holland, Brian
See Holland-Dozier-Holland **5**
Holland, Eddie
See Holland-Dozier-Holland **5**
Holly, Buddy **1**
Hornsby, Bruce **3**
Hutchence, Michael
See INXS **2**
Ian, Janis **5**
Idol, Billy **3**
Iglesias, Julio **2**
Jackson, Freddie **3**
Jackson, Joe **4**
Jackson, Michael **1**
Jagger, Mick
See the Rolling Stones **3**
James, Rick **2**
Jarreau, Al **1**
Jennings, Waylon **4**
Jett, Joan **3**
Joel, Billy **2**
John, Elton **3**
Johnson, Brian
See AC/DC **4**
Johnston, Tom
See the Doobie Brothers **3**
Jones, Brian
See the Rolling Stones **3**
Jones, George **4**

Jones, Mick
See the Clash **4**
Jones, Quincy **2**
Jones, Rickie Lee **4**
Joplin, Janis **3**
Judd, Naomi
See the Judds **2**
Kantner, Paul
See Jefferson Airplane **5**
King, Albert **2**
King, B.B. **1**
Knopfler, Mark **3**
Kravitz, Lenny **5**
Krieger, Robert
See the Doors **4**
Kristofferson, Kris **4**
Lake, Greg
See Emerson, Lake & Palmer/Powell **5**
L.L. Cool J. **5**
Lamm, Robert
See Chicago **3**
Lang, K.D. **4**
Leadon, Bernie
See the Eagles **3**
LeBon, Simon
See Duran Duran **4**
Lennon, John
See the Beatles **2**
Lennon, Julian **2**
Levene, Keith
See the Clash **4**
Lightfoot, Gordon **3**
Little Richard **1**
Llanas, Sammy
See BoDeans **3**
Loggins, Kenny **3**
Loughnane, Lee
See Chicago **3**
Loveless, Patty **5**
Lovett, Lyle **5**
Lynn, Loretta **2**
Lynne, Jeff **5**
Lynne, Shelby **5**
MacDonald, Barbara
See Timbuk 3 **3**
MacDonald, Pat
See Timbuk 3 **3**
Madonna **4**
Manilow, Barry **2**
Manzarek, Ray
See the Doors **4**
Marley, Bob **3**
Marley, Ziggy **3**
Martin, Jimmy **5**
Marx, Richard **3**
Mattea, Kathy **5**
McCartney, Paul **4**
Also see the Beatles **2**
McDonald, Michael
See the Doobie Brothers **3**
McVie, Christine
See Fleetwood Mac **5**
Medley, Bill **3**
Miller, Roger **4**
Meisner, Randy
See the Eagles **3**
Mellencamp, John "Cougar" **2**
Merchant, Natalie
See 10,000 Maniacs **3**
Miller, Steve **2**
Milsap, Ronnie **2**
Mitchell, Joni **2**
Morrison, Jim **3**
Morrison, Van **3**
Mullen, Larry
See U2 **2**
Myles, Alannah **4**
Near, Holly **1**
Nelson, Rick **2**

Nelson, Willie **1**
Neville, Art
　See the Neville Brothers **4**
Newman, Randy **4**
Newmann, Kurt
　See BoDeans **3**
Nicks, Stevie **2**
Nugent, Ted **2**
Ocasek, Ric **5**
Ocean, Billy **4**
O'Connor, Sinead **3**
Orbison, Roy **2**
Osbourne, Ozzy **3**
Oslin, K.T. **3**
Owens, Buck **2**
Page, Jimmy **4**
　Also see Led Zeppelin **1**
Palmer, Robert **2**
Pankow, James
　See Chicago **3**
Parton, Dolly **2**
Paul, Les **2**
Paxton, Tom **5**
Pedersen, Herb
　See Desert Rose Band **4**
Penn, Michael **4**
Perez, Louie
　See Los Lobos **2**
Perry, Joe
　See Aerosmith **3**
Pierson, Kate
　See B-52s **4**
Plant, Robert **2**
　Also see Led Zeppelin **1**
Pop, Iggy **1**
Presley, Elvis **1**
Prince **1**
Rabbitt, Eddie **5**
Raitt, Bonnie **3**
Ray, Amy
　See Indigo Girls **3**
Redding, Otis **5**
Reed, Lou **1**
Reid, Vernon **2**
Rhodes, Nick
　See Duran Duran **4**
Rich, Charlie **3**
Richard, Keith
　See the Rolling Stones **3**
Richie, Lionel **2**
Ritchie, Jean **4**
Robertson, Robbie **2**
Robillard, Duke **2**
Robinson, Smokey **1**
Rodgers, Jimmie **3**
Roth, David Lee **1**
Rotten, Johnny
　See the Sex Pistols **5**
Rutherford, Mike
　See Genesis **4**
Sade **2**
Sager, Carole Bayer **5**
Saliers, Emily
　See Indigo Girls **3**
Satriani, Joe **4**
Schmit, Timothy B.
　See the Eagles **3**
Schneider, Fred III
　See B-52s **4**
Scott, Bon (Ronald Belford)
　See AC/DC **4**
Scruggs, Earl **3**
Seals, Jim
　See Seals & Crofts **3**
Sedaka, Neil **4**
Seeger, Pete **4**
Seraphine, Daniel
　See Chicago **3**
Sheila E. **3**

Shocked, Michelle **4**
Simmons, Gene
　See Kiss **5**
Simmons, Patrick
　See the Doobie Brothers **3**
Simon, Carly **4**
Simon, Paul **1**
Simonon, Paul
　See the Clash **4**
Skaggs, Ricky **5**
Slick, Grace
　See Jefferson Airplane **5**
Smith, Patti **1**
Smith, Robert
　See The Cure **3**
Spector, Phil **4**
Stanley, Paul
　See Kiss **5**
Stanley, Ralph **5**
Starr, Ringo
　See the Beatles **2**
Stevens, Cat **3**
Stewart, Rod **2**
Stills, Stephen **5**
Sting **2**
Stipe, Michael
　See R.E.M. **5**
Stookey, Paul
　See Peter, Paul & Mary **4**
Strait, George **5**
Streisand, Barbra **2**
Strickland, Keith
　See B-52s **4**
Strummer, Joe
　See the Clash **4**
Summers, Andy **3**
Taylor, Andy
　See Duran Duran **4**
Taylor, James **2**
Taylor, John
　See Duran Duran **4**
Taylor, Mick
　See the Rolling Stones **3**
Tilbrook, Glenn
　See Squeeze **5**
Timmins, Margo
　See Cowboy Junkies **4**
Timmins, Michael
　See Cowboy Junkies **4**
Tone-Lōc **3**
Torme, Mel **4**
Tosh, Peter **3**
Townshend, Pete **1**
　Also see The Who **3**
Travers, Mary
　See Peter, Paul & Mary **4**
Tubb, Ernest **4**
Tyler, Steve
　See Aerosmith **3**
Vai, Steve **5**
　Also see Whitesnake **5**
Vandross, Luther **2**
Van Shelton, Ricky **5**
Vega, Suzanne **3**
Vox, Bono
　See U2 **2**
Waits, Tom **1**
Walker, T-Bone **5**
Walsh, Joe **5**
　Also see the Eagles **3**
Waters, Muddy **4**
Waters, Roger
　See Pink Floyd **2**
Watts, Charlie
　See the Rolling Stones **3**
Weir, Bob
　See the Grateful Dead **5**
Welch, Bob
　See the Grateful Dead **5**

Williams, Deniece **1**
Williams, Don **4**
Williams, Hank Jr. **1**
Williams, Hank Sr. **4**
Williams, Paul **5**
Willis, Pete
　See Def Leppard **3**
Wilson, Brian
　See the Beach Boys **1**
Wilson, Cindy
　See B-52s **4**
Wilson, Ricky
　See B-52s **4**
Winter, Johnny **5**
Winwood, Steve **2**
Womack, Bobby **5**
Wonder, Stevie **2**
Wood, Ron
　See the Rolling Stones **3**
Wyman, Bill
　See the Rolling Stones **3**
Wynette, Tammy **2**
Yarrow, Peter
　See Peter, Paul & Mary **4**
Yoakam, Dwight **1**
Young, Angus
　See AC/DC **4**
Young, Malcolm
　See AC/DC **4**
Young, Neil **2**
Zappa, Frank **1**

Soul
　The Blues Brothers **3**
　Bolton, Michael **4**
　Brown, James **2**
　Charles, Ray **1**
　Cooke, Sam **1**
　Franklin, Aretha **2**
　Gaye, Marvin **4**
　Holland-Dozier-Holland **5**
　Jackson, Freddie **3**
　Knight, Gladys **1**
　Little Richard **1**
　Medley, Bill **3**
　Morrison, Van **3**
　The Neville Brothers **4**
　Pendergrass, Teddy **3**
　Reeves, Martha **4**
　Redding, Otis **5**
　Reid, Vernon **2**
　Robinson, Smokey **1**
　Ross, Diana **1**
　The Temptations **3**
　Vandross, Luther **2**
　Wilson, Jackie **3**
　Womack, Bobby **5**
　Wonder, Stevie **2**

Trombone
　Pankow, James
　　See Chicago **3**
　Watts, Eugene
　　See Canadian Brass **4**

Trumpet
　Armstrong, Louis **4**
　Benson, Ray
　　See Asleep at the Wheel **5**
　Berigan, Bunny **5**
　Bumpus, Cornelius
　　See Chicago **3**
　Coleman, Ornette **5**
　Davis, Miles **1**
　Hirt, Al **5**
　Jones, Quincy **2**
　Loughnane, Lee **3**
　Mills, Fred
　　See Canadian Brass **4**

Musicians Index

Volume numbers appear in **bold.**

O'Connor, Mark **1**
O'Connor, Sinead **3**
O'Donnell, Roger
   See The Cure
Ohanian, David
   See Canadian Brass
Orbison, Roy **2**
Osbourne, Ozzy **3**
Oslin, K.T. **3**
Osmond, Donny **3**
Ott, David **2**
Owen, Randy
   See Alabama
Owens, Buck **2**
Owens, Ricky
   See the Temptations
Page, Jimmy **4**
   Also see Led Zeppelin
Palmer, Carl
   See Emerson, Lake & Palmer/Powell
Palmer, Robert **2**
Pankow, James
   See Chicago
Parazaider, Walter
   See Chicago
Parker, Charlie **5**
Parton, Dolly **2**
Patinkin, Mandy **3**
Paul, Les **2**
Pavarotti, Luciano **1**
Paxton, Tom **5**
Payne, Bill
   See Little Feat
Pearl, Minnie **3**
Pedersen, Herb
   See Desert Rose Band
Pendergrass, Teddy **3**
Pengilly, Kirk
   See INXS
Penn, Michael **4**
Perez, Louie
   See Los Lobos
Perlman, Itzhak **2**
Perry, Joe
   See Aerosmith
Pet Shop Boys **5**
Peter, Paul & Mary **4**
Petra **3**
Phelps, Doug
   See Kentucky Headhunters
Phelps, Ricky Lee
   See Kentucky Headhunters
Philips, Anthony
   See Genesis
Phillips, Chynna
   See Wilson Phillips
Phillips, Harvey **3**
Phillips, Sam **5**
Phungula, Inos
   See Ladysmith Black Mambazo
Pierson, Kate
   See B-52s
Pilatus, Rob
   See Milli Vanilli
Pink Floyd **2**
Plant, Robert **2**
   Also see Led Zeppelin
Pop, Iggy **1**
Porter, Tiran
   See the Doobie Brothers
Powell, Cozy
   See Emerson, Lake & Palmer/Powell
Presley, Elvis **1**
Price, Louis
   See the Temptations
Pride, Charley **4**
Prince **1**
Public Enemy **4**
Rabbitt, Eddie **5**

Raitt, Bonnie **3**
Ray, Amy
   See Indigo Girls
Reagon, Bernice Johnson
   See Sweet Honey in the Rock
Redding, Otis **5**
Redpath, Jean **1**
Reed, Lou **1**
Reeves, Martha **4**
Reid, Christopher
   See Kid 'n Play
Reid, Vernon **2**
R.E.M. **5**
Rhodes, Nick
   See Duran Duran
Rich, Charlie **3**
Richard, Keith
   See the Rolling Stones
Richie, Lionel **2**
Ritchie, Jean **4**
Robertson, Robbie **2**
Robillard, Duke **2**
Robinson, Smokey **1**
Rodgers, Jimmie **3**
Rogers, Kenny **1**
The Rolling Stones **3**
Romm, Ronald
   See Canadian Brass
Ronstadt, Linda **2**
Rosas, Cesar
   See Los Lobos
Rose, Axl
   See Guns n' Roses
Rosenthal, Phil
   See the Seldom Scene
Ross, Diana **1**
Roth, David Lee **1**
Rotten, Johnny
   See the Sex Pistols
Rourke, Andy
   See the Smiths
Rudd, Phillip
   See AC/DC
Ruffin, David
   See the Temptations
Run-D.M.C. **4**
Rutherford, Mike
   See Genesis
Ryland, Jack
   See Three Dog Night
Sade **2**
St. John, Mark
   See Kiss
Sager, Carole Bayer
Salerno-Sonnenberg, Nadja **3**
Saliers, Emily
   See Indigo Girls
Sanborn, David **1**
Sanger, David
   See Asleep at the Wheel
Santana, Carlos **1**
Satriani, Joe **4**
Savage, Rick
   See Def Leppard
Schormic, Joe
   See Three Dog Night
Schickele, Peter **5**
Schlitt, John
   See Petra
Schmit, Timothy B.
   See the Eagles
Schneider, Fred III
   See B-52s
Scott, Bon (Ronald Belford)
   See AC/DC
Scruggs, Earl **3**
Seals & Crofts **3**
Seals, Jim
   See Seals & Crofts

Sears, Pete
   See Jefferson Starship
Sedaka, Neil **4**
Seeger, Pete **4**
The Seldom Scene **4**
Seraphine, Daniel
   See Chicago
Severinsen, Doc **1**
The Sex Pistols **5**
Shabalala, Ben
   See Ladysmith Black Mambazo
Shabalala, Headman
   See Ladysmith Black Mambazo
Shabalala, Jockey
   See Ladysmith Black Mambazo
Shabalala, Joseph
   See Ladysmith Black Mambazo
Shallenberger, James
   See Kronos Quartet
Sheila E. **3**
Sherba, John
   See Kronos Quartet
Shocked, Michelle **4**
Shogren, Dave
   See the Doobie Brothers
Shorter, Wayne **5**
Sills, Beverly **5**
Silva, Kenny Jo
   See the Beaver Brown Band
Simmons, Gene
   See Kiss
Simmons, Joe "Run"
   See Run-D.M.C.
Simmons, Patrick
   See the Doobie Brothers
Simon, Carly **4**
Simon, Paul **1**
Simonon, Paul
   See the Clash
Sinatra, Frank **1**
Sixx, Nikki
   See Mötley Crüe
Skaggs, Ricky **5**
Slash
   See Guns n' Roses
Slick, Grace
   See Jefferson Airplane
Smith, Bessie **3**
Smith, Patti **1**
Smith, Robert
   See The Cure
Smith, Smitty
   See Three Dog Night
Smith, Willard
   See DJ Jazzy Jeff and the Fresh Prince
The Smiths **3**
Sneed, Floyd Chester
   See Three Dog Night
Snow, Don
   See Squeeze
Snow, Phoebe **4**
Solal, Martial **4**
Sonnenberg, Nadja Salerno
   See Salerno-Sonnenberg, Nadja
Sosa, Mercedes **3**
Spector, Phil **4**
Spence, Skip
   See Jefferson Airplane
Spencer, Jeremy
   See Fleetwood Mac
Squeeze **5**
Stanley, Paul
   See Kiss
Stanley, Ralph **5**
Starling, John
   See the Seldom Scene
Starr, Ringo
   See the Beatles
Starship

See Kentucky Headhunters
Zappa, Frank **1**
Zimmerman, Udo **5**
Zukerman, Pinchas **4**
ZZ Top **2**